MW01126826

FROM WELFARE TO WORKFARE

Gender and American Culture

FROM **WELFARE**

TO **WORKFARE**
The Unintended Consequences of Liberal Reform, 1945–1965

Jennifer
Mittelstadt

*The University of
North Carolina Press*

Chapel Hill and London

Designed by April Leidig-Higgins

Set in Monotype Garamond by Copperline Book
Services, Inc.

Manufactured in the United States of America

The paper in this book meets the guidelines for
permanence and durability of the Committee on
Production Guidelines for Book Longevity of the
Council on Library Resources.

Library of Congress Cataloging-in-Publication Data
Mittelstadt, Jennifer, 1970–
From welfare to workfare: the unintended conse-
quences of liberal reform, 1945–1965 / by Jennifer
Mittelstadt.
    p. cm.— (Gender and American culture)
Includes bibliographical references and index.
ISBN 0-8078-2922-6 (cloth: alk. paper)
ISBN 0-8078-5587-1 (pbk: alk. paper)
    1. Aid to families with dependent children
programs—United States—History—20th
century.   2. Poor women—Government policy
—United States.   3. Welfare recipients—
Employment—United States.   4. Public welfare
—United States—History—20th century.
I. Title.   II. Gender & American culture.
HV699.M565   2005
362.71'3'097309045— dc22   2004013684

cloth   09 08 07 06 05   5 4 3 2 1
paper   09 08 07 06 05   5 4 3 2 1

To my parents —
Peter and Linda Geiss
and Paul Mittelstadt

CONTENTS

ILLUSTRATIONS AND TABLES

ACKNOWLEDGMENTS

Numerous individuals and institutions helped bring this book to fruition. From my first research forays into the archives in 1996, I was fortunate enough to encounter people generous with their encouragement, resources, time, and ideas, and for that I am sincerely grateful.

This book began as a dissertation at the University of Michigan. There, I was lucky to have Nancy Burns, Sonya Rose, Maris Vinovskis, and Terry McDonald to guide me. They provided me with the flexibility to pursue my interests and the structure to make sure the project succeeded. Maris stoked my passion for social policy, and his unflagging energy inspired me. Sonya helped me widen the scope of this project, and her enthusiasm buoyed me. Terry's astute comments and questions, from the beginning of the dissertation through the revision of the manuscript, not only directed this project but also shaped my whole approach to the craft of history.

As I researched the book, I met archivists and librarians whose help was essential. Tom Rosenbaum of the Rockefeller Archive Center supported this project from the moment he heard about it. I benefited from both his technical assistance and his insights about history and welfare politics. Dave Klaasen made my long stay at the Social Welfare History Archives in Minneapolis a pleasure. He brought important, little-known collections to my attention, discussed characters and events from the collections, and was just plain fun to spend time with. Librarians at the Center for American History helped me wade through the uncataloged collection of the Field Foundation. And I could not have completed this project without the help of archivists and librarians at the Wisconsin Historical Society, the Bentley Library at the University of Michigan, the Library of Congress, the National Archives, the Lyndon Baines Johnson Presidential Library, and the Schlesinger Library at Radcliffe.

Several institutions provided support for the completion of the project. The Rockefeller Archive Center and the Social Welfare History Archives both generously provided travel and research grants for the use of their collections. The Mellon Dissertation Fellowship and the Rackham Predoctoral Fellowship at the University of Michigan helped me conduct the initial research and writing for the project. My department heads at Pennsylvania State University, Gregg Roeber and Carolyn Sachs, allowed me to focus on finishing this manuscript, and the College of Liberal Arts at Penn State supported the final preparations of the manuscript and publication of the book.

As this project wended its way from dissertation to completed manuscript, I received suggestions and comments from participants and audiences at conferences and seminars for which I am grateful. These include the Institute for Research on Women and Gender Seminar at the University of Michigan, the Brooklyn College History Seminar, the Journal of Policy History Conference, the Social Science History Association Annual Meetings, and the Organization of American Historians Annual Meeting. Readers at *Social Politics* also helped me hone my arguments.

I am lucky to have colleagues willing to share their own research with me, including Alan Derickson, Rick Perlstein, and especially Andy Morris. Many were generous enough to read portions of the manuscript or the entire manuscript, helping me correct, rethink, and improve the project. I owe heartfelt thank-yous to Edward Berkowitz, Eileen Boris, Marissa Chappell, Lori Ginzberg, Alice Kessler-Harris, Sonya Michel, Andy Morris, Alice O'Connor, Ann Orloff, and Gina Morantz Sanchez. Cynthia Harrison read the manuscript twice (and one chapter many times!), and our email conversations over several years forced me to rethink my major assumptions, dive back into the archives, and focus my arguments. I am grateful for her engagement with this project. Joanne Goodwin read this manuscript three times by my count, and her expertise and guidance —not to mention her enthusiasm—were invaluable. She is largely responsible for any contributions this book can be said to make, and I am indebted to her beyond measure. I was also fortunate to have my dissertation catch the eye of Kate Torrey at UNC Press. Her initial suggestions and Chuck Grench's later guidance have reshaped this book. Amanda McMillan and Paul Betz at UNC Press led me through the editorial process from beginning to end skillfully and efficiently.

Over the years, in various institutions, I found colleagues who helped make my work enjoyable. At Brooklyn College, Ted Burrows, Phil Gallagher, Arline Neftleberg, and Jocelyn Wills encouraged my early progress on the book. My new colleagues at Penn State—Alan Derickson, Lori Ginzberg, Joan Landes, Sarah

Lawrence, Sally McMurry, Holloway Sparks, Maria Truglia, and Nan Woodruff—are already like old friends, and supported me as I completed the book.

As I worked on this project, I gained inspiration from my close friends. Chris Bass, Barbara Cole, Catherine Foley, Maria Mesner, Laura Minikel, Jack Quigley, Shalei Simms, Susan Stolar, and Simone Wennik buoyed me through the many years of this project. Alexander Shashko rose above and beyond the obligations of friendship, not only providing encouragement and letting me blow off steam, but reading every single line of the manuscript several times over, valiantly (and I hope not vainly) attempting to turn me into a better writer.

Without my family, I could not have completed this book. My grandparents, Alice Keery and Olga and Fred Mittelstadt, provided love and kindness, and in not talking about the project, reminded me that many things are more important than writing books. Bob, Roberta, and Rebeca Matthews were close to me while I was writing this book (across the street!), and were always interested and supportive. My brother, Joel Mittelstadt, and my sister-in-law, Mueni Maingi, made the final years of writing this book in New York much more fun. My parents, Paul Mittelstadt and Linda and Peter Geiss, have supported all of my choices for many years. My mother watched the news on welfare closer than even I did, and passed on every relevant article and reference she came across. Together, my parents provided a haven for me when I was worn out, and always believed in my work and me. They are my biggest cheerleaders, and this book is dedicated to them. Finally, I was lucky to share this intellectual journey with Aaron Matthews, who is a storyteller of a different kind. His insights and questions, through the many drafts of the book that he read, improved the book immeasurably. More important, being with him made the time spent writing the book—and not writing the book—the best years of my life.

FROM WELFARE TO WORKFARE

INTRODUCTION

In the 1950s, amid unprecedented economic growth and prosperity, American policy makers rediscovered poverty. In 1955 Democratic congressman John Sparkman of Alabama convened hearings to try to "assess the size and characteristics of the low-income group" in America, basic data that the country sorely lacked.[1] Nearly ten years of affluence had obscured the persistence of poverty. Sparkman's hearings were not the only hint of a renewed interest in the poor. In 1957 the state of New York, under the leadership of Democratic governor Averell Harriman and his deputy, Daniel Patrick Moynihan, undertook a study of "the distribution and the characteristics of the low income population and the causes of their depressed condition," a first step in a pioneering state-level "War on Poverty."[2] That same year, the Committee for Economic Development, an elite economic policy think tank in Washington, commissioned a survey on the extent and nature of poverty in America. Also in 1957 the prestigious and well-endowed Russell Sage Foundation provided a large, multiyear grant to the University of Michigan to begin a study of poverty. Nearly ten years before Democratic presidents John F. Kennedy and Lyndon Johnson launched the War on Poverty, the problem of poverty was on the agendas of a small but growing number of scholars and policy makers.

One of them was Wilbur Cohen, former Social Security analyst for the Social Security Administration, later to become secretary of the Department of Health, Education, and Welfare under President Johnson, and one of the most influential social policy experts in postwar America. In the mid-1950s, Cohen was a professor of public administration at the University of Michigan's School of Social Work. There, he spearheaded several of the 1950s poverty studies, including the Committee on Economic Development's poverty study and the Russell Sage Foundation's University of Michigan Seminar on Income Maintenance.[3]

By most measures, poverty constituted a less widespread problem than in the past. Only one-fifth of Americans were poor in the 1950s, as compared with nearly two-thirds in the early twentieth century.[4] Nevertheless, Cohen and his colleagues at the University of Michigan viewed the contemporary poverty problem as serious. While economic growth had raised many out of poverty, it had not eliminated it for too many Americans, creating what came to be known as a paradox of prosperity.

Members of the Michigan seminar explained this paradox of prosperity by positing the existence of a new kind of recalcitrant poverty they labeled "fundamental poverty." While some of the poor in the 1950s found themselves in "situational poverty"—temporarily unemployed, for example—others, they asserted, were mired in long-term poverty, and it was this group that caused concern. "Fundamental poverty," the Michigan seminar claimed, was defined not only in terms of length of time in poverty but also in terms of other characteristics associated with these poor people. It was portrayed "as a situation in which the individual or family unit is not only unable to supply itself with a certain minimum level of living but . . . is usually associated with a syndrome of other defects, lack of education, medical problems, or low levels of skill and ability to work." The fundamentally poor were poor for the long term because they faced psychological and social challenges that increased the likelihood that they would remain poor.[5]

Who constituted this category of the "fundamental" poor? In his study of the problem of low incomes for the Committee for Economic Development, Wilbur Cohen singled out one group for special notice—"unmarried mothers . . . [or] broken families."[6] At that time, they constituted approximately one-quarter of the nation's total poor.[7] But looking to "the immediate future," Cohen forecast that "the number of broken families is bound to increase."[8] Cohen and his colleagues were not the only experts in the postwar period to worry about rising numbers of single mother households. These women were the focus of anxieties about family, gender, and race that had long existed but were accentuated in the 1950s, when deviations from the prescribed norm of the nuclear family were met with caution, disapproval, or fear.[9] Unwed, divorced, or deserted mothers were cast as immoral, psychologically troubled, or pathological by a variety of professionals.[10] But unlike child welfare experts, adoption counselors, or psychologists, Cohen and his colleagues were concerned with the implications of single motherhood for poverty and social welfare in America.

Single mothers stood out as a visible poverty problem because of their association with the Aid to Dependent Children (ADC) program, a federally funded, categorical public assistance program. In the mid-1950s, 3.1 million poor people received Aid to Dependent Children payments, and nearly 90 percent of its clients lived in single-mother households.[11] Behind these numbers lay significant changes in the ADC clientele over several decades. ADC was an outgrowth of mothers' pensions programs of the Progressive Era, which provided income support to needy mothers deprived of the wages of a male breadwinner. Though mothers' pensions were important new forms of government welfare, their reach was modest. By 1931, for example, only 250,000 children were covered by mothers' pensions in the United States each month, and the program reached only 6 percent of all single-mother households.[12] The small scope of the program was in part due to moral, social, and racial strictures. A 1933 Children's Bureau review of mothers' pensions programs revealed that only 3 percent of mothers' pensions recipients were nonwhite. In addition, only morally "worthy" mothers, most often widows, were able to take advantage of the program, leaving divorced or never-married women with less access to government resources.[13] Fully 80 percent of recipients were widows.

In 1935, as part of New Deal legislation, the federal government took over mothers' pensions and transformed them into the federal Aid to Dependent Children program. With increased funding and federally established standards for eligibility, the coverage of children more than tripled from the days of mothers' pensions, growing from 250,000 each month in 1933 to 925,000 children each month in 1940–41. By 1950, 1.6 million children each month received ADC, serving 25 percent of all American female-headed families, and more than quadrupling the percentage that mothers' pensions had reached.[14] By 1957, moreover, ADC's caseload was larger than the other three categories of federal public assistance programs—Old Age Assistance, Aid to the Blind, and Aid to the Totally and Permanently Disabled. The rising numbers told another story, too: different kinds of clients were receiving ADC. No longer did widows dominate the program. Divorced, deserted, and never-married mothers, as well as nonwhite mothers, entered the program in large numbers in the 1940s and early 1950s.

It was the growing ADC program, therefore, that Cohen and his fellow poverty investigators focused on in their inquiry into postwar poverty and single motherhood.[15] Women and children on ADC were more likely to be poor because they lacked a male breadwinner and were therefore deprived of additional wages. But more important in Cohen's mind was the fact that these "broken homes" of ADC clients distorted family and social patterns in such a way as to aggravate or create economic problems. "Matriarchy" and "social maladjustments" were, in the view of Cohen and his colleagues, apt to foster additional problems such as maintaining health, caring for children, and finding and keeping jobs.[16] All of these problems, in turn, increased the likelihood of remaining in poverty.

Long familiar with the ADC program through his work at the Social Security Administration, Cohen concluded that it would have to be radically altered if it was going to address the poverty problems facing its new clients. As it was, ADC gave money to clients, albeit paltry sums, to reduce their economic distress. But Cohen maintained that "money is not the entire solution of many of the cases receiving assistance. In fact, continued payment of assistance may only serve to perpetuate the problem."[17] ADC, in Cohen's view, was alleviating but not remedying the "fundamental" poverty of single mothers, offering a temporary palliative rather than a cure for the social and psychological maladjustments associated with it. "I don't know how to solve all of these [problems]," Cohen continued, ". . . but I believe there are lots of other elements we must emphasize other than [money] assistance."[18] In the end, Cohen's inquiries into poverty in the affluent society generated a simple analysis: the thorniest of America's poverty problems was single mothers and the solution was to change welfare.

Cohen's determinations about poverty, women, and welfare were crucial because he was a leader in an emerging coalition of welfare and social work professionals, researchers, foundations, and interest groups whose work was related to the ADC program. Today we would call them welfare reformers. In the two decades after World War II, they studied the program and its clients and proposed, lobbied for, and enacted major changes in federal welfare law. Their labor resulted in three reforms of the ADC program in 1956, 1961, and 1962.

Nearly five decades before the elimination of welfare and the substitution of "workfare," three decades before the studies of the "underclass" and the debates about "welfare queens," and one decade before the War on Poverty, Cohen and his allies in the field of public welfare confronted what had already become charged, intertwined issues in postwar America: gender, race, poverty, and welfare. Their story reveals a neglected aspect of the history of poverty and the welfare state in postwar America—that national policy makers were focused determinedly on poor women and welfare programs much earlier than has been recognized. Early welfare reformers' leadership of national policy challenges our understanding of the history of public policy regarding the poor in other ways, too. Neither Cohen nor his colleagues were social scientists; they were not part of the cohort of sociologists and economists whom poverty historians have labeled America's poverty intellectuals and policy makers.[19] They were a far less exalted group that was affiliated with schools of social work and the administration of federal welfare programs. Yet, in the two decades after

World War II in which they dominated the field of national welfare policy, this coalition of welfare reformers created distinct perspectives and proposed policy solutions that would provide models for what subsequent policy makers of the 1960s and beyond would—or would not—do.

The Influences of Postwar Welfare Reform

The standard historical narrative of the twentieth-century American welfare state has focused almost exclusively on the Progressive Era, the New Deal, and the Great Society.[20] But it was in the 1950s and early 1960s that programs from earlier eras—like ADC—were transformed, laying the groundwork for further social welfare policy in the late 1960s and beyond. The affluent society provided opportunities and inspiration for policy makers like Wilbur Cohen who were committed to studying poverty and social welfare. Guided by an evolving liberal political ideology and new theories and methods in the social work profession, they found the 1950s and early 1960s a hospitable, though not unlimited, environment for studying poverty, women, and welfare, and using their insights to change federal welfare law.

All of the individuals associated with postwar welfare reform were self-designated liberals, and postwar liberal ideology shaped their approach to poverty and welfare programs in the 1950s and early 1960s. Many had long cared about poverty and social policy as Democrats and participants in the New Deal. Wilbur Cohen, the most influential member of the welfare advocacy coalition of the postwar era, cut his teeth as a policy maker during the New Deal when he started at the Social Security Administration as an assistant to Social Security Commissioner Arthur Altmeyer, a fellow University of Wisconsin alumnus. Other postwar welfare leaders, all friends and colleagues of Cohen, also took part in the New Deal expansion of the welfare state. Loula Dunn, for example, was director of the American Public Welfare Association (APWA), the professional organization representing public welfare administrators, policy makers, and social workers. Created in the early 1930s as a liaison between the various New Deal federal welfare agencies and state and local governments, the APWA formed a core professional constituency actively involved in the federal welfare state. It became the most influential institution within national welfare circles, as many of its leaders moved fluidly between state and federal agencies.[21] Dunn ran the APWA from the 1940s through the 1960s, but she began her career as a state welfare administrator in Alabama during the 1920s and 1930s, and then worked in the New Deal's Federal Emergency Relief Administration and the Works Progress Administration. Ellen Winston, an active leader in the APWA who would become commissioner of the federal Welfare Administration in the early 1960s, also began her career in the New Deal. She worked in the Works Progress Administration and the Farm Security Agency and was on the National Resources Planning Board, becoming an administrator of New Deal welfare programs in North Carolina by the early 1940s. Elizabeth Wickenden, a colleague of Dunn and Winston at the APWA, a lifelong friend of Wilbur Cohen, and the most influential welfare lobbyist of her day, also began her career in the Works Progress Administration and parlayed that first position into a long career in federal welfare policy.

As the 1940s dawned, these public welfare leaders allied themselves with other liberals to try to continue the New Deal's momentum. Wickenden left the federal government and joined Dunn and Winston at the American Public Welfare Association as a legislative consultant in their new Washington, D.C., office.[22] There she and Cohen, also an APWA member while in the Social Security Administration, became strategists and foot soldiers in the liberal campaign to expand social welfare programs, which they saw many Western European countries doing. Banding together with other government and wartime agencies, they lobbied for expanding Social Security, increasing public welfare, creating national health insurance, and guaranteeing employment—an encore to the New Deal.

Welfare professionals and federal agency officers were joined in this effort by liberal allies outside the world of welfare, who would in the 1950s support them in their bid for welfare reform. These included the AFL-CIO labor union, particularly its Community Service Activities division, and the National Urban League, the national civil rights organization. Both the AFL-CIO and the Urban League played a role in welfare policy making in the 1950s, usually with the aim of getting legislation passed or of presenting legislative issues to the public.[23] Their support for welfare in the 1950s derived from their initial political investment in the New Deal and their hopes for expanding the welfare state during the 1940s, as part of their respective agendas on labor and civil rights. Both sustained the efforts of welfare professionals and federal agency officers in lobbying for the expansion of social security and the creation of new employment and health care programs during the 1940s.

Another liberal organization that joined the coalition of welfare reform advocates in the 1950s was the foundation created by department store and newspaper magnate Marshall Field III. The well-endowed and influential Field Foundation was a crucial source of financial support for research and public relations, promoting ADC reform and pursuing opportunities to shape legislation in the early 1960s.[24] Its initial interest in welfare programs arose in the

1940s, however, in hopes of expanding New Deal liberalism. Founded in 1944, the Field Foundation was explicitly political, a rare characteristic in the world of philanthropy. Left-leaning, it was an advocate for the welfare state and for expanding social programs for the poor and minorities.[25]

Although the efforts of liberal welfare professionals, federal agency officers, foundations, and interest groups to expand and improve New Deal–era welfare programs were rejected in the immediate postwar period, these advocates continued to try to effect liberal policy change in the 1950s. Yet there were significant differences between the liberalism of the New Deal and the 1940s and the liberalism of the 1950s. Cohen's and his allies' postwar analysis of poverty and welfare emerged within the bounds of Keynesian growth liberalism, the economic ideology to which most liberals and Democrats in the affluent society subscribed. No better articulation of this ideology existed than a renowned midcentury assessment of American life in the late 1950s, the Rockefeller Brothers Fund Special Studies Project called "Prospect for America," in which Wilbur Cohen participated. Rather than trying to regulate the capitalist economy in order to protect and improve the welfare of citizens, as some of the most ambitious New Deal proposals had, the Rockefeller Brothers Fund project concluded that projected economic growth would raise incomes and provide jobs. Economic growth was also expected to provide enough tax revenues to fund social policy, making additional taxation for social spending unnecessary. Neither Cohen nor fellow welfare policy makers questioned that the economy could provide enough government revenues for programs to aid citizens who did not share in its growth.[26] They believed, as Cohen wrote to the Rockefeller Brothers Fund, that "we can also accomplish the expansion of our services without reducing the existing standard of living of producers. In other words, as our gross national product increases, we can allocate a portion of the increase for needed improvement in services, thus making it possible to increase the income of producers at the same time that services are increased."[27] In sum, Americans could have all they wanted materially and reduce economic inequities at the same time. This acceptance of the market and its abilities to provide security differed markedly from liberal attitudes of the 1930s and 1940s, and constituted a central tenet of the liberal political culture that in 1949 Arthur Schlesinger termed the "vital center"—a broad, nonideological, and moderate-liberal political consensus.[28]

Recent historical studies of political liberalism in postwar America, however, have shown that the liberal consensus was more complicated and contested than Schlesinger implied. Welfare reformers and their allies, despite their faith that Keynesian growth liberalism could solve social and economic problems, formed a distinct subgroup of liberals.[29] Their interest in poverty and welfare programs and their accompanying concern with single mothers set them apart from many other liberals in the 1950s. The Rockefeller Brothers Fund project, for example, reflected the interests of most leading liberals, who, in focusing almost solely on national security and economic growth, gave poverty and welfare short shrift.

Working within the confines of a less comprehensive and ambitious liberal vision of the welfare state in the postwar years, welfare reform advocates and their allies nevertheless considered themselves revolutionaries of sorts. Much of the novelty they claimed derived from their association with the social work profession, which was undergoing a change in the 1940s and 1950s that would influence federal welfare policy. Most welfare advocates were either trained as social workers or affiliated with social work–based organizations. The APWA was one such organization, and others included the National Social Welfare Assembly, an organization of private social welfare organizations, and the National Association of Social Workers (NASW). The latter two would not become significant actors in national policy making until the late 1950s and early 1960s, but individual members of these organizations and faculty in schools of social work, such as Wilbur Cohen and Elizabeth Wickenden, played important roles in welfare reform. Other allies of welfare reform were also affiliated with the field of social work. National Urban League leaders of this period, Lester Granger and Whitney Young, were social workers, and their organization provided social services. In addition, some national foundations funded social work research that was then applied to the field of public welfare. The most influential was the William T. Grant Foundation, which funded agency-based experimentation in applying social work methods to public welfare programs. Social work's ideas and practices thus formed a common language and practice for all those professionals coalescing around welfare in the 1950s.

In the early postwar years, changing views of poverty, women, and welfare were closely tied to a transformation in the social work profession. Though casework had lain at the heart of the profession since the 1920s, its popularity waned during the depression. Now, after the war, social work leaders embraced casework again. But they recast it. By midcentury, psychology and social psychology reigned as dominant frameworks for understanding human behavior, and social casework became sharply focused on the therapeutic treatment of small groups, families, and individuals. Most casework was performed by private agencies and social welfare organizations where pay and prestige was high. But therapeutic ideology and practice also began to influence the social workers associated with public welfare programs. Group and individual casework among public program clients became increasingly popular, and researchers conducted pilot projects attempting to demonstrate how the "trained professional" using professional methods could better solve the problems of public welfare clients. As policy makers like Cohen contemplated the paradox of poverty in the affluent society and he and his fellow liberal supporters of welfare programs considered how to augment and improve ADC in the 1950s, casework provided inspiration and guidance.

Social work researchers thus became important allies in promoting the welfare reform agenda for which Cohen and others proselytized. Some of the research on ADC originated in private social welfare organizations that were members of the National Social Welfare Assembly, including the Family Service Association of America and the Child Welfare League of America. More research on welfare derived from schools of social work, including the one at the University of Michigan, where Wilbur Cohen pursued his studies. Among the most influential institutions researching welfare programs was the consulting firm Community Research Associates (CRA). Founded by social worker Bradley Buell and the past president of the APWA, Harry O. Page, CRA took contracts from local and state welfare agencies as well as grants from private foundations to conduct research and demonstration projects on welfare.[30] They and other social workers created a substantial new body of information on welfare.[31] Working closely with the APWA and leading policy makers, CRA and other researchers blended their research with advocacy for ADC reform, using it to fuel public relations and recommend changes in policy.

Just as liberal ideology and social work provided inspiration and tools for welfare reform, other forces limited it. To be sure, social workers and welfare administrators operated with relative autonomy in the area of poverty and welfare reform, as few other liberals during this period demonstrated interest. In addition, until the mid- to late 1960s, there were no poor people's movements and no welfare rights organizations to represent welfare clients and contest welfare policy makers' authority.[32] Policy makers therefore spoke of and for the poor with little challenge. But because many welfare reformers were employed in the public welfare programs, federal, state, and local officeholders held them accountable, as did a public increasingly concerned about welfare clients and welfare spending. Welfare policy makers thus had to negotiate their reform agenda with opponents.

The most challenging negotiation in this period was with conservative politicians — at the local, state, and national levels — who opposed public assistance programs in general and ADC in particular. Mainstream political conservatism surged in the postwar years with the election of more conservatives to Congress in the 1940s and 1950s and Republican Dwight Eisenhower to the presidency in 1952. Though postwar conservatism was as varied as postwar liberalism, it rested on several principles opposed to federal welfare programs. Many conservatives were fiscally cautious, opposing discretionary spending on social welfare programs as unaffordable or wasteful. Other conservative politicians, particularly in the South and the West, also supported the ideology of states' rights, which opposed the attempts of federal authorities to dictate how the states should act. Some conservatives of both the Republican and Democratic parties subscribed to racist ideologies and sought to prevent federal social programs from reaching African Americans. And, finally, many conservatives subscribed to a concept of social morality hostile to the new welfare clientele that appeared after the war—divorced and unwed mothers. They viewed these women as immoral and therefore undeserving of public support. Welfare advocates faced one or more of these objections to welfare nearly every time they came before Congress. They were often forced to calibrate their requests based on the power of conservatives to block their proposals. Across the country, from the 1940s to the 1960s, conservative opposition to welfare grew, evolving into a nearly impenetrable political resistance.[33]

Welfare policy makers faced another limitation to their influence. Though welfare reformers were an expertise-based policy elite, they were a group apart from, and generally lower in professional status than, the social science experts who, as Alice O'Connor's recent work demonstrates, would soon gain power over the national social policy agenda. Social science experts—namely economists —directly influenced federal social policy on poverty after 1961, through the Council on Economic Advisers, the Juvenile Delinquency Program Office, and the Office of Economic Opportunity.[34] Unlike these experts, welfare policy makers claimed knowledge not through complex macro- and microeconomic theory, but largely through the concrete experience of social work practice. And while many social work leaders took pride in what they considered to be advances in their profession at midcentury, welfare policy makers who invoked social work expertise nevertheless felt, correctly, that their specialized knowledge was not deemed as legitimate as more esoteric social science knowledge. They occupied a vulnerable political space, one whose weakness would be revealed as social scientists gained power over the federal poverty and social welfare agenda in the early to mid-1960s.[35]

Gender, Race, and Rehabilitation

By the mid-1950s, liberal social work professionals, researchers, government officials, and allied organizations such as foundations created a consensus to reform welfare to address their concerns about poor women in the affluent society. The contours of this policy agenda emerged in studies that placed ADC and welfare clients under the microscope. In one such pioneering study of welfare in St. Paul, Minnesota, Community Research Associates, the private consulting firm that researched public welfare, conducted an in-depth study examining why welfare clients used welfare. Though the most obvious answer was lack of income, CRA did not accept that. Its study examined the lives, relationships, and personalities of welfare clients in great detail, concluding that welfare use was not necessitated by the economy or social composition of St. Paul, but rather, "in 96% of the families, the primary cause of continuing dependency lay in some serious handicap to self-maintenance."[36] In nearly all cases, the "handicap" was a deep-seated personal problem of the welfare recipient. "Vicious clustering of human ills" and personal "maladjustment," CRA concluded, were predominant causes of welfare need.[37] If America was going to solve the problem of the so-called hardcore poor, CRA believed that welfare programs needed to address the personal ills of welfare clients, and this required fundamental change in the welfare system. None was more important than "rehabilitation," which became the centerpiece of postwar poverty and welfare policy.

Rehabilitation embodied the political and professional beliefs of its architects, typifying their centrist liberalism and their faith in therapeutic solutions to social problems. The policy did not aim to change the economy, social structure, or social relations of American society. To the contrary, the rehabilitative ethos assumed that American society and its economy were healthy and functional and that the welfare poor simply needed to be helped or compelled to participate in both more effectively. In the words of President Dwight Eisenhower, instead of aiming to reduce poverty, rehabilitation strove to "reduce need and increase self-help among those who depend on public welfare," keeping them from welfare or helping them get off welfare expeditiously.[38] Casework provided the discourse and methodology guiding the rehabilitative process. Rehabilitative services would determine the individual psychological and social problems faced by the poor—establish a diagnosis, in the jargon of social workers—and then provide therapies to fix them. In concrete terms, social workers would provide tailor-made services on a client-by-client basis to rehabilitate the welfare poor from "dependency" to "independence."

Beneath rehabilitation's individualistic and therapeutic ethos lay other motivations. Rehabilitation did not grow simply out of a general interest in poverty, nor was it targeted to all people with low incomes. Rather, rehabilitation grew out of Wilbur Cohen's and others' identification of the poverty problem with poor single women. The clearest evidence of this was that rehabilitative methods were not incorporated equally into all four existing categorical federal public assistance programs; they were primarily made part of the ADC program, the program that these women populated. The logic of rehabilitation, therefore, was inextricably tied to researchers' assessments of the "problematic" status of ADC clients. This meant that as the welfare reform coalition honed their vision of a rehabilitative welfare state for the poor, they did so through the lenses of race and gender ideologies, which animated their views of their target population. To put it another way, the political moderation of rehabilitation, its individualistic analysis of poverty, and its therapeutic mode derived in large part from policy makers' assumptions about poor single mothers.

This was evident as early as the very first successful reformist legislation instituting rehabilitation at the federal level: the 1956 Social Security Amendments. According to the law, the new rehabilitative ADC program was to "encourage self-care and self-support" among clients.[39] Self-care and self-support were defined according to policy makers' views of poor single mothers. Self-care referred to mothers' caring for themselves and their children adequately, and translated into a goal of "strengthening family life." Tapping into broader social debates about the importance of families in American society and the role of parents and children within families, welfare reformers attempted to "rehabilitate" welfare clients whose family patterns deviated from white middle-class norms. While they rarely envisioned turning single-parent households into two-parent households—that seemed beyond their capabilities—they did imagine altering the sexual and social behavior of mothers and supervising the relationships between mothers and children in order to improve the care at home.

The rehabilitative goal of "self-support" referred to "encouraging independence," which meant being self-supporting through wage work. Welfare reformers took sides in an emerging debate about working mothers in 1950s America that pitted "traditional" domestic expectations for women against the desire of and need for women to work. They made a virtue of what they perceived as necessity—that women heads of households would have to work and support themselves and their families with earnings. Expounding on the psychological and social value of work, they argued that employment could be positive for some mothers and their children. Social services in the welfare program there-

fore attempted to "rehabilitate" welfare clients by training them for employment and encouraging them to find jobs.

The two goals of rehabilitation—self-care and self-support—rested on
two different prescriptive roles for a woman: woman as mother and woman as
economic provider. This was an important historical shift in the program. As
welfare historian Joanne Goodwin has shown, mothers' pensions and ADC had
never formally incorporated the simultaneous goals of protecting family life
and encouraging women's employment.[40] So welfare policy makers of the 1950s
broke new ground in imagining women's roles as encompassing both responsibilities. The new goals, however, were arguably contradictory. Could women
who were encouraged to leave their children to support their families be the
kind of "functional" mothers that rehabilitation prescribed? Conversely, would
"strengthening family life" in a one-parent family require the mother to forgo
earning to spend more time on family responsibilities? Given such tensions,
which role would rehabilitation rank higher? Were women on welfare to embrace primarily the familial role as mothers or the economic role as workers?

These were questions that welfare reformers did not fully acknowledge,
even though they faced pressures to lean toward one or the other conclusion.
The institutional history of ADC favored encouraging women to care for their
families: its original stated purpose was to help poor mothers without husbands
to remain in their familial roles, raising children. Moreover, in actual implemen-
tation, the program sometimes achieved this goal, especially for white women
and northern women. The strong cultural bias toward traditional, feminine domesticity in the 1950s also seemed to support keeping mothers in the home.
Yet ADC's support of mothering was not, and had never been, secure. Despite
the ostensible purpose of the program, some local welfare agencies distinguished among poor mothers, often on the basis of race, forcing some to work
and allowing others to become eligible for welfare. This was increasingly common in the South and in agricultural states of the West in the 1940s and 1950s.
At the same time, in the 1950s, unprecedented numbers of married women, many
with children, entered the labor force. Their paid employment implicitly challenged the social and cultural representation of women as solely stay-at-home
mothers. Welfare policy makers grappled with the question of how, for the
purpose of social entitlements, welfare should envision women's roles throughout the period from 1945 to 1965, never fully resolving the contradictions in-
herent in their rehabilitative policy.

The complexity and contradictions of the rehabilitative agenda took other
forms, too. Rehabilitation was predicated on negative perceptions of poor single mothers: they had serious personal problems that contributed to their pov-

erty and only individual intervention could solve them. To justify the need for rehabilitation, its advocates stigmatized their target population. Yet the public presentation of rehabilitation simultaneously projected a more subtle and positive image of poor single mothers. With the growing and changing clientele of the ADC program, welfare advocates rightly feared political opposition. In the late 1950s, they developed public relations strategies to sell welfare to the public and to protect the program from opponents. This tactic had one central goal: preventing the stigmatization of the ADC program. Altering their gendered discourse, welfare reformers billed ADC as a program "for families," rather than a program for troubled single mothers. Placing the word "family" in the title of the program—Aid to Families with Dependent Children, which occurred in 1962—was symbolic of this effort. In the process, single-mother families were often publicly portrayed as "just like other families." They provided warm, functional homes where children grew up normally. When welfare reformers admitted ADC families had problems that traditional families might not, they pointed to the "self-care" goals of the new rehabilitative ADC program as important, and as yet underutilized, tools in the battle to restore these families. Presented in its best light, ADC looked like a means of protecting and invigorating American families and communities.

In this light, ADC was also oriented toward whites. The corollary to the destigmatizing gendered rhetoric was an equally strategic response to the racialization of the program. As more African Americans gained access to ADC in the 1940s and 1950s, hostility to the program rose. Though the majority of eligible African American women did not receive ADC, opponents of welfare and African American rights nevertheless implied that welfare opened its doors to huge numbers of African American women. Welfare advocates were keenly aware of this misrepresentation. They feared its potential to destroy the program and hamper their bid to reform ADC. As a result, they developed a public relations strategy whereby they erased the race of ADC clientele. In their minds destigmatizing welfare meant not merely emphasizing "family" but also emphasizing the whiteness of ADC families. Only on rare occasions were ADC families revealed publicly as nonwhite families. Often, race was simply not mentioned. But when welfare advocates chose positive stories of "rehabilitated" ADC families to present to the public, they overwhelmingly chose white families.

The public erasure of race in welfare reform discourse was typical of midcentury "Myrdalian" racial liberalism. Welfare advocates, like sociologist Gunnar Myrdal and many liberals, acknowledged the "American dilemma" of racial inequality. Yet they viewed direct and aggressive confrontations over discrimination as dangerous.[41] Moreover, they, like many other race liberals, believed that racial discrimination was probably going to be eliminated through formal legal challenges, such as *Brown v. Board of Education* (1954), and through the "modernization" of American society. Those who supported welfare in this period created a rhetoric in which positive portrayals of family life shrouded references to race.[42]

Through their reform efforts, welfare policy makers created a complex and seemingly contradictory postwar discourse on poverty, race, women, and welfare. On the one hand, their ideas for welfare reform rested on racial and gendered ideologies of the postwar era that positioned poor single mothers as objects of social anxieties about family life and race. Yet, on the other hand, welfare advocates had professional and political investments in the ADC program, and these required them, when presenting ADC to the public, to deny or circumvent the very ideologies they relied on. Moreover, the effort to cast a positive light on poor women and welfare produced unpredictable results, such that contemporary assumptions about welfare clients and the realities they faced were subverted in the service of policy reform.

The Politics of Welfare Reform

Postwar welfare reformers struggled to implement rehabilitation, but their success depended on the broader political context in which they operated. This context shifted markedly over the twenty years in which reformers led national welfare policy. In the 1940s, American liberalism was at the tail end of the New Deal; in the 1950s, it appeared more accomodationist; and in the 1960s, it stood at the dawn of a seemingly new era—the Great Society. Changing political winds from the 1940s through the mid-1960s help account for the rise and subsequent fall of welfare policy makers' control over the national agenda on poverty and form the chronological backdrop of this book.

The politics of the 1940s are crucial to understanding the subsequent welfare reform agenda because the notion to reform the ADC program emerged from the ashes of liberals' failed drive to expand the New Deal welfare state in that decade. As is discussed in chapter 1, the defeat of a comprehensive vision of social welfare required actors in the federal agencies, such as Wilbur Cohen, Elizabeth Wickenden, and their colleagues in the APWA, to reconsider their legislative strategy and their philosophy of welfare provision. Disappointed but not defeated, they scaled back and redefined "comprehensive social welfare" to meet new political realities. In the late 1940s, welfare advocates created a new strategy to seek change and improvement within the existing ADC program, making ADC more "comprehensive," as they put it, through an array of social services for welfare clients. With that, however, the promise of truly comprehensive social welfare withered. In the 1950s, policy makers would not discuss poverty and solutions to it in a bold, universal manner, but rather within a context narrowed by the structure of the existing categorical ADC program and the gender and race politics adhering to it.

In the late 1940s, as this accommodation was made, it was still unclear what kind of services would be added to welfare to make it more "comprehensive." But by the mid-1950s, it was clear: the answer was rehabilitation. Chapter 2 describes the main elements of the new rehabilitative paradigm and how they reflected the changing social and political concerns of the 1950s—concerns about the confluence of poverty and family life, and faith in therapeutic methods. In 1956 welfare advocates took the first step toward permanent reform—passing the Social Security Amendments. With this law, the purpose of ADC was altered to emphasize rehabilitation. ADC would no longer merely provide income support to the poor; it would also "strengthen family life" and "encourage independence." The rest of the decade continued to provide a hospitable environment for welfare reformers. Chapter 3 describes how they built on their legislative success, promoting their ideas to groups with looser affiliations with welfare, including private social welfare agencies in the National Social Welfare Assembly, the AFL-CIO, and the National Urban League. Rehabilitation's emphases on increasing social services and improving family life resonated with the priorities of these organizations in the 1950s.

New political developments of the early 1960s, however, would challenge the growing coalition and its reform ideology, and chapters 3, 4, and 5 detail how these events influenced welfare reform. Though welfare advocates generated broader support for rehabilitative welfare reform, they were profoundly shaken when two national welfare crises exploded in the early 1960s. In Louisiana in 1960 and in Newburgh, New York, in 1961, angry local politicians vowed to eliminate the welfare system, punish undeserving welfare clients, and enforce morality and the need to work. Print and television reporters, and George Gallup's pollsters, conducted "man-on-the-street" interviews in which the public revealed dissatisfaction with welfare. The crises irrevocably altered the political landscape of welfare.

One change caused by the crises pertained to how welfare reformers navigated racial politics. In the late 1940s and early 1950s, during the relative quiet of the Eisenhower years and the when the Democratic Party was relatively silent on civil rights, it was feasible for the overwhelmingly white welfare policy makers to erase race from their discourse. But this strategy faltered in the early 1960s, as chapters 3, 4, and 5 explain. The attacks on ADC in the two explosive welfare crises in Louisiana and Newburgh placed race at the center of welfare politics and created a national public debate about race and welfare. In addition, in the early 1960s, the national civil rights movement garnered wide notice and wielded influence within the Democratic Party. When racial issues became paramount in welfare and in politics in the early 1960s, the limitations of a race-blind political strategy became evident. On the one hand, welfare reformers' nonracial discourse did nothing to confront the increasingly racialized opposition to welfare. On the other hand, within the liberal coalition, welfare reformers had difficulty working alongside or within a newly invigorated civil rights lobby and agenda that began to take different perspectives on racial rights and welfare.

The same dynamic was reflected in the changing gender politics of welfare and the overall strategy of presenting ADC as a "family" program, as is described in chapter 3. During the Louisiana crisis, the governor called the 6,000 women cut from the welfare rolls "a bunch of prostitutes," hardly an endorsement of ADC's family image. Likewise, in Newburgh, the city manager implied that women on ADC were not doing useful work when caring for their children, but were, instead, shiftless people who should be in the labor market. These critiques of single mothers on welfare boldly denied the central strategic contention of welfare supporters—that ADC was a necessary family services program—and that it contributed positively to family life. Instead, the welfare crises portrayed welfare as a program that destroyed families and allowed lazy women not to work. What happened in Louisiana and Newburgh suggested that many Americans were unwilling to accept a definition of family that included low-income single mothers.

The welfare crises jolted the welfare reform agenda, especially its embrace of the contradictory goals of improving family life and encouraging paid work for women. Chapter 4 explains how many members of the welfare reform coalition—none more important than Wilbur Cohen—responded by reducing rehabilitation's emphasis on family and women's roles as caregivers and increasing the emphasis on work and women's roles as potential wage earners. In 1961 Cohen assumed a leadership position in the Department of Health, Education, and Welfare; as assistant secretary of legislation, he pursued the further institutionalization of his vision of rehabilitation. With the passage of two laws, one in 1961 and the other in 1962, Cohen stressed work goals for women on welfare, articulating the view that new services and new work and training programs should encourage low-income single mothers to enter the labor force.

By 1962 it looked as though the welfare state offered poor women only one option for addressing their needs: a rehabilitative welfare program that encouraged them to work. But in 1963, with Democrats holding the presidency and in charge of Congress, and an array of liberal activist organizations exerting influence on national political developments, new policy agendas flowered in Washington, D.C., as chapter 5 shows. For the first time in postwar America, federal government policy directly addressed issues that welfare reformers had confronted for at least fifteen years: poverty, race, and women. Two of the most important policy initiatives included the President's Commission on the Status of Women, which helped give birth to a second-wave feminist women's agenda, and the War on Poverty, which raised the prospect of new, larger, and better-funded programs for dealing with the paradox of poverty in the affluent society. What would these policy initiatives mean for welfare reform and poor women?

Because welfare administrators, social workers, researchers, and foundations had been debating these issues since the 1940s, and because they had successfully pushed for passage of relevant legislation, they believed they had an effective model for how the War on Poverty and the President's Commission on the Status of Women might address poverty as it affected women. Yet welfare advocates could not successfully integrate their ideas or their policy recommendations into new arenas. Nor did policy makers in the new arenas generate new models for directly addressing the increasingly pressing relationship between women and poverty. Multiple factors accounted for this. One was the growing political unpopularity of AFDC (ADC having been renamed Aid to Families with Dependent Children in 1962), which caused the new-arena policy makers to shy away from direct association with welfare. But there were also serious ideological differences among liberals: architects of the War on Poverty and members of the President's Commission on the Status of Women acknowledged the relationship between gender and poverty, but they had different ideas about how to address it. In particular, neither believed it necessitated creating new policies solely for poor women, single mothers, or welfare clients. As a result, neither the poverty programs nor the new initiative on women made poor women or welfare programs a priority. In the end, poor women were left only with the recently reformed, rehabilitative AFDC program.

By 1965 welfare reformers had both succeeded and failed. They had created a discourse and a policy to address poverty in an era when few fellow liberals paid notice. But that discourse and policy existed within the narrow political and ideological boundaries of a public assistance program for poor women. Reformers were able to implement their rehabilitative goals in federal law. But when the goals shifted over the years, they left women on welfare in a more precarious position than ever before, with a growing emphasis on their need to work. Welfare itself was also in a precarious position by 1965. Isolated from logically related liberal agendas on poverty and women's rights, it was vulnerable to attack. Low-income single women had little but welfare to serve them, even as their numbers in America grew. Finally, welfare reformers began to lose their influence in the arena of poverty studies and poverty policy, as other policy makers systematically rejected them.

This book tells the story of the origins, development, and outcome of liberal efforts to confront poverty within the ADC program. It details how the professional identities of policy makers, the social politics of race and gender, and the political context of liberalism in the 1940s and 1950s produced a welfare reform agenda that altered women's relationship with the state and produced a novel discourse of poverty in postwar America. It then explores how the reform agenda changed in the early 1960s, examining the public politics of welfare, the move toward work-based goals in rehabilitation, and the unpredictable politics of gender, race, and class in the emerging liberal social agenda of the Great Society. The book concludes by tracing the legacy of postwar welfare reform, after the postwar welfare coalition was dismantled and drifted from influence in the latter half of the 1960s. Paradoxically, while liberal welfare reformers lost power, aspects of rehabilitative rhetoric, particularly the rhetoric of self-support, gained momentum. Drawing on the precedent of rehabilitation, welfare law after the 1960s increasingly focused on forcing poor "dysfunctional" women out of "welfare dependency" and into mandatory "self-support." "Rehabilitation" evolved into "responsibility," and welfare became workfare.

CHAPTER ONE

A New Postwar Paradigm for Welfare

From Comprehensive Social Welfare to Welfare Services

In 1943 a wartime agency called the National Resources Planning Board (NRPB) released a grand plan for the future of America's economic and social security. The NRPB's "Security, Work and Relief Policies" offered a blueprint for a new welfare state. It inspired two ambitious bills in Congress in 1943 and 1945, whose purpose was to augment and alter the infant programs of the New Deal.[1] The bills proposed legislation to guarantee "comprehensive social welfare" for Americans by enlarging the social safety net and providing social and medical services programs to a wide swath of the population. In the judgment of contemporary supporters, and of historians since, passage of these bills would have ensured a larger welfare state and enhanced the power of New Deal liberalism.[2] One important, but seldom noted, outcome of the comprehensive social welfare bills of the early 1940s would have been a new way of providing assistance to the poorest people in the United States.[3] The future of the Aid to Dependent Children (ADC) program in postwar America therefore was tied to the fate of these two bills.

In 1935 the Social Security Act created the first federal programs for helping the poor. One of these was ADC, the federal version of the longstanding mothers' pensions programs in the states. In 1935 ADC became one of several federal public assistance programs that provided aid to special categories of needy Americans—in this case, to dependent children in the care of a needy adult, usually the mother. However, from its inception in 1935, ADC was hamstrung. New Deal policy makers wrested public assistance for women and children from the control of its champion at the federal level up to this time, the Children's Bureau, and instead placed it in the newly created Social Security Administration. There, it was envisioned by administrators as a small, relatively unimportant public assistance program. The Social Security Administration portrayed welfare provision for mothers as a "residual" program for one particular group of the poor, "less desirable and less popular than the new and untried insurance programs," which supported many more American workers and their dependents.[4] As a result, ADC was generally overlooked by the public and overshadowed by the larger and more popular program, Social Security. As Linda Gordon has argued, the creation of ADC in 1935 was a crucial moment, enshrining the undesirability of ADC and its clients while legitimizing Social Security and its clients.[5]

Ten years later, the two comprehensive welfare bills of the early 1940s might have altered the fate of public assistance, for they had the potential to correct some of the negative outcomes of the 1930s for welfare. The two comprehensive welfare bills proposed abolishing ADC and replacing it and the other categorical assistance programs with an all-encompassing, noncategorical public assistance program. The proposals would have changed the demographics of public assistance, serving not only single women with children and an increasing number of nonwhites—a politically vulnerable group—but also a broader cross section of the population, including men and women, white and nonwhite, married and unmarried people, old and young, disabled and able-bodied. This would have enlarged federal public assistance rolls significantly, challenging the "residual" position of welfare, if not the preeminence of Social Security. Had the bills passed, the social welfare proposals of 1943 and 1945 would have created a new program and new faces of welfare in America.

Though the bills had support in the administration and, to some extent, in Congress, as well as among many liberal interest groups, they failed to pass in the conservative-dominated congressional sessions of 1943 and 1945. Conservative hostility to the New Deal welfare state continued after 1945, making future plans to radically augment the American welfare state unlikely. With the defeat of comprehensive social welfare, the promise of altering the fate of ADC evaporated.

The future of welfare then became uncertain. Would ADC remain in its unimportant position in the federal social welfare system? Would it be even more neglected and demeaned? Observers of welfare policy at the time were not sure and could conclude only the obvious: "Today we stand at the crossroads in public welfare."[6] But in the years immediately following the defeat of the proposed innovative legislation, welfare did start down a different path. Just as the mid-1930s were a pivotal period for women and welfare in America, so, too, were the years from 1943 to 1949. This chapter reconstructs the legislative, political, and policy-making moments of the 1940s. It describes the possibilities that comprehensive social welfare offered for welfare programs and the defeat of this liberal vision. It then examines the subsequent "crossroads" at which welfare policy stood and the direction in which it headed afterward.

During the difficulties of the 1940s, new historical actors emerged in welfare policy. The most important was the American Public Welfare Association (APWA), the national organization representing administrators and social workers affiliated with federal welfare programs. The APWA influenced the proposals for comprehensive social welfare and responded to their defeat with new strategies for welfare. Indeed, the defeat of comprehensive social welfare forced welfare advocates to reconsider the way in which they approached legislation, positioning it so that it could survive a conservative Congress wary of enlarging the welfare state. At the same time, welfare advocates sought a way to wield greater political power vis-à-vis Congress. The defeats of the comprehensive social welfare bills of 1943 and 1945 spurred a major effort to politicize APWA members and redefine the organization as the voice of federal public assistance programs, especially ADC. With greater influence, APWA leaders hoped for legislative success.

In practical terms, welfare policy makers repeatedly failed to win legislative successes. But their work in the 1940s was fundamental nonetheless. The ups and downs of the 1940s prompted new thinking about the philosophy of welfare provision. The failure of broad legislative proposals prompted a diminishment of the meaning of the term "comprehensive social welfare." Chastened by the defeat of grand plans for massive reform, welfare advocates settled on a modest strategy to change and improve the existing ADC program in the late 1940s. The APWA carved out a new philosophical position on welfare that emphasized making ADC more "comprehensive," not by replacing the program with a broad noncategorical system as the 1943 and 1945 bills had proposed to do, but instead by providing an array of social services to welfare clients from within the ADC program itself. By the end of the 1940s, "comprehensive" meant something far less bold.

Comprehensive Social Welfare in the Early 1940s

Although the New Deal social welfare system had just been created in the mid-1930s, by the 1940s liberal policy makers were already deconstructing and reconstructing it, in a sweeping attempt to refurbish the system. Two cornerstones of this effort were the Wagner-Murray-Dingell bills of 1943 and 1945, sponsored by congressional allies Robert Wagner (D-N.Y.), James Murray (D-Mont.), and John Dingell (D-Mich.). The presidential administrations of Democrats Franklin Roosevelt and Harry Truman, respectively, proposed major improvements and changes in the New Deal through new health care policy, full-employment policy, and social welfare programs.[7]

Though the proposals came only ten years after the Social Security Act, the cast of characters involved in social policy had changed. Some actors from 1935 were no longer as influential. One was the Children's Bureau. As Linda Gordon has demonstrated, the Children's Bureau was handed a political defeat when the ADC program, a program it had overseen in its state-level mothers' pensions incarnation, was wrested from its control in 1935. That defeat spelled the declining influence of the bureau; it would never play a decisive policy-making role in ADC again. Of course, the Children's Bureau did not abandon its interest in ADC simply because of its declining power. In the 1940s and 1950s, the Children's Bureau continued to review legislative and administrative proposals regarding ADC and advocate for the program. Yet in general in the postwar years, the Children's Bureau spent more of its resources on promoting child welfare and child care than on ADC. Moreover, leadership in the Social Security Administration, the Bureau of Public Assistance, and later incarnations of the federal welfare administration were not inclined to grant the Children's Bureau any greater role.[8]

Aside from the declining power of Children's Bureau, the conception of the Wagner-Murray-Dingell bills reflected the creation of the Social Security Act in the 1930s in several ways. Just as in 1934–35, no major Progressive Era organizations were involved in the lobbying for or deliberations of the bold new laws being proposed. The National Consumer's League, the American Association of University Women, the General Federation of Women's Clubs, and the Women's Trade Union Leagues, which had vigorously supported the creation of state-level social welfare legislation in the early twentieth century, were no longer actively lobbying in the early 1930s for social welfare legislation, and did not, therefore, contribute to the legislative process in the 1940s. Rather, both the Social Security Act of the 1930s and the Wagner-Murray-Dingell bills of the 1940s were products of government insiders—officers in government agencies. Just as a temporary government agency—the Committee on Economic Security —had crafted the Social Security Act, so, too, did a temporary agency—the National Resources Planning Board—inspire the comprehensive social welfare bills of the 1940s. In addition, some actors from the 1930s continued to wield power in the 1940s. The Social Security Administration and its staff, created in 1935, and the Bureau of Public Assistance, remained crucial actors in the early 1940s, major planners of comprehensive social welfare.[9]

One Social Security civil servant wielding influence in the 1940s was Wilbur Cohen. In 1943 Wilbur Cohen was serving as technical adviser to the commissioner of Social Security, Arthur Altmeyer. He had been working for Altmeyer for eight years, and Altmeyer treated him "almost like a son," as one mutual friend put it.[10] Through Altmeyer, Wilbur Cohen found himself deeply involved in the proposals for comprehensive social welfare, an active policy maker unlike most technical advisers to commissioners of Social Security.[11] Throughout his five-decade career in government, spanning from the 1930s to the 1980s, Cohen was a skilled architect of public policy. He frequently wrote legislation for his agency, and also for members of Congress, whether trying to gain their sponsorship for a bill or helping them win an election. As Edward Berkowitz points out, in the early 1940s, Cohen built a relationship with Senator Robert Wagner of New York, educating him about the Social Security system and helping him craft positions on social welfare in general. Working with the senator and his staff, Cohen wrote key sections of the Wagner-Murray-Dingell legislation on Wagner's behalf.[12]

The Wagner-Murray-Dingell bills of 1943 and 1945 reflected an ideology of "comprehensive social welfare" unique to the early 1940s, part of what some scholars call the "third New Deal." Beginning in 1939, with the creation of the National Resources Planning Board, members of Roosevelt's administration began to plan for the postdepression economy. Composed of federal agency officers with slightly varying ideologies, the NRPB collectively envisioned both an opportunity and a necessity to create fiscal and welfare policies to ensure prosperity, employment, and welfare for the American people in the coming decades.[13] This philosophy envisioned a sweeping social safety net for Americans. At its core was the old-age insurance program, Social Security. Surrounding it were various social programs, from unemployment insurance to public assistance, which were seen as necessary to ensure total security, but ancillary to social insurance. The bills were a bold attempt to secure many different kinds of social welfare legislation at once, and they would have changed social welfare in the United States significantly.

Notably, the bills proposed major changes in federal public assistance programs. The rhetoric of public assistance surrounding the bills reflected the traditional preeminence of Social Security. Comprehensive social welfare advocates argued that eventually social insurance—both old-age and unemployment insurance—would expand its coverage of citizens so as to obviate the need for public assistance; public assistance might then "wither away." Yet in their details, the bills belied this rhetoric, the authors' being mindful of the fact that the public assistance rolls were growing in the late 1930s and early 1940s, though they declined temporarily during the war. The bills' authors recognized that public assistance was not likely to wither away, so they proposed overhauling and enlarging it.[14] They suggested replacing the existing 1935 categorical assistance programs—Aid to Dependent Children, Aid to the Blind, and Old Age Assistance—which were aimed at helping specific target populations of the needy, with one large, noncategorical federal public assistance program that would cover all needy people. Single mothers and children, the blind, and the needy elderly would no longer be the only people covered. Any needy adults could receive benefits.[15] This change would protect more of the poor under federal public assistance programs, rather than leaving them to the whims of local and state general assistance programs, which were notoriously underfunded and unreliable.

In addition, the new large, noncategorical program would have featured greater national-level administrative control of welfare. Because the existing categorical programs were strongly federal, with shared monies and administration and rules between the federal government and the states and localities, significant discretionary authority over welfare existed across the country. Such discretion allowed for states to provide small welfare payments if they so desired and to interpret federal rules with considerable latitude. Many southern and western states exercised their own discretion to limit or deny aid to nonwhite ADC clients. The new, national, noncategorical program might have reduced the power of state and local governments to determine eligibility for public assistance.

Some of those included in the existing categorical public assistance programs feared that a noncategorical federal public assistance program would threaten their status. Advocates for the blind, for example, worried that a new universal program would obscure the special needs of the blind.[16] Some children's advocates, such as the Child Welfare League of America, expressed concern about a program that lumped children's welfare in with the welfare provided to adults, fearing it would reduce the sympathy associated with aid for children.[17] Indeed, no one group would have received special benefits or recognition under a universal plan.

For single women with children in the ADC program, however, inclusion in a broad, noncategorical public assistance program for all needy adults and dependents would likely have improved their experience in the program—and their children's—though such an outcome was neither foreseen nor intended by policy makers at the time. Because the new programs would have served all kinds of needy people, the beneficiaries of ADC might have faced less scrutiny and disapproval as single mothers or as representatives of "broken families." Indeed, the poverty of single mothers might not have been interpreted as an exceptional issue and, instead, could have been subsumed within a larger debate about problems of low income.

The changes to the social welfare system promised by the Wagner-Murray-Dingell bills garnered solid support from the AFL and CIO, civil rights organizations, and a range of other groups and individuals interested in Social Security, disability, child welfare, and health.[18] The support of one organization was particularly significant for the future of public assistance—that of the American Public Welfare Association (APWA). Founded in 1931, it was "financed by the Laura Spellman [Rockefeller] Fund . . . [and] devoted to Public Administration." In its early years, it was closely associated with New Deal programs, particularly the Federal Emergency Relief Agency (FERA) and assisted in getting the programs of the Social Security Act off the ground. As the latter programs became institutionalized, the field of public administration grew in the late 1930s and 1940s. The APWA then turned its attention to professionalizing welfare administrators and to representing local and state-level workers and administrators in public welfare offices.[19] The APWA was also a conduit for information about welfare between different levels of government, keeping "membership informed of state and federal developments in legislation and administration."[20]

The American Public Welfare Association became closely involved in federal policy, particularly once it was clear that federal assistance programs were institutionalized. In the 1930s, Frank Bane, one of the founders of the APWA, was selected to serve on the Social Security Board, and "the APWA acted in close consultation with, and as an extended arm of, the board," according to one historian.[21] In the early 1940s, because of World War II, the APWA became more involved in the policy-making process at the federal level. The war disrupted traditional patterns of social welfare provision and created new ones. The mobilization of soldiers and civilians, and the conversion from a civilian economy to a wartime one, required a mammoth and coordinated response by cities, communities, and families. To expedite this, the government turned to partnerships with nongovernmental organizations. Although such relationships were most evident in the guidance of wartime industrial production, with business and labor unions playing key roles, there was also a partnership of government and the private sector in the field of social welfare.[22]

During the war, various offices in the federal government, including the War Department, the Labor Department, the Federal Security Agency, and the Children's Bureau, worked with the APWA, as well as other nongovernmental groups. The APWA's leaders promised to do anything they could for any agency as part of the war effort. The organization loaned personnel to the government and staffed committees such as the U.S. Committee for the Care of European Children and the Toland Committee on Migration of Workers during the war. APWA director Fred Hoehler "was all over the War Department, the State Department, every department of government figuring out what APWA could do for them." As one overwhelmed APWA staff member recalled, "As he [Hoehler] went about on these missions he would drop various promises that the APWA would be glad to help them with problems in the camps or crowded communities or whatever came up."[23] The APWA used the wartime emergency to raise its profile in the federal government.[24]

Yet despite its successful government partnerships, the APWA was not always able to influence federal policy through its connections to the state. Its impact on the Wagner-Murray-Dingell bills stemmed from its unofficial activities, not its formal ties to government. In the early and mid-1940s, key federal policy makers behind the comprehensive social welfare proposals had joined the APWA. Social Security Commissioner Arthur Altmeyer was an APWA member. His assistant Wilbur Cohen was also a member and an active leader within the APWA's committee structure. Moreover, Cohen was beginning a close friendship with an ambitious woman named Elizabeth Wickenden, who was appointed to be the APWA's legislative consultant in 1940. Wickenden served as a sounding board and informal consultant to Cohen on social legislation, including the Wagner-Murray-Dingell bills of 1943 and 1945. As Wickenden reported, the APWA leaders, who had access and influence, "were really engaged in a considerable amount of lobbying" with regard to World War II–era social legislation.[25]

Interestingly, the APWA's support for the Wagner-Murray-Dingell bills highlighted social insurance, a program in which APWA members had no direct interest. The APWA actually downplayed the importance of public assistance, even though APWA members were responsible for programs providing it. They embraced the comprehensive social welfare policies of the Roosevelt and Truman administrations and agreed that public assistance "should not blow its own horn, especially with being competitive with Social Security." Although APWA members oversaw categorical federal public welfare programs, they nevertheless supported a welfare state that aimed to create security for Americans through insurance rather than public assistance. To the APWA, comprehensive social welfare promised a broader, more effective safety net for Americans than the existing piecemeal, categorical assistance programs. Legislative consultant

Elizabeth Wickenden explained that in the early 1940s "we [the APWA] lent our strongest support to Social Security as a means of preventing the need for assistance. I think we were rather remarkable in the fact that we were always trying to do ourselves out of a job."[26]

Liberals had rallied behind comprehensive welfare legislation, but conservatives had not. Despite the support of the federal government agencies, the Social Security Board, the Bureau of Public Assistance, the APWA, many Democratic congressional representatives, and the AFL and the CIO labor unions, the Wagner-Murray-Dingell bills of 1943 and 1945 faced an uphill battle in Congress. While liberal members of Congress were planning dramatic new legislation, the political composition of Congress was changing. In the 1942 elections, Republicans made their first significant gains in Congress since before the Great Depression. Although they did not have a majority, the new Republicans became allied with conservative Democrats already in Congress, many of whom opposed the New Deal and any further growth of federal social programs. Together, Republicans and conservative Democrats formed a loose bipartisan conservative majority that effectively opposed any expansion of the social welfare programs and hoped to weaken existing liberal social welfare legislation. In their view, the Wagner-Murray-Dingell bills epitomized a massive and unnecessary expansion of federal involvement in the private realm of the market and the lives of individuals. The conservatives also considered the legislation to be too costly. As the majority, they were able to squelch the bills and thus the hopes of liberals for a comprehensive social welfare system.[27] The prospect for legislative success grew even dimmer after the election of 1946. In that year, Republicans, capitalizing on an economy suffering from postwar inflation, recaptured Congress for the first time since 1928.[28]

Conservative congressional opposition was not the only stumbling block to enacting comprehensive social welfare. The rising wave of conservatism was driven by the empowerment of big business and the declining power and shifting goals of big labor unions. By 1945 the National Association of Manufacturers was beginning to spearhead an effort to roll back the welfare state, curb the power of unions, and preserve the prerogatives and profits gained by business during the war. At the same time, union leadership in both the AFL and CIO turned quickly to negotiating substantial bread-and-butter contracts, including private pensions, with major manufacturers. Though the AFL and the CIO supported the Wagner-Murray-Dingell bills in 1943 and 1945 (as well as other liberal legislation of the period, such as a bold version of the Full Employment Act of 1946), labor historians argue that their pursuit of bread-and-butter issues and private pensions diluted their commitment to a vigorous left-liberal-labor alliance in support of bold social welfare measures and high social welfare spending.[29]

As the Wagner-Murray-Dingell bills went down to defeat, the federal government embarked on a new sort of welfare program that was comprehensive in a different way. In 1944 Congress passed the Servicemen's Readjustment Act, better known as the G.I. Bill. Rather than focusing on economic security for vulnerable workers and nonworkers, the G.I. Bill created a system of entitlements ranging from education to job training to medical and housing benefits exclusively for veterans and their families. Aimed in part at staving off the return of economic depression through an infusion of government spending, the G.I. Bill funded the creation and the protection of a new middle class in America. Congressional support for the G.I. Bill did not necessarily translate into opposition to social welfare proposals, such as the Wagner-Murray-Dingell bills. Yet Congress's focus on returning servicemen, and the amounts appropriated to support them, actually represented a distraction from legislating for the poor and a diversion from overhauling the welfare state.

The APWA and the New Meaning of Comprehensive Social Welfare

The success of conservatives in Congress, the growing power of big business leading to the diminished left-liberalism of unions, and the increasing focus on middle-class entitlements forced liberal policy makers who supported social welfare programs to face new political realities. In the second half of the 1940s, therefore, some of the same actors who had been behind the comprehensive social welfare bills of 1943 and 1945 changed course. They pursued a different strategy for passing social legislation and sought new policy goals.

The American Public Welfare Association was deeply involved in transforming the strategy and goals of welfare legislation. But the process was not easy. The end of the war and defeat of the second Wagner-Murray-Dingell bill marked a crucial moment for the APWA. From 1941 to 1945 the APWA had gained a foothold in the federal arena by supporting the war effort and lobbying for comprehensive social welfare. But in 1945, with the war over and its legislative agenda defeated, the organization faced obscurity. Although the APWA helped the federal government solve social welfare problems during the war, this aid did not solidify the APWA's influence at the federal level. Wartime agencies ceded little real power to nongovernmental groups. Moreover, the wartime agencies dealing with social welfare issues were temporary and were dismantled at the end of the war. Few government agencies that had worked with nongovernmental welfare groups remained.[30] Demobilization thus threw the ad hoc relationship between the APWA and the federal government into disarray. The influence of APWA over legislative matters was no more certain than its general status with the federal government. There was no formal structure to the APWA's legislative activity and no mechanism for generating organization-wide discussion or consensus on legislative issues. Cohen and Wickenden's personal relationship facilitated the organization's participation in the Wagner-Murray-Dingell bills. And with the defeat of these bills and the success of conservatives in the 1946 elections, the APWA's future in promoting legislation was in doubt.

During this postwar crisis, the APWA's fate lay in the hands of three dynamic women who assumed formal and de facto leadership roles in the organization: Elizabeth Wickenden, Cohen's friend and the APWA's legislative consultant; Loula Dunn, the mild-mannered but politically savvy and efficient new director of the organization beginning in 1949; and Ellen Winston, North Carolina's commissioner of welfare and a tireless advocate for welfare and ADC, who would eventually run the federal Welfare Administration in the 1960s.[31] Wickenden and Winston were politically active in the Democratic Party and legislative circles and wanted to make the APWA a more influential policy-making institution. Dunn, while not as active in legislative affairs, was nevertheless hoping to redefine and stabilize the APWA after a decade of desultory and somewhat inefficient leadership. Beginning with her formal tenure as director, Dunn encouraged Wickenden and Winston to create new structures within the APWA devoted to policy making and advocacy. She allotted Wickenden a large budget and granted her autonomy for her legislative consulting activities.[32] Together these leaders of the APWA prevented the organization from returning to its modest prewar relationship with the federal welfare administration and pushed it to become a more sophisticated policy-making institution.

One crucial way these women secured the influence of the APWA was by helping to redefine the defeated philosophy of "comprehensive social welfare" in the late 1940s. The vehicle for this redefinition was the APWA's Welfare Policy Committee, which was originally a temporary wartime activities panel, created to monitor and guide the APWA's assistance to the government. When the war ended, Wickenden recognized the value of the committee as an organizing and policy-making tool, and decided to retain it, converting it into the Welfare Policy Committee. A coterie of APWA members with the greatest interest in legislative affairs joined. In the late 1940s they included Wickenden, who ran the committee, Ellen Winston, and notably, Wilbur Cohen, who joined in 1947. The committee's purpose, according to Wickenden, was to articulate a formal legislative agenda for welfare and communicate it to federal agencies and Congress. Yet it also performed another important role for the APWA. The committee raised the consciousness of leaders and members about the need to clearly define a "fundamental conception of what public welfare ought to be."[33]

The Welfare Policy Committee provided a context in which philosophy and practical politics combined to reshape the meaning of welfare in the early postwar years. In 1945 Wickenden suggested that the Welfare Policy Committee create formal statements of the association's beliefs about welfare. Such documents could be used, she said, to create social work curricula, administer the program, and respond to legislation. The first statement to emerge was the "Platform for Public Welfare," which laid out policy goals for the upcoming year of legislation.[34] It was followed up by a more permanent and formal statement on welfare policy that came to be known as the "Essentials of Public Welfare." In the end, it took almost seven years to write, involving national meetings, surveys, circulated reports, and formal and informal debates. In the process of crafting the "Essentials of Public Welfare," the APWA raised consciousness among its members about the need to pay more attention to welfare policy making. As Wickenden later recounted: "It took a long, long time. . . . At first the committee wrote a draft—that is they had a draft submitted to them, they kicked it around, they made changes. They then sent that draft out to every state and local public welfare agency for comment and suggestions. . . . This was as much an educational process as it was a policy formulating process—a policy making procedure—because obviously in the process of working over this document they learned a lot about what they were doing in the country."[35] Because the "Essentials of Public Welfare" was a collaborative and educational effort, "it was the most broadly subscribed to statement" in public welfare history.[36] The unanimity behind the statement provided force for the ideas it contained.[37]

The official statements of the APWA in its "Platform on Public Welfare" and its "Essentials of Public Welfare" openly recognized for the first time the centrality of federal public assistance programs in the welfare state. To be sure, the "Essentials" did not claim that public assistance was as important as Social Security, much less a competitor with it. In fact, point nineteen of the document reemphasized the need for social insurance as "the best governmental method to assure maintenance of income."[38] Arthur Altmeyer, commissioner of Social Security, praised the APWA for recognizing that social insurance remained "a first line of defense" while public assistance was "more definitely a second line of defense."[39] There remained in these documents, however, a firm acknowledgment of the importance of federal public assistance programs. Public assistance was not played down; rather, it was openly claimed as a viable and legitimate "line of defense." And instead of withering away, "public welfare would grow," the APWA's testimony before Congress in 1940 claimed.[40] The "Platform on Public Welfare" "marked a definite shift of thinking away from the piecemeal concept of public welfare . . . toward acceptance of its role as one of the basic areas of governmental services."[41] Likewise, the "Essentials" reflected the belief that future federal welfare programs should be bolder, larger, and more elaborate, rather than small, disparate residual programs designed to absorb the people ignored by the social insurance system.

The formal statements of the APWA were meant to influence new social welfare legislation in the late 1940s. The APWA's Welfare Policy Committee worked with Wilbur Cohen in his official capacity at the Social Security Administration, as well as with Jane Hoey and Kathryn Goodwin at the Bureau of Public Assistance, to develop legislative welfare proposals that would come before Congress in 1946, 1947, and 1949.[42] There was a significant difference between the bills that emerged in the latter part of the decade and the ones put forward earlier in the decade. The comprehensive bills of the early forties had assumed that public assistance and social insurance legislation were necessarily linked, suggesting that insurance for retirement or unemployment reduced the need for public assistance. In the late forties, however, Cohen, the government agencies, and the APWA pursued a legislative strategy focusing on public assistance programs alone—separate from social insurance. In 1946, 1947, and 1949, this coalition wrote and lobbied for public welfare bills that dealt solely with securing advances in public assistance programs.

The separate focus on public assistance bills was practical. A smaller bill addressing one single program may well have been easier to shepherd through a hostile Congress.[43] But the sole focus on public assistance also reflected the growing recognition by the APWA that public assistance deserved intense, concentrated consideration. Echoing the beliefs stated in the "Platform on Public Welfare" and the "Essentials of Public Welfare," Cohen told Elizabeth Wickenden that, "for the long-run, public assistance rolls will continue to increase."[44] Through their sole focus on public welfare, the public welfare bills of 1946, 1947, and 1949 recognized that public assistance was a permanent and important program in its own right.

Focusing on public assistance alone marked a strategic and philosophical shift. But there remained the question of what kind of public assistance program to advocate. Although Cohen, Wickenden, and the Welfare Policy Committee limited their late 1940s bills to address just public assistance, they nevertheless wanted to maintain the spirit of broad comprehensive social welfare within the narrowed context of federal public assistance programs. To do this, the public welfare bills of 1946, 1947, and 1949 maintained one of the goals of the earlier Wagner-Murray-Dingell bills: that of creating a new federal, noncategorical welfare program to serve any and all needy adults. The new noncategorical program was to be "comprehensive" by making "assistance available to needy individuals . . . whose resources are not sufficient to enable them to maintain a minimum standard of economic security."[45] The commitment to a broad, noncategorical program was consistent with the APWA's "Essentials of Public Welfare," which favored an expansive program with the maximum possible federal control over public welfare as an essential function of the federal government.

The harsh reality of the political process tempered the hopes of those involved in welfare policy. The authors of the public welfare bills hoped to create a noncategorical welfare program, but they knew that it was unlikely to pass Congress. Elizabeth Wickenden reported to APWA members that "it [was] apparent that the Ways and Means Committee was not prepared to consider Federal matching for assistance to employable people," that is, to people not already in the existing categorical programs for the elderly, the blind, and children.[46] Diminished hopes forced a built-in compromise plan. While the public welfare bills of the late 1940s continued to propose the new noncategorical welfare program, public welfare leaders also requested the continuation and extension of the existing categorical programs. Kathryn Goodwin in the Bureau of Public Assistance explained to Social Security Commissioner Arthur Altmeyer that "in the event the comprehensive bill is rejected and general assistance not enacted, we [the Bureau of Public Assistance] believe that Congress should be urged to expand the aid to dependent children program."[47] Goodwin and other policy makers in the bureau and the APWA hoped to strengthen the existing public assistance programs since, in their view, comprehensive welfare was bound for defeat—as Jane Hoey put it, "That name [i.e., comprehensive] seems to wreck us."[48] Specifically, they sought to increase the federal funds for the ADC program and expand coverage to include the caretaker of children on ADC rather than just the children themselves.[49] The APWA was so convinced that the ADC program and categorical welfare would remain the only form of welfare that they began planning for a national, multiyear study of the ADC program in 1948.[50] The attempt to continue to legislate within the existing categorical ADC program constituted an admission that the noncategorical proposal would not survive consideration in congressional committees, and that ADC would remain intact.

With their eyes open to this reality, Cohen, the APWA, and the Bureau of Public Assistance also made one final, decisive change in their conception of "comprehensive" welfare. If comprehensiveness would not mean exploding the categories of needy people served by public assistance, it would mean providing a more comprehensive coverage within the existing categories. What did the APWA, Cohen, and Wickenden want the federal government to provide that it had not provided before? They reconceived "comprehensive" to mean a wide range of social services provided within existing categorical social programs. The bills of the late 1940s presented ADC as a collection of "comprehensive" services for the needy, including, but no longer limited to, giving money. They aimed to "enable each State, as far as practicable under the conditions in such State, to develop a comprehensive public welfare program, including assistance and medical services to needy individuals, and social welfare services, including welfare services for families and adults and child welfare services."[51] The public welfare community believed that by adding services to assistance, assistance came as close as practically allowable to meeting the goal of a comprehensive, full-fledged social program, even if it did not create one large noncategorical program.

Though "comprehensive services" seemed innovative to welfare policy makers of the late 1940s, it was a new policy with old roots. The emphasis on social services in welfare programs reprised the reform orientation of an earlier era. Late-nineteenth- and early-twentieth-century reformers, who had helped craft the field of social work itself, advocated a social casework approach—individual interaction between a patient and a professional—to "aid" the poor. In the era of scientific charity, poverty was often attributed to intemperance, ignorance, and debauchery, and late-nineteenth-century social reformers hoped that through personal intervention they could rid the poor of these behaviors. In the Progressive Era, settlement houses like Jane Addams's Hull-House served communities of poor urban dwellers by modeling good behavior for the poor and by providing social services. New schools of social work churned out caseworkers to work individually with poor clients in, for example, mothers' pensions programs. This model continued into the 1920s and was particularly strong in the Children's Bureau, the federal agency that ran and monitored welfare programs for children and women.[52]

Though crucial to the profession of social work and to early social provision, social casework services were largely removed from public assistance programs after the onset of the Great Depression and the federalization of the welfare function in the New Deal programs of 1935. New Deal welfare philosophy emphasized structural causes of poverty and advocated straightforward solutions to poverty: giving the poor money or jobs. As Bureau of Public Assistance Director Jane Hoey explained it at the time, "I think public assistance [money grants] is one of the most important services to people, when you are starving." In addition, because the pay and prestige of social workers increased in private social work, social workers and casework left public welfare and the ADC program.[53]

But, with the redefinition of "comprehensive social welfare" programs in the late 1940s, social casework began to blossom again in public welfare. The impetus came from private social agencies, where most social workers worked and which most social work organizations cared most about. With the emergence of new social strains during and after the war, private social welfare organizations serving families and children, like the YMCA, for example, had grown, offering casework to more and more people. By the mid-1940s, a small cross-fertilization between private casework and public programs began to occur again. On the one hand, some social workers were beginning to recognize the permanence of public welfare programs and their potential relevance to their work, though those workers were a minority.[54] On the other hand, and more important, professionals in public welfare began to gain a "sympathetic comprehension of the need for security in social and emotional life" as essential to a broader conception of "welfare."[55] More willing to recognize the usefulness of services, Jane Hoey now argued to Frank Bane of the Council of State Governments in late 1947 that "expansion of services, including extension of child welfare services and the development of child and adult welfare services, is needed to enable people to meet the demands of our highly complex and dynamic society." She cautioned, however, that "comprehensive welfare services can be developed only if there are additional trained workers," thus placing professional casework firmly within the domain of the public welfare system.[56] The American Public Welfare Association also began to argue for providing social services in prominent articles in its journal, *Public Welfare*, in the late 1940s and early 1950s, and panels titled "Services in ADC" became part of the APWA's national conferences.[57]

What the new services mantra in welfare meant was not clear in minds of its supporters. All of the policy makers crafting the 1946, 1947, and 1949 public welfare bills took stabs at defining comprehensive services. Often these amounted to philosophical statements on the spirit of welfare services, such as this one by the Welfare Policy Committee of the APWA: "To be effective welfare services must be based upon respect for individual rights, affection and warmth toward people, understanding of society, and full knowledge of the specific institutions which serve human needs."[58] Wickenden, for her part, viewed adding welfare services to welfare as an institutional recognition of the "fundamental inter-relatedness of all welfare functions" in society.[59]

When statements on welfare services moved beyond philosophy to specifics, a common theme emerged: prevention of social problems. Jane Hoey wanted the definition of "'adult and family welfare services' to emphasize the preventative aspects."[60] The APWA's Welfare Policy Committee also emphasized the preventive nature of welfare services. The APWA legislative statements in 1947 and 1949 argued that "the Federal Government [should] recognize the expanding preventive role of service functions in a total public welfare program . . . as part of a comprehensive state welfare plan."[61] Still, prevention was not clearly defined—prevention of what? The APWA thought preventive services included a wide range of possibilities: "those in which the welfare agency exercises a protective function; . . . those which are necessary to bring together the individual and the social program; . . . and those which facilitate relationships between individuals and the social environment in which they live."[62] The Social Security Board was more precise. A memorandum on welfare services for the bills in 1946 and 1947 stated that "the term 'welfare services' means family and adult welfare services and child welfare services, including, . . . with respect to family and adult welfare services, social services designed to help families and individuals to become self-supporting, to meet individual or family social problems, and to make use of community resources and to contribute to community life."[63] Preventive welfare services, then, meant not only curbing the social problems of welfare clients but even ending the use of welfare.

Welfare policy makers wanted social services for welfare clients to augment the existing program, but did not yet know how this would be accomplished. Congress, however, made sure it would not be accomplished at all. Once again, in the late 1940s, Congress resisted new legislation. Although the Social Security Board, the Bureau of Public Assistance, and the APWA had scaled back and changed their conception of social welfare, their legislative proposals in 1946, 1947, and 1949 were rejected by Congress. Conservatives in Congress viewed even the limited concept of "comprehensive welfare services" as thinly disguised efforts to expand the welfare state. The echoes of New Deal–Fair Deal language in the aim of achieving "comprehensive coverage," albeit in a far less ambitious manner, may well have alienated anti–New Dealers in Congress.[64] Cohen went so far as to alter the 1949 public welfare bill further, to moderate language about the extent and expense of new welfare services, but it still drew objections from conservatives in Congress.[65]

There was, however, one final public welfare bill of the late 1940s. Proposed in 1949 and enacted the next year, the bill was designed to improve the ADC program by providing payments to cover not only the dependent children in a household but also the caretaker of the children, be it the mother, grandparent, or other adult in the home. The "caretaker amendment," like the 1946, 1947, and 1949 public welfare bills, was premised on the idea that incremental improvements in welfare programs might pass Congress more easily—and for once the strategy worked. The 1950 caretaker amendment marked a small but important victory by raising the profile of the ADC program alongside other federal insurance and assistance programs. But it was symbolic of the accommodation liberal welfare advocates had made over the course of the 1940s to keeping categorical programs, and aiming to make them more "comprehensive" in coverage and services.

THOSE WHO TOOK PART in the legislative battles of the 1940s never forgot them. To Wilbur Cohen and Elizabeth Wickenden, the Wagner-Murray-Dingell bills, with their comprehensive, bold approach to social welfare, remained touchstones, markers of what-might-have-been in the American welfare state. The failure to enact them, however, was never considered a tragedy, only a hurdle to be surmounted. By scaling back legislative proposals and redefining the concept of "comprehensive" welfare to mean simply social services, Cohen, Wickenden, the Bureau of Public Assistance, and the American Public Welfare Association crafted a flexible, practical response to the political realities of welfare. Exactly what this historic shift would bring in the long term remained to be seen. Yet in the late 1940s there were already hints of what a new era might yield.

Although most public welfare bills of the late 1940s failed to win congressional approval, the process of writing and trying to pass legislation fostered interest in and created information about federal welfare programs that was absent before 1945. The Social Security Board, particularly Wilbur Cohen and Commissioner Arthur Altmeyer, relied on the Bureau of Public Assistance and the APWA in this process and, as a result, learned a great deal more about the programs. In the process of crafting legislation, the Social Security Administration developed numerous fact sheets about, political justifications for, and fiscal rationales concerning welfare policy that raised the consciousness of employees —and other welfare supporters—about welfare.

Perhaps no single group was more important in generating a concern about federal welfare policy in the 1940s than the APWA. It played a significant role in the redefinition of comprehensive welfare in the 1940s, and as a result its major focus became federal welfare policy and the ADC program. Thus the events of the 1940s irrevocably tied the APWA and its members—welfare administrators —to the fate of the ADC program. The organization's Welfare Policy Committee and its "Platform for Public Welfare" and "Essentials of Public Welfare" represented a serious and lasting institutional investment in welfare programs. And its leadership—Loula Dunn, Ellen Winston, Elizabeth Wickenden, and, above all, Wilbur Cohen—would assume even more prominent roles in welfare policy in the future.

The legislative actions and reactions of the APWA, the Bureau of Public Assistance, and the Social Security Administration also foretold the future. With the failure to create a broad, noncategorical program, the retention of narrow categorical programs, and the acceptance of a more circumscribed, services-based concept of welfare in the late 1940s, public assistance would remain less important politically and philosophically compared to social insurance. In addition, the possibility of eliminating distinctions among the nation's poor was also gone. In early postwar America, policy makers no longer offered universal, comprehensive solutions to poverty, but instead worked within a narrow political and legislative context to revise existing programs.

The new plan for welfare consisted of adding new services to ADC. But what services welfare clients needed, and how they would be obtained, was vaguely defined. Answering these questions was complicated, both practically and politically, from the inception of the service idea: because new welfare services were attached to a narrow categorical program that served a designated target population, not to a broad, noncategorical welfare program that served a cross section of the population, close scrutiny of clients on ADC was sure to follow. Those clients were poor women without husbands, and it was their behavior —or the perception of their behavior—around which the new ethos of welfare-as-services would be defined. To make matters more difficult, just as attempts at comprehensive welfare failed and the new services mantra emerged, the clientele of ADC was changing. No longer mostly white widows, the clientele comprised increasing numbers of divorced, deserted, and never-married women, and a growing number who were not white. The program as a whole, furthermore, was expanding. These changes would be noted by the public and politicians and by welfare professionals themselves. As the next decade began, welfare policy makers would debate how to implement their new concept of welfare services to low-income women and growing numbers of racial minorities.

CHAPTER TWO

Strengthening Family Life and
Encouraging Independence

Gender and the Postwar
Rehabilitation of the Poor

"Mix into any public welfare program a fairly substantial number of persons
with little moral orientation and little capacity for wearing the cloak of exter-
nal conformity, add the fact that they are being supported without having to
work, and a conflict situation can well blow into a storm of disapproval." Rudolph Danstedt, executive director of the Social Planning Council in St. Louis,
Missouri, believed this was precisely what was happening in the Aid to Dependent Children (ADC) program in the early 1950s. Divorced, deserted, and unmarried mothers with moral, social, and psychological impairments were entering the program and creating a public relations problem for ADC. "The average
John Joe citizen," Danstedt wrote in *Public Welfare*, "has doubts . . . about these
Aid to Dependent Children cases." And he believed the public welfare community had to address these doubts. We "have to get the angels on our side by identifying a plan with progress" for welfare clients, one that would address the problems he and the public believed ADC clients possessed. His solution? In a word,
"rehabilitation": "Let us create a social rehabilitation center analogous to the
physical rehabilitation centers . . . for A.D.C. mothers. . . . Let us provide for
services of case workers, psychiatric and medical consultation, psychological
testing, educational and vocational counseling, planned vocational training, job
placement, and of course, day-care or homemaker services . . . right on the
firing line in the public agency."[1]

Four years after Danstedt wrote his article, these services were institutional-ized in the ADC program through a new federal law: the 1956 Social Security Amendments. The amendments embodied the change in thinking about pub-lic welfare that began in the previous decade, after the defeat of a more com-prehensive vision of social welfare. When welfare advocates started to discuss altering ADC in the late 1940s, it was unclear what form this change would take. But the 1956 law clarified it. As Danstedt's article indicated, welfare advocates believed that new elements needed to be added to the ADC program. And none was more important than rehabilitation.

Rehabilitation changed the purpose of the Aid to Dependent Children pro-gram. It was no longer an income support program. It was a combination in-come support and social services program whose purpose was to prevent and reduce dependency while giving aid to needy women and children. Although the 1956 amendments to ADC produced only modest results in service provi-sion, they announced major changes in welfare philosophy and altered the fu-ture of postwar welfare reform. With the passage of the law, ADC aimed at re-habilitating welfare clients, and this goal assumed greater rhetorical importance than the money grant, which was at the very root of public assistance.[2] The emergence of rehabilitation as an objective of postwar welfare shifted the pol-icy community's view of poverty from the social and structural perspective common in the 1930s to an individual perspective.[3] Rather than regarding pov-erty as the result of inadequacies in the economic or social system in which peo-ple live, policy makers began to see poverty as the result of an individual's in-adequacy. And that inadequacy had to be remedied.

Though the concept of rehabilitation heralded an era of intense focus on the individual, the most salient features of this individualized interpretation of poverty have gone virtually unnoticed by historians. The individuals targeted in the rehabilitative paradigm were those typical of the rapidly changing ADC cli-entele. Beginning in the 1940s, the program's clientele was increasingly made up of unmarried, divorced, and deserted women, more and more of whom were nonwhite. Moreover, the program grew at its fastest rate thus far in history. The growth and change in the ADC clientele ignited a furious public and polit-ical response, in which the program was attacked by journalists and politicians, and cut and altered at the state level to become more restrictive. Thus the shift in welfare policy from the vague emphasis on services of the late 1940s to the consensus on rehabilitative services in the mid-1950s occurred amid, and partly because of, tumult and change in the ADC program itself.

Welfare professionals like Rudolph Danstedt and organizations like the Amer-ican Public Welfare Association (APWA), who had cast their lot with the ADC program, had to respond to the attacks while absorbing changes in the program. Already attempting to expand and improve the program through services, they tried to fit those services to what they saw as the needs of the new and controversial ADC clientele. The APWA was joined in this effort by new organizations, including consulting firms, foundations, and schools of social work. All performed research on ADC in various locales across the country, aiming to determine what services were needed. In the politically charged atmosphere, and the narrowed context of expert research on ADC, the consensus on rehabilitation emerged, heralding a shift in the philosophy behind welfare, welfare law, and the treatment of women welfare clients by the state.

The rehabilitative discourse of postwar America was profoundly shaped by gendered and racialized assumptions about the social status and value of the welfare poor, its logic intertwined with the ADC clientele. This chapter describes the origins and main elements of the new welfare paradigm of rehabilitation in postwar America and its importance as a gendered and racialized discourse of poverty. As policy experts undertook research and demonstration projects on rehabilitation, they engaged, explicitly and implicitly, in a discussion about what roles women could or should play in society. They also determined how the state should intervene to affect these roles. Beneath therapeutic themes of rehabilitation lay a deeper set of concerns about family life and women's employment. The services that researchers and advocates put under the rubric of rehabilitation sought to address perceived problems in both areas of poor women's lives by "strengthening family life" and "encouraging independence."

ADC's Changing Clientele: The Attacks

In 1950 the American Public Welfare Association registered a growing and unprecedented wave of negative sentiment directed at the ADC program. "There has been a barrage of criticisms and adverse comment," the director of public welfare for the city of Baltimore told the APWA's annual conference in 1950. He cited "recent articles in the *Saturday Evening Post* on Detroit and New York" that "strike hard, rough blows at the welfare program." In addition, he said, "there have been numerous investigations of local and state welfare departments, among which have been studies in Baltimore, Detroit, New York and Boston."[4] Another APWA conference in 1951 followed up with a session that addressed the fact that the "aid to dependent children program has been the target of so much recent criticism."[5] Winifred Bell—a friend of Elizabeth Wickenden, a grantee of the Field Foundation, and a welfare policy maker who would later join the Department of Health, Education, and Welfare and write the first definitive historical analysis of the ADC program—remembered this period vividly, "For ADC the late forties were remarkable for the inception of violent and pervasive attacks."[6]

The attacks coincided with public recognition of the change in the clientele of the ADC program. In 1939 Congress passed the Survivor's Insurance program for widows of insured male wage earners. This program siphoned off many of the widows in the ADC program. By 1941–42, therefore, only 20 percent of children receiving ADC had a widowed mother, a dramatic difference from the 80 percent levels in the mothers' pensions program. In addition, with the onset of federally administered uniform eligibility rules, some women overlooked by mothers' pensions programs finally did receive government support. Nancy Cauthen and Edwin Amenta demonstrate, for example, that the numbers of nonwidowed mothers on ADC increased dramatically from 1935 onward so that by 1941–42 39 percent of children receiving ADC came from homes in which the mother was never married or homes where the father was absent due to desertion, separation, or divorce. In addition, African American women and other minority mothers gained access to ADC. Although their access was incomplete, it was improved from the days of mothers' pensions programs. The number of nonwhite children covered by ADC rose to 14 percent nationally in 1937–38, and to higher levels in the South, where the majority of African Americans lived. By 1948, ten years later, nonwhite families were 30 percent of ADC recipients.[7] As ADC's rolls changed in their demographic composition, they also grew. Between 1945 and 1950, the number of families on ADC more than doubled.[8]

The reaction to this shift in ADC's clientele intensified over time. At first, few people took note of the growing and changing ADC clientele. Cauthen and Amenta insist that during its passage ADC "sparked little debate . . . and encountered little opposition in Congress," and that "the expansion of ADC over the next 15 years [after 1935] was similarly uneventful" in Congress.[9] Yet, by the end of the 1940s, the growth and change in the ADC clientele fostered controversy.[10] Conservatives at the state level led the charge in attacking ADC. Their dissatisfaction with welfare was in part fiscal. There was an apparent discrepancy between rising ADC rolls and the state of the economy. During World War II, public assistance rolls had declined. Wartime mobilization had drawn millions of workers, including less-skilled and less-experienced mothers and minorities, into the workforce. As a civilian, peacetime economy became reestablished, many war workers were forced out of their jobs to make room for returning male veterans. The result was a rise in public welfare rolls. Yet the economy remained strong. Consumers unleashed a flurry of pent-up demand; civilian production utilized wartime technological gains to increase worker productivity; and military spending continued at high rates. Soon, many fired war workers found new jobs in the civilian economy, and overall postwar affluence raised wages in nearly all income categories. Many observers had expected welfare rolls to decline, but they did not. ADC rolls climbed persistently, increasing from 1945 to 1950.[11] This presented a troublesome paradox: amid rising affluence, welfare use was increasing.

A second fiscal complaint against ADC in this period related to taxes. To pay for wartime mobilization, Congress and President Franklin D. Roosevelt had raised taxes on income during World War II. In addition, property taxes began to rise after World War II, while growing proportions of local and state budgets went to welfare spending.[12] This tax burden appeared high and unwarranted to many conservatives, and they resented the use of tax revenue for relief.[13] As the APWA saw it, "Taxpaying citizens, hard-pressed by the double burden of paying for the war both directly through taxes and indirectly through skyrocketing prices seek relief in re-examination of one of the most costly of public functions, the support of those in need."[14]

Fiscal concerns, however, were secondary to worries about the racial and familial-sexual status of new ADC clients. Since support for social programs is often based on the perceived attributes of their target populations, changes in the composition of social programs can have important policy outcomes.[15] As feminist historians of welfare provision have shown, entitlement programs for women in the United States were supported in conjunction with a distinct ideology regarding women's proper role in society. Mothers' pensions were justified as programs that "protected motherhood." Motherhood was considered the greatest social role for women, far greater than the wage-earner role. Low-income mothers, mothers' pensions advocates argued, were forced by economic necessity to forgo their mothering duties. Mothers' pensions would reverse this necessity and allow low-income mothers to stay at home and perform a more important duty for society: raising children. When federal public assistance programs were created during the Great Depression, New Dealers incorporated the basic premise of state-level mothers' pensions into national law and provided the categorical public assistance program, Aid to Dependent Children, to foster the same social roles as the legislation for mothers' pensions: to allow some needy mothers to stay at home and care for their children.[16]

Mothers' pensions and ADC's support for poor women's mothering role, however, depended on the perceived social value of the individual mothers themselves, as Joanne Goodwin has pointed out. The most "valuable" mothers were considered those who reflected the demographics of the majority of Americans and whose social and moral standards reflected white, middle-class norms.[17] When mothers' pensions and ADC rolls had reflected these norms, there was little criticism. However, once it became clear in the late 1940s that ADC's clientele had permanently shifted to nonwidowed, single mothers and, increasingly, minorities, the program was called into question.

Many politicians, particularly in the South, were outraged by the new clientele of the ADC program. In response, state politicians added new regulations to their existing laws respecting welfare. In 1943 the state of Louisiana passed the first restrictive state-level law concerning ADC. By 1952 several southern and western states had also passed laws that severely limited the eligibility of needy women for ADC, based on either "suitable home provisions," usually strictures against giving aid to unwed mothers, or employability laws, laws aimed at preventing employable mothers from receiving ADC. These "vilifying attacks" on welfare, according to public welfare professionals, were a reaction to the new clientele.[18] The hostile laws pushed some women off ADC and into the workforce, guaranteeing labor for local agricultural elites during the planting and harvesting seasons.[19] Such laws were also aimed at punishing behavior considered immoral or deviant: for example, by excluding unwed mothers from ADC. National politicians also attacked ADC, passing the Notice to Law Enforcement Officials (NOLEO) in 1950. This law forced public assistance employees to get information on deserting fathers from mothers who applied for ADC, so that law enforcement officials might pursue the father for financial support.

The pressure from antiwelfare rhetoric, local investigations, and harsh local and state welfare laws forced welfare advocates at the national level to respond. In the late 1940s and early 1950s, the APWA's *Public Welfare* began to run articles —such as "The Local Public Welfare Administrator and the Legislator"—that tried to advise welfare administrators about outmaneuvering negative publicity in their dealings with state politicians.[20] One article explained how to conduct, as its title said, "public relations on a local level"; it told readers what local administrators were "doing about public relations."[21] Another directed welfare administrators to communicate with welfare skeptics: it featured examples of "a business man's questions" followed by "how to give the answers."[22]

But simply combating the attacks on welfare with words would not work. Welfare professionals felt they had to do something about the underlying conditions that helped precipitate the attacks—the changing face of the ADC program. In the late 1940s, the APWA began what one author called a "soul-searching phase," in which welfare professionals grappled with the changes occurring within the program.[23] In 1947 the APWA launched a series of articles in *Public Welfare* meant to respond to a blunt question: "Is Aid to Dependent Children effective?" One author answered, "Implicit in the Aid to Dependent Children program is the philosophy that children should grow up in a normal family setting." But "now, after a number of years' experience with the ADC program we are asking ourselves how closely have we been able to translate this philosophy into practice."[24] Were the homes of unmarried mothers "a normal family setting?"

As much as advocates for public assistance in the APWA were upset by conservative attacks on welfare, they were equally unhappy with the changing and growing clientele of the program. As one scholar put it, "They, too, were affronted by the broken and besieged families who reflected the ways and values of poverty."[25] These were not the clients that social workers had been accustomed to handling, either professionally or politically. The changing clientele therefore raised questions for the APWA's members. Were the new types of mothers seeking to benefit from ADC fundamentally the same as white widows or fundamentally different? Was providing them with government funds somehow different from providing white widows funds?

Welfare professionals responded to the criticisms and perceived needs of the changing clientele of the program by creating a new agenda, an adaptation of the "comprehensive" agenda conceded to by welfare advocates in the late 1940s. It promoted several changes, including expanding and improving the program and adding services to it.

Welfare advocates argued that the ADC program needed to be expanded, and not cut, as critics desired. Although welfare professionals were alarmed by the ADC demographics, they did not want to alienate clients from welfare or cut them from the rolls. Instead, they felt obliged to aggressively bring the poor further into the welfare system. In their minds, the new ADC clientele needed more help from government programs, not less. *Public Welfare* author Fred Steininger, for example, insisted: "The problem is not going to be solved by eliminating the ADC grants to the mothers and children. . . . Making life more miserable for the mothers and children by starvation, punishment, and embarrassment are methods that are unscientific and combine to make an unfair attack on those who are the victims of this social problem."[26]

The APWA countered calls to restrict the program by continuing to insist on "the comprehensive nature of public welfare responsibility."[27] This included raising welfare payments. As an author in the APWA journal *Public Welfare* put it, "States which continue to limit their grants by going only so far as the federal matching will allow, we believe, are not able to achieve the purpose for which ADC was established."[28] APWA leaders also felt that "the Federal Government has a responsibility for equalizing the capacity of the states to care for needy people," so that needy people across the nation would have access to the same benefits. Moreover, they thought the federal government had a responsibility to maintain better national standards in order to ensure that "benefits of the assistance program may be available on a reasonably equitable and consistent basis throughout the country."[29] Welfare leaders also wanted to "broaden the coverage of the ADC program" to incorporate more needy children.[30]

The most important part of the new welfare agenda—adding welfare services to the program—proved more complicated. Just what services did ADC clients need? How would they be implemented? What would be their goals? The APWA did not have answers to these questions while facing the barrage of antiwelfare sentiment. Trying to specify what welfare services should be included as part of the ADC program took the APWA down a new path on which, joined by a range of new institutions in the welfare field, it embarked on fresh research on welfare and used it to create an innovative and specific welfare services agenda.[31]

Defining Welfare Services: Gender and Rehabilitation

In 1944 Bradley Buell, a social work administrator from the Community Chests and Councils of America, and Harry Page, a past president of the American Public Welfare Association, formed Community Research Associates (CRA), a policy research consulting firm.[32] Such institutions were new to social welfare. Research and consulting boomed after World War II, reflecting the increasing reliance of government on science, technology, and new management processes. For example, large, nonprofit research consulting firms—think tanks—emerged in the fields of military science and economics.[33] The research consulting firms formed by social workers differed from large think tanks, however. They were smaller, composed of nonscientists, and operated in a less prestigious field, public welfare. Yet the birth of CRA was significant and spawned similar organizations in the welfare field such as Greenleigh Associates and Laurin Hyde Associates. And they reflected the larger trend toward cultivating expert knowledge in other fields of government policy.[34]

CRA's goal was to create expert knowledge about public welfare—government programs—rather than private welfare, where social work research was already concentrated.[35] As CRA's director Buell put it, "To free its [public welfare's] unrealized potentialities, . . . thoughtful attention of [the] professional . . . is required."[36] Other welfare researchers heeded his call, joining Buell in arguing that they must begin to "give important place in our field—as the other sciences have—to the research worker."[37] CRA hoped to use new expert knowledge to guide federal, state, and local welfare offices and administrators toward

Bradley Buell was cofounder and executive director of Community Research Associates from 1947 to 1963; in 1967, when this photograph was taken, he was chief consultant to CRA. The promotional pamphlet in which the portrait appeared touted his past leadership with the national Community Chests and Council and his executive editorship of *Survey Midmonthly*. Courtesy of Social Welfare History Archives, Minneapolis, Minnesota.

Harry O. Page, former president of the American Public Welfare Association, helped Bradley Buell establish Community Research Associates. He served as director of the organization's Public Welfare Research and thus was in charge of many of the ADC surveys that CRA performed. Courtesy of Social Welfare History Archives, Minneapolis, Minnesota.

improving the provision of public welfare. It was successful: CRA played a decisive role in determining what services the ADC program should provide to clients.

CRA received help in claiming a leadership role in welfare services from the William T. Grant Foundation.[38] Traditionally, major national foundations had been reluctant to provide funding in the area of public welfare, but the Grant Foundation was one of several institutions that ventured into the field in the early postwar years.[39] The rationale was to "create new public policies which combine the best of 19th Century humanitarianism with the best we can borrow from 20th Century scientific thought. To our sympathetic concern for the person in trouble, we must add the desire to get the facts about the size and shape of the problems in our communities, and the willingness to follow where the facts lead."[40] The Grant Foundation complained that "leaders [in public welfare] . . . concentrate upon the *maintenance* of activities to which they are traditionally committed. Ambitions for expansion express themselves in promoting customary patterns, rather than in new creative directions." This, the foundation suggested, posed problems for innovation; public welfare leaders were only responding to older stimuli and not to the new challenges of the postwar world.[41] They believed welfare programs had to be allowed to meet the conditions of the postwar era.

According to Harry Page, one anachronism to which social workers and welfare administrators held was the most serious. "The underlying trouble is that . . . we have looked upon . . . dependency . . . primarily as a condition which affords good reasons for giving people money enough to keep alive. . . . [N]either we nor our public policy makers have looked upon dependency as a *problem* to be solved."[42] With funding from the Grant Foundation, CRA began several multiyear studies of welfare in the late 1940s. In these studies, CRA administrators observed welfare clients with serious personal problems and were dismayed that "provision of money payments was alleviating but not remedying this situation."[43] This was especially true of ADC: "In many of these families far more than an Aid to Dependent Children money grant is needed, if the children are to be given a fair chance to grow into normal adult Americans."[44]

Pushed by CRA, a consensus emerged on the specific nature of welfare services. They should prevent and reduce dependency—in a word, "rehabilitate." The discourse of rehabilitation caught on quickly and was embraced by the public welfare world. When Governor Adlai Stevenson of Illinois addressed the APWA's annual conference in 1950, he invoked the association's increasing support for rehabilitation. He told the approving crowd, "Grant assistance is not an end in itself—it is a means to an end. . . . The basic purpose of grant-ing financial aid is to rehabilitate the individual so that he can take care of him-self."[45] Welfare advocates believed, as one welfare historian put it, that they had "the power and the duty to reform the poor."[46]

Rehabilitation in welfare was inspired in large part by a massive labor force rehabilitation effort that occurred during World War II, when virtually all po-tential sources of labor were mobilized.[47] Among them were the ill and disabled —those normally left out of the labor market. Medical and vocational experts in the field of vocational rehabilitation—represented by the National Rehabil-itation Association and administered through the Office of Vocational Reha-bilitation—provided medical services, occupational therapy, and counseling to thousands of disabled Americans to allow them to participate in the war effort. Particularly interesting to social workers observing the mobilization was the fact that so many disabled and sick individuals became self-supporting after having been on welfare and gone through the process of rehabilitation.[48] So-cial workers thus adopted, and then adapted, rehabilitation to encompass not merely the medically or physically disabled but also those who came to be deemed "socially disabled" welfare clients. In doing so, they utilized a medical-ized model of rehabilitation. As James Leiby has written, "The professionals conceived of their method by analogy with that of the physician: they made a *diagnosis*—a systemic assessment of a situation—and applied a *treatment*."[49] Rudolph Danstedt's proposal for "a social rehabilitation center analogous to the physical rehabilitation centers" was the perfect embodiment of this "clin-ical approach."[50]

One major "social disability" cited by public welfare researchers was "the handicap of inexperience and lack [of] training to meet the job market."[51] Al-though a pervasive lack of job skills and education among the welfare poor might have implicated the failure of society to meet the needs of citizens, wel-fare professionals articulated these problems as personal ones for the individ-ual. CRA's pioneering studies of welfare epitomized this tendency. In 1947 CRA conducted an influential study of the poor and welfare services in St. Paul, Minnesota. Staff members determined that "in 96% of the families, the pri-mary cause of continuing dependency lay in some serious handicap to self-maintenance" that had little or nothing to do with outside economic forces.[52] CRA was not alone. Other researchers across the country began to find or sus-pect the same thing. The chief of South Carolina's Division of Child Welfare services believed, for example, that in the public assistance cases in that state "the requests coming to the agency are different" than they used to be.[53] Welfare researchers and administrators observed that social and psychological problems—a "vicious clustering of human ills" and "maladjustment," according to CRA—were predominant causes of welfare need.[54]

While rehabilitation was a significant departure from New Deal–era federal welfare policy, the clue to its most important feature—gender—lay in the individual on whom rehabilitation was focused, the ADC client. The great bulk of research and discourse on rehabilitation in welfare programs was aimed at ADC. So it was not just any poor person that interested rehabilitation advocates; it was primarily poor single women with children, mostly white, but increasingly nonwhite, too.[55] Behind general statements about the maladjustment and social disability of welfare clients and the need for rehabilitation lay specific concerns about the problems of poor single mothers on welfare and specific ideas about how to solve those problems. To put it another way, the individualized perspective on poverty and welfare in the 1950s was created and shaped by gendered assumptions. In pursuing rehabilitative services, welfare reformers determined what roles women should play in society and how the state should intervene to help them or force them to play those roles.

One of the roles that most interested rehabilitation advocates was the family role—whether poor single women were caring properly for their children and performing as mothers. Family relations were an overriding popular and intellectual concern of the 1950s. The cultural symbolism of the nuclear family —the two-parent, mother-at-home family—was cultivated and widely deployed in popular culture as well as in social science. Freudian psychoanalytic theory in conjunction with theories of psychosocial development formulated by Talcott Parsons and his followers during and after World War II shaped a model of healthy adult psychology, for which a sound nuclear family life and good family relationships were crucial.[56] Popular discourse in the 1950s implied that deviations from sanctioned white, middle-class family norms would spell disaster for parents and children.[57]

Welfare professionals applied these powerful cultural ideas about the family to their own work with welfare clients. One such application was the belief that the structure of ADC families led to dependency. Families with only one parent were identified as "broken" and seen as closely associated with, or even causing, welfare dependency. The root of the problem was in part simply financial: the father was no longer providing support, thus putting the family in financial jeopardy. But single motherhood was also associated with nonfinancial difficulties that supposedly encouraged dependency. The burden of parenting on the single mother, the lack of a paternal presence in the home, and even the resulting reduced guidance and supervision were all thought to make families vulnerable to welfare dependency.[58]

TABLE 1. Community Research Associates' Assessment of Problems in the ADC Caseload of Boston, 1959

Problem	Number of Families	Percent
Dependency (total caseload)	298	100.0
Dependency only	8	2.7
Dependency with other problems	290	97.3
Indigent disability	35	11.7
Disordered behavior	280	94.0

Source: Community Research Associates Boston ADC Study, 1959, "New Directions in ADC," November 23, 1959, folder 2, box 17, Community Research Associates Collection, Social Welfare History Archives, University of Minnesota, Minneapolis, Minn.

Note: The CRA ADC study in Boston reveals the thoroughgoing pathologizing of ADC clients in studies of rehabilitation. Only 2.7 percent of ADC clients were seen to have dependency (defined as welfare use) as their only "problem." Of the "other problems" of ADC clients, few constituted disability while the overwhelming majority constituted "disordered behavior."

Yet to some the more troubling feature of certain "broken families" was unwed motherhood. Although unwed mothers had historically been cast as morally degenerate, in the 1950s this language gave way to the putatively objective discourses of sociology and psychology.[59] Welfare professionals, like other experts in psychology at the time, presented unwed mothers as individuals who were maladjusted: "Virtually all of the research on the subject appears to point its collective finger toward . . . personal insecurity . . . which tend[s] to thwart proper personality development, . . . ignorance of the biological facts of life, . . . feeblemindedness and low mentality."[60] Although welfare professionals did not believe, as some in the public might, "that welfare was a breeding ground for illegitimacy," they nevertheless thought "that dependency and illegitimacy are first cousins of a sort." One author argued that they constituted "two social ills which are related in the sense that they arise from approximately the same circumstance," that circumstance being social disability or maladjustment.[61]

Worries about family structure were intertwined with assumptions about race.[62] "The problem of illegitimacy among Negroes merits special consideration," an article in *Public Welfare* stated. "It is a well known fact that for the United States as a whole, the illegitimate birth rate for Negroes is considerably higher than the rates for both native and foreign-born whites." The writer con-

TABLE 2. Community Research Associates' Measure of Pathology in the
ADC Caseload of Boston, 1959

Area of Family Functioning	Percent of Caseload Judged to Show Each Level of Pathology		
	Good	Moderate	Poor
Financial	2.2	85.8	12.0
Child	26.2	64.4	9.4
Child rearing	25.8	62.2	12.0
Adult	10.7	71.3	18.0
Marital*	13.3	56.0	30.7

*For cases where marriage is currently in effect

Source: Community Research Associates Boston ADC Study, "New Directions in
ADC," November 23, 1959, folder 2, box 17, Community Research Associates Collection, Social Welfare History Archives, University of Minnesota, Minneapolis, Minn.

Note: In the CRA ADC study in Boston, moderate functioning and poor functioning
constituted grounds for recommending rehabilitative services. Note the low scores
CRA gives clients on marital functioning and on adult functioning. Adult functioning
was defined as "the capacity for meeting the demands of mature adulthood," a broad
criterion that included everything from psychological adjustment to ability to maintain employment.

cluded that "cultural attitudes are partially responsible for a higher illegitimacy
rate among Negroes." Drawing on E. Franklin Frazier's study of the African
American family, the author of the *Public Welfare* article argued that "from a historical standpoint, the observance of strict monogamy, so long the goal among
the white population, is at best imperfectly realized" in the black community.
Although such frank identifications of race with the problem of unwed motherhood were often avoided, racial assumptions about illegitimacy remained
prevalent among welfare professionals, and discussions of race and unmarried
motherhood were often conducted through coded terms such as "community
attitudes toward illegitimacy," "deviance," or simply "culture."[63]

When social workers and welfare administrators spoke of the problem of
"family breakdown" in the 1950s, they were not merely referring to a breakdown
in structure. They were also talking about a "deadly process" of breakdown in
family psychology.[64] Rehabilitation's concerns with the family plunged into the
very psychodynamics of family life. Because the institution of the family was
central in models of individual psychosocial development, welfare profession-

als theorized that the family—irrespective of structure—was the site where degenerate and dependent thinking and behavior emerged. CRA led the charge in formally linking dependency and degeneracy to family life. In 1951 CRA's director argued that these "basic problems tend to converge within the family group."[65] Moreover, according to research by welfare professionals, they tended to occur in "the same family groups." CRA's study of welfare services in St. Paul, for example, found that "a small group comprising 6 per cent of the community's families were commanding over 50 per cent of all the dependency, health, and maladjustment services in the city." These welfare families were thus identified as "multi-problem families." According to CRA, "The reason for the . . . high incidence of serious problems clustering in certain families . . . is obvious enough. One almost instinctively knows that a serious problem suffered by one family member becomes part and parcel of that family's life and in one way or another, each member suffers from its consequences."[66] Using a functionalist analysis typical of the period, welfare observers portrayed the family unit as a machine that, when a problem was introduced, short-circuited and broke. Once broken by dependency, psychological degeneracy ensued. Alternatively, once broken by psychological degeneracy, dependency was likely to follow.

Although the family problems of welfare clients were portrayed in a negative, even pathological fashion, a "hopeful view of human personality and a more constructive idea of the role of services" coexisted among social work professionals with beliefs about the problems of "personal disorganization."[67] APWA president John Tramburg expressed faith that "there is much that can be accomplished among public assistance recipients . . . to help rebuild family life for children."[68] Rehabilitation advocates believed that providing the "multi-problem family" with social services would produce successful outcomes. CRA's director Bradley Buell insisted that "professional workers long ago learned that family strength . . . constitutes a powerful asset . . . in the handling of many different kinds of problems."[69] A representative of the Grant Foundation even made a rather strained but revealing scientific analogy: "The discovery of the family approach to this problem [of dependency] is an instrument, a method which may be compared to the discovery that drainage and DDT gave us [for] the control of malaria."[70]

CRA and other public welfare officials only vaguely defined what constituted the "powerful tool" of "family services." Social workers at the Bureau of Public Assistance began working with social workers in the Children's Bureau in 1954 to define the nature of "skilled help with personal family problems." But they came up with few concrete suggestions, such as endorsing the idea that "estranged husbands and wives might be reunited and the deserting parent helped to resume the responsibilities and satisfactions of family living." Such a definition of family services blurred the lines between counseling and law enforcement, which in some states consisted of tracking down so-called deserting dads in ADC cases.[71] Another effort of Bureau of Public Assistance staff, with the help of the APWA, produced a list of family services provided in existing research and demonstration projects on rehabilitation. It included disparate examples. One told of "helping a family to maintain relationship with father in a TB Sanitarium," while another told of "providing housekeeper and homemaker services," which were essentially cooking and cleaning services. Others reported "helping family with a mentally ill father by referral for psychiatric treatment" and "helping a mother and the absent father to consider their parental responsibilities and encouraging them in carrying out their efforts at reconciliation." Though these attempts at providing aid focused on "improving family life," they often consisted of referral to medical or psychiatric services rather than family casework services per se.[72]

Though efforts to "improve family life" defined one part of rehabilitative services, another part revolved around promoting "self-support" among mothers on welfare. Welfare professionals were not only concerned with the family responsibilities of low-income women. They were also concerned with their economic role—the implications of women taking on the role of household head. Popular and specialized discourses of the 1950s cast mothers' employment as a controversial issue. Child-rearing experts debated whether women's work disrupted child rearing and should be discouraged.[73] Welfare advocates believed they could and should encourage mothers to work. "A major function of public welfare programs," an APWA resolution stated in 1955, must be "to assist individuals . . . in finding the means to achieve economic, social and personal self-sufficiency."[74] In practice, encouraging self-support meant "to assist . . . mothers to obtain employment."[75]

When welfare policy makers began encouraging women on welfare to work, they looked in part to national trends to justify their position. They were aware that women's employment rates were generally rising, while those of mothers were rising even faster. According to Sonya Michel, "From April 1948 to March 1958, the number of employed married women with children under eighteen rose from 4.2 million to 7.5 million, an increase of almost 80 percent. More than half of all women who had at least one child under twelve were working full time."[76] A few welfare leaders suggested that ADC ought to conform with social values about employment, if only to retain its relevance and some semblance of public acceptance. Elaine Burgess, an APWA official, wondered, "Is it any longer wise to have as a basic proviso 'keeping the mother in the home' since this conflicts with what has become an accepted phenomenon—the working American mother?"[77] Winifred Bell, who was a social work researcher at that time, also discussed the importance of the general trend toward working mothers for the ADC program in the context of a study of rehabilitation that she conducted in 1957. But, for Bell, the issue was not conformity but socio-economic mobility and opportunity. "Is it possible," she asked, "that the increased employment of women has heightened the relative deprivation of families on ADC and turned opportunity into frustration?"[78]

Women on welfare were certainly deprived, as welfare professionals knew. Despite their hopes, welfare policy makers had not been able to pass legislation raising or equalizing welfare payments around the country. Welfare payments "were not adequate to provide a minimum standard of living," an APWA study of ADC concluded; "68% of the ADC families have total incomes of less than $2,000."[79] Because of the inadequacy of welfare, welfare professionals like Winifred Bell concluded that they should help clients earn their own income, at, it was hoped, higher levels than ADC would pay. An author of a *Public Welfare* article put it this way: "A.D.C., despite our hopes of a number of years ago, is not at present designed in terms of services and financial grants to provide more than a temporary and insecure status to motherhood." Wage earning, therefore, offered better long-term opportunities for welfare clients.[80] Bell's study of welfare and work suggested that "the availability of work might increase the freedom of choice which does not now exist for the poor and untrained mother."[81]

Welfare policy makers were not alone in thinking that work could offer a better standard of living than welfare; some welfare clients agreed. Surveys of welfare clients in this period revealed that a significant number of clients on ADC wanted to work. An APWA study of ADC found that 50 percent of ADC clients used the program for eighteen months or less, supporting themselves otherwise. At the same time, even while women were on ADC, in about 60 percent of the cases, "homemakers . . . did something, or tried to do something, to help the economic situation while receiving ADC." They reported that "32% obtained full-time, part-time, or seasonal work; 16% tried but failed to obtain a job; 15% farmed or raised produce or livestock to supplement income." Welfare clients reported to Winifred Bell's research team that they sought work because they "were weary of second-class citizenship" that went along with being poor and on welfare; they simply "wanted to provide more material goods for their children and themselves." Bell reported that ADC clients in her demonstration project said that they "had always wanted to work but had never been able to find employment."[82]

Welfare professionals were also interested in the psychological component of employment. Drawing on the psychosocial discourse of rehabilitation, some argued that work was good, psychologically speaking, for welfare clients. A welfare professional named Alice Mertz believed that families needed someone in the family, usually the father, to work outside the home as a crucial source of socialization for children: "The child sees father get up in the morning, perhaps not too eager to work, yet having to meet his responsibilities to his family and his employers. At the job he must relate to an employer who may be an 'easy,' 'hard,' or a 'kind' boss. . . . These experiences with their profound meaning are and should be shared in some way in the home." Through exposure to a working parent, children learned about the demands of the outside world, about concepts such as responsibility, unfairness, duty, sacrifice, and getting along with others. In families without a father, Mertz reasoned, the mother should assume the role of wage earner rather than deny her children this crucial opportunity for socialization. Work was also good for families because it would temper an overweening mother by teaching her "to share her child emotionally with others who give care when she is away." By leaving the home each day to go to work, the ADC mother reduced the risk of concentrating too much on her children, thus becoming too neurotic to allow the children the opportunity to socialize with other people.[83] Psychology also promised another benefit of work to family life—psychological fulfillment of the mother. As Mertz put it: "The mother may gain social growth for herself . . . , creative self-expression. . . . A mother may get release from the emotional strains and worries at home; get perspective on her problems; get practical help from fellow employees in rearing her children. . . . The mother may get direct emotional satisfaction on the job in being liked and wanted by the employer and fellow employees, and in having healthy companionship."[84]

Such glowing appraisals of the psychological value of work were rare, however. More often, the positive psychological result of work cited by welfare professionals was not "creative self-expression" but the value of not being "dependent." Winifred Bell, for example, reported that her welfare clients told her they "felt useless because they were 'doing nothing.' . . . All they could see in the future was non-ending weariness and defeat."[85] Whether Bell's clients were typical was impossible to know. But welfare professionals believed that being poor and on welfare was psychologically impairing women and their families, and that work could benefit them. Wilbur Cohen performed a study of rehabilitation at the University of Michigan, for example, in which he referred a woman to job services who was diagnosed as "apathetic . . . in caring for the children." Cohen's research partner Sydney Bernard explained that the woman's apathy resulted from a general lack of responsibility in her life. Work would help her "take more responsibility for herself and the children." The study found her a job as a "baby-sitter-housekeeper, earning $65.00 [per] month. This is very little," Bernard admitted, "but is more than she has ever earned before. . . . We have had to learn that in some cases change is measured in such small steps as this one."[86] A small job, he and other advocates of rehabilitation implied, could provide big gains in overcoming the supposed psychological burdens of dependency.

While welfare professionals easily enumerated the reasons why single mothers on ADC who did not work would have problems, they struggled to develop solutions. Welfare clients had to overcome serious obstacles if they were to obtain employment and become self-supporting. CRA found, for example, that the average level of educational achievement among ADC clients was only the ninth grade. An APWA survey confirmed the low level of education attained by ADC clients and also reported that "only 16% of homemakers had special skills or training that were being or could be used in the labor market." Unsurprisingly, Winifred Bell's study of rehabilitation in Detroit reported that "one of the persistent problems in families living at the edge of poverty is that their efforts to find employment are so frequently unsuccessful due to the lack of skills, confidence, education and experience."[87]

Ideally, welfare professionals would advocate employment-based rehabilitative services that were fairly comprehensive, including "psychological testing, educational and vocational counseling, planned vocational training, [and] job placement" for welfare clients.[88] But, in practice, rehabilitative demonstration projects varied greatly in the way they helped welfare clients obtain jobs. At one end of the spectrum were the very intensive efforts of social workers in small studies. Bell's study of ADC in Detroit, for example, had only five clients referred to her from the Detroit public welfare department. With so few cases, Bell used extensive "therapeutic work . . . [for] . . . a year and a half." Bell counseled the women about choosing work, obtained funds from community agencies for "vocational training," helped them find child care, provided the fees for them to take "Civil Service tests" and "simple intelligence tests," tutored them in "vocabulary, spelling and simple arithmetic," and placed them in jobs—all for $2,000.[89] Wilbur Cohen's demonstration project on rehabilitation in Washtenaw County, Michigan, was also relatively small, helping about fifty families per year for four years. Cohen's study provided "intensive casework" that included "job finding, psychiatric consultation, vocational education, and a wide variety of referrals by caseworkers to community agencies."[90]

At the other end of the spectrum were city- or countywide research demon-

TABLE 3. Community Research Associates' Assessment of ADC Caseload Requiring Rehabilitative Social Services in San Francisco, 1962

Specialized Social Welfare Services	Percent of Families Needing Specialized Social Service
Authoritative or protective supervision	22.2
Foster home care—for placement	14.7
Foster home care—for adoption	1.1
Institutional	2.5
Homemaker	1.5
Extra financial assistance	0.8
Education and training	17.4
Job placement	59.5
Other	20.8

Source: Community Research Associates San Francisco ADC Study, 1962, "Rehabilitation for Independence," November 29, 1962, folder 10, box 17, Community Research Associates Collection, Social Welfare History Archives, University of Minnesota, Minneapolis, Minn.

Note: N = 2,481. The CRA ADC study reveals the range of services involved in rehabilitation and the heavy emphasis on education, training, and employment for women on ADC.

stration projects conducted by CRA, which classified and attempted to treat the entire ADC caseload in large cities like Boston, San Francisco, and St. Paul, Minnesota. These offered precious few services to welfare clients. In Boston, CRA had between 245 and 298 clients in one year. Only twenty-two of the clients received "education and training," the extent and auspices of which were not explained, while eighty-one clients received direct "job placement" with no preparatory services. In San Francisco, CRA handled 4,617 families on ADC, and singled out 2,481 for "specialized social services." Of the clients receiving some kind of services, CRA recommended that only 432 receive "education and training" of some kind, whereas 1,475 were to get direct "job placement."[91]

While most rehabilitative programs with employment-based individual services were started voluntarily by social workers and researchers, some welfare administrators were forced to provide employment services in response to antiwelfare legislative mandates in the states. The quality of these services was likely lower because of the fiscally conservative, antiwelfare atmosphere in which they were created. In California in 1951, for example, the antiwelfare state legislature passed multiple laws aimed at reducing welfare eligibility, including requiring "employable" welfare recipients to take any suitable work offered to them. At the same time, however, they passed a different but related code regarding the provision of services within the ADC program: "It is the intent of the Legislature that the employment and self-maintenance of parents of needy children be encouraged to the maximum extent and that this chapter [California's Aid to Needy Children program—the special state name for ADC] shall be administered in such a way that needy children and their parents will be encouraged and inspired to assist in their own maintenance." A pilot rehabilitation project in California was created to link the ADC program to the Bureau of Vocational Rehabilitation, the state employment service, and other related agencies to effect self-support rehabilitation in the ADC program.[92] Its success, compared to the programs of welfare professionals who supported the ADC program, was not clear.

While the extent and quality of job-related rehabilitative services varied, the kinds of jobs for clients did not. Even in the demonstration projects where clients received relatively greater services and spent more time in rehabilitation, women on welfare were generally referred to low-wage, unskilled positions in typically female-dominated fields. Wilbur Cohen's project in Michigan reported finding clients jobs in "waitressing," "baby-sitting," and "cafeteria work." Winifred Bell reported placing clients in jobs as "nurses' aids."[93] Large projects, such as those run by CRA, did not record the kinds of jobs taken by women on ADC. But it is unlikely, given the relatively few clients in these programs who received education and training and given the size of the projects in general, that these women received the education, training, or guidance that would have led them into higher-paying, nonfemale-oriented fields.[94] Such no-frills job placement demonstration projects were probably rather common. One such program, reported in *Public Welfare* in 1953, provided volunteer welfare clients in East St. Louis, Missouri, the opportunity to participate in the "Domestic Workers Training Program," a three-week crash course in being a maid.[95]

The advocacy of such employment-based services by federal welfare policy makers, and their use in the ADC program, marked a significant moment in the history of the welfare state's dealings with women. With the advent of rehabilitation in the 1950s, the historical vacillation between the ostensible purpose of ADC—allowing mothers to remain in the home—and the digressions from the state policy—trying to force some mothers to work—ended.[96] Rehabilitation's advocates pushed federal law to openly embrace both goals for the first time.

But this created ambiguity. Was stay-at-home mothering and family functioning more important than encouraging employment among welfare clients? Did advocating work undermine the quality of mothers' care for their children at home? The research and demonstration projects provided no answers to such questions, in large part because welfare advocates themselves were ambivalent. The APWA, CRA, social work researchers, and policy makers like Wilbur Cohen did not know how to resolve the tension in rehabilitation.

Although welfare advocates embraced the idea of encouraging single mothers to work, they qualified their support of this goal. Participation in employment-related services was, officially, voluntary. Moreover, policy makers' stance on ADC was, as Wilbur Cohen put it, that "for most mothers, whether on relief or not, the care of children, particularly young children, is a full time job."[97] CRA prefaced its studies of rehabilitating ADC clients with statements about how "a mother's first responsibility is the care of her children."[98] Yet support for the mothering role was easily overlooked. While CRA stated that "mothers with young children cannot work," it also asserted in the same report that, "in the absence of other problems, she [the ADC client] should be considered a potential wage earner."[99] And in fact, on close inspection, CRA's categorization of mothers by their "employability" seemed to cast the majority of mothers on ADC as employable. Even mothers whom CRA categorized as "unemployable for limited period" were considered, essentially, "employable" from a policy perspective. CRA categorized only one-eighth of all the mothers on ADC in San Francisco, for example, as "unemployed for an indefinite period." Fully seven-eighths of ADC mothers were either immediately employable or only temporarily "unemployable for a limited period." It recommended, therefore, that 77 percent of ADC clients in San Francisco be referred either for education and training or job placement.[100]

Wilbur Cohen's study on rehabilitation in Michigan followed a similar pattern, drawing a fuzzy line between upholding the role of the mother and insisting that wage earning was important. In several of the few cases reported in detail in the study, case workers attempted to keep the mother in the home and caring for her children instead of working. For example, Mrs. Jones, a young twenty-three-year-old mother with two young children, was provided with social services to try to reconcile with her husband and was encouraged to be a more attentive mother. Yet in many other cases mothers were advised to seek work. Cohen's research partner, Sydney Bernard, reported two cases of large families, the Clarks and the Edwardses, in which each mother had eight children. Despite the enormous workload of caring for eight children, both mothers were encouraged to find employment.[101] In another case, a mother who had been deemed unfit to care for her three young children, and had her children removed on several occasions, was also referred to "counseling concerning her capabilities for working."[102] Cohen and Bernard did not explain the criteria used for making these determinations. Nor did the report indicate why they recommended work for a mother. Cohen's study made clear that for many welfare researchers, even the most influential, determining whether the mother-role or the wage-earning role took priority rested on subjective factors.

Rehabilitation in Federal Law

The ambiguity and ambivalence that marked welfare policy makers' rehabilitative agenda for helping the female poor was institutionalized in federal law. At the same time that APWA members, CRA, and social work professors pursued research on rehabilitative social services and created a consensus on family and employment-based services, they began a political strategy to incorporate rehabilitation in a new federal ADC amendment.

Wilbur Cohen remained with the Social Security Administration until 1955 —a lone liberal in the Eisenhower Department of Health, Education, and Welfare (HEW). Though he was not entirely comfortable, he found allies.[103] Throughout this time, Cohen worked to change federal welfare law to reflect the emerging consensus on rehabilitation, and leaders in the Eisenhower administration were sympathetic.[104] In 1953 HEW requested that the APWA prepare, for the use of the Bureau of Public Assistance, a "statement on increased emphasis on services to public assistance recipients and development in helping recipients of public assistance become self supporting."[105] Then in 1954 Charles Schottland, the commissioner of Social Security, announced that he wanted to develop legislative proposals under the rubric "Rehabilitation for Public Assistance Recipients" and that he wanted "outside groups and individuals" to "consult" on the preparation of these proposals, including the APWA.[106]

Through this process of engagement with HEW, leaders in the APWA honed their proposals alongside the Eisenhower administration. In late 1954 the draft of the statement procured by Schottland for the Bureau of Public Assistance laid out the first specific legislative goals for rehabilitative welfare reform. The proposal was "to clarify the purpose of Federal Grants to the States for the needy that in addition to enabling the States to provide financial assistance, . . . [would] also . . . assist the needy to regain economic and social self-sufficiency." The objective of a change in federal law, according to the APWA, was "to reduce dependency and to obtain greater social benefits from Federal and State assistance expenditures by encouraging the states to place greater emphasis on offering opportunities to the needy to achieve maximum economic and personal independence." The APWA proposal was accompanied by a list of thirteen "illustrations of services in public assistance." These included both family-based and employment-based services culled from the APWA's monitoring of rehabilitative research and demonstration projects.[107]

In 1955 and 1956 the discussions about rehabilitation resulted in several legislative initiatives. The first was an administration bill that Wilbur Cohen helped author. It addressed issues of matching funds, medical services, and, of course, the basic goal of rehabilitation—"federal funds for self-support and self-care."[108] This first bill failed. But in 1956 the new secretary of HEW, former Kodak executive Marion Folsom, introduced a second bill for rehabilitative services.[109] Folsom, an enthusiastic supporter of rehabilitation, published an article on the subject— in *Nation's Business*—while he was secretary.[110] Although Cohen left the federal government for the University of Michigan in 1955, he nevertheless helped Folsom write the bill and navigate it through the department and Congress. While working on the bill, Cohen brought the APWA into the policymaking process. He proposed to Folsom the APWA's "Federal Legislative Objectives—1956," thirteen of which Folsom supported, including rehabilitative services aimed at both improving family life and encouraging independence among welfare clients.[111] Thanks to a new Democratic majority elected in late 1955, the proposed legislation did not meet the kind of resistance it would have in the past.[112] Jere Cooper, Democratic chair of the Ways and Means Committee from Tennessee, enthusiastically introduced the administration's bill before the House. In the Senate, it received strong support from Democrat Robert Kerr of Oklahoma. The bill passed overwhelmingly in both houses of Congress.[113]

The 1956 legislation, included as part of the Social Security Amendments of 1956, codified the new welfare agenda of the 1950s. First, it was committed to the extension and improvement of payments of assistance. The bill included an increase in federal financial provisions for public assistance by raising the federal matchable maximums to fourteen-seventeenths of $17 plus half the balance up to $32 for the first child and the caretaker and $23 for each additional child. It also slightly broadened the coverage of ADC by including needy dependent children who were living with first cousins, nephews, or nieces. Finally, it deleted the provision that required school attendance for ADC eligibility between ages sixteen and eighteen. The amendments also allowed federal payments on a limited matching basis for medical services to public assistance recipients including those on ADC.[114]

But while extension of coverage and provision of money payments were improved, the centerpiece for rehabilitation advocates was that, "in addition to enabling states to give financial assistance to needy people, the purpose is also to enable states to furnish appropriate public welfare services to help assistance recipients toward independent living." The law authorized the federal government to "share in the states' costs in providing appropriate public welfare services, as well as assistance, to needy people."[115] The ADC program was now officially assisting clients in the two areas that rehabilitation advocates cared about: maintaining and strengthening family life and encouraging "self-support" among clients.

While providing rhetorical, administrative, and financial support for rehabilitative services, the new law failed to resolve a central tension embedded in rehabilitative welfare services. The 1956 Social Security Amendments embraced both family-based and employment-based goals in ADC, but did not prioritize them. Because welfare professionals did not formulate recommendations, much less official guidelines, for encouraging mothers to work, there was the risk that work would become required as a condition of welfare.

In 1957 Wilbur Cohen's mentor and former boss, past commissioner of Social Security Arthur Altmeyer, warned about the threat rehabilitation posed to the rights of women on welfare. "I am afraid that in the name of rehabilitation, increased self-help, and provision of constructive social services we will depreciate the need for effective income maintenance programs and weaken such principles as . . . the right of needy persons to assistance." Altmeyer focused on the trade-off between needy women's rights as mothers and the recommendation that they work. Anticipating the transformation of therapeutically motivated, voluntary recommendations about work into obligation-motivated requirements for work, he told an audience of social workers that a "mother had a right to assistance even if she refused to go to work."[116] Altmeyer reported to Wilbur Cohen that his audience had been "shocked" at his views on poor single mothers' right to stay at home and care for children. So, too, was Cohen. His faith in rehabilitation as a positive force was so strong that he did not understand Altmeyer's fears. Few advocates of rehabilitation believed that providing social services encouraging low-income women to obtain employment and achieve independence could be seen in any other way than as an improvement on existing welfare programs.

LOOKING BACK ON the success of rehabilitative welfare reform, Wilbur Cohen gushed to his friend and colleague Elizabeth Wickenden, "We are living a kind of charmed life in an Eisenhower era."[117] In only six years, welfare advocates had accomplished a great deal. With the joint efforts of established organizations such as the APWA and new ones such as CRA, and with the aid of foundations and social work researchers in universities, they succeeded in redefining welfare dependency as a new and compelling problem for postwar society. Next, they created a solution to that problem in the form of rehabilitation. By 1956, with a new Democratic majority in Congress, rehabilitative legislation could be passed. From the perspective of liberal welfare professionals like Cohen, the 1956 Social Security Amendments were "the most important legislative enactment since the original law of 1935."[118] The APWA's director, Loula Dunn, who had also worked hard for their passage, echoed Cohen's sentiments in a special address in *Public Welfare* titled "1956—Year of Significance." She wrote, "The actions taken by the Congress and the state legislatures put public welfare on the threshold of wide and new opportunities for serving people."[119] At a national welfare conference after the passage of the new law, "there was a general sense of rejoicing at the new opportunities these amendments give for better services to people."[120] For welfare advocates, the 1956 amendments marked a watershed in federal welfare provision.

The amendments were in other ways a crucial turning-point. For welfare recipients, federal welfare law now sought to intervene both in their family lives and in their economic lives, with ambiguities about which area would be prioritized and why, and about how the potentially clashing objectives would be achieved. The passage of rehabilitative welfare reform also proved to be a significant moment in the discussion about poverty in America. The 1956 amendments represented a policy view that was increasingly oblivious to broader social structures that caused poverty and thus primarily focused on individuals. Moreover, because this discussion of poverty occurred within the accepted boundaries of the categorical ADC program, it was, by definition, a narrow discussion, driven mainly by its gendered and racialized focus on "family life" and "independence" among welfare clients.

Though welfare advocates were pleased with the 1956 amendments, many realized that they were but a small first step toward a fully rehabilitative welfare program. At the National Conference of Social Welfare in 1956, "there was general recognition that their [the 1956 amendments] passage alone was not the full answer to public welfare's needs."[121] Restating the purpose of welfare was crucial, but not sufficient to meet the promises made to reduce serious social disabilities among welfare clients or to render clients self-supporting. While Congress had authorized the reimbursement of states' spending on services at a fifty-fifty rate (the states and the federal government sharing costs evenly), this rate was less than the one at which the federal government reimbursed states for welfare money payments.[122] States, therefore, would have to pay more, dollar per dollar, to create services than they would in simply raising money payments to clients. There was little fiscal incentive in the 1956 legislation for states to provide rehabilitative services to clients.[123] In addition, rehabilitation remained a concept of specialists. It was developed by public welfare experts in response to public attacks on ADC and the perceived change in the clientele of the program. And at the time of the passage of the 1956 amendments, it was unlikely that many Americans outside the arena of public welfare policy debates had heard about rehabilitation or understood the vision of welfare that it proposed and the promises it made. Welfare reformers girded for an advocacy campaign for rehabilitation in the late 1950s and early 1960s. But it would be a struggle. Welfare policy makers would have to present the concept of rehabilitative welfare reform to an audience that was far larger and broader in its opinions of these issues, not just to each other and to Congress. How they chose to portray ADC clients and rehabilitation in this context, and their successes and failures in doing so, would reveal both the opportunities and limitations of postwar welfare reform.

CHAPTER **THREE**

Selling Welfare

The Gender and Race Politics
of Coalition and Consensus

In the late 1950s Maxwell Hahn, director of the Field Foundation, began compiling a public relations portrait of the Aid to Dependent Children (ADC) program, measuring the media's perception of it. He clipped articles on ADC from the *Tribune* and *Sun-Times* in Chicago and filed them away. Most of the articles were direct appraisals. About half of those were purely negative. The other half were backhandedly positive, concluding that ADC was not as bad as the general public might think. The articles that were not directly about ADC concerned issues Hahn considered relevant to the program, including pieces about unwed motherhood among African Americans and the migration of African Americans to Chicago.[1] Viewed in its entirety, Hahn's file on the media's perceptions of ADC was representative of the Field Foundation's two historic mandates. Since its inception in 1944, it primarily had funded projects in the domain of child welfare and ADC and the arena of race relations.[2]

Hahn's clippings showed that in the late 1950s the two primary areas of concern to the Field Foundation were overlapping: ADC was becoming increasingly identified with African Americans both directly, as more of them received ADC, and indirectly, through issues like unwed motherhood and migration. Hahn also correctly sensed that the two issues, whether alone or in combination, were garnering more negative public attention. He wanted to build a political coalition behind ADC and a consensus on the value of reforming the program along the lines of rehabilitation. "The Social Security Amendments of 1956 permit some things to help dependent families to become independent—to get back on a self-sustaining basis," he told a colleague, "and not much is being done about that."[3] Yet galvanizing support for ADC required countering the negative, interconnected ideas about ADC and African Americans that the press was reporting. He feared that he could not gain support for rehabilitation among whites if welfare was perceived as a program primarily for African Americans.

In response, the Field Foundation and other organizations and individuals that had been involved in ADC reform earlier in the 1950s tried to broaden the appeal of rehabilitative welfare reform at the end of the decade. The Field Foundation, the American Public Welfare Association, Community Research Associates, and leaders in these organizations, including Hahn, Wilbur Cohen, and Elizabeth Wickenden, promoted welfare reform to a range of institutions: private social welfare agencies, the AFL-CIO, and the National Urban League, among others. Their interests in this period dovetailed with the new rehabilitative tenor of the ADC program, and they became political allies in seeking to improve and reform ADC.

Welfare advocates successfully appealed to these institutions with a strategic discourse that destigmatized ADC and prevented its racialization by invoking the concept of family. Whenever possible, they projected a "family image" of ADC. They acknowledged that the program was aimed at single-parent families, but they refused to suggest that such families could not be deemed "normal." In terms of rehabilitation as a specific policy, this meant emphasizing the family services rather than the employment programs among the new rehabilitative elements in welfare. Welfare advocates pointed to their goal of "improving family life" for ADC mothers as an important and under-utilized tool in the battle to preserve America's families and communities. For welfare advocates, promoting the family also meant remaining silent on the issue of race. The advocates' public references to families and communities did not specify race and, more often than not, implied that ADC families were white. By infusing their research, advocacy, publicity, and outreach with an explicitly nonracial, profamily discourse, welfare advocates like Max Hahn hoped to build a political coalition for supporting and rehabilitating America's needy families.

Building coalitions with national interest groups was not the same, however, as persuading the public that welfare was a family-friendly program for whites. Though welfare advocates gained some initial support for rehabilitative welfare reform, Max Hahn's fears, reflected in his ADC newspaper clippings, were soon realized. In 1960 legislators in Louisiana threw nearly 30,000 individuals off of the ADC program. In 1961 a city manager in Newburgh, New York, declared a one-man "war on the welfare state," with the seemingly overwhelming approval of the populace. Grumbling assessments about ADC turned to a roar when the two national welfare crises hit newspapers and television screens across the country.

The furor generated by these events threatened the power and unity of the small coalition behind ADC, and it challenged the strategic decision to present welfare as a family-based, essentially "white" program. Both crises directly put into question the racial composition of welfare programs. They also undermined welfare supporters' central contention that ADC was a necessary family services program—and thus cast doubt on the idea that ADC had anything positive to contribute to family life. Facing open racial hostility to ADC and the injunction that welfare clients be made to work, welfare's supporters responded in different ways, with important consequences for the public presentation of welfare and the success of welfare reform.

This chapter examines the public presentation of welfare in the crucial period from 1956 to 1962. It explores in depth the strategic discourse of family and race, and why it appealed to organizations outside the traditional realm of welfare. It then describes the crises over welfare in Louisiana and Newburgh and how these events challenged and redefined the way welfare advocates and their allies sold ADC and welfare reform to the public.

The Consensus for Rehabilitation: Emphasizing Family and Erasing Race

For Max Hahn and other welfare advocates, promoting rehabilitation and destigmatizing welfare in the late 1950s took the form of marketing specialized, professional, and expert knowledge about welfare. Welfare advocates published research in the professional journals of social workers and welfare administrators and in the professional journals of allied professions such as county administration and public health. Occasionally, they attempted to speak to the public about their research. University of Michigan professor Wilbur Cohen and Community Research Associates (CRA), for example, published reports on their rehabilitative demonstration projects in local papers where they conducted their research in order to increase public awareness. CRA also published a compendium of all rehabilitative studies conducted in public welfare programs; they donated it to state and federal legislators, whose votes for further research dollars CRA sought. Through these efforts, welfare advocates hoped to build practical political relationships and ideological support for their ideas.

By selling welfare through research and statistics, its advocates mirrored the growing trend in postwar America toward using increasingly sophisticated science and research techniques to produce knowledge for public consumption.[4] In the realm of popular culture, for example, Americans took in the seemingly shocking results of the Kinsey Report's questionnaires on sexual activity, and both accepted and contested the results as a true representation of themselves. Gallup polls reported with authority the opinions of Americans on virtually every topic.[5] And advertisers relied on increasingly sophisticated nationally collected data to market their products. In the realm of law and politics, sophisticated research techniques were used to evaluate and recommend policies. This was most notable in defense policy, but increasingly in fiscal policy and social policy as well. In the case of social policy, the use of such techniques was evidenced in diverse instances, ranging from the work of social scientists who testified on behalf of school desegregation in *Brown v. Board of Education* to the evaluation of area redevelopment plans and low-income housing.[6]

Emphasizing Family

The most important research tool used to market welfare was launched in 1959. At the end of that year, the director of the American Public Welfare Association (APWA), Loula Dunn, requested funding for a new project from Max Hahn at the Field Foundation. Ten years before, with Field Foundation assistance, the APWA had conducted the first-ever national survey of the ADC program, called "Future Citizens All." Now, on the cusp of a new decade, Dunn made the case that, "while there was widespread interest in this program at the time the earlier study was made, there is even greater concern now because of changes in the character of the program and incomplete understanding on the part of the public of the purposes and effects of the program."[7] Max Hahn agreed. In early 1960, they began the process of locating researchers, deciding on a team at the University of North Carolina at Chapel Hill. Shortly thereafter, the APWA began discussions on the goals and needs for the study, and created a blueprint to meet them. A new national survey of ADC began.

For the APWA and the Field Foundation, the study represented more than an attempt to generate new knowledge about the ADC program. It was an opportunity to cast the ADC program in a new light. The survey's subtext was promoting rehabilitation, and its major themes, therefore, reflected the rehabilitative ethos. None was more central to this agenda than "family." Presenting ADC as a "family" program became the main strategy of welfare leaders in the period from 1956 to 1961. Thus they emphasized the family services offered through rehabilitation, which portrayed ADC families—especially those who received such services—as potentially positive, functional social units. The rhetoric of welfare leaders met three goals: to destigmatize the program, to tap into cultural concern for family life and thereby gain support for the program, and to present themselves as experts with the solution to tough family problems.

Changing the name of ADC and the agencies that administered it was one component of this strategy. The key, according to Wilbur Cohen, was to place the word "family" somewhere in the title. Though ADC's name would not officially be changed to incorporate "family" until late 1962, efforts to redesignate the program began earlier. In a meeting in 1961 with Max Hahn he said he wanted "to start re-orienting people to a new concept and to have a break with the past." Rather than the Bureau of Public Assistance overseeing Aid to Dependent Children, a new "Bureau of Family Welfare" would have federal responsibility for an "Aid to Families with Dependent Children" program.[8] Loula Dunn at the APWA also tried to utilize the word "family" in the context of ADC. From 1957 to 1959 the APWA undertook a communications campaign about the 1956 welfare reform directed at state legislators and state welfare departments, the people who would be responsible for implementing the 1956 amendments at the state level.[9] The APWA encouraged state and local welfare departments to adopt the designation "Family Welfare Department," and some did. They were told to describe their role as serving "families and individuals in the community including recipients and non-recipients" and "meeting educational, health, and social needs of all members of the recipient's family."[10]

The effort to associate ADC with the word "family" guided the APWA's national survey of the program. Whereas the 1950 survey, "Future Citizens All," had "as its chief focus the effects of the program upon the children," the 1960 study, titled "An American Dependency Challenge," was focused "on the families themselves."[11] In part, the new emphasis reflected real changes in the program. In 1957 ADC replaced Old Age Assistance as the largest federal welfare program. As a result, the APWA argued that "the number of families now involved in ADC compared with other programs . . . pointed to the need for the shift in emphasis." But the APWA chose the family focus primarily to garner public support for the program, especially among skeptics. One of the study's coordinators, Elaine Burgess, acknowledged that growing criticism of the families on ADC had previously been answered only by noting that "changes in the ADC load reflect important changes in the basic social structure." Now, she said, this was "not a sufficient answer for those who are raising questions." Instead, researchers had to answer specific questions about family structure and functioning, and provide specific solutions. "The weaknesses of ADC, real or imagined, are according to critics centered in ADC as a *family* program not as a child welfare program." Thus, she argued, "it is important to emphasize the total family unit far more extensively."[12]

As Burgess's response to public criticism suggested, the APWA did not expect its study to uncover a trouble-free picture of ADC. Indeed, welfare advocates' research and demonstration projects related to ADC in the early 1950s and their lobbying for the 1956 amendments had made the case that ADC families were troubled and needed help. The directors of the study, therefore, anticipated that they would find serious family-based problems in the survey, more serious ones than the 1950 survey did. They even designed the study's questions to locate these problems. The survey questionnaire included a section on the "existence and alleviation of problems in the family," the first subgroup of which concerned "behavioral problems." The familiar grouping of "dysfunctional" behaviors associated with "multi-problem families" appeared here: "unmarried parenthood," "promiscuity or prostitution," "desertion or abandonment," and "marital conflict." In addition, the study surveyed clients directly about illegitimacy in previous generations of the family. Other survey questions targeted educational problems, economic problems such as "lack of vocational skill or training," and health problems, including "emotional and other nervous disorders." A final section of the survey explored "other problems"—for example, "inadequate housekeeping or neatness."[13]

Though aware of the danger of stigmatizing ADC clients, the APWA believed that it could place negative findings in the context of larger changes in American family life. Moreover, it was anxious to present solutions to these problems in the form of the family-based rehabilitative services. "In order to meet the growing reaction to ADC," survey coordinator Burgess wrote, the APWA would also have to present ways "to cope with the underlying causal factors rather than the symptoms of the families involved."[14] The study would not merely summarize facts but interpret them and suggest the focus of appropriate policy recommendations—namely, that the best way to deal with ADC families was through rehabilitation. The study would offer "information about the existence and alleviation of behavioral, health, educational, economic, housing, and environmental problems in our sample." In addition, the study sought to prove that rehabilitative services could succeed. Researchers expected that the study would show that welfare agencies that "allow for a maximum number of home and office visits with clients . . . will realize the greatest success in coping with ADC family problems."[15] The APWA and the Field Foundation anticipated that the study would produce a more sympathetic portrait of individuals on ADC as members of needy families, and thus would create broader support for rehabilitation.

Sympathy was the goal of an unusual project promoted by the APWA at the same time—a play. Titled *The Pink Telephone*, the play was conceived as a dramatic vehicle by which welfare advocates could "make use of the excitement and penetrating effect of live drama to interpret the much-maligned and misunderstood Aid to Dependent Children program." The narrative concerned the quotidian difficulties of a seemingly normal, everyday family. In the course of the play, the audience learned that the family was actually on ADC. By portraying the protagonists as living in circumstances not so different from other mothers and children, and as caring about the same issues as other families, the play was designed to convince the public that ADC clients were similar to themselves. As New York's commissioner of public welfare, James Dumpson, put it in his endorsement of the play, "'The Pink Telephone' . . . clearly shows that families receiving ADC differ from self-supporting families only in their source of maintenance."[16]

As the APWA's planning for "An American Dependency Challenge" progressed, the Field Foundation sponsored another study that promoted ADC as a family program: a pilot project that linked ADC clients to the foster care program. Conducted by the New York City Departments of Welfare and Child Welfare, the study originated as an attempt to solve a foster care crisis. In the late 1950s New York City had "upwards of 100 babies, mostly under two years of age, waiting for foster home placement." Although public and voluntary organizations had tried to place them, they were "unable to keep pace with the . . . acute and desperate need." This was where the ADC families came in. The program placed the babies "with carefully selected families who are receiving public assistance."[17]

The study was billed as "a unique project which demonstrates that public assistance families can offer wholesome family life to babies needing foster care." The project director lamented the "cynical pessimism about the possibility of finding any families with strengths among the recipients of public assistance," reflecting the negative image of the typical ADC client found among the public and among many relief recipients themselves.[18] Yet she hoped that the study would give the public a more positive impression of ADC clients. "Recognizing the interest that the community has in the project and the fact that it is 'newsworthy,'" the project administrators explained to the Field Foundation, "it is our hope to use whatever media can be made available to us for continued publicity and interpretation."[19]

The New York ADC/foster care project eschewed alarmist rhetoric about ADC families, whether used by welfare critics or by practitioners of rehabilitation. Notably absent from the study's background papers was concern about the negative effects of single parenthood, whether moral or psychosocial in nature. Instead, the study asserted that "any recipient regardless of age, present marital status or family situation can be considered; the primary consideration will be the evaluation of the stability of their home and their personal, emotional and physical ability to provide the kind of care for a child which meets the generally accepted standards of child care." The study's architects specified that "single women who are temporarily heads of homes, or women who are separated or divorced may be considered."[20] In the end, such women were not merely considered but chosen as foster parents. Of the twenty-two families selected to participate in the program, nineteen were families headed by women.[21]

Considering these ADC families to be "proper" ones in which to raise foster children placed them on equal footing with two-parent or non-poor families that participated in the foster care system. The program director emphasized the "normal" family values that the ADC foster families possessed. "There is one thing," the program director stated, "that all these women have in common. This is their devotion to their children and their concern and effort to provide a stable, happy family life." Although the director of the program talked about the "warm loving arms" of public assistance families, she also emphasized the "strengths" of public assistance families: "integrated into the immediate communities," the mother "maintains close ties with her family or a small group of neighbors." The families were characterized as "planful, resourceful and ingenious."[22]

It was this image of the warm, ingenious, loving ADC family—well adjusted and capable—that the Field Foundation and the New York Department of Welfare hoped to use to improve the image of the ADC program. Yet one fact was absent from the publicity: of the first twenty-two families who were awarded foster children, twenty were African American. In the publicity for the initial successes of the study—through vignettes about the families—the families were presented without reference to race.[23] The program's administrators erased it from the picture.

Erasing Race

Omitting race from the visual imagery of ADC families was the corollary to the strategy of portraying ADC as a profamily program, and it occurred in all efforts to build a coalition and consensus on welfare. But hiding the connection between race and welfare was difficult considering the demographics in American society and within the ADC program in the late 1950s and early 1960s. African American families were more apt to be poor than white families. In addition, because the ratio of single-mother households among African Americans was higher than that among whites, and single mothers were more likely than single fathers or two-parent families to be poor, African American single mothers were predictably indigent. Fully 70 percent of African American female-headed households were below the poverty line, while 42 percent of white female-headed households were below the poverty line. Not surprisingly, then, African Americans were more likely to need welfare than whites. In 1959, 40 percent of clients on public assistance were African American, a percentage exceeding their proportion of the national population.[24]

Welfare leaders understood that African Americans were disproportionately poor and that this contributed to their presence on welfare. As the APWA noted in a resolution on public assistance by the board of directors, "Non-white families were only one-tenth of the total of all families in the nation while more than two-fifths of families receiving ADC were non-white."[25] Welfare policy makers traced this phenomenon to racial discrimination in employment practices. At the University of Michigan, Wilbur Cohen undertook a study of poverty for the Committee for Economic Development, and in it he noted that "Negroes, Puerto Ricans, [and] Mexicans" (he sometimes referred to members of these groups as "migratory workers") suffered from a lack of "employment opportunities."[26] Cohen realized that confronting poverty and welfare use among African Americans required that society determine "what steps can be taken to minimize discrimination against the full utilization of minority groups" in the labor market.[27] At Michigan, Cohen took part in a faculty seminar on income maintenance that supported the "elimination of Negro-White differentials."[28] In 1959, as members of an advisory panel on welfare, Wilbur Cohen and Elizabeth Wickenden acknowledged the role of "insufficient opportunities for minority groups" in creating the need for welfare.[29]

Some welfare advocates were even aware that discrimination stood in the way of their success with the policy of rehabilitation in ADC. Two studies of ADC and rehabilitation in Detroit, Michigan, took note of the special difficulties of rehabilitating African American women on ADC because of racial discrimination. University of Michigan professor Josephine Williams studied a sample of African American ADC clients in Detroit to determine the possibilities and limitations these women faced in trying to become independent of welfare through rehabilitation. She noted that although low-income African American women typically had more work experience than low-income white women, they nevertheless faced greater difficulty finding adequately paid jobs.[30] Winifred Bell took these insights further. In 1957 she supervised the rehabilitation of "four Negro mothers . . . and one white woman" on ADC. Obtaining employment for African American mothers proved difficult in Detroit, however. "Two of them [the mothers] wished to work in stores, two of them in offices." But, unfortunately, "there were few local stores hiring Negro sales people, unless the poorly paid soda fountain jobs were considered the goal. The other two [Negro mothers] not only had to face the usual discrimination, but they had no office skills." After finding employers willing to hire African American women, however, Bell discovered that "there were no day care facilities available in [the mothers'] neighborhoods." Outside African American neighborhoods, day care facilities were often segregated. Bell found that on multiple levels race affected the process of rehabilitating ADC clients.[31]

Welfare scholars and professionals were also aware of racial discrimination in the administration of the ADC program itself. In the late 1950s Max Hahn was upset by the increasingly punitive actions initiated by local politicians or police against African Americans on welfare. Southern whites, for example, had "economic and racial conflicts . . . so intertwined as to be inseparable."[32] Hahn and other welfare advocates knew that welfare laws that increased employment expectations for ADC clients or cut off payments due to "unsuitability" of the families' homes were used to force African American clients from welfare and into the labor market.[33] "I consider [it] a really shocking attitude," Hahn wrote to a fellow welfare supporter, "which I am afraid is only too prevalent."[34] In 1960 Winifred Bell confirmed this prevalence. Her dissertation on state welfare laws reported what many welfare leaders already knew: racially motivated uses of employability standards and suitable home provisions were common in the South in the 1950s.[35]

Knowledge of racism, however, did not translate into action on civil rights. Though some welfare professionals recognized that racial discrimination contributed to poverty and welfare use, and existed within the ADC program itself, welfare policy makers in the late 1950s did not add fighting racial discrimination to their agenda for helping the poor. Though leaders like Max Hahn deplored the racism exhibited in the ADC program, they did not fight for civil rights within the welfare system. Welfare policy makers distinguished between recognizing the existence of racial discrimination and incorporating this analysis into their policy agenda.[36]

Not one of the APWA's legislative objectives regarding public assistance addressed racial discrimination within the ADC program. The board of directors did not demand an end to racial discrimination within the federal welfare system, or even identify southern states as committing racial discrimination. Nor did the organization make any formal statement about the equal treatment of minority clients on ADC before the law. In addition, although the APWA often made legislative recommendations that extended beyond its bailiwick of welfare, such as recommendations on health care policy and social insurance, minutes of APWA meetings suggest that the board did not even debate making any general statement on civil rights. The APWA declined to link its legislative objectives in any area of social policy to a national policy on civil rights.[37]

In addition to avoiding civil rights in policy statements, welfare reform advocates eschewed the use of racial statistics and descriptions in their research and reports. Welfare organizations accepted what one observer termed "an unofficial ban on racial identifying statistics." HEW followed this "unwritten law," discouraging the use of racial statistics in welfare surveys, research, and reports.[38] Furthermore, most research and demonstration projects on welfare in the late 1950s did not keep track of the differential patterns or experiences of African Americans on welfare. For example, the most prominent demonstration projects on rehabilitation, conducted by the consulting firm Community Research Associates, did not utilize race as a variable in welfare studies until the mid-1960s.[39] The two studies of rehabilitative services done by scholars at the University of Michigan in 1957 and 1958 also failed to report on racial differentials among clients, services, and outcomes. Elizabeth Wickenden, policy consultant for the National Social Welfare Assembly, joined the New York School of Social Work in 1960 to undertake a study of the structural reorganization of federal welfare programs around the rehabilitative services ideal; she, too, failed to incorporate racial statistics on welfare use or to describe service provision for African Americans. Nor did Wilbur Cohen's studies of welfare and rehabilitation record the outcomes of the demonstration project by race. He would use these studies as models for legislative proposals when he joined in 1961 the Kennedy administration as HEW's assistant secretary for legislation.[40] As Elizabeth Wickenden put it with characteristic frankness, welfare policy makers' silence about racial discrimination revealed that they had a "fear of identifying assistance with race."[41] If racial discrimination was a problem, fighting for civil rights was too dangerous a solution.

Welfare policy makers' stance on race and welfare reflected both political and ideological considerations. Some welfare administrators believed that the administrative politics of welfare prohibited fighting racial discrimination in welfare programs. Racial discrimination tended to occur at the state and local level of the program's operation. National welfare leaders argued that the federal-state nature of the administration of ADC law prevented attempts to impose national antidiscrimination standards on the states.[42] The congressional politics of welfare in the late 1950s also influenced welfare advocates' attitudes regarding race. The policy makers had to work with three of the most powerful congressional leaders in the late 1950s—Democrat Wilbur Mills of Arkansas, chair of the House Ways and Means Committee, and Democrats Robert Byrd of West Virginia and Russell Long of Louisiana, both of the Senate Finance Committee, which they chaired at different times. All led the committees that determined the fate of welfare legislation. All were southerners. And none could be characterized as liberal on the issue of race.[43] In order to get welfare legislation through Congress, Wilbur Cohen believed he and other welfare advocates had to be extremely sensitive to "the character of [a congressional leader's] constituency; . . . his own personality and ambitions; . . . [and] whether he's a Northerner or a Southerner, a rural or urban man, a conservative or liberal, a populist or reactionary."[44] Welfare advocates avoided raising the ire of these men and other southern Democrats and conservatives whenever possible. For a program already barely tolerated by congressional leaders, pursuing vigorous antidiscrimination codes in dictating policies to the southern states was dangerous.

Yet liberals shared responsibility for this racist political atmosphere through their embrace of a postwar racial strategy that did not dislodge discrimination. In 1944 Swedish sociologist Gunnar Myrdal published *An American Dilemma*, the first major study of racial discrimination in America. As historian Walter Jackson has demonstrated, Myrdal's "moral exhortation and social engineering won converts . . . and his program of civil rights, integration, assimilation, and equal economic opportunity became liberal orthodoxy among American intellectuals."[45] In his book, Myrdal argued that the treatment of African Americans by whites posed a moral dilemma for Americans. The founding principles of the nation prized individual rights and equality, but the treatment of African Americans countered these principles. Myrdal argued that the treatment of African Americans was America's "greatest scandal." Racial discrimination was a threat to America's moral stature and even its long-term success as a democratic, capitalist nation.[46]

Ironically, although Myrdal identified racial discrimination as a problem and created a consensus in favor of mitigating it, his book inadvertently produced nearly opposite results. Liberals agreed with Myrdal that racism was a dilemma for American society, but their beliefs about how and why this dilemma would be resolved actually discouraged direct action on civil rights.[47] Many liberals in the late 1950s believed that racial discrimination was nearing extinction as modern American society evolved. As Walter Jackson has pointed out, "An argument that liberals would often make in the 1950s and 1960s [was] that 'industrialism' as well as the democratic political system was creating a society in which people were treated more uniformly in the market place, on the job, and in the distribution of public services." As these trends progressed in American society, segregation was "not feasible" in the long run.[48] Many liberals, including welfare policy makers, thus abandoned more active, immediate goals for civil rights action: "Gradual . . . change," they reasoned, "would . . . be more effective than moralistic pleas for immediate racial justice."[49]

To many liberals in the late 1950s, moreover, it seemed that this gradual change was occurring. In 1954 the Supreme Court decision of *Brown v. Board of Education* had set the stage for the gradual ending of segregation across the South. Welfare leaders revealed their philosophy of gradual change in some pointed disagreements with the National Association for the Advancement of Colored People (NAACP) about when to stand up for civil rights. Welfare organizations wanted to hold conventions in cities in the South where segregation was practiced, but the NAACP "took the view that you shouldn't come there as long as any restaurants [in the cities] are segregated." Welfare advocates thought otherwise. They reasoned that "as long as the hotel [where the conference takes place] writes that it's going to have an open policy," then civil rights groups should not object. Max Hahn of the Field Foundation told Joseph Reid, executive director of the Child Welfare League of America, that letting African Americans into hotel lobbies was enough of a step forward: "They [African Americans] were happy that they could hold a meeting in the Biltmore Hotel[.] [T]hey could stand around in the lobby—[but] they couldn't sleep there." This, Hahn believed, was "progress—this is a softening up that is going on."[50]

Some liberal social scientists were less hopeful that racial prejudice would disappear quickly or easily. They believed that racism was a deeply emotional, psychological phenomenon. Yet because they viewed racism as irrational, even atavistic, they were pessimistic about any strategy that directly confronted it. In 1947, just three years after *An American Dilemma* had appeared, Robin Williams, a student of the prominent sociologist Talcott Parsons, published a study on the social psychology of prejudice called *The Reduction of Intergroup Tensions*. Williams argued that "since prejudice could be so deeply rooted in an individual's personality . . . direct moral appeals to prejudiced people . . . could have a 'boomerang' effect and make certain individuals feel under attack and hence unwilling to change." In 1950 Theodor Adorno expanded the thesis of the dangerous, intractable nature of racism in *The Authoritarian Personality*. His study concluded that "prejudice . . . was so deeply rooted in the personality that it would not yield easily in response to moral suasion, educational efforts, or intergroup contact." Racial liberals felt that avoiding the direct issue of racial discrimination was a wiser course. They promoted "a strategy of indirect approaches" that served to help minorities, increase shared experiences between whites and blacks, and encourage universal benefits to African Americans and whites.[51] While such a strategy would improve the lot of African Americans, it would not, in the process, enrage the deep racial prejudices of some whites, especially in the South. Fearing angry reactions, liberals strategized to "minimise the danger of racial conflict" in a way that "amounted to a kind of voluntary self-censorship" on race, as historian Frank Füredi has put it.[52]

Welfare advocates followed suit by engaging in racial censorship in the APWA's "An American Dependency Challenge." Early on, study leaders demonstrated their understanding of the discrimination African Americans suffered in society and within the ADC program. Elaine Burgess was referring to racially motivated welfare restrictions when she said that "the real targets are the parent or parents and/or some specific racial groups who deviate from certain white middle class norms."[53] In addition, the study was originally planned to collect racial statistics, and these might have been analyzed to highlight the problems faced by African Americans in general and those on ADC in particular. Yet the study's advisory council changed its focus. One member of the committee stated that she "would like to see the figures given on a combined basis for all races." The rest of the committee "agreed that the racial differences should not be hidden but neither should they be overplayed." The danger, they agreed, was that "separation on the basis of race compounds the problem," the problem being the link in the public mind between race and welfare use.[54] As a result, they censored themselves. The study's data were to "be given in combined form . . . where there . . . [were] . . . not significant differences."[55] ADC families would, wherever possible, be presented as a monolithic group, without reference to race.

Avoiding race-based evidence was central to the aims of the study. Though "An American Dependency Challenge" gathered data on ADC, it was mainly designed to confront and subvert both the stigmatization of families on ADC and the association between ADC and racial minorities. As a result, those findings that were too controversial, too complicated, or not defined as directly related to ADC were not expected to be directly addressed. Rather, the intent was to have the study present those realities that ADC leaders felt they could and did address well—and ones that placed ADC in a less stigmatized light. This meant focusing on families and erasing race while extolling the benefits of rehabilitation.

A Coalition for Rehabilitation and ADC

The efforts of the APWA, the Field Foundation, and individual welfare leaders to destigmatize ADC and forestall its association with nonwhites garnered some wider political support for ADC and rehabilitation. The discourse of family resonated with several types of organizations in the late 1950s, including private social welfare groups and the AFL-CIO.

Private social welfare organizations such as the Young Women's Christian

Association, National Jewish Charities, and the Family Service Association of America, all of which belonged to the National Social Welfare Assembly, got involved in welfare because of their own direct involvement in family services.[56] In the 1940s and 1950s private social welfare groups attracted large numbers of social workers and developed therapeutic family services for private clients. With the advent of rehabilitation, a massive effort at developing social services for public welfare clients meant that private social welfare organizations potentially had something to gain by lobbying for the ADC program and rehabilitation.

The AFL-CIO's interest in family services in public welfare came from union support for the traditional two-parent, male-breadwinner family. Since the New Deal, the AFL and the CIO (then separate) had advocated social programs for women lacking breadwinners.[57] Both far preferred social insurance—Social Security—to public assistance as a way to meet this social need; but if deceased male breadwinners had not qualified for Social Security, labor wanted programs for widows to keep them from destitution.[58] In addition, the 1959 Constitutional Convention of the AFL-CIO supported the specific concept of rehabilitation: "We urge that . . . the administration of public assistance shall respect the dignity of the individual and promote his self-reliance and his independence. Funds should be included for more effective programs of rehabilitation."[59]

While private social welfare organizations and labor were allies of welfare, the National Urban League (NUL), was also an important—and unique—partner. Formed in the early twentieth century, the NUL was one of the two major national civil rights organizations, the other being the NAACP. The NUL had long been interested in welfare as part of its overall civil rights agenda, but in the 1950s and 1960s it increasingly distinguished itself as an important civil rights force by pursuing social welfare issues, in contrast to the more legal-oriented NAACP.[60] Moreover, as the NUL pursued a social welfare agenda in the postwar era, it tied that agenda to an effort to strengthen and improve family life among African Americans.[61]

Following in the tradition of research by W. E. B. Du Bois and E. Franklin Frazier, the NUL's leadership tried to document and understand the postwar African American family. The organization's research maintained that African American families were particularly vulnerable members of American society. Poverty, discrimination, and a changing family structure threatened the strength and stability of African American families.[62] To combat these ills, the NUL developed family-focused projects. Jobs had always been a priority for the group, and in the 1950s the NUL undertook a research project called "The Negro Family —Its Search for Economic Security." In 1956 its annual conference focused less on economics and more on psychology, featuring results of social work projects and studies under the heading "The Negro Family—Social Adjustment for Children and Adults."[63] Echoing the discourse of rehabilitation, in 1959, the annual conference of the NUL explored "strengthening family life in our metropolitan areas."[64] And to that end, the NUL worked throughout the 1950s on "expanding public and voluntary agency services to children and families."[65] When Whitney Young took over the leadership of the NUL in 1961 from Lester Granger, the NUL stepped up its family rhetoric and research.[66]

First Granger and then Young developed regular working relationships with the social work and public welfare communities.[67] The NUL had always backed the ADC program as part of its institutional mandate to ensure equal-access basic income support for African Americans. In 1954 it strengthened its commitment to ADC, placing public welfare on a list of six main priorities for the NUL's national agenda and establishing a committee on public affairs to monitor federal public welfare policy in 1955.[68] In the 1950s and early 1960s, the NUL folded its commitment to family life into its support of ADC. The organization's leaders articulated their championing of ADC by pointing out that the program helped African American mothers and children survive. Moreover, with rehabilitative social services, it helped improve family life.

Unlike private social welfare organizations and the AFL-CIO, the NUL took refuge in the family discourse of welfare reform because of fears similar to those of public welfare professionals: that ADC was stigmatized as public assistance for shiftless people and that race was increasingly a factor in how it was being perceived. There was ambivalence within the national civil rights movement in the 1950s as to whether to pursue an aggressive antidiscrimination strategy or to be "aware of the political delicacy of the issue" and use "less obvious language" in gaining civil rights benefits in federal legislation.[69] As Dona and Charles Hamilton have demonstrated, in the 1940s and 1950s national civil rights organizations, generally speaking, handled the open discussion of race cautiously. In many areas of American life, such as housing or education, they spoke openly of discrimination. But with regard to more controversial political issues, such as welfare, they preferred to handle racial identification in much the same way that welfare groups did—by downplaying it. They avoided association with "politically vulnerable . . . public assistance programs" like ADC.[70] On more than one occasion in 1960, for example, Max Hahn and the Field Foundation had suggested in private meetings with southern civil rights leaders that they might consider taking up the issue of discrimination in federal welfare programs. But the civil rights leaders declined. They said that they and others in the South were not interested in using their scarce resources to fight for integration of federal welfare programs when their approach to "lunch counter" issues—the integration of public space—was proving successful.[71] They knew that welfare was not likely to be a popular cause for them.

In the minds of civil rights leaders, welfare, while necessary to African American families, was a program that underscored the poverty and vulnerable family status of many African Americans and raised the unpopular issue of public spending for the poor. Echoing the views of welfare organizations, civil rights advocates believed that relative silence on the relationship between race and welfare would decrease controversy and hostility. Whitney Young stated that "for many years I was personally in favor of this . . . unofficial ban on racial identifying statistics by various agencies . . . including the Urban League." To have done so was, he said, quite logical, "for the obvious reason that these facts were used to our disadvantage."[72]

With similar concerns regarding indigent families and similar worries about the association of welfare and race, the NUL and welfare advocates could agree on the usefulness of family-friendly rhetoric and presenting ADC through the lens of family services. The NUL supported rehabilitation in ADC because it offered hope not merely for the survival but also for the improvement of African American families and communities. Its leaders testified before Congress for ADC reform in 1956, published positive articles on ADC, raised awareness among NUL members, and served on federal commissions on welfare in the early 1960s. The NUL also sought to protect African Americans from the attacks that welfare could generate against them. And the organization wanted to emphasize its own positive efforts to help solve the problem of "family breakdown" and present African American families in a positive light. The NUL's leaders therefore formed a comfortable political coalition with welfare organizations, both public and private, that began portraying welfare as a family program in the late 1950s and early 1960s.

The National Attack on ADC

In late 1960 and 1961 a bomb exploded during the campaign to promote welfare and rehabilitation to a wider public. Louisiana's governor Jimmie Davis launched the attack in July 1960 when he instituted a sweeping law eliminating nearly 30,000 women and children from the ADC rolls. In 1961 the war on welfare escalated when in the small town of Newburgh, New York, an obscure city manager implemented a harsh antiwelfare code. The godfather of postwar Republicans, Senator Barry Goldwater of Arizona, was one of many politicians who weighed in on Newburgh, proclaiming the code "as refreshing as breathing the clean air of my native Arizona." Newspaper articles, magazine covers, and television programs chronicled new and escalating accusations against the ADC program. Although a full-blown, sustained national public crisis over welfare would not occur until later in the 1960s, when the size of the ADC program grew enormously, the war of words began in Louisiana and New York in 1960 and 1961.[73] And it was a war that undermined the premises on which welfare policy makers' political consensus was based. When it was all over in late 1962, the effects of the Louisiana and Newburgh crises on welfare reform were evident. The emphasis on family life and family services receded in favor of a new emphasis on work. But the silence on race by welfare advocates, despite overheated and offensive racist accusations, would persist.

The Welfare Crisis in Louisiana

In July 1960 the Louisiana state legislature passed a "suitable home" law that forbade providing ADC payments to women who had children out of wedlock. The law condemned the homes of such women as morally "unsuitable." Governor Jimmie Davis, with the support of many residents of the Crescent State, referred to the targeted ADC clients as "a bunch of prostitutes" who did not deserve public funds.[74] Although southern states had passed restrictive welfare laws in the past, none were as drastic or ruthless as the Louisiana law. Some 6,000 mothers, caring for more than 23,000 children, were struck from Louisiana's rolls in the next two months. The press picked up the story, and the Louisiana ADC program hit newspapers around the country.

The suitable home provision derived from the precursor to the ADC program, the state-level mothers' pensions programs, and was incorporated into the Aid to Dependent Children program under the Social Security Act in 1935. It stated that the ADC program was obligated to ensure that dependent children lived only in "suitable homes" where their health and well-being were not threatened by physical, emotional, or moral danger. The definition of "suitable," however, had been open to interpretation by the states, as part of the relatively broad powers given to them in the federal-state structure of the federal public assistance programs. When Louisiana acted in 1960, eight other states had restrictive suitable home laws already on the books, which in several cases pertained specifically to the marital status of the ADC mother. The Louisiana legislature argued, therefore, that it was within its rights to interpret the suitable home provision as including unwed mothers; their out-of-wedlock births, the legislature stated, rendered their homes "morally" unsuitable for their children.[75]

Although the Louisiana ADC law ostensibly affected only unmarried mothers, it also implied a wider criticism of single mothers in general. When Governor Davis called the targeted ADC clients "a bunch of prostitutes," he cast aspersions not only on those mothers but on all single mothers on ADC. Since by 1960 widows were almost entirely absent from the program, the remaining women were generally divorced or deserted by their husbands. Divorce and desertion, historian Gwendolyn Mink has argued, were perilously close to the moral degradation implied by unmarried motherhood, in the eyes of welfare's critics: "Divorced, deserted, or never married, 'welfare mothers' could . . . be blamed for their single motherhood: perhaps they drove their husbands away; obviously they had weak family values; undoubtedly they were oversexed and promiscuous; by definition they were matriarchs."[76] If divorced and deserted ADC mothers were not technically immoral, they were at least weak willed or weak minded, unable to hold a family together. Their illegitimacy lay not in the literal illegitimacy of their children but in the illegitimacy of their family structure and their failure to produce positive family outcomes. The Louisiana law was a harsh attack on the family status of ADC clients, a rejection, in fact, of the premise that they were "families."

This kind of attack on welfare families was precisely what liberal welfare policy makers had been working against. Their strategic discourse had attempted to portray all kinds of ADC families as legitimate, viable families that, while perhaps troubled, presented opportunities for achieving positive family outcomes. But the tone of the debate in Louisiana made it impossible to acknowledge these ADC clients as families. In addition, when Louisiana politicians said that these clients should be cut off from ADC to isolate and punish them, they challenged the premise that rehabilitation in ADC was a valuable family service. This created a conundrum for welfare advocates. While they might agree with critics of ADC programs that single mothers, especially unmarried mothers, were weak and vulnerable to a host of negative outcomes that could pose potential social problems, they did not believe that the appropriate response to such potential problems was cutting women off from public support and social services. To deny ADC assistance to unwed mothers and their children would, welfare advocates rightly argued, only make broken families worse off. It would reduce those families to the kind of abject poverty that would bring on even more serious dislocation and disintegration.[77] By contrast, the premise of rehabilitation was that "troubled" single mother households should be the target of aggressive interventionist tactics; they should be drawn even more into the public support system and rendered services aimed at strengthening their families. Only rehabilitative welfare services could help strengthen the family lives of single mother households. But this part of the argument for welfare fell on deaf ears in Louisiana.

Louisiana's law challenged the racial silence of rehabilitative discourse as well. The Louisiana suitable home law was passed as part of a legislative package of segregation bills that year. Other segregation bills targeted education, housing, and voting. The goal was to isolate African Americans from the political process and eliminate them from public spending programs in Louisiana. The stigmatizing of unwed motherhood within the suitable home provisions was also, therefore, a proxy for racism. It was not merely coincidence, as some Louisiana officials would later claim, that 80 to 90 percent of the mothers affected by the Louisiana law were African American.[78] Liberals had left a vacuum on issues of race and welfare, and segregationists rushed to fill it.

Faced with family-based and race-based attacks on ADC clients, the institutions that had been involved in welfare reform since the early 1950s were horrified. This crisis, besides hurting ADC clients, challenged the premises of the reform agenda that welfare advocates had struggled to implement. They had invested over ten years in creating and implementing what they thought was a positive model for welfare, and now it was being thwarted. As Louisiana legislators impugned the reputation of the ADC clients and the ADC program, welfare policy makers were forced to fight back.

When Louisiana's punitive ADC law was enacted in the summer of 1960, local organizations were the first to object. None was more important than the New Orleans chapter of the National Urban League (NUL), to which "hundreds of mothers came . . . for assistance."[79] The local chapter responded swiftly to the passage of the law, calling a meeting of African American ministers to "enlist their aid in raising funds to provide for the children who were affected by the legislation." Throughout July and August 1960, the local chapter of the NUL pressured state officials, enlisted the support of other local organizations, and "agreed that a program disseminating the facts should be launched at once."[80]

The National Urban League's local and national branches built a network of organizations that strategized together to change the punitive Louisiana welfare law. Many groups that had been cooperating in welfare matters during the late 1950s joined. The NUL provided instant reports on developments in Louisiana and routed them to the National Social Welfare Assembly (NSWA). The NSWA's policy consultant, Elizabeth Wickenden, then passed the information on to the major organizations active in public welfare and their leaders: the APWA and its director, Loula Dunn; the Child Welfare League of America (CWLA) and its director, Joseph Reid; and the Field Foundation and its director, Max Hahn. They exchanged phone calls, letters, memos, updates, and articles about the situation.[81]

Despite their cooperation, these groups fought the Louisiana law in different ways. The NUL used both public relations and political and legal pressure to overturn it. From the outset, the NUL and its local allies in Louisiana—the Interdenominational Ministers Alliance, the Family Service Society, the International Longshoreman's Association chapter, and other labor, civic, and religious organizations—were remarkably successful in publicizing their critiques of the law. They gained "considerable publicity in the press," as one Louisiana state official ruefully noted, by issuing press releases and using national conferences and meetings to promote their cause. They even started an international relief campaign called "Operation Feed the Babies," which produced "bundles of cash from mothers . . . [in] Britain."[82] At the same time, the NUL augmented publicity strategies with policy strategies. Leaders contacted the governor and state officials to question the legality of the law. They also contacted the secretary of HEW, Arthur Flemming, to let him know their interpretation of the law and to ask him to review its legality. In addition, the NUL's work with welfare groups reflected their interpretation that the Louisiana crisis was a policy problem. They hoped that a coalition of like-minded national social welfare organizations could exert even more pressure on HEW to evaluate the law and rule it illegal.[83]

Though welfare organizations gained most of their knowledge about the case from the NUL, the APWA, the NSWA, the CWLA, and the Field Foundation were nevertheless inclined to see the public crisis in Louisiana differently. They did not mimic or even augment the NUL's publicity strategy. They never created relief drives or protests. Nor did they develop press releases about the dire situation in Louisiana. They never contacted welfare correspondents for newspapers or magazines. Instead, welfare groups fought the Louisiana law through political and legal means.[84]

After months of pressure from welfare organizations, HEW secretary Arthur Flemming agreed to conduct a federal administrative hearing on November 14, 1960, to determine whether the Louisiana law was legal. Welfare organizations responded by filing legal briefs with HEW to overturn the decision. Initially, there were two briefs circulating. Alanson Wilcox, former general counsel for the Social Security Administration and soon to take a position in HEW, wrote a brief on behalf of the American Civil Liberties Union (ACLU), an organization that previously had not been very active in litigating welfare rules or law, and would not become more so until the late 1960s, when it helped develop the field of welfare and poverty law.[85] The more influential brief in the social welfare world was initiated by the CWLA. Its director, Joseph Reid, asked Shad Polier, a lawyer and the husband of Field Foundation board member Justine Polier, to write a second brief on the CWLA's behalf. Most welfare organizations signed on to that brief. While the one prepared by the ACLU emphasized the constitutional aspects of the Louisiana law, the CWLA, or Polier brief, emphasized the welfare law aspects of the Louisiana law, a side of the law with which welfare organizations, professional groups, and social workers were more comfortable.[86]

The NUL, however, did not sign on to either brief. It agreed with welfare groups that amicus curiae briefs were important tools with which to have the Louisiana law overturned. But the Polier brief did not meet the approval of NUL staff because it once again erased race. Despite the overwhelming evidence that Louisiana's suitable home provision was a segregationist law passed by a segregationist legislature aiming to punish African Americans, welfare groups ignored the issue of race. In keeping with this historically nonracial discourse in welfare circles, the Polier brief avoided using the words "race," "Negro," or "racial discrimination." Instead, welfare advocates phrased the problem with the Louisiana law in terms of discrimination against families—unwed mothers and their innocent children—or as a strict legal question of authority in the shared federal-state administration of the ADC program.[87]

In sharp contrast, the NUL viewed the suitable home law first and foremost as a racial issue. Jerome Wilson of the NUL placed the Louisiana ADC law squarely in the context of "racial brush fires. One does not know where they are going to crop up. Little Rock [the Arkansas capital, where school desegregation orders were hotly contested] . . . or New Orleans." The NUL explained that the ADC law was a "blatantly anti-Negro bill" sponsored by a "rabid segregationist crowd" who had a larger segregationist agenda. They wanted to keep African Americans from benefiting from any public programs or privileges, from voting and education to housing and welfare.[88]

As a result, the NUL filed its own brief for Secretary Flemming's review at HEW. Written by its legal counsel, Lisle Carter, who would eventually join HEW under Kennedy, the NUL's brief mentioned race and racial discrimination prominently. In keeping with the NUL's understanding of the Louisiana case and the relationship between welfare, families, and race, the brief argued that welfare was a program that addressed the special needs of African American families and that to deny assistance to them was a violation of the family-based goals of the welfare program as well as a civil rights violation.[89]

When Flemming handed down his decision at the end the year, all of the organizations that filed briefs were pleased: he ruled against the Louisiana law, calling it a violation of the letter and the spirit of ADC law. This vindication, however, could not erase the problems that the Louisiana crisis posed. Welfare policy makers now faced an uphill battle to convince the public that rehabilitation was a legitimate new approach to welfare. As the passage of the Louisiana law indicated, the premise that rehabilitation was a family-friendly policy was contradicted by open hostility toward unwed mothers. As if pursuing this uphill battle were not hard enough, the public crisis over the Louisiana law also revealed that the liberal alliance for ADC was divided over how to address race. While welfare organizations declined to address the obvious racial aspects of the Louisiana ADC case, the NUL chose to face the racial issue squarely and openly. The Louisiana crisis signaled trouble ahead.

The Welfare Crisis in Newburgh

The public outcry over welfare intensified one year after the Louisiana emergency, in the summer of 1961. That July, the city manager of the Hudson River community of Newburgh, New York, announced his "declaration of war on the welfare state." Joseph Mitchell described his war as a "campaign to banish 'chiselers, loafers and social parasites' from the relief rolls."[90] He began by mustering all of the town's relief recipients—young and old, sick and disabled and healthy—to the police station to investigate the legitimacy of their status. After that, he initiated a follow-up study of welfare, concluding that there were abuses and fraud in Newburgh's welfare programs. Mitchell then instituted a new "thirteen-point plan" aimed at preventing able-bodied, employable, or "immoral" people from receiving welfare, and limiting all citizens to only three months of welfare support each year. State welfare administrators and the state courts immediately began to challenge the veracity of Mitchell's claims about welfare in Newburgh and the legality of his provisions. A fight was on over welfare's legitimacy.[91]

The welfare code in Newburgh garnered unprecedented national attention, far more than the Louisiana crisis did the year before. Major New York City newspapers from the *New York Times* to the *Wall Street Journal* covered events in Newburgh as they occurred. After August 1961, when Mitchell's plan ran into stiff objections from the local, state, and federal governments, newspapers and periodicals around the country picked up the story of the "Battle of Newburgh," and welfare became a national media topic. Whereas in 1960, the year Louisiana passed its restrictive welfare law, there were only eight public welfare articles in nationally circulating periodicals, in 1961, the year of Newburgh, there were twenty-nine such articles.[92] In addition, there were hundreds of articles and editorials published in local newspapers from the *Minot Daily News* in North Dakota to the *Chicago Sun-Times*. Newburgh even prompted an hour-long NBC *White Paper* television documentary in 1962, the first-ever prime-time show devoted to welfare.[93] Widespread press attention turned Newburgh into a national political issue. Politicians of all stripes tramped through New-burgh either to praise Joseph Mitchell or to attack him. Though the Republican Party had never before placed ADC on its national platform, rivals for the 1964 Republican presidential nomination took opposing stances on Mitchell and his Newburgh plan, with Nelson Rockefeller (who was governor of New York) condemning it, and Arizona senator Barry Goldwater praising it. Goldwater even met with Mitchell in Washington, D.C., to congratulate him on his "stand on welfarism."[94] A *New York Times* reporter commented that the Newburgh plan had been publicly debated "with a vehemence normally reserved for de-bate on such cosmic matters as nuclear bomb tests or the fate of Berlin."[95]

The media coverage of Newburgh's welfare plan indicated that Mitchell's at-tack on welfare programs and their recipients resonated with many Americans. A Gallup poll in October 1961 showed that there was "wide-spread public ap-proval of the so-called Newburgh . . . program."[96] An editorial from Connecti-cut's *Hartford Courant* concluded, "There is no doubt that Dr. Gallup is accurate in reflecting public concern over chiselers and lazy bums on the relief rolls."[97] *Look* magazine reported that "an almost visible wave of resentment has begun to roll across the land against the rackets and abuses that plague the vast, ever-growing American welfare programs."[98] A professor of social work admitted in an article in the *University of Chicago Magazine*, "We cannot dismiss the New-burgh controversy as a minor rebellion which has been squashed nor as mere headline seeking by a politically ambitious city manager. The favorable response to the plan was too widespread to be ignored. The amount of attention which it received gives us some idea as to the amount of dissatisfaction there is with our present social welfare system, particularly with public assistance."[99]

Louisiana was wiped from the memories of policy makers as the horror of Newburgh and the public reaction to it was seared into their minds. Initially, most leaders in public welfare were surprised. New York State's commissioner of social welfare, Raymond Houston, commented, "We're all startled to know the least little thing that comes up [in welfare] is a matter of public concern."[100] The shock galvanized welfare advocates even more than the Louisiana law. In this case, however, welfare leaders did not have to fight to have the Mitchell plan overturned. By early fall, the New York State courts and the New York State Department of Public Welfare had already demonstrated that nearly all of Mitchell's claims regarding welfare in Newburgh were false and ruled that Mitchell's plan was illegal in most respects. The job of welfare leaders and or-ganizations, therefore, was not to roll back Newburgh's law but confront the public support it enjoyed and the potential spread of its ideas.

The anti-Newburgh campaign was led by many of the same individuals and

Political cartoons in support of Joseph Mitchell's antiwelfare code in Newburgh, New York, proliferated in upstate New York cities like Rochester in the weeks and months after the code was created in July 1961. Almost uniformly, they portrayed welfare programs as corrupt, state officials and social workers as inept bureaucrats or foolish do-gooders, and Mitchell and his supporters in the city as protectors of taxpayers and public virtue. Courtesy of the Rochester *Democrat and Chronicle*.

organizations that had taken the lead in Louisiana a year earlier—the Field Foundation and its director Max Hahn and board member Justine Polier; Loula Dunn of the APWA; Elizabeth Wickenden of the NSWA; and the National Association of Social Workers. It also included various individual leaders in the field of welfare: Wilbur Cohen, now assistant secretary for legislation at HEW; Raymond Houston, New York State's commissioner of welfare; James Dumpson, New York City's commissioner of welfare; and Leo Perliss, director of the AFL-CIO's Community Service Activities. Welfare advocates found solace in the degree to which they were able to unite against Mitchell. Justine Polier confided to Max Hahn, "I am very heartened about the public welfare thing—that forces and people are being moved together."[101]

Deciding which direction to move in, however, was difficult. The "visible wave of resentment" of welfare that *Look* magazine described outstripped the public reaction in the Louisiana crisis not only in its magnitude but also in its depth and complexity. Whereas the Louisiana law and the discussion about it focused on one group of ADC clients—unwed African American mothers— the Newburgh incident generated discussion aimed at virtually all aspects of welfare.[102] But some themes stood out.

The first important theme of the Newburgh welfare crisis was revealed by the comments of a young Newburgh resident who had been watching the fallout from Mitchell's plan for several months. Asked what he made of the situation by a visiting reporter, he complained, "No little town ever got so famous so fast except Little Rock."[103] The comparison to Little Rock, Arkansas, site of the national showdown over racial integration of public schools, was apt. Both public policy controversies—one over schools, the other over welfare—generated for the small cities involved unprecedented notoriety. And the lightening-rod issue in each instance was the question of providing public services to African Americans. The prominence of race in the public debate over Newburgh demonstrated its centrality in the new national-level public debate about welfare in the early 1960s.

The racial theme of Newburgh also demonstrated that the racial politics of welfare were not limited to the South.[104] African Americans had begun migrating to the North in large numbers after World War I. Starting in 1940, with the onset of mobilization for World War II and the mechanization of agriculture in the South, additional African Americans migrated to the North for jobs. They settled largely in industrial and commercial centers, where they were more likely to find employment. Although African Americans were the last hired and the first fired in almost every field of employment, many nevertheless found some economic improvement in the North. As migration continued through the 1950s and early 1960s, however, and unemployment inched up, African Americans coming to the North had a harder time finding regular employment. This was how Newburgh's fate met that of African American migrants: some African Americans moved out of big cities and into smaller ones like Newburgh, and newcomers from the South entered the migrant agricultural labor market in the Northeast, such as the one surrounding the Hudson Valley area near Newburgh. Their arrival was not welcomed. African Americans in Newburgh were not only economically displaced but also socially displaced, confined to small, decaying areas of the city by the river, in substandard housing with substandard social services. Welfare was the only way that many could survive their social and economic dislocation.[105]

The attack on welfare in Newburgh was inextricably connected to the changing racial, social, and economic demographics of the small city. "Those most ardently on [Joseph] Mitchell's side," one reporter wrote, "believe the real problem in Newburgh has been the increase in its Negro population in the last decade—from one-sixteenth of the total population in 1950 to one-sixth last year [1960]."[106] According to Mitchell, African Americans were "undesirable newcomers," the "dregs of humanity" whose presence encouraged the creation of slums, social blight, and the degradation of social values in Newburgh.[107] Moreover, he and others argued that the reason African Americans came to Newburgh was "to get public assistance." A retired grocer in Newburgh stated that "the Negroes who are moving up here these days want everything for nothing. . . . Mitchell is right in keeping the riffraff out." Some Newburgh residents even asserted that there were signs in North Carolina train stations that encouraged African Americans to go north to Newburgh to get welfare.[108]

Since race was just as prominent an issue in Newburgh as it had been in Louisiana, it again posed the question for institutions, organizations, and leaders involved in national welfare policy: how should they address the relationship between race and welfare? Finding an answer one year after the Louisiana crisis was as difficult as it had been in 1960. Now, however, the responses of welfare advocates and their allies were less predictable than might have been expected.

In contrast to how they confronted the Louisiana case, a few welfare policy makers began to discuss racial matters, at least among themselves. Max Hahn confided to New York State welfare commissioner Raymond Houston that he was "a little afraid [that] the combination of Newburgh plus the Puerto Rican situation here in New York [referring to the disproportionate numbers of Puerto Rican immigrants on welfare in New York City] might have repercussions around the country and snowball, and set welfare back."[109] Some even spoke publicly about the racial nature of the attack on welfare in Newburgh. Leo Perliss of the AFL-CIO's Community Service Activities, for example, wrote a series of articles and memoranda and gave several speeches in the late summer and early fall of 1961 in which he railed about racism. In describing those who attacked welfare programs, he left no doubt as to the truth of the relationship between race and welfare. The opponents of welfare "are against it," Perliss said, "because they are prejudiced and bigoted, because they don't like the Negro and the Puerto Rican, because they distrust anyone who is not quite like they are."[110]

Winifred Bell, beginning further research on welfare in 1961, also publicly aired the dilemmas of race and welfare. Inspired by the defeat of the Louisiana ADC law in 1960, Bell began a history of the nationwide use of the suitable home provision.[111] Her study broke from previous ADC research, including her own in Detroit in the late 1950s, by focusing on the racial aspects of the ADC program. She argued that by allowing too much state and local discretion, federal law and federal policy makers had allowed states to discriminate against African Americans and especially African American unwed mothers. Bell's conclusions were potentially explosive. Yet when she sought to have her work published, she received support from key leaders in the welfare field. Both Wilbur Cohen, now at HEW, and Elizabeth Wickenden, Bell's mentor, strongly encouraged the Field Foundation to pay for publication. Influential board member Justine Polier agreed and told Max Hahn that "this could become a very impressive piece . . . on the discrimination against the non-white mother." She went on: "[Bell's] conclusions—the last 20 or 25 pages—if re-edited could be turned into a tremendously significant public affairs pamphlet *on the way in which over the years* the development of Mothers Pensions for nice white widows to [the] Social Security [Act in 1935] . . . help[ing] N[egro] families[,] and then with it came the building in of dodges and ways for excluding the non-white community."[112]

Bell's work prompted Elizabeth Wickenden to question the legitimacy of the tacit ban among welfare groups on using racial statistics. Wickenden wondered "whether our fear of identifying assistance with race is not actually self-defeating." She thought it might be better for African Americans "to get more rather than less racial identification in . . . studies and statistics" in order to show more clearly "how attitudes toward Negroes play a major role" in welfare policies.[113] By 1963 Wickenden was openly writing about racial discrimination in the APWA's journal *Public Welfare*. "Twenty years ago," she cautioned, "Gunnar Myrdal, in *The American Dilemma*, said we were going to have a tremendous welfare problem if we did not remedy discrimination against Negroes. Now, twenty years later, we do have a heavy incidence of Negroes on public welfare rolls just precisely as he predicted."[114] By acknowledging that there was an association between race and welfare, that it was not positive, and that it likely required action, Bell, Wickenden, and Cohen began to challenge the welfare community's, and their own, long-standing silence on race.

Yet their foray into an open discussion of race and welfare was not supported by the wider community of welfare policy makers. Just as in the Louisiana case, the primary response to the racist element of the attack on welfare in Newburgh was silence. Many welfare advocates preferred to mute the racial aspects of Newburgh and focus on other issues instead. At most, they used oblique references to race, or code words, in public. They referred, when pressed, to African Americans as "migrants from the south," or "newcomers."[115] They referred to racism as "xenophobia . . . a fear of and often hatred of strangers," rather than the historically specific phenomenon of northern discrimination against African Americans. In general, however, in the early days of the crisis, welfare advocates simply did not address the racism directed at welfare and welfare's clients.[116]

In particular, some welfare professionals resented the implication in Bell's dissertation on the suitable home provision: that they had been complicit in allowing racism to affect ADC through their silence on the issue. When considering publication of Bell's research, the Field Foundation received excoriating replies from some welfare experts. Joseph Reid of the CWLA, and Florida's influential state public welfare commissioner Robert T. Lansdale were both dead set against Bell's study. Although Lansdale and Reid provided several rationales for opposing the study's publication, it was clear that the most important reason was Bell's interpretation of the racial dimensions of the ADC program. Lansdale was defensive about Bell's argument that federal policy makers had ignored their responsibility to exert pressure on states to prevent racial discrimination through the suitable home provision. He wrote to Hahn: "Either Miss Bell does not understand the powers of the Federal agency or she is advocating a course of action designed to change the basic Federal-State relationships provided in the Social Security Act. One may well advocate a change in this statute but to state that 'it is not clear' why the Federal Government does not engage in an effort to put outside pressures on the states [regarding discrimination] reflects a lack of comprehension of the provisions of the present law."[117] Joseph Reid was far more blunt about his opinion of Bell's work when he spoke to Hahn on the phone. "Did you note this thing of [Bell's] stating that [']thru [sic] the years, in the absence of united and harmonious federal leadership, services lagged and problems remained unsolved. The fate of Negro illegitimate children and their mothers had been particularly affected by the situation.[']?" Reid was outraged. "I think the thing absolutely stinks," he said. "I would be very glad to write you to that effect. . . . This is a tract."[118] Like Lansdale, Reid could not abide Bell's conclusion that policy makers had been complicit in the poor treatment afforded African Americans by the ADC program.[119]

With welfare professionals divided, the NUL, which had been vocal about race and welfare during the Louisiana crisis the year before, now had an opening for demanding that the relationship between race and welfare politics be confronted. Yet the organization did not exploit the chance. In the wake of the furor in Newburgh, the NUL retreated somewhat from its aggressive stance on race and welfare. To be sure, its leaders recognized that Newburgh's antiwelfare code was racially motivated. In his last months as president of the NUL, Lester Granger jumped on the Newburgh incident just after it began and fired off a memorandum to local affiliates. Granger stated that "the Newburgh action is very plainly stimulated not only by rising welfare costs but by the steady increase in the city's non-white population. The Negro population has been growing, and the Negro proportion of the relief load is roughly three to one." Granger linked the racial politics of Newburgh back to those of Louisiana. "This is the Louisiana . . . plan more smartly handled, with the obvious race bias muted and with a profession of concern for the welfare dollar." But Granger also added that race might not be the most important issue at hand in welfare. He told local affiliates that "there is a racial angle in this matter as we all know; but it is more than even this; it is a matter of truly efficient and enlightened welfare practices."[120] In other words, Newburgh was, at its root, a welfare problem, not a race problem.

While the NUL's files are replete with accounts of the Louisiana crisis and the organization's public relations and policy strategies to solve it, there is comparatively little about Newburgh to be found. The NUL did not mount any public relations campaign comparable to "Operation Feed the Babies," nor did it organize local or national groups to join the fight. One reason for the diminished effort was that the thirteen-point welfare code Mitchell instituted in Newburgh did not generate the massive and frightening consequences of the Louisiana law. Whereas nearly 30,000 African Americans were cut off from assistance in Louisiana, Mitchell found only about a dozen people in Newburgh to throw off the rolls. So the NUL simply was not needed as a community organization to help African Americans in the same way it had been in Louisiana.[121]

But another event in the wake of Newburgh suggested that the NUL had other reasons for not taking on Newburgh as it had Louisiana. When John F. Kennedy took office in 1961, the NUL asked to address the Kennedy administration about its agenda. On May 17, 1962, NUL leaders from around the nation and the national leadership were invited to HEW's offices to discuss that department's programs and how they might benefit African Americans. The meeting offered the NUL an unprecedented opportunity to present their views publicly.

When welfare was broached that day, NUL leaders raised their concern over racist attacks on the ADC program such as the one in Louisiana. "The reason we in the Urban League have such a stake in this," an NUL member explained, "is the fact that we are fighting for a goodly, or high percentage of ADC families, who are minority families, and this is one of the reasons why we find . . . punitive measures being proposed."[122] As a remedy, the NUL proposed that HEW undertake a national public relations campaign. In a seeming repudiation of their strategy in Louisiana two years earlier, however, the NUL did not ask the department to talk openly about racial discrimination. Instead, its representatives suggested that HEW simply try to improve the overall image of the ADC program: "The Bureau of Family Services [formerly the Bureau of Public Assistance] could do a little more in terms of interpretation, to build an image along the lines of the tremendous values to be received from the programs of aid to dependent children." Their specific recommendations for the publicity campaign echoed the strategy that professional welfare organizations had been using to promote ADC. NUL representatives suggested that the HEW avoid controversy and instead promote the fact that welfare was now a rehabilitative program, a more constructive, profamily program than before. The HEW representatives agreed: "The idea of helping families sets [sic] better with a lot of people than public assistance, or handouts. . . . It is a much better connotation, family service, you are trying help families get over a rough spot." The NUL and HEW officials agreed that day to rely on general family-focused and rehabilitative rhetoric and practice as a defense against racist attacks on welfare programs even when such defenses were evidently failing.[123]

The public strategy expressed by the NUL in this meeting with HEW differed from the strategy it had taken in the Louisiana case. It revealed that its leadership was wary about the relationship between race and welfare. Speaking frankly, NUL leaders agreed with an HEW official who said during the May 17 meeting, "Welfare is a dirty word in this country." If possible, the NUL wanted to avoid muddying its civil rights agenda with that "dirty" word. Although in dire circumstances it would aggressively pursue welfare issues, in the wake of Newburgh its leaders seemed reluctant to link their primary agenda too closely with the increasingly controversial issue of public assistance.[124]

The dealings with race after Newburgh revealed complex and not necessarily expected developments within the welfare coalition. While liberals agreed in the late 1950s that a nonracial approach to publicizing ADC was best, in 1960 the Louisiana attack challenged that, and Newburgh did again in 1961. Some key leaders within welfare groups—such as Winifred Bell, Elizabeth Wickenden, and Wilbur Cohen—were beginning to question the ban on discussing race in connection with welfare. Most others, however, including the NUL, remained tied, albeit ambivalently, to the nonracial public discourses of welfare. While it was clear that some welfare groups and leaders were still hesitant to make welfare a *racialized* issue, civil rights groups and their leaders may have been reluctant to make racial rights a *welfare* issue.

The Newburgh crisis reprised the racial theme of the Louisiana case, but it also raised a new issue. Whereas the Louisiana ADC crisis had challenged the contention that ADC families were legitimate families, the Newburgh crisis was largely about other matters. For Mitchell, the key issue was employment: welfare clients were "loafers," objectionable not merely because of their sexual or marital status but because of their failure to earn a living. Mitchell accused welfare programs of harboring able-bodied people who collected public funds for doing nothing. He believed that welfare clients should be punished and made responsible for finding work.

While Mitchell inveighed against loafers on welfare, he was ambiguous about whether women on welfare should be forced to work. His comments on laziness cast aspersions on all able-bodied adults who might be "cheating" the system by refusing to support themselves. One of Mitchell's thirteen points stated that no person could receive relief who had quit a job, for whatever reason. Mitchell argued that welfare recipients were encouraged to quit perfectly good jobs when they knew that they could easily obtain relief afterwards. A second stated that no person on relief could refuse to take paid employment offered him (or her), no matter what. Finally, Mitchell declared that no person (except someone who was blind or disabled) could receive relief funds for more than three months per year. This was aimed not only at reducing costs but also at forcing recipients into the labor market. Suggesting that all able-bodied people should work certainly implied that many women raising children ought to work. And the declaration that no able-bodied person could receive relief for more than three months clearly meant that women raising children on ADC would be forced to work.[125]

The sweeping nature of Mitchell's statements was mirrored in the broader public debate over Newburgh. In articles about welfare ensuing from Newburgh, reporters frequently referred to stereotypes of welfare clients either as factual representations of welfare clients or in order to point out their inaccuracy. Often, these stereotypes differed by gender, and specifically in terms of which gender was considered employable. One article, for instance, stated that "the prototype of the person 'on welfare' is either an unemployed but able-bodied man or a woman of questionable morals."[126] Men were stereotyped as lazy, while women were stereotyped only as immoral, bearing illegitimate children in order to get welfare money.[127] Other articles criticized women on welfare for being not just immoral but lazy, too: "The public image [of an ADC client]," one article stated, "is of a mother who is shiftless and lazy, unwilling to work, promiscuous, and neglectful of her children."[128]

The ambiguity in federal law over whether women on welfare ought to be encouraged to work made fighting the negative publicity against welfare clients difficult.[129] Welfare advocates themselves bore some responsibility for making the issue of ADC mothers' employment status unclear. When they developed rehabilitative welfare reform during the 1950s, they might have anticipated that a moment like the Newburgh crisis would arrive in which they would have to be clear about the issue of women, work, and welfare. After all, though the original 1935 ADC law was predicated on the belief that needy mothers with children ought to be considered not employable and allowed to remain at home caring for children, the rehabilitative welfare reform that liberal welfare policy makers pursued contradicted this. Their demonstration projects, articles, discussions at conferences, and, especially, their legislative reform—the 1956 Social Security Amendments—all stated that the goal of the ADC program was both "promoting family life and encouraging independence." Clearly, they were not opposed to employment for ADC mothers per se. When employment was the result of opportunity-oriented, well-designed rehabilitative programs, the welfare community was in favor of it. Yet welfare advocates opposed *forcing* mothers to take employment. Moreover, in their bid to destigmatize welfare and gain support for the program, welfare advocates' preference had been to present ADC as a family-based program offering family-based services. Now, Joseph Mitchell and the media were raising the question of "self-support" for welfare clients—work. But they were not raising it in the way that public welfare advocates would have liked. While welfare advocates focused on both work and family life, Mitchell made no mention of family life and focused on responsibility and punishment. Welfare policy makers believed that the distinction between punitive employability standards applied by hostile critics of the program and voluntary, helpful employment rehabilitation programs was clear to any rational observer.

Yet welfare advocates were nevertheless responsive to the charges of "loafing" and the insinuations that welfare discouraged work. In the year after Newburgh some members of the welfare community began to address the question of whether mothers on ADC should be encouraged to work. And when they did, it seemed that they, too, were beginning to question the legally-based definition of ADC clients as "nonemployables," though in a more subtle fashion than opponents of welfare.

As welfare organizations mobilized against the Newburgh backlash, they contacted a slew of reporters. By October 1961 Loula Dunn of the APWA told Max Hahn, "We are building quite a file on it and we think that the stories are really running against the Newburgh thing rather than for it."[130] The APWA and other welfare professionals encouraged the writing of these articles, often providing the factual information and editorial slant for them. In the positive articles about ADC appearing in late 1961 and 1962, the aspect of ADC lauded most was that rehabilitation could, and did, encourage women on welfare to work. In late 1961, for example, the *Wall Street Journal* reported approvingly that in the wake of Newburgh, HEW was touting "more federal funds for day care centers to watch the children of welfare mothers while they are being trained for work."[131] In 1962 the *Chicago Sun-Times* ran editorials and articles based on APWA and Field Foundation information under headlines such as "To Help Them Help Themselves" and "Relief Recipients Take to Schooling Program" (in order to build their job skills).[132] That fall, the *Chicago Daily News* ran an article called "How ADC Families Get Back on Feet," which described five cases that showed the ways in which welfare recipients entered the workforce: an ADC "restoration team tries to find work for ADC mothers."[133] The *Philadelphia Inquirer* used APWA information to run a series of articles called "ABC's of Relief" —with headlines like "Most Families on ADC on the Level Despite Wrong Public Image" and "Image of Recipients Wrong." Key to these positive corrective portrayals were two themes: that "the mother hopes to become independent" and "would like to work," and that the "only way to help relief families permanently, officials say, is to rehabilitate them."[134]

In the months after Newburgh, some welfare policy makers argued that work ought to become a more important feature of rehabilitation for women on ADC. Elizabeth Wickenden, for example, acknowledged to the leader of a private welfare organization in early 1962 that "current debate about the ADC program . . . raise[s] some very interesting questions about the relationship of mothers to the labor market and the extent to which the public is willing to support them." As a result, Wickenden began to support more aggressive rehabilitative projects in various states and localities that blurred the line of gendered definitions of employability by coming perilously close to forcing mothers into rehabilitation.[135] One of the most remarkable of these projects, never fully implemented, was a plan by Raymond Hilliard, the influential director of Chicago's Cook

County Department of Public Aid. In early 1962 he proposed "Project Jubilee": "A plan to undertake a massive attack on illiteracy in Chicago and to inaugurate a city-wide network of training and educational programs especially for Chicagoans who receive public assistance." Wickenden approvingly circulated copies of Hilliard's plan—a mandatory plan that would have targeted 34,000 ADC mothers.[136]

The most important of those welfare advocates who, in the aftermath of Newburgh, turned his attention increasingly to the issue of employment for women on ADC was Wilbur Cohen. Though Cohen had been, and still was, a strong proponent of the strategy of destigmatizing ADC through invoking the discourse of family, he was increasingly convinced that presenting ADC as a program that helped women on welfare find work was important. His own research at the University of Michigan partly embraced the notion that rehabilitation should encourage employment for some women on welfare. In the wake of Newburgh, Cohen wrote to Max Hahn about how the Field Foundation should consider spending its money to improve welfare. "One of the areas I believe needs encouragement," he stated, "is related to . . . ADC mothers who wish to work."[137] As assistant secretary of HEW, of course, Cohen was himself in a position to shape the direction of welfare policy, and his increasing interest in presenting ADC as a program that encouraged independence for women both measured the change that the welfare crises had caused and foreshadowed what was to come in federal welfare policy.

The subtly increasing emphasis on linking ADC to work after Newburgh was also evident upon the final publication of the APWA's ADC study, *An American Dependency Challenge*, in 1963. Even this family-based study, which was to highlight family services, ended up being publicized as promoting self-support and employment for ADC mothers far more than its early planners probably would have anticipated. The *Chapel Hill Weekly* published the most extensive review of the study because the University of North Carolina at Chapel Hill had helped conduct the study. Researchers speaking to the North Carolina reporters stressed the employment problems and potentials facing ADC clients and how rehabilitation in ADC programs addressed the question of work before addressing any family issues or illegitimacy. The article quoted the studies' authors as saying, "The combination of low education, low occupational positions and lack of strong skills strongly suggests that the potential for employment and self-support may be poor." "However," the authors added, "with improved job opportunities, vocational rehabilitation and accelerated vocational education, the majority of adults in our ADC families could conceivably realize an adequate standard of self-sufficiency."[138] Other articles on the landmark study followed suit. The headline from the *Christian Science Monitor* focused on the vocational issue: "Child Welfare Aid Solutions Posed—Education and Training." Its opening paragraph reflected the responsiveness of the APWA to the Newburgh situation. The "study on aid to dependent children," recommended that "in addition to financial aid, there must be education and training in occupational skills in this era of automation so families will be able to exist without welfare assistance."[139]

In the year or so after Newburgh, the public and policy discourse regarding gender, work, and welfare grew muddier. Contradictory images of mothers as stay-at-home care givers were juxtaposed with images of them as potential workers. Criticisms of their laziness were given as much stress as criticisms of their care-giving or sexual status. Critics of welfare like Mitchell in Newburgh argued that all ADC mothers, if they were simply able-bodied, were de facto employable. Welfare advocates opposed this broad claim and drew a line in the sand. But they nevertheless found themselves responding subtly to such criticism by beginning to publicly emphasize how rehabilitation promoted work for ADC mothers.

IN 1962 NBC AIRED ITS FIRST, and only, prime-time television documentary on welfare. Producers of the *NBC White Paper* series trekked up the Hudson River from New York City to Newburgh to investigate the dramatic events that had occurred months before when Joseph Mitchell had announced a "war on welfare." Though not a complete endorsement of welfare policies as they existed, the documentary, "Battle of Newburgh," represented a critique of Mitchell and the virulent antiwelfare ideology that motivated him and his supporters. Using stark black-and-white film, producers entered small, spartan, and often dilapidated homes to introduce viewers to families on welfare. An African American woman with six children said she struggled to buy food and winter clothes. An elderly white man, staring forlornly at the floor, spoke of his feelings of inadequacy. A man with his ill-clad child on his lap and his wife by his side broke into tears telling of his repeated, failed attempts to secure work. The "Battle of Newburgh" strongly suggested to viewers that the so-called war on welfare had really been a war on the poor. And it further suggested that a fair, decent welfare policy that aided needy clients financially and otherwise was the only proper response.[140]

The documentary must have pleased welfare advocates. Not only did it take their side in the battle of Newburgh; it represented the social and political issues surrounding welfare in much the same way that welfare advocates themselves did.[141] It advocated helping welfare clients through social policy, not punishing them; and it showed an awareness of poverty that welfare advocates had been trying to promote for nearly ten years. The "Battle of Newburgh" followed the "race-blind" stance of the welfare community as well, showing both white and black welfare clients while avoiding the history of the recent migration of African Americans to Newburgh and the difficulties they had faced there finding jobs and getting services.

The documentary suggested that, in the wake of Newburgh, cooler heads prevailed, and welfare policy—and its advocates—had bounced back from the public attacks. But in fact they had not recovered from the nadir of Newburgh. Antiwelfare sentiment continued unabated, with national conservatives in both the Republican and Democratic parties making political hay with the issue in local, state, and congressional elections. And welfare policy makers were shaken. In the late 1950s they had begun to destigmatize the program and prevent its racialization by using the discourse of family and presenting ADC as a necessary program for troubled families. But the national public crises over ADC generated significant challenges to the ideological premises on which the national welfare reform agenda was based.

For one, how could they promote ADC as a family program and rehabilitation as a positive plan for families when critics denied, as in Louisiana, that ADC clients were legitimate families, and denied, as in Newburgh, that family issues were even important in comparison to work? The welfare coalition's ambiguous response to these charges after Newburgh suggested that they, too, were considering the value of attaching a stronger discourse of employment to ADC. During these intensely political years in ADC's history, welfare advocates defined and then redefined their presentation of rehabilitation and ADC based on the politicized crises in Louisiana and Newburgh.

But they did not redefine their treatment of the nexus between race and welfare. Those who defended welfare generally maintained their silence on race. The long-term effectiveness of such a strategy was questionable, however, when racism had been a precipitating factor in both of the national outbursts over welfare. Welfare advocates' determination to avoid the discussion of race, as part of selling their rehabilitative strategy, rendered them less effective in countering publicly expressed racism with regard to welfare. This strategy raised another question: could future racial attacks on welfare mimicking those in Louisiana and Newburgh be effectively combated when civil rights groups were nervous about being associated with the increasingly unpopular policy of welfare and welfare groups were fearful of talking about race?

Questions about strategy and substance were no longer hypothetical in the early 1960s, either. In the year between the Louisiana crisis and the Newburgh crisis, Democrat John F. Kennedy was elected president of the United States and gave welfare professionals what they had wanted since 1956: the chance to be directly involved in elaborating and improving the rehabilitative components of the ADC program established in the 1956 Social Security Amendments. Paradoxically, at the height of the attack on welfare, welfare policy makers were given more power over the national agenda than ever before. As their responses to the welfare crises of 1960 and 1961 suggested, however, their ability to shape new welfare laws was likely to be limited by the increasingly controversial public politics of welfare.

CHAPTER FOUR

A "New Spirit" in Welfare

Women and Work in the
Kennedy Administration

On a Saturday night in January 1961, Wilbur Cohen received a phone call from
an adviser to newly elected Democratic president John Kennedy who told him,
"The President is going to announce your appointment tomorrow as Assistant
Secretary [of Health, Education and Welfare]." At the time, Cohen was a professor of social work at the University of Michigan and had been advising the
candidate on social policy matters. The appointment came as somewhat of a
surprise, however, because Cohen had told the president only days earlier, "You
don't need to bring me into the Administration." Kennedy, apparently, had different ideas, and Cohen later recalled that the president refused to take no for
an answer. So Cohen finished grading his student's final exams at 4:45 A.M.,
showered, packed, and left for Washington, D.C., on a 7:00 A.M. flight. "I left
my office, my papers, my home, and walked out," Cohen remembered. He reported directly to the Department of Health, Education, and Welfare (HEW),
where he was sworn in as assistant secretary for legislation. He was to stay in
Washington for nearly a decade.[1]

Though the appointments of assistant secretaries seldom merit acknowledgment, Wilbur Cohen's new job represented the kind of moment historians
like: when small events create larger consequences. Cohen's appointment ush-
ered into power the de facto leader of the coalition of liberals who for over ten
years had been championing major national-level reform of the Aid to Dependent Children (ADC) program. With Cohen's appointment, welfare reform ad-

vocates gained unprecedented access to federal policy making. When Kennedy promised during the election to "get the country moving again" and to push the country toward a "new frontier," he did not have welfare policy in mind. But welfare advocates did. They hoped that with the new Democratic administration and Wilbur Cohen in power, their welfare reform agenda would be enacted.

Yet the public politics of welfare suggested that the early 1960s were not necessarily an auspicious moment for reaching new frontiers. The welfare crises in Louisiana in 1960 and Newburgh, New York, in 1961 shocked the welfare establishment, revealing deep antipathy toward welfare among conservatives and dissatisfaction with welfare among the general public. Welfare professionals and their allies had carefully constructed a public face for ADC that was family based and race neutral, hoping to gain support for welfare and rehabilitation among politicians and the public. Yet both images were blurred in the welfare debacles. Welfare advocates had planned on promoting rehabilitation by emphasizing family services, but the welfare blow-ups prompted many of them to reconsider whether emphasizing family services was the best defense of welfare. In order to answer welfare's critics, some began to underscore how rehabilitation promoted employment and job training for welfare clients.

Though welfare reformers gained an unprecedented opportunity to implement their ideal welfare agenda through Cohen's new position, the damaging public debate about welfare echoed through welfare policy making in the early 1960s, nonetheless. In 1961 and 1962 two welfare laws were passed: the ADC–Unemployed Parent provision (ADC-UP) and the 1962 Public Welfare Amendments. The new legislation, whose passage was engineered by Cohen with the help of welfare allies and Congress, fulfilled hopes of a new era of Democratic Party rule; it broadened ADC's coverage, institutionalized rehabilitation, and funded rehabilitative social services at an unprecedented level. The 1962 law also changed the name of the program from Aid to Dependent Children to Aid to Families with Dependent Children (AFDC), seeming to reinforce the importance of family services in welfare law.[2] Yet at the same time, the new laws reflected the persistent fears of political attack on welfare. Cohen adjusted the themes of welfare reform to combat the political reverberations of the welfare crises of 1960 and 1961. Just as the public presentation of welfare began to move away from family services and toward portraying rehabilitation as a way to encourage women on welfare to work, so, too, did welfare law. The new laws of 1961 and 1962 continued to support family services for welfare clients, but above all they emphasized employment. Women's status as officially nonemployable was abrogated within the ADC program.

The new emphasis of welfare law came about both unintentionally and intentionally, and this chapter explores both paths in detail. The first step coupling welfare and work came unintentionally, from the expansion of ADC called the ADC-UP provision in the early spring of 1961. This program brought together two previously separate categories of social policy for the first time: unemployment policy and ADC. It did this through a provision that allowed some unemployed men with families to receive ADC payments. Incorporating officially designated "employables"—able-bodied, unemployed men—into a program officially designated for "nonemployables"—mothers with dependent children—challenged the existing gendered basis of federal welfare programs and work expectations. Though ADC-UP was passed in order to combat the recession, broaden welfare coverage, and improve the family-friendly image of the program by adding two-parent families to the welfare rolls, the chapter explains that the intersection of these categories of policy unintentionally created a closer association between ADC benefits and work.

Yet Wilbur Cohen also intentionally chose to further blur the gender distinctions between welfare and work. The chapter describes how after the passage of the ADC-UP law in early 1961, Cohen consciously pursued a set of policies whereby a woman's welfare entitlement was related increasingly to her status as a potential wage earner. Through the 1962 Public Welfare Amendments, he emphasized rehabilitative services that encouraged women on AFDC to work.

"Employable" Men and ADC: The ADC-UP Program

Although the status of women's claims to welfare would soon shift, this was not the initial goal of Wilbur Cohen or the Kennedy administration. In early 1961 their immediate interest was the economy. When Kennedy won the election in late 1960, the United States was entering a recession, the latest in a series of recessions that had plagued the second administration of Republican Dwight Eisenhower. The recession had slowed economic growth and enlarged the already growing pockets of unemployment and poverty in various regions and economic sectors throughout the country.

With the pressure of the recession looming just after his election, Kennedy began exploring remedies in the form of stimulus programs and tax cuts, and he asked Wilbur Cohen to begin exploring some social policy solutions.[3] Named chair of Kennedy's transition team on social policy, the Task Force on Health and Social Security, Cohen was given the mandate to produce short-term, attainable legislative goals for the new administration.[4] He picked his friend Elizabeth Wickenden, a policy consultant and welfare expert, to work with him on welfare proposals.[5]

Cohen and Wickenden had been juggling ideas for changes in welfare through-out the 1950s, and they believed that one in particular would meet Kennedy's short-term economic needs.[6] They recommended that the Aid to Dependent Children program expand its eligibility to include the children of unemployed men who were not covered by federal or state unemployment insurance programs. This was the Aid to Dependent Children–Unemployed Parent provision.[7]

In ADC-UP, Cohen and Wickenden hoped to hit several birds with one stone. Cohen sold it to Kennedy as an antirecession measure. He argued that providing ADC payments to the families of unemployed fathers would introduce more money into the economy, increase consumer spending, and, according to Keynesian economic theory, prime the economic pump to help raise the country out of the recession. This argument was probably more political rhetoric than truth, however. The ADC-UP program was projected to reach only a couple hundred thousand families in its first year, hardly enough people to bolster the economy. Moreover, it was questionable whether those at the bottom of the economic scale could spend enough money to significantly influence economic growth anyway.[8]

But Cohen had more justifications for ADC-UP than its antirecession qualities. The antirecession bill provided a cover for what was, in reality, a small step in the direction of noncategorical federal public assistance to all needy adults. In the early 1940s Cohen and Wickenden strongly advocated eliminating categorical federal welfare programs—such as Old Age Assistance, Aid to the Blind, and Aid to Dependent Children—and replacing them with one federal noncategorical public assistance program for all needy individuals. The Wagner-Murray-Dingell bills of 1943 and 1945 and the public welfare bills of the late 1940s all strove for this goal. Cohen and Wickenden saw ADC-UP as a small measure that might provide a wedge with which to pressure Congress toward the slow, incremental expansion of federal public assistance coverage beyond the existing categorical programs. Because the recession was exacerbating poverty, Cohen figured that 1961 would be an auspicious political moment to achieve a modest expansion of federal welfare coverage.[9]

Cohen and Wickenden had yet another reason for proposing the ADC-UP provision: to advance their public relations campaign for welfare reform. The ADC-UP program was a way to contribute to a neutral and palatable profamily image of ADC. This image was under siege with the Louisiana and Newburgh attacks that lambasted welfare mothers as immoral and deviant, and ADC-UP provided an opportunity to strengthen it. Cohen and Wickenden told President Kennedy that the existing ADC laws, because they turned away two-parent, father-headed families, actually encouraged families to break up. Kennedy's

Wilbur Cohen (center right) is pictured with President John F. Kennedy, Secretary of Health, Education, and Welfare Anthony Celebrezze (left), and HEW's commissioner of education, Frances Keppel, in Miami Beach, Florida, in early 1963. Courtesy of the Social Security Administration History Archives, Baltimore, Maryland.

report to the House of Representatives later echoed their views: "Too many fathers [who are] unable to support their families . . . have resorted to real or pretended desertion to qualify their children for help. Many other fathers are prevented by conscience and love of family from taking this route, thereby disqualifying their children under present law."[10] ADC-UP was to remedy this by allowing needy unemployed fathers to get assistance. Although there was little evidence at the time or later to support this argument, Cohen, Wickenden, and other welfare allies were willing to argue that ADC-UP would help prevent family disintegration.[11] As Cohen explained this political calculus, "The bringing together of needy unemployed families with other needy family units who now receive AFDC, would tend to strengthen the provision for both groups, and would perhaps help to minimize some of the controversy which tends to surround many AFDC programs."[12]

Kennedy's staff liked the ADC-UP recommendation for all the reasons Cohen laid out. After appointing him to HEW, Kennedy had Cohen immediately write the ADC-UP legislation and lobby Congress for its passage. As part of an antire-

Elizabeth Wickenden had her portrait taken in 1960 for her appointment at the New York School of Social Work. While there, she conducted research and continued to lobby and consult on welfare legislation. Courtesy of the Wisconsin Historical Society, Madison, Wisconsin.

cession package of bills, ADC-UP passed easily by voice votes and took effect in May 1961.

Although ADC-UP's supporters intended it to combat the recession, expand welfare coverage, and improve the image of ADC as a family-friendly program, the most important consequence of ADC-UP lay elsewhere. Throughout American history, able-bodied men, even the unemployed, had been considered officially "employable." As a result, unemployed men historically had difficulty getting access to public assistance at any level—local, state, or federal. ADC, for example, was designated officially for "nonemployables." The ADC-UP provision "introduced, for the first time, an identifiable group of employable people unto [*sic*] the federally aided public assistance programs."[13] In doing so it challenged the precedent on which ADC entitlements were predicated.

Adding "employable" unemployed men to the ADC caseload not only challenged the federal program's basis for entitlements; it also brought work relief to the doorstep of the ADC program for the first time. Historically, what public assistance "employable" men obtained had often required performing some kind of work in exchange. In the nineteenth century this work was done in community-operated workhouses and in the twentieth century in local work relief programs. The Great Depression and the New Deal brought work relief to the federal level for the first and only time. Franklin D. Roosevelt created various public works projects, most notably the Works Progress Administration, to help the millions of unemployed and destitute. But after 1943, when the economy recovered, the federal government abandoned work relief and its support of able-bodied, low-income unemployed men. After that, able-bodied unemployed men lacking insurance could get relief only through state and locally funded general relief programs, often performing work in return for assistance.[14]

Because of these historical precedents regarding gender, welfare, and work, Cohen and his colleagues in the Kennedy administration knew that when they proposed ADC-UP, Congress and many members of the public were unlikely to approve of official "employables" collecting welfare checks without having to work in return. The administration therefore approved the House of Representatives' demand "that provisions must be made [by states] to deal with the problem of useful work for the unemployed parent."[15] Legislators at the federal level wanted to follow the long-established precedent in state and local programs of requiring able-bodied men who received relief to work. When the ADC-UP bill passed, then, it contained work requirements for the needy unemployed fathers on the program. It stated that "an unemployed individual whose family is receiving aid under this program should accept any reasonable offer of employment." In addition, to encourage ADC-UP recipients to work, "the bill require[d] that a State agency administering the expanded aid to dependent children program must enter into cooperative arrangements with the State agency administering the public employment offices" and vocational education programs.[16] Finally, states would have to create work relief programs for ADC-UP clients. Through training or employment, the new male recipients of the

ADC-UP provision would have to comply with work requirements.[17] By compelling states to create work programs for ADC-UP clients, the Kennedy administration thought that it had solved the problems associated with incorporating employable men into the ADC program.

Soon after the passage of the ADC-UP legislation, however, Cohen and the secretary of HEW, Abraham Ribicoff, realized that the problem of employable men and ADC-UP was not solved by the law's requirement for states to use work relief. Though popular in public rhetoric and sentiment, work relief was not prevalent in the United States in the early 1960s. HEW performed a nationwide review of the extent of work relief in May 1961 and revealed that "work programs as an organized, planned operation, are not very extensive; . . . [they] tend to be a local operation[;] . . . projects, in general, appear to be poorly devised and administered[;] . . . [and] public welfare agencies generally have difficulty finding suitable projects" even when they wanted to use them. Moreover, only twelve states used work relief as a test of eligibility for general assistance, and eight of those programs were not mandatory. And only eight other states reported "some" use of work relief. Despite the fact that ADC-UP required states to create suitable work for ADC recipients, states would be reluctant to comply because creating and running work programs for all the new ADC-UP clients was likely to cost more than simply disbursing the welfare payments to new clients.[18]

Yet if able-bodied men receiving ADC-UP were seen receiving welfare without being compelled to work by the states, it would create a political problem for the administration. The Newburgh welfare crisis arose just months after the passage of ADC-UP, bringing work relief to the attention of the nation. City manager Joseph Mitchell's attempt to force all able-bodied welfare clients to work in return for their payments met with great popular support. As one welfare analyst put it: "The persons who are able bodied and unemployed and still on the public welfare rolls present a difficulty in the problem of public relations which tends to force a program of work relief. If no initiative is assumed in setting up training and employment opportunities . . . , public welfare cannot sit back and do nothing."[19]

Cohen was sensitive to political pressures and worried that the public controversy about welfare and work would hinder the legislative success of ADC-UP and further welfare reform, and worked to neutralize the threat. Secretary Ribicoff pointed out to President Kennedy that "conservatives are up in arms over the reports of welfare abuses," and he exhorted his staff to be sure that the ADC-UP program did not play into their accusations.[20] Ribicoff was personally desperate to portray welfare in a way that made it seem politically palatable because midway through his first year on the job, he privately decided to run for the Senate in Connecticut in the 1962 election. He wanted policy proposals at HEW that suited his campaign strategy—to effectively counter conservative charges. He started and ended meetings with HEW staff by reminding them of the public perception of welfare. He arrived at one legislative session for welfare carrying "the current copy of *U.S. News and World Report* which had on its cover, 'the Growing Scandal in Relief.'" He exhorted the staff, "You are dealing with sensation." [21] Above all, he wanted to "find ways of emphasizing [to the public] how well our welfare programs are helping people."[22] "If we can show," Ribicoff said, "that a welfare worker does more than act as a conduit for money, we might make some progress with legislators and the public."[23]

Cohen knew quite well that Ribicoff was hoping to make progress with voters with the welfare reform bill, and though he was later critical of Ribicoff's politicking, he was nevertheless responsive to Ribicoff's requests and the overall political needs of the Kennedy administration. Cohen therefore determined that work programs in ADC-UP could not be left to the potentially wayward states.[24] For the first time since the New Deal, the federal government was going to undertake "work relief programs for able-bodied unemployed assistance recipients" in the ADC-UP program.[25]

But adding a federally funded work relief program to ADC was going to be difficult to get by many of Cohen's closest allies in the world of welfare and social work, with whom Cohen was forced to negotiate in order to get the federal work relief program passed into law. Having gotten ADC-UP passed, in the late spring of 1961 Cohen and Secretary Ribicoff convened a committee of experts to advise them on pursuing further reform of the ADC program along the lines of expanded and enhanced rehabilitative measures—what would come to be called the 1962 Public Welfare Amendments. The group was called the Ad Hoc Committee on Public Welfare, and Cohen stacked it with his colleagues and allies in welfare reform circles—members of the American Public Welfare Association (APWA), the National Social Welfare Assembly, and the NUL.[26]

The National Association of Social Workers and its director Joseph Anderson led the committee. The NASW (created through a merger of social work organizations in 1955) represented all social workers, those who worked in private agencies and those in public programs. The organization generally concerned itself with issues of professionalization and practice, and had not been actively involved in the 1940s or early 1950s in lobbying for federal policy. However, there was a cadre of NASW leaders who were interested in federal welfare policy, looking for increased opportunities to expand social work's role in the programs and ensure that programs met the social work profession's standards. In the mid-1950s the NASW created a Washington, D.C., office to act on legislative priorities and objectives established by the NASW board of directors. The leadership of the Ad Hoc Committee was perceived by NASW leaders to be their first chance to directly influence the federal ADC agenda.[27]

Having hatched the idea for the Ad Hoc Committee on Public Welfare before the Newburgh crisis and before passing ADC-UP, Cohen now faced the challenge of clarifying with this group all federal law regarding men and women on welfare and the issue of work. The effort was more than Cohen bargained for. Though many of the participants advocated the stance that ADC recipients could be rehabilitated through education, training, and job placement, they were nervous about the way in which employment was discussed by Cohen and Ribicoff in the ADC-UP program. In the minds of committee members, it was one thing to talk of rehabilitation and invoke independence and self-support, but it was quite another to discuss work relief programs, or make-work programs for those receiving welfare. Although the difference between the two approaches may have seemed marginal, to the welfare community they were not. They never conceived of their rehabilitative demonstration projects as having anything to do with work relief. Work relief was a separate program category. Unlike local administrators in state-run general relief welfare programs, they were not trying to punish ADC clients by making them work. Nor was their goal simply to make clients "useful" by having them work. Advocates of employment-based rehabilitative services believed that they were helping ADC mothers who wanted to work, preparing them for the workforce through an array of social services. They were trying to provide welfare recipients with opportunities, not make them debtors to the cities or towns they lived in. From the perspective of the welfare community, work relief was antithetical to their rehabilitative employment programs.

The members of the Ad Hoc Committee thus forced Cohen and Ribicoff to debate the creation of a federal work relief program associated with welfare. The minutes of the third meeting of the committee reported that "one point of view held that the responsibility of public welfare is to provide assistance, not to train . . . not to provide work relief. Public welfare agencies would take leadership in stimulating and cooperating in the development of training and job opportunities," but they themselves would not provide them.[28] In addition, four committee members officially dissented from any recommendation that work relief be associated with federal welfare programs. Edwin Witte, one of the founders of Social Security, for example, objected to changing the historical distinction in federal programs between public welfare and work relief. So, too, did Trude Lash, head of the Children's Committee of the City of New York.[29]

Work relief was an especially hard pill to swallow for two African Americans on the committee, the two other dissenters from recommendations on work relief. They were James Dumpson, commissioner of the New York City Department of Public Welfare, and Whitney Young, president of the NUL. Concerned about the association of African Americans with welfare use during the Louisiana and Newburgh welfare crises, Young was unwilling to have ADC further stigmatized by an association with work relief. He explained to Secretary Ribicoff and Wilbur Cohen that coupling work and relief would produce negative rather than positive public sentiments: "They [work relief programs] tend to perpetuate the myth that public welfare encourages idleness," by sanctioning the view that those who receive welfare need to be forced to work. This, he explained, would be an especially negative result for African Americans, who suffered disproportionately from unemployment but were not well covered by federal and state unemployment insurance. A "large percentage of the unemployed are Negros [*sic*]," he told Ribicoff, and, with this proposal, "society's answer to their needs would be asking them to 'sweep the streets.'" He went on, "Some of the [work relief] projects talked about are those now performed by prisoners," hardly an appropriate policy response to the needs of African Americans, and one that would compound discriminatory views of them. With Dumpson echoing his remarks, he concluded that work relief programs could not be construed in any way to be positive for relief recipients. Invoking the liberal consensus on rehabilitation, he argued, "This [work relief] is the kind of a program that does not rehabilitate, but perpetuates dependency."[30]

The welfare community was now arguing about something that they had thought, prior to the convening of the Ad Hoc Committee, they had agreed on. They had all supported a rehabilitative welfare program that promoted both self-care and self-support for families. But now, in the context of a federal work relief program in ADC, they were not so sure.

In the face of the Ad Hoc Committee's discomfort with federally funded work relief in ADC, Cohen and Secretary Ribicoff astutely deployed rhetoric that they believed would capture the hearts of committee members. Rather than talk about work relief as an obligation, Ribicoff presented work relief in a more positive light: "Perhaps this [the issue of work relief] could all be viewed in terms of a program that is constructive and rehabilitative. Perhaps training could be provided against some sort of an apprenticeship formula. It might be possible . . . to direct some of these assistance funds to constructive projects for which persons applying for assistance could be referred. Perhaps the definition of the use of federal funds could be broadened so as to include training and employment, and so forth, and the development of small limited public works projects on which the person would work—not for his relief, per se, but until re-training or an employment possibility had developed."[31] Though Ribicoff had not been steeped in the decade-long effort to define a new vision of welfare, Cohen had. And, through Cohen, Ribicoff had adequately grasped the protean rhetoric of rehabilitation. The issue of work relief could be incorporated into recommendations on welfare reform, but not so obviously as to look regressive. Instead, the report would use the language that the welfare community itself used, the language of rehabilitation and opportunity. As Ribicoff intoned, "With freedom there must be opportunity. And this is what we seek—the creation of opportunity to become educated, to find employment, to earn decent wages, to enjoy good health. With these opportunities established and strengthened, each individual can enjoy a free life and make his utmost contribution to our free society."[32]

Shifting work relief from the discursive context of punishment and obligation to the discursive context of rehabilitation worked. Ribicoff and Cohen convinced the members of the welfare and social work organizations on the Ad Hoc Committee to endorse a federally funded work program for the ADC-UP clients if the work program was viewed as rehabilitation, not as work relief.[33] In late 1961 the APWA released a formal statement supporting work relief in ADC-UP, adding that "such work should, where possible, provide training and be directed toward the preservation and development of work skills" of welfare clients. The NASW stated that while it formally disapproved of "work for relief," it would support programs that aimed to usefully train and rehabilitate low-income unemployed males.[34]

After the close of the Ad Hoc Committee's work in the fall of 1961, Cohen began to craft legislation for the new work programs in ADC, the Community Work and Training Programs (CWTPs). They were federally funded, locally operated work and training programs for the training and employment of fathers brought into the ADC program through the extension of the Unemployed Parent provision. Ribicoff and Cohen reiterated that the CWTPs would not be considered old-fashioned work relief programs. They and the staff at HEW described the CWTPs "under the concept of rehabilitation." "Community work projects [were] oriented to job training," not punitive make-work.[35]

Regardless of their orientation, the CWTPs and the ADC-UP program opened a Pandora's box of conflicting interpretations of gender, welfare, and employability. After the ADC-UP provision passed, it was arguable whether the ADC program was still a program for "nonemployables." With the advent of the CWTPS, moreover, ADC was, for the first time since government entitlements had been created for women, a combination welfare-work program. Even more important, however, CWTPS directly endangered women's claims to ADC based on their nonemployable status: the initial administration bill introduced before Congress did not specify that only men were to be subject to the work relief requirement. It left the gender of participants ambiguous, referring to clients merely as "individuals."[36] In doing so it muddied the existing gendered definitions on which entitlements were based. Whether and how these concepts would be clarified, and how they would affect the overall ADC program, was unclear. It was evident, however, that although the CWTPS were developed for the needy unemployed "employable" fathers on ADC, they placed the "nonemployable" status of mothers on ADC in jeopardy.

The 1962 Public Welfare Amendments

After the passage of ADC-UP in the spring of 1961, and after the decision to pursue federal work relief programs was made, the status of low-income women's claims to welfare balanced on a fence. On one side was the traditional nonemployable claim of low-income single mothers. On the other side was the new employable, work-relief requirement for ADC fathers. Although the consequence of linking women to work through the ADC-UP program and the CWTPS was almost certainly unintended, what happened afterward was not. In the fall of 1961 and the spring and summer of 1962, as Wilbur Cohen continued work on the proposals for the 1962 Public Welfare Amendments, he pushed women's claims to ADC decisively off the fence. ADC emerged as a welfare program for employables, with work-based goals for its clients.

Although the Ad Hoc Committee had spent time debating the relationship between the new ADC-UP program and work relief, that was not its main purpose. Its central mission—for which it had been convened by Cohen—was to make recommendations on expanding and improving the ADC program along the lines implied by rehabilitative ideology. And in the end, despite the intense debate over the issue of work relief in the last committee meetings, the final Ad Hoc Committee report issued in November 1961 was, indeed, focused on long-term rehabilitative welfare reform. "The very essence of a vital [ADC] program," the report read, "should be full use of all rehabilitative services."[37]

There was little to distinguish the Ad Hoc Committee's report from past remarks on the need for rehabilitation in ADC. Like earlier public statements, the report had no recommendation regarding racial discrimination, either in creating the need for welfare or in creating unfair treatment within the ADC program itself. Only on two occasions did the committee even discuss racial discrimination. Both times Whitney Young raised the issue: once, to offer his critique of work relief; the other time, to demand that federal agencies attempt to employ African Americans as social workers. Young did not press for any further treatment of racial discrimination in the report.[38]

The final report also reflected established themes of welfare reform when discussing goals for family and employment. Following models from social work research and demonstration projects of the 1950s, committee members conceived rehabilitation as a full-fledged social services program within the ADC program that both strengthened family life and encouraged independence. Although the Ad Hoc Committee stated that "the ultimate aim [of rehabilitation] is to help families become self-supporting," it was also careful to balance goals for independence with safeguards for protecting ADC clients from forced or ill-advised work. The safeguarding language invoked the theme that the welfare community was comfortable with and that it had pursued in the late 1950s and in lobbying for ADC-UP: preserving the family. "It should be recognized," the Ad Hoc Committee's Wayne Vasey wrote, "that the goal of service for some cannot be restoration to employment. There are situations in which the mother, carrying alone the burden of care of children, may make a better and more significant contribution to society by remaining at home to take care of her children."[39] In addition, in the specific recommendations of the report regarding welfare services, family problems—not employment—received the most attention. Counseling, child welfare services, day care, homemaker services, juvenile delinquency services, and other family support services were named as crucial elements of rehabilitative services.

The administration bill, unveiled in December 1961, followed the general guidelines of the Ad Hoc Committee report. As Cohen and others wrote the bill, the central feature was "the importance of the rehabilitative factor in the public assistance programs," though Cohen left the precise interpretation of rehabilitation and services open to the secretary of HEW and subject to administrative direction.[40] He and the Kennedy administration did, however, try to ensure that services of whatever kind would actually be provided by the states. The law contained unprecedented federal reimbursement for welfare services, 50 percent higher than before.[41] For welfare advocates such as those on the Ad Hoc Committee, the 1962 amendments' historic support for social services in welfare marked a victory. The APWA, the NASW, and the NUL and many others hailed the bill as "the greatest advance in social legislation . . . since the Social Security Law passed in 1935."[42]

Yet these organizations may have rejoiced too soon. Although their broad vision of rehabilitation made it into the general language of the law, there was considerable evidence that Cohen had begun to guide welfare reform toward emphasizing that women on welfare should work. Welfare and social work organizations overlooked hints throughout the legislation that the rehabilitative measures it contained were focused subtly, but clearly, on encouraging independence for ADC mothers through employment. On close inspection, it was evident that despite the general rhetoric in support of family-based services, "the key provisions of this bill" were "services to help families become self-supporting and independent."[43]

In drafting the bill and ushering it through Congress, Cohen remained closely attuned to the charged national political context of welfare, and this shaped the emphasis he gave work in the bill. He faced an uphill battle in Congress, where he had to sell the amendments to important welfare skeptics concerned more about waste and fraud than rehabilitation. Ribicoff tried to assuage Wilbur Mills (D-Ark.), chair of the House Ways and Means Committee, and Robert Byrd (D-W.Va.), chair of the Senate Finance Committee, by listing administrative steps he would take to tighten up welfare such as "locating deserting fathers and fraud."[44] But Congress wanted more from federal administrators. The House authors of the bill were anxious to deal with "complaints . . . concerning the practices of some recipients of aid to dependent children in not spending the . . . payments for the best interest of the child." The 1962 Public Welfare Amendments therefore established "additional authority [for] States to prevent abuses in . . . payments" and mandated the "appointment of advisory council and other advisory groups."[45] The very first sentence of the House report on the bill stated that "the proposals embodied in H.R. 10606 . . . are designed to improve, redirect, and tighten up the Federal State cooperative welfare programs." With key congressional leaders fastened on issues of waste, fraud, and cost, Cohen believed that a program that provided education, job training, and rehabilitation to encourage independence would be easier to sell.[46]

Cohen pursued employment goals for ADC clients in several ways in the 1962 Public Welfare Amendments. First, and perhaps most significantly, Cohen opened the CWTPs to mothers. The CWTPs had been created to provide work relief and work training programs for the fathers who qualified for the ADC-UP provision. The original administration bill presented to Congress had been ambiguous with respect to the gender of eligible ADC clients, leaving the gendered definition of eligibility for work and training programs open to interpretation. Through the process of administrative and congressional debate about the 1962 Public Welfare Amendments, however, Cohen paved the way for specifying that women were eligible for participation in the CWTPS. The gender ambiguity in the original administration bill, it turned out, had masked what Wilbur Cohen knew was a crucial legal opening for states: the vague language of the bill allowed states, if they so desired, to open the CWTPS for female ADC clients. "Any relative over 18 years of age who is part of the family and included in the ADC payment . . . could be required to participate in the Work and Training Programs," Cohen wrote in an internal memorandum for HEW.[47] Cohen, moreover, believed that this opening was good. He acknowledged that "the bill [for CWTPS] seems . . . designed to encourage mothers to work" and thought that "it may help the mother and the children if the mother works."[48]

During congressional debate over CWTPS, Congress went even further and amended the language in the administration bill to make the gendered eligibility clear. The Committee on Ways and Means wrote: "Although the committee expects that the program [CWTPS] will be used primarily for the unemployed fathers of children in the aid to dependent children program, States may, if they wish, make the program available to mothers."[49] The Senate Finance Committee was also clear about the overall goals of the CWTPS. The introduction to the Senate report read: "The bill is . . . designed to encourage and assist the States to provide more rehabilitation services in order to get individuals off the welfare rolls."[50] Women on ADC could be considered officially "employable" for the first time in federally funded work-relief programs associated with the ADC program.[51]

There were also more subtle aspects of the 1962 Public Welfare Amendments that encouraged women on welfare to work. One was income incentives. Under existing welfare law, any income that welfare clients earned—including day labor, caring for neighbors' children, or occasional domestic or laundry work —was tallied and subtracted from their monthly welfare payment. Welfare advocates had long argued that this practice was unwise. Taking away small sums of income reduced the already low standard of living of welfare clients. In the late 1950s some advocates of welfare reform began to argue that counting earned income against welfare payments not only further impoverished welfare clients but also reduced their incentive to work. "Some method should be found," Elizabeth Wickenden wrote in 1960, "for making exceptions [in ADC law] . . . to encourage employment of adults and older young people on assistance by permitting them a progressively higher income, when earnings are involved, until the level of full self-support is effectively reached."[52] The Senate Finance Committee also wanted to promote work through income incentives. It was distressed that the subtraction of all earnings from the welfare payment punished clients for earning money, and it argued that "if work expenses are not considered in determining need, they have the effect of providing a disincentive to working."[53] In keeping with these concerns, Cohen designed the 1962 Public Welfare bill to include an "incentive for employment through consideration of expenses" incurred in association with work, such as education, training, travel, clothing, or child care. Welfare clients' costs in this area would be subtracted from the earnings deduction from their welfare check.[54]

Cohen also promoted the ability of ADC clients to work by supporting day care services for ADC mothers. The federal government had not provided significant funding for day care services except during the temporary crisis of World War II, when emergency mobilization drew millions of mothers into the workforce. After the war ended, however, the temporary federal child care provisions were abandoned. Since that time, day care advocates had not succeeded in getting any further substantial federal funding. In part, this failure was due to a historical dispute among child care advocates about the definition of day care. While some day care advocates saw child care primarily as an early childhood education program, others viewed it as a social services program for working mothers. The distinction suggested different auspices for day care. Education advocates conceived of day care as a highly specialized education program to be run by experts and available to all, while social services advocates saw it simply as a nonspecialized welfare services program that should be available generally only for mothers who had to work. Within the social service perspective lay yet another fissure: some policy makers argued that day care should be available on a limited basis to mothers who needed to work in order to support their families; others contended that mothers of all backgrounds or classes should be able to have day care services funded by the government. These divisions among proponents of day care had, after World War II, led to a fatal weakening of support for the policy.[55]

The 1962 Public Welfare Amendments revived the quest for federal funding for day care, taking the general social services approach rather than the early childhood education approach, and seeming to favor universal entitlements for all mothers who worked. The House of Representatives report on the bill argued that increased day care funding was necessary as a response to "the great increase in the number of working mothers in recent years. Of the 22 million women now working, about 3 million have children under age 6." Children's needs for safe, affordable care might be compromised if the government did nothing to help these mothers. So the bill asked for $10 million per year for three years for day care services.[56]

Though at first glance the administration's justification for day care seemed to invoke universalistic references to all working mothers, the fine print and subtext of the legislation and the testimony in hearings revealed that day care was aimed only at some mothers. It was to be used as a tool in the arsenal aimed at encouraging mothers on welfare to work. The administration's official request for child care, for example, stated that "many women now on assistance rolls could obtain jobs and become self-supporting if local day care programs for their young children were available."[57] In addition, welfare advocates and administration officials who testified in favor of the bill almost invariably cited child care services as necessary components of rehabilitation because they allowed welfare mothers who wanted to work to take employment. "In accordance with the rehabilitation concept of ADC," one welfare commissioner testified, "adequate day care facilities, especially for low-income families, are a necessary resource in carrying forward a program for the preservation of family life and the prevention of dependency." The link between ADC work goals and day care was also evident in the administration of the program. Though the child care programs of the 1962 Public Welfare Amendments were authorized as part of the Children's Bureau's child welfare services—services technically open to all women—they were closely linked to welfare agencies, the Bureau of Family Services at the federal level and administrators of ADC at the local level. To be sure, the administration and the supporters who testified cautioned that "the development of day-care facilities should not be promoted as a means for exerting pressure on ADC mothers to take employment, but rather to facilitate employment when it is in the best interest of the family."[58] Yet by presenting day care as a pro-employment service for mothers on welfare, Cohen and the administration emphasized that welfare mothers ought to be considered employable.

One final element of the 1962 Public Welfare Amendments also served Cohen's goal of encouraging self-support for women on welfare: federally funded research on rehabilitation. Since 1956 Cohen and his allies in the world of social work had been arguing that the government could improve welfare programs by funding experimental cooperative research projects with universities, local welfare departments, or research consulting firms. In 1962 Cohen and others finally persuaded Congress to appropriate funding.[59] Cohen told the APWA that research on rehabilitation would "find better ways to help people help themselves" and generate a continuing source of innovative ideas about welfare services, directly linked to the federal welfare administration.[60]

Since Cohen was a researcher himself, he took special interest in federally sponsored welfare research, carefully picking staff, and encouraging people and institutions that he knew to apply for research funds.[61] Friends and colleagues from the wider world of welfare advocacy helped him fan the flames of interest. Elizabeth Wickenden, for example, was pursuing her own welfare research at the New York School of Social Work during this period and sent many research proposals to Cohen from various people and institutions with whom she worked. Ellen Winston, commissioner of welfare in North Carolina and soon to be named HEW's commissioner of welfare in 1963, was also a research enthusiast and passed on research projects for Cohen's perusal.[62] Cohen hired Elizabeth Wickenden's former research assistant, Winifred Bell, herself the author of an authoritative historical study of the ADC program, to oversee the new HEW research office.

While federal funding was technically open to any study that contributed to the general rehabilitative goals of the 1962 Public Welfare Amendments, Cohen promoted research and demonstration projects that focused on independence for welfare mothers through education, job training, and job placement. "One of the areas I believe needs encouragement is related to . . . ADC mothers who wish to work," he wrote in late 1962.[63] In the planning phases for the program, Cohen solicited projects such as this one from Ellen Winston: "a demonstration project in providing day care for children in families receiving Aid to Dependent Children (ADC), to encourage the mother to become partially or fully self-supporting by freeing her either to accept work for which she is qualified or to take vocational training."[64] Elizabeth Wickenden sent Winifred Bell several projects that attempted to help welfare clients find work. She told Bell that one project in Fulton County (Atlanta), Georgia—an "intensive counseling-training-day care etc. project for AFDC mothers[—]sounded like the kind of practical approach you and I have so often discussed," something she knew would appeal to Cohen as well.[65]

In Detroit in 1957 Bell herself had studied rehabilitative programs that encouraged women on welfare to work.[66] Now, as welfare research director at HEW, she followed Cohen's lead, pursuing many projects that stressed welfare mothers' potential to become self-supporting through employment. Her reports, for example, touted a program offering "intensive services and job training to a group of ADC mothers" in Delaware, and a program in California in which ADC mothers "had received training as motel maids, nurses' aids, cafeteria or diet kitchen helpers, hospital housekeeper, typist," along with child care and follow-up services.[67] She also approved programs in Indiana and Vermont that provided "vocational education for . . . AFDC mothers."[68] Bell explained to Wickenden that one of her main goals was "raising standards of assistance, or budgets . . . and then coupling this . . . with some vocational training for mama [ADC mothers], who may shortly be released from the necessity to stay at home."[69]

Through CWTPs, income incentives, day care, and research, Cohen helped resituate welfare reform in 1962, shifting the rehabilitative agenda toward promoting employment for mothers. This suggested a future in which women's welfare entitlements were no longer discussed in terms of their historical status as "nonemployable" mothers, but were instead characterized as potentially "employable" heads of households. Secretary Ribicoff readily accepted this perspective in a television interview with NBC's *Today* program. Touting rehabilitation and the 1962 Public Welfare Amendments, he told the audience only about the new services they offered in job placement and training, and stated that while the elderly, blind, and disabled might be considered nonemployable, mothers with children were to be considered employable.[70]

Postscripts to the 1962 Public Welfare Amendments

Cohen was right that a rehabilitative welfare program supporting work goals would be accepted by conservative Democrats and moderate Republicans in Congress. The 1962 Public Welfare Amendments passed Congress easily, with the conference report winning by 358–34 in the House of Representatives and by a voice vote in the Senate. After Newburgh, many congressional representatives felt pressured to do something about welfare. In addition, as congressional observers pointed out, the bill "had powerful political appeal in an election year," which 1962 was.[71]

Yet despite the overwhelming congressional support, there was evidence that conservatives in the Democratic Party and Republicans viewed the issues of welfare, work, and rehabilitation somewhat differently than the administration liberals who proposed the bill and those who testified in its favor. While liberal welfare supporters talked about the 1962 Public Welfare Amendments as providing recipients of assistance with new economic opportunities, many conservatives talked about how the same amendments injected more responsibility into a welfare system that was, in their eyes, rife with abuse and tolerant of laziness and irresponsibility. For conservatives, encouraging women on AFDC to work was part of the overall theme of tightening-up welfare practices.

Although many conservative members of Congress favored formally encouraging women on welfare to work, they opposed the spending required to provide the extensive employment services that liberals had advocated. The U.S. Chamber of Commerce, for example, testified that while "job training" programs for welfare clients were "constructive," increasing spending on public assistance was not.[72] Conservatives had historically opposed dramatic increases in spending. The most fiscally conservative, antiwelfare state politicians, in fact, had "no appetite for the rehabilitation idea." As a *New York Times* reporter put it, they regarded it "as a dream word invented by 'welfare bureaucrats and empire builders' to encourage taxpayers to pour more money down the drain."[73] Ten Republican members of the House Ways and Means Committee thus "opposed the increase in federal spending for welfare services."[74] But even the many conservatives of both parties who supported the bill nevertheless worried that increased federal funds might be misused. Above all, they hoped that "the possibility of eventually reducing the costs of . . . aid through rehabilitation" would make higher spending in the bill worth it.[75]

Because of the rebellion of far-right conservatives and the worries of moderate conservatives, the fullest possible funding of welfare services did not pass in the final bill. The Senate scuttled the ambitious federal funding plan advocated by liberals in the House of Representatives. It provided federal funding incentives to states to take up rehabilitative services by reimbursing states at a level of 75 cents for every dollar a state spent on services. It also penalized states that did not provide social services to welfare clients by lowering the normal federal portion of spending on AFDC payments—50 cents for every dollar—to the lower amount of 25 cents for every dollar. Incentives for services, therefore, were coupled with sanctions for failure to comply. The Senate, however, determined that the sanction part of the funding plan was too harsh and removed it. The final bill was weakened, therefore, and left only the incentive of the 75:25 federal-state payment ratio for services, and no penalty. That meant that states could continue doing things as usual, with no new services, and suffer no financial setback. Providing services, on the other hand, would cost more, albeit at a discounted rate.[76]

The final public welfare bill in 1962 reflected the ambiguous backing of conservative Democrats and Republicans who supported the administration's rehabilitative welfare program. They favored the rhetoric of independence and policy goals that encouraged work and responsibility, but they reined in the spending for the services that accomplished these goals. Funding for job training, education, clothing allowances, transportation allowances, day care, and other employment-support services was limited, while the rhetoric of work and responsibility was expanded.

WHILE SECRETARY RIBICOFF was in the midst of lobbying for welfare reform and gearing up for his own senatorial election, he unveiled a new acronym. Sounding perhaps more like a cheerleader than a cabinet member, Ribicoff explained that he planned to inject a "new S-P-I-R-I-T" into the nation's welfare system. "The letters of the word SPIRIT spell out the ingredients of our new program . . . : Services, Prevention, Incentives, Rehabilitation, Independence, and Training." Though Ribicoff's SPIRIT acronym was a public relations gimmick, the ideas behind it were serious. When the 1962 Public Welfare Amendments passed six months later, they were the culmination of over ten years of research and advocacy by liberal welfare and social work organizations in favor of changing the AFDC program from a simple income support program to a more ambitious social services program that aimed to "rehabilitate" clients to independence.[77]

Yet when Ribicoff embraced rehabilitation in the early 1960s, he and his assistant secretary for legislation Wilbur Cohen pushed it in a new direction. Under the leadership of Cohen, Kennedy-era welfare reform renegotiated the status of women's claims to government entitlements. After 1962 the AFDC program focused much more strongly on women's potential status as independent wage earners and financial heads of households than ever before. Ribicoff's SPIRIT acronym for reform revealed this new focus: nowhere in "Services, Prevention, Incentives, Rehabilitation, Independence, and Training" did the words "Family" or "Mother" or "Children" appear. Instead, the elements of SPIRIT were clearly directed at encouraging welfare clients to work.

Under the Kennedy administration, the two new welfare laws, ADC-UP and the 1962 Public Welfare Amendments, altered the gendered definitions on which federal entitlement claims had previously been based. The ADC-UP provision redefined ADC as a program that included "employables" for the first time. Women's claims to welfare entitlements based on motherhood, in turn, began to crumble. Their potential for economic independence became more important. Wage work replaced mothering in defining poor women's value to the state and society.

Rather than helping welfare mothers, as members of the Ad Hoc Committee on Public Welfare and Cohen had surely hoped would be the case, the change in orientation may have harmed them. Although the 1962 amendments had broad liberal and conservative support, Cohen and the Kennedy administration, and indeed the overall liberal coalition, may have misunderstood the nature of its appeal to members of Congress, especially conservative Democrats and centrist Republicans. Because Congress gave more extensive support to work and responsibility rhetoric and proportionally less support to funding the services associated with rehabilitation, it was questionable whether social services would ever be implemented by money-conscious states. Many states might choose not to take on new rehabilitative services because of their high cost. Some might simply provide whatever services they already provided, which were often minimal. Rehabilitation was in danger of being a program in which "social service is little more than a relatively infrequent, pleasant chat. It is somewhat supportive, . . . but also not too meaningful in the sense of either helping poor people get things they want or of changing their lives."[78] With services like that, the outcome of the 1962 amendments would not meet the hopes of welfare advocates and Cohen. Would they simply comprise an injunction for welfare mothers to become self-supporting, to work? Welfare advocates like Cohen could not have yet known. However, they did know that the funding of the amendments fell short, and that further efforts were needed to promote rehabilitative welfare reform.

They would soon have the opportunity. Welfare reform emerged at almost the same time that new policies on civil rights, poverty, and women's rights were being created in the Kennedy administration, to be followed up on by the administration of Lyndon Johnson. As a program for low-income, often minority, women, AFDC clearly seemed to be relevant to these new agendas. The question for Cohen, HEW, and welfare advocates outside government would be, how did a program that focused on low-income single mothers fit amid the new agendas?

CHAPTER FIVE

Doing Enough for Broken Families

The Liberal Social Agenda on Welfare,
Women's Rights, and Poverty, 1962–1964

In 1958 author and economist John Kenneth Galbraith declared America to be "the affluent society." His book of that title detailed the many new problems unprecedented economic growth and private wealth brought to Americans' doorsteps.[1] Though it became a popular bestseller, it did not portray the economic reality facing many Americans in the 1950s. One of them was Miss B. (as her case record identified her), a single mother from the Midwest. Miss B. and the millions of single mothers like her never confronted Galbraith's dilemmas. The 1950s brought them problems quite different from affluence.

In the early 1950s Miss B. moved from rural Arkansas to Michigan in search of better opportunities for herself and her family. But events did not unfold as she hoped. By 1958 she lived alone with her four children after the youngest child's father "ran away." At first, they "lived in a terrible apartment"; but then Miss B. lost her job as a laundress, and she and her family were forced into a succession of cheap hotels and relatives' homes. Eventually, Miss B. found work "babysitting" and "clean[ing] apartments for students," but she still could not make ends meet. Her son Billy was an epileptic, and she struggled to pay for medical treatment. Billy often went without medicine and had "convulsions" as a result. Miss B.'s own health declined, too. At the very end of the decade, when social workers in the Aid to Dependent Children (ADC) program met up with Miss B., her caseworker reported that "her physical condition is not good."[2]

This young mother obviously needed assistance. What were her options? By

1962 the federal government could offer Miss B. and other poor single mothers like her one thing: the Aid to Families with Dependent Children (AFDC) program. The triumph of rehabilitative ideology in federal welfare law meant that poor single mothers like Miss B. were offered more than they had been fifteen years before, when payments were lower, eligibility was restricted, and social services were unavailable. AFDC now provided her with more income support than before. In Michigan where she lived, payments would be above the national average of public assistance payments. In addition, the AFDC program allowed Miss B. to receive services to aid her with "self-care and self-support." The caseworker who gathered Miss B.'s complicated ten-year history concluded in fact that she needed rehabilitation: "The record indicates that Miss B. is not a very stable person and could be referred to the Family Service Agency. She also needs counseling concerning her capabilities for working." In sum, what Miss B. would get from the federal government in the early 1960s was income support, as well as advice and assistance with improving her mothering skills and getting a job.

While an improvement over the past, these options were not vast. In addition, the injunction to become more "stable" and to work may have galled Miss B., since it appeared that she had been trying to do those very things on her own for ten years.[3] Moreover, the rehabilitative elements of AFDC had only been passed into law in 1956, and while strengthened with the 1962 Public Welfare Amendments, it was unclear whether they would remain securely ensconced in the law for the long term—and how successful they would be in meeting their goals.

As Miss B. worked her way through the AFDC system, other political events unfolding in Washington, D.C., suggested the possibility that the federal government might be able offer more than AFDC and rehabilitation to America's low-income single mothers. After eight years of the Republican administration of Dwight Eisenhower, the victory of Democrat John Kennedy elevated hopes for expanding the liberal agenda and building on the existing welfare state. Kennedy had already acted in 1962 to expand and reform the renamed AFDC program. And in 1963 his administration began to turn its attention to new policy concerns. One was a women's agenda. Through the creation of the first-ever President's Commission on the Status of Women, the Kennedy administration raised the possibility of a modern-day formulation of political objectives by women for women, a possibility lost since the early twentieth century when suffragists fought for the Nineteenth Amendment to the Constitution. Another new area of social policy pursued by Kennedy was poverty. Kennedy famously "rediscovered" the poor and crafted a nascent War on Poverty, which was eventually implemented by President Lyndon Johnson after Kennedy's death. For the first time since welfare advocates and policy makers began coalescing around the ADC program in the 1940s, a broader collection of policy makers and a more general political will seemed to be developing around the issues of women and poverty. The new agendas on women's issues and poverty presented possibilities for low-income single mothers.

Whether poor single mothers would see tangible results from these developments depended in part on the fate of the AFDC program. Since welfare policy makers were the experts with the closest association with poor single mothers, they thought of themselves as representatives of not only the AFDC program but also its clients. In addition, they believed that their experience of dealing with these issues in the previous twenty years qualified them as leading thinkers on questions of women's poverty. When welfare experts looked at the intersection of poverty and gender, they saw a clear diagnosis: socially disabled single mothers. And their solution was now institutionalized in law: give poor single mothers the services they needed to overcome disability—income, of course, but also counseling, family services, and above all job training and employment so they could be self-supporting heads of households. Armed with a clear plan, welfare advocates lobbied to have the AFDC program, rehabilitation, and poor single mothers be of central concern to the President's Commission on the Status of Women and the Office of Economic Opportunity, which headed the poverty programs.

But a question remained. Would other policy makers see the issues of women, poverty, and welfare in the same way that welfare policy makers did? To welfare professionals, the solution was to focus on single mothers, welfare, and social and employment services, but policy makers on the President's Commission on the Status of Women—including members from national civil rights organizations—and those involved in the War on Poverty concluded differently. The latter were not apt to view the intersection of poverty and gender as grounds for devoting special attention to poor single mothers. They acknowledged that such women existed and that they faced serious problems. But they did not target them directly. And neither the President's Commission on the Status of Women nor the War on Poverty embraced welfare or the 1962 Public Welfare Amendments as priorities.

Multiple factors generated the diverging views of liberal policy makers about whether and how to deal with gender and poverty. One was the growing political unpopularity of welfare. Conscious of the two national outbursts over welfare in 1960 and 1961, and of congressional investigations into welfare fraud in 1962 and 1963, poverty planners and members of the President's Commission on the Status of Women were undoubtedly reluctant to associate themselves directly with the AFDC program and its clients.[4] In addition, some in the administration did not support all aspects of the 1962 Public Welfare Amendments. In particular, they objected to encouraging poor single mothers to work outside the home.

Yet even without the controversy over welfare and disagreements over the new AFDC law, it was unlikely that poor single mothers and welfare programs would have become significant components of the women's rights and poverty agendas. There was also an ideological barrier to be overcome. Over the previous fifteen years, welfare policy makers had effectively abandoned a working model of the family in which two parents operated in traditional fashion, with the mother staying at home. Their reason for this was practical: over 90 percent of their low-income clients were unmarried or divorced single mothers, so it was not realistic to craft welfare policy around the two-parent family. They therefore accepted the single mother household as a valid mode of family life —albeit an imperfect one.Through their reform of AFDC, they altered the program to serve what they defined as the practical needs of low-income single women: income support, social and psychological services, and especially work experience or jobs.

By contrast, in addressing the public policy needs of women and the poor, women's rights advocates and antipoverty campaigners sought to reconstitute the two-parent family and protect the traditional roles of men and women within that family. National civil rights organizations including the National Urban League—fellow lobbyists with welfare reformers in the 1950s—also pursued these goals in the early 1960s. This Kennedy-era focus on reviving and preserving traditional two-parent, mother-at-home families across different areas of social policy meant that low-income single mothers and the welfare programs that served them did not fit easily into the women's rights, civil rights, or poverty agendas. As a result, the policy discussions about women and poverty of the early 1960s produced no major new proposals directly aiding poor single mothers, and the rehabilitative AFDC program remained the primary source of government aid for them.

This chapter explores the diverging views among liberal policy makers who addressed the overlapping issues of women and poverty. It describes the strategies by which welfare policy makers tried to insert low-income single women, AFDC, and rehabilitative welfare reform into the President's Commission on the Status of Women and the War on Poverty. The single most important advocate was Wilbur Cohen. Ambitious and committed to the project of welfare reform, he wanted the stamp of the Department of Health, Education, and

Welfare (HEW) on new social programs. But he and HEW met with little success. The chapter analyzes why no new programs or initiatives besides AFDC were created for single mothers on the burgeoning liberal social agenda. It also explores the outcomes of the policy decisions for policy makers, social policy, and indigent women across America such as Miss B.

Welfare and the Emerging Women's Agenda

The beginning of a "second-wave" revival of a national women's rights agenda began during the Kennedy administration. The "first wave" of feminist activity in the early twentieth century culminated in women's right to vote and the creation of a proposal for an equal rights amendment, a constitutional amendment guaranteeing equal treatment regardless of sex, which never passed. Shortly after this period, however, women's political activities changed. From the 1930s through the 1950s, rather than being solely focused on women's issues in women's organizations, women political activists addressed more general issues and moved into institutions not solely for women, such as the Democratic and Republican party structures, interest groups, and national civic and political organizations. While women's rights and women's issues remained topics for many politically active women, they did not generate the amount of debate that was conducted in the early twentieth century.[5]

The Kennedy administration marked the end of this interim period. In late 1961 Esther Peterson, undersecretary of the Department of Labor and head of the Women's Bureau, a division of the Department of Labor dating from the Progressive Era, created a plan for a full-scale inquiry into the status of American women. Such a study had never before been undertaken at the federal level. Over the years, Women's Bureau leaders had periodically attempted to start national commissions on women's status by appealing to Congress, but were rebuffed by representatives wary of raising the contentious issue of the equal rights amendment.[6] A veteran activist and former lobbyist for the Amalgamated Clothing Workers of America, Peterson crafted a politically savvy plan to avoid the failures of the past. She circumvented Congress and approached the White House directly, suggesting that Kennedy issue an executive order to create a presidential commission. Kennedy assented and announced the groundbreaking President's Commission on the Status of Women (PCSW) in December 1961.[7]

As Cynthia Harrison has argued, the PCSW "had an impact" by putting women's rights and roles back onto the national political agenda. Harrison states that it "provided both a psychological foundation and a structural basis for the organization of the first women's rights group of the new [second-wave feminist] era." In particular, it brought attention to "long-standing discrimination [against women] in the law and in practice." In doing so, the PCSW launched a debate about women's rights that would contribute to the national feminist political movement of the 1960s.[8]

The PCSW was timely because women's lives and status recently had undergone dramatic change. One of the most important shifts concerned women's participation in the labor market and its effects on family life. The rate of employment for married women grew by 42 percent during the 1950s, so that by 1960 "30 percent of married women were employed, and 39 percent of all mothers with school-age children were in the labor force."[9] In light of these changes and others, the commission approached the study of American women's status in two ways. First, the PCSW hoped to accurately represent the altered everyday private life of American women in regard to family, community, and work. Second, the commission hoped to analyze women's relationship to federal law, policy, and programs in light of these changes. The commission planned to examine women's legal and civil rights, their political activities and their place in the tax system and social welfare programs.[10]

Welfare, Single Mothers, and the PCSW

Because of its multiple approaches, the PCSW promised the possibility that a wide range of groups, institutions, and individuals might participate. Moreover, the commission's exploration of women's relationship to the federal government and its laws and programs meant that the PCSW's contributors would not be limited merely to self-described feminists or representatives of women's organizations. Individuals and organizations involved in federal policies or programs that affected women would also have relevant perspectives to share with the PCSW. Welfare policy makers in HEW, in particular, had a strong position from which to claim relevance to the PCSW. As a rule, welfare advocates did not consider themselves feminists, nor were they involved in women's issues per se; nevertheless, they had been concerned with low-income women, family structure, and economic opportunity for the fifteen years in which they had been pursuing their national reform of the ADC program.[11] They saw their mandate as working to improve the status of low-income single women through social policy, and they therefore wanted to be included in any programs ensuing from the commission and hoped to participate in what was widely considered a historic undertaking for women.

Daily oversight and staffing of the PCSW were given to the Women's Bureau in the Labor Department, where the idea for the commission originated. The commission was an "interdepartmental" endeavor, with HEW taking part, too. The secretary of HEW—first Abraham Ribicoff and then Anthony Celebrezze —was granted a leadership position on the commission. In terms of day-to-day involvement, Wilbur Cohen's assistant at HEW, Grace Hewell, served as a liaison to the PCSW.[12] Yet there was little additional presence from traditional welfare organizations. Notably absent from the commission were traditional welfare institutions like the American Public Welfare Association, the National Association of Social Workers, or the National Social Welfare Assembly.[13]

As the PCSW took shape, its subcommittees tackled a wide range of issues that reflected not only the changes in women's lives but also the Women's Bureau's historical interests—and welfare and poverty were not direct points of inquiry. Since its inception, the Women's Bureau had been involved in matters related to the legal, civil, and political status of women in employment. Social programs had generally not been their bailiwick, particularly welfare. Nevertheless, there were several forums in which welfare issues might have been discussed: the Committee on New and Expanded Services (which became the Committee on Home and Community), the Committee on Social Insurance and Taxes (which addressed income support), and the Committee on Private Employment (which discussed wages and discrimination among other things). In the end, it was the Committee on New and Expanded Services that took up welfare issues, broadly defined.[14]

At the outset in early 1963, the New and Expanded Services Committee members began to address social welfare in general and the AFDC program and its new rehabilitative services in particular. Committee chair Cynthia Wedel announced that she planned to explore how AFDC helped women and how it could be improved and strengthened.[15] HEW liaison Grace Hewell thought that the committee was making a good start. But as a strong supporter of HEW's rehabilitative program, especially the family services provided through the 1962 Public Welfare Amendments, Hewell encouraged the New and Expanded Services Committee to think broadly, considering not only what AFDC provided its clients but also social and family services for all low-income women and their families. Another commission member, historian Caroline Ware, was also pushing the PCSW to focus on single mothers. Ware wrote several background papers for the commission urging them to pay "special attention . . . to women who are heads of families." She asked that the PCSW look into both their "status" and their extra need for social and economic services.[16]

In the spring of 1963, after the whole commission's preliminary report was edited by the commission's staff, HEW officials reviewed it and discovered, to their surprise, little discussion of welfare, low-income women, or single mothers in the Home and Community Committee section of the overall report (soon after the committee that was designated New and Expanded Services began its work, its name was changed to "Home and Community," nomenclature that portended less attention to welfare issues). The Home and Community section of the overall report advocated "community services," public and private, which "should be available without regard to the individuals' . . . income." It also mentioned the 1962 Public Welfare Amendments with respect to child care, approvingly noting that the law "authorized the first appropriation of federal funds specifically for the care of children in peacetime." And it said that "preventive services, those which reduce the incidence of problems requiring community action" be implemented, a nod, perhaps, to the idea of rehabilitation. Yet the report of the Home and Community Committee did not reflect the initial discussions of its earlier incarnation, and it neither mentioned the AFDC program by name nor referred to welfare programs in general. Nor did it discuss poverty or single motherhood.[17]

Through April, May, and June 1963, Ellen Winston, commissioner of the Welfare Administration, Grace Hewell, Wilbur Cohen, and others at HEW mounted a protest. Winston made a formal request to have references to welfare, rehabilitative services, and single mothers put into the report. Liaison Grace Hewell, however, reported to Wilbur Cohen that "I know Mrs. Peterson is not carrying out for [sic] my satisfaction . . . a sincere written request from Dr. Winston."[18] Hewell had previously complained to Cohen of "major questions" and "substantial omissions" regarding HEW programs: "This second draft does not offer a recommendation or strong statement dealing with services to families for the purpose of strengthening family life"—in other words, the services of the 1962 Public Welfare Amendments. Nor did it adequately mention the rehabilitation of women, which was in Hewell's view the keystone of welfare reform: "This report also does not include significant recommendations on the . . . rehabilitation needs of women, or the services needed to rehabilitate women who have physical or mental disabilities that obstruct their ability to function in the home, in the community, or in employment."[19]

As a result of objections like these, Philip Des Marais, deputy assistant secretary of HEW, negotiated with Peterson to include family services, rehabilitation, and welfare in the commission report. Des Marais wrote Peterson that "the report . . . makes no mention as such of family services. As you know, the whole concept of the emphasis on the family and welfare services has been the underlying theme of President Kennedy's welfare program. The focus of the 1962 welfare amendments is on increasing services to families first of all and we renamed the Bureau of Public Assistance the Bureau of Family Services as a consequence."[20] Not including mention of this important piece of legislation, he suggested, was not merely to overlook an important program for low-income women; it was bureaucratic bad form and bad politics for the Kennedy administration.

By June 1963, however, HEW seemed resigned to failure. Finally admitting her poor chances of changing Esther Peterson's mind, Grace Hewell reported to Wilbur Cohen, "The best that can be hoped for is fairly generalized statements in each of our areas of special concern."[21] In the end, when the PCSW's final report was issued in October 1963, it did mention the issues of poverty and low-income women on two pages and made references to rehabilitative services. The family services that were cited in the special Home and Community section had no direct association with welfare. Overall, there was scant discussion of low-income single women or welfare. The report did not even mention by name the AFDC program—the sole federal social welfare program directed overwhelmingly at women.[22]

By suggesting that lack of attention to the 1962 Public Welfare Amendments in the report was a political faux pas, Philip Des Marais and HEW tried to prod Peterson into including welfare, but she had in fact compelling political reasons *not* to bring up welfare in any substantive way. Having convened a historic panel to explore the status of women, Peterson wanted to avoid controversial issues if she could. This was most evident in the way that she guided the commission to bypass the most sensitive and potentially explosive issue related to women's status: the long-standing debate among feminists concerning the equal rights amendment.[23] Peterson was surely aware of other political land mines and sought to avoid them. In late 1962 and early 1963, she may well have seen welfare as one of them. After the welfare crises of the previous two and a half years, lingering public controversy over the policy, and some caustic congressional debates during the passage of the 1962 Public Welfare Amendments, it was logical that Peterson would seek to skirt the matter of welfare. Featuring it prominently as a program for women might risk tainting the commission, or at least burdening it with an unpopular issue.

But there was another more direct political reason for Peterson's decision to ignore welfare: she did not support the 1962 Public Welfare Amendments. She had, in fact, already declared her doubts about them to the administration, through a memorandum from her boss, Secretary of Labor Arthur Goldberg, to the director of the Bureau of the Budget regarding new manpower training programs. In the memo, which Peterson approved, the secretary outlined why the agency opposed the proposed 1962 Public Welfare Amendments: they went too far in encouraging mothers to work. Peterson did not want the Community Work and Training Programs—added to AFDC through the ADC-UP program—to be construed to include mothers, which by 1962 was the case. The memo reminded the administration of the original intent of ADC in 1935: "the care of dependent children in their own home . . . and help to 'maintain and strengthen family life'." The Community Work and Training Programs "might result in children being placed under the care of others outside the home when it would be better from the standpoint of the family that they be cared for by their mother in the home."[24] When Peterson decided not to place AFDC and its attendant issues prominently in the PCSW's report, she simply may not have wanted to accentuate her opposition to the employment components of the 1962 Public Welfare Amendments in such a public manner. Nevertheless, she did take a risk and include in the report an oblique reference to her opposition. "It is regrettable," the report stated, "when women with children are forced by economic necessity or by the regulations of welfare agencies to seek employment while their children are young."[25]

Yet it was not only Peterson's opposition to the 1962 Public Welfare Amendments that accounted for the report's reticence on the issues of welfare and poor women. A determining factor shaping the commission's overall approach was the view of Peterson and commission members about the proper role of women and the way in which the state ought to support that role. As Peterson's objections to the 1962 Public Welfare Amendments hinted, she and the commission subscribed to the view that the traditional two-parent, mother-at-home model of the family was ideal. According to Cynthia Harrison, the PCSW presupposed that "women's obligation to be the primary nurturers of children remained immutable."[26] Peterson embedded the commission's recommendations on policies for women within the framework of the two-parent family and women's fundamental obligations to husband and children. The recommendations for home and community services, for example, recognized "the fundamental responsibility of mothers and homemakers and society's stake in strong family life." To be sure, the report's authors did not shy away from demanding that women be allowed to break boundaries and do more than just be homemakers. And they were keenly aware of the challenges facing mothers who struggled to balance work and family life. But the commission was careful to reassure its readers that "widening the choices for women beyond their doorstep does not imply neglect of their education for responsibilities in the home."[27] In general, both Peterson and the commission were unwilling to recommend policies that could be seen as undermining a woman's primary role as nurturer.

These normative assumptions about women and families had, however, the consequence of privileging the needs of some women. Only certain mothers would be able to balance their work and family lives in order to favor their mothering roles: they were likely to be working-class and middle-class married women who lived in two-parent, male-breadwinner families, and could afford to do so. The commission admitted that it chose to focus on what it saw as the "norm" for American women—economically stable two-parent families: "Though the Committee recognized that the needs of some women and their families are obviously more pressing than the needs of others, . . . it aimed its recommendations at the needs of *all* women."[28] From the commission's perspective, focusing on working- and middle-class married mothers made sense statistically. Single mothers, especially those with a history of receiving AFDC, were a minority of mothers in America. It was arguable whether they merited significant discussion in a report targeted at American women in general. In addition, the commission surely believed that in focusing on the majority of women in America they would nevertheless help poor women indirectly. Certainly, the report was not hostile toward poor women and single mothers. To the contrary, many of the report's final recommendations stood to benefit them. Proposals for protective labor legislation, eliminating job discrimination, increasing Social Security coverage for women, and federally funded day care were all policies that, if enacted, would benefit poor single women just as much as —if not more than—they helped working- and middle-class married women.

Yet the commission's decision to uphold two-parent, male-breadwinner ideology and traditional gender roles for women, and to thereby focus on working- and middle-class married women, had the effect of rendering low-income single women and their needs less visible, which did not escape the attention of HEW. Irvin Walker, a staffer in Wilbur Cohen's office, remarked to Cohen that though the commission's overall report was impressive, his "only serious quarrel with the report is its failure to seek out and present vigorous new proposals intended to narrow the gap between those with the least opportunity and those with the most."[29]

Welfare, Civil Rights, and the PCSW

While welfare advocates at HEW negotiated with Peterson over welfare in the spring of 1963, they discovered a second means by which to force poor single mothers and welfare onto the PCSW's agenda. In May 1963 Grace Hewell noted that the commission neglected a particularly relevant topic: the status of African American women. Hewell pointed out to Wilbur Cohen "a lack of planned effort to improve the status of women in minority groups. . . . [I]t is strongly felt that a recommendation or strong statement is needed to direct attention to . . . the great masses of women who fall into this category."[30]

Grace Hewell was joined in her call for more attention to African Americans by the deputy assistant secretary of HEW, Lisle Carter, who had been a lawyer for the National Urban League (NUL). Just days after Hewell protested to Cohen, Carter reviewed Peterson's version of the PCSW report and wrote to Hewell: "I am disappointed that the draft report makes no recommendation which gives specific attention to the more acute problems of the status of women in minority groups."[31] Carter's personal history made him particularly concerned about the need of some African American women for welfare services. In 1960, before joining HEW, he authored a legal brief for the NUL regarding racism in the welfare program. His brief to Secretary of Health, Education, and Welfare Arthur Flemming succeeded in helping overturn the state of Louisiana's decision to cut 6,000 African American women and their children from its ADC rolls.[32] With support from national civil rights organizations including the NUL, Carter demanded more attention be given to the issue before the final PCSW report was published.

Esther Peterson faced pressure to consult African Americans not only from HEW and national civil rights groups but also from President Kennedy himself. In the spring and early summer of 1963, Kennedy was beginning the tensest months of his administration regarding civil rights. Under mounting pressure from civil rights groups, the president activated the National Guard to desegregate the University of Alabama. Soon thereafter, riots would break out in Birmingham, Alabama, civil rights activist Medgar Evers would be killed, and the March on Washington would take place at the end of the summer.[33] On June 1, 1963, Cohen and other HEW staffers met with the president, the vice president, their aides, and cabinet members to try to address growing African American demands for action by the administration. Although President Kennedy told the meeting, "Almost anything we do won't satisfy them," he nevertheless directed cabinet officers to sort through their existing policies and programs to see "what could be done to relieve Negro unemployment."[34] Within days Cohen produced several documents on "the potential opportunities for increased employment of Negroes under the 1962 Public Welfare Amendments," noting that through the new rehabilitative titles "a substantial number of Negro mothers who are now receiving public assistance [will] . . . make satisfactory plans for their children and undertake employment."[35] The civil rights review served as fuel for HEW's demand that the PCSW take up the status of African American women. Hewell told Cohen in a private memorandum that "since they [the commission] did not . . . incorporate a recommendation on Negro women . . . , they are leaving this Administration open for wide criticism."[36] The civil rights review also reinforced HEW's hope that a special consideration of African American women's status might force the PCSW to address welfare and low-income single women. In the circumstances, Peterson felt compelled to create a special, one-time "Consultation on the Status of Negro Women." Dorothy Height, president of the National Council of Negro Women, led the discussion. The consultation committee included African American "educators, editors of black magazines, . . . and government officials." It also included the NUL.[37]

Despite the hopes of HEW staff, the Consultation on the Status of Negro Women hardly aired the issues of welfare and single mothers. Discussion in the consultation demonstrated that it was not merely the PCSW leaders who saw the confluence of gender and poverty differently from welfare advocates. At that moment, so, too, did civil rights leaders.

In the consultation, questions about single mothers and welfare were dispatched quickly. Dorothy Height and others in the meeting shifted the discussion away from welfare and single mothers and from women to men. Height explained that "if the Negro woman has a major underlying concern . . . it is the status of the Negro man . . . and his need for feeling himself an important person, free and able to make his contribution in the whole society in order that he may strengthen his home." Height believed that in some ways it was simplistic to focus on the phenomenon of African American single mothers. "The Negro woman," she argued, "becomes head of the household generally through necessity. Therefore, . . . if the Negro male had employment opportunities . . . there would be less of the matriarchal characteristics in Negro families." According to Height and other members of the consultation, welfare and single mothers were symptoms of the problems faced by African American men rather than policy problems in and of themselves.[38]

When civil rights leaders proposed that the real interest of female heads of households lay in the economic opportunities of men, they showed that they envisioned women playing a traditional role in a two-parent family supported by a male breadwinner. But even though Dorothy Height's conclusions about social policy were in accord with those of Esther Peterson and members of the PCSW, they came from a somewhat different source. Height and other civil rights leaders on the consultation drew on the historical experience of African American men and women in the home and in the labor market. While the majority of white women, especially married women, had stayed out of the paid labor force until the 1950s, African American women, most mothers included, had generally been forced by economic necessity to work outside the home.[39] African American men historically had suffered high unemployment rates and low wages, a combination that made many unable to support a family as the chief breadwinner. Many African American leaders believed that these patterns undermined the strength of African American families, contributing to the higher rates of divorce, desertion, and out-of-wedlock births that increased the number of single-mother households. Single motherhood and its attendant poverty were, in other words, indicators of racial discrimination in the labor market against African American men.[40]

In the 1940s and 1950s civil rights leaders had been unable to force the federal government to address the racial discrimination in the labor market that, in their view, caused family breakdown and poverty. As a result, national civil rights organizations like the NUL had pursued social policy agendas that served these goals indirectly or modestly. Their support for welfare and rehabilitation in the 1950s was indicative of this approach. The NUL advocated the improvement and reform of welfare services, and, in addition, strongly endorsed welfare reformers' idea of rehabilitation as a way to obtain more income and services for needy African American families.

In the early 1960s, however, the civil rights movement gained momentum and seized a historic opportunity to follow the logic of its analysis of race, family, and poverty in order to try to force the government to address its concerns. As a result, organizations like the NUL discarded a modest social agenda concerning social services such as welfare, which helped mostly poor, single-mother households. Just as the PCSW was getting started, in fact, the NUL entered into discussions with the Kennedy administration on new policy priorities for African Americans. In meetings with Lyndon Johnson and HEW's leaders, the NUL's president, Whitney Young, and his staff avoided discussing welfare programs or rehabilitation, programs for which they had lobbied in the recent past. Instead, they talked almost exclusively about a fuller social welfare and socioeconomic agenda for African Americans that they called a "Domestic Marshall Plan." The NUL told the Kennedy administration that it wanted a major effort to produce education and jobs for African American men, in the belief that this would strengthen African American families and raise them out of poverty.[41]

With their desire to take advantage of the political opportunities of the early 1960s, civil rights leaders, as represented by the Consultation on the Status of Negro Women, did not want to focus on single mothers. The consultation made it clear that from their perspective, talk of single mothers, AFDC, and the welfare services of the 1962 Public Welfare Amendments distracted precious attention from the new, more ambitious agenda to help African American men and thus restore the two-parent, male-breadwinner family. At the moment when welfare advocates were hoping to place single mothers and welfare on the women's agenda, members of the Consultation on the Status of Negro

Women were looking past these issues with a different understanding of the relationship between women and poverty.

Welfare and the Poverty Programs

At the same time that Wilbur Cohen, Grace Hewell, and others in HEW were trying to influence the President's Commission on the Status of Women, they were also trying to include welfare programs and clients in another new area of social policy: poverty programs. The War on Poverty was the product of two presidential administrations and multiple political motivations. Although the legislation was enacted under President Lyndon Johnson after John Kennedy's death in November 1963, much of it was crafted under Kennedy. In part, the War on Poverty grew out of a renewed appreciation among liberals in the Kennedy administration of the people and places left behind during the era of affluence after World War II. It was also, however, a reflection of Kennedy's desire to address persistent unemployment, which he feared would slow economic growth. In addition, the poverty programs offered recognition and resources to African Americans; they allowed President Kennedy, who was reluctant to pursue civil rights programs openly and aggressively, to address the disproportionate poverty of African Americans and thereby appease national civil rights leaders.[42]

Before it was a full-fledged "war," however, the poverty agenda was merely a collection of programs that Kennedy pursued in different parts of his administration. Many of them were already existing programs in HEW and the Department of Labor. Although Kennedy had successfully enacted manpower training programs, education programs, and welfare programs in 1961 and 1962, he was having trouble expanding them further in 1963. As welfare policy consultant Elizabeth Wickenden remembered it, "Kennedy . . . couldn't get anything passed in the Congress and he was very frustrated." Kennedy's advisers suggested that he cast these diverse programs in the light of antipoverty initiatives. By linking existing programs under existing agencies to an overall message of antipoverty, the administration hoped to bolster "several different programs that were flagging, where [Kennedy] couldn't get help."[43]

But some fresh policy initiatives were developed as part of the poverty agenda. One was the juvenile delinquency program of Attorney General Robert Kennedy, aide David Hackett, and Professors Lloyd Ohlin and Richard Cloward. Modeled on a community program in New York City, the juvenile delinquency initiative eventually developed into the signature program of the War on Poverty, the Community Action Program.[44] Along with Walter Heller and the

Council of Economic Advisers, the juvenile delinquency program staff became the vanguard of poverty program planning in Kennedy's administration.

Although welfare leaders in HEW were not among the select groups planning the War on Poverty, Assistant Secretary Wilbur Cohen was nevertheless hoping to influence them. When Cohen first learned of Kennedy's developing program on poverty, he acted to ensure that the welfare community's programs and knowledge were incorporated. With the help of Elizabeth Wickenden, he developed his own ideas about how a Kennedy antipoverty program should look. Wickenden recalled that throughout 1963 she "worked with Wilbur Cohen on an alternative proposal to the poverty program." Though the two never crafted a full-fledged proposal to counter what the poverty planners had in mind, they did offer, in keeping with their long-held perspective on how best to fight poverty, modifications and alternatives to the plans of the Council of Economic Advisers and the Office of Juvenile Delinquency.[45]

The proposals made clear that Cohen believed welfare programs could make several contributions to the development of poverty programs. First, Cohen argued to the Kennedy administration that welfare programs needed to be important components of a poverty strategy because welfare clients, notably single mothers, were a large and growing segment of the poor. As early as 1956 Cohen had identified "unmarried mothers" and "broken families" (the result of "desertion, divorce, [and] separation") as an important subgroup of the poor.[46] In 1959 the ADC program served 3.1 million clients, approximately 10 percent of the nation's poor.[47]

In addition, Cohen believed that welfare advocates should be included in poverty planning because they had expert knowledge about the poor based on their experience and research in the 1950s. They were, in fact, some of the few policy makers in the 1950s who had thought extensively about the problem of poverty and had real contact with poor people. In 1956 the American Public Welfare Association had assisted the path-breaking congressional inquiry into low income, the "Sparkman Committee." In addition, Cohen himself had conducted two major inquiries into poverty in the late 1950s, one with colleagues at the University of Michigan—the Faculty Seminar on Income Maintenance —and one on his own for the Committee for Economic Development, a major Washington, D.C., think tank.

More than knowledge, however, Cohen believed that welfare leaders had an effective strategy for helping the poor: rehabilitation. In speeches that he gave around the country in the early 1960s, Cohen explicitly advocated rehabilitation as a way of "fighting poverty." From his perspective, rehabilitation was not merely a welfare services program; it was a new social right crucial to helping the poor. Cohen announced that "rehabilitation as a professional service . . . constitutes another right of the individual. To achieve strengthened family life, maximum possible economic independence, and an enhanced sense of self-worth, some families need services . . . [and] will have to be helped to utilize it [*sic*] through dependable, continuing assurance of society's concern and helpfulness."[48]

In addition, rehabilitation was not merely a theory; it was now the law. The 1962 Public Welfare Amendments provided unprecedented federal support—in legislative language, administration, and funding—for rehabilitative services that strengthened family life among AFDC clients and encouraged them to become financially independent through work. Cohen saw the poverty agenda as an opportunity to follow through on the 1962 Public Welfare Amendments and "augment . . . [the] existing programs." He promoted the "flexible and imaginative work with public assistance" to the poverty planners in the Council of Economic Advisers.[49]

Moreover, the War on Poverty was essentially a rehabilitative program anyhow. The work and training programs mandated by the Economic Opportunity Act, such as the Job Corps program and the Manpower Development and Training Program, enabled poor men to acquire skills, while the sums paid them kept them temporarily from dependency. As Gareth Davies has written, such programs were not radical departures but instead constituted nothing more than "rehabilitative and preventive services" as a solution for the problems of the poor.[50] This approach was precisely that of the welfare advocates who had first developed the use of rehabilitative services for the dependent poor in their reform of the ADC/AFDC program in the 1950s and early 1960s.[51]

Despite Cohen's arguments about the relevant expertise and strategies that welfare professionals could offer to the War on Poverty, poverty planners overlooked welfare programs. As they proposed drafts of legislative goals in 1963, Cohen "argued especially [for] the need for more welfare" programs to be included, and complained when early proposals did "not do enough . . . for broken families where the women have to support the family."[52] Yet poverty planners were reluctant to incorporate welfare. They knew that welfare was often perceived negatively by the public, and they exploited this view in order to create a distinction between nascent poverty programs and existing welfare programs: they considered the poverty programs to be "a hand up" rather than "a handout." As if to finally cut off all further debate on including welfare in the proposals, William Capron of the Council of Economic Advisers called Cohen's suggestions and arguments "garbage."[53]

Welfare advocates resented these attacks on welfare and rehabilitation. Rudolph Danstedt, who headed Washington, D.C., operations of the National Association of Social Workers, objected to the poverty planners' "pretty stiff hands-off attitude to what they call a 'handout' welfare program." Social workers and welfare experts, he said, "would like to demonstrate that they [poverty planners] ought to start where they are and not go off in the wild blue yonder" without the help of established poverty experts in the field of welfare.[54] But "going off into the wild blue yonder" was precisely what the poverty planners wanted to do. They were certain that they needed to break away from the existing federal agencies in order to have fresh, successful antipoverty programs. Poverty planners actually began with the central thesis that they should "bypass what they considered the dead hand of welfare bureaucracy—'professionalism run rampant, meaning the professional social workers, [and] bureaucrats in existing federal agencies.'"[55] Their effort to wrest control of the poverty agenda from the existing federal departments and agencies caused deep resentment, as Wilbur Cohen revealed in later years when he called the Office of Economic Opportunity (OEO) "high-handed."[56]

Institutional prejudice partly accounted for poverty planners' desire to avoid welfare programs. But it did not explain why they would refuse to create new programs that helped the people on welfare, especially low-income single women. The answer to that question lay in deeper assumptions among poverty planners about who should be targeted for poverty programs and why. In 1964, testifying before Congress, OEO director Sargent Shriver revealed these deeper assumptions in response to sharp questions from Representative Edith Green (D-Ore.) about why women were not given many spots in the Job Corps. "The principal purpose [of poverty programs]," he explained, "was to give young men, who we hope will be heads of families and wage earners, an opportunity."[57] Shriver's agenda, and that of the entire OEO, was specifically to reduce poverty among men. As Eileen Boris and other historians have pointed out, reducing poverty among men was expected to restore the traditional two-parent, male-breadwinner family among the poor.[58] Though many poor families were already single mother households, poverty analysts nevertheless theorized that these mother-headed households would become two-parent households if poor men could find jobs. The "Moynihan Report," which was leaked in 1964, represented the distillation of this view of gender roles, family, and poverty. According to the theory, fathers and mothers in two-parent families were to play the proper social roles of the father providing economic support and the mother supplying the caregiving. Such roles kept parents and children out of poverty and safe from the ills of family "disorganization" or "matriarchy." War on Poverty programs were supposed to help poor men assume "proper" breadwinning roles and thus eliminate the danger of single-parent households.[59] The war's major programs, such as Manpower Development and Training, were, as Wilbur Cohen pointed out, aimed at "training . . . mostly men."[60] Within this framework for understanding poverty, family, and work, poverty planners simply could not see any gain from addressing the needs of welfare clients.

Eventually, though, poverty planners were forced to consider how welfare clients should be dealt with. Kennedy's advisers finally agreed with Cohen that at least one component of the federal AFDC program should be included in the poverty legislation, now called the Economic Opportunity Act of 1964. That component was the Community Work and Training Programs (CWTPS), created in 1961. The CWTPS were initially meant to be federally approved local employment projects—a kind of work relief—for the few needy married male heads of households who had become eligible for ADC. But the 1962 Public Welfare Amendments increased appropriations for them and opened them officially to women on what was now called AFDC. Whether the CWTPS offered economic opportunity, as welfare advocates contended, or a step toward welfare-to-work programs was debatable. But they were the only existing federal training programs that served the lowest-skilled, poorest Americans. The Kennedy administration and HEW had been trying unsuccessfully to get more funding to expand the CWTPS, and they wanted to include it in the poverty proposal if it meant a better chance of congressional support.[61]

Despite the insistence of poverty planners that the poverty programs were radically different from existing "handout" welfare programs, the CWTPS clearly fit within the rehabilitative orientation of the Job Corps and Manpower Development and Training. Moreover, the CWTPS were probably better suited to meeting the rehabilitative goals of the War on Poverty. While the Manpower Development and Training Program "creamed" the best potential trainees off the top of the pool of applicants and focused on semiskilled rather than low-skilled job training, the welfare-based CWTPS focused on the poor with the least education and skills.

Although injecting the welfare-based CWTPS into the Economic Opportunity Act of 1964 may have seemed to be a coup for Wilbur Cohen, it ended up being a Pyrrhic victory. The CWTPS were rechristened Work Experience Programs (WEPS), included as Title V of the act.[62] The OEO now handled legislative affairs regarding the WEPS, such as requesting appropriations and legislative changes in the programs. And the OEO neglected them.[63] The OEO stated in 1964 that it intended to try to serve "30,000 of the 100,000 mothers [on AFDC] seeking employment (there were 900,000 mothers total on the program, with 13 percent, or roughly 95,000, already doing some kind of work)" by giving them "basic literacy education and vocational training."[64] But these goals were never reached. As early as 1965 it seemed that the OEO had begun to follow through on its priority of helping men in its funding requests to Congress. In 1964 Congress had not appropriated the requested amount of funding for the Economic Opportunity Act. In 1965, therefore, the OEO requested that Congress double the appropriations for the Economic Opportunity Act programs. Notably, however, the OEO did not include Title V of the Economic Opportunity Act, the WEPs, in this higher funding request. Instead, the OEO left its funding request for the WEPs in 1965 exactly the same as it had been in 1964: $150 million. But since the WEPs, like the other poverty programs, had never received close to the requested funding in 1964 (it received $112 million), the flat appropriations request for 1965 meant that the WEPs would probably remain underfunded. Furthermore, the WEPs became disproportionately underfunded in relation to the other OEO programs, whose funding requests—and, eventually, their actual appropriations—were raised in 1965. By fiscal year 1967 the WEPs were allocated only $100 million, and by 1968 only $70 million.[65] In their first year the WEPs only succeeded in assisting 13,000 welfare clients to become self-supporting. The Manpower Development and Training Program, by contrast, grew in the same period and did not attempt to make up for the small scope of the WEPs by reaching out to public assistance clients. HEW complained to President Johnson in 1965 that "*present* training and education *programs* [of the War on Poverty] largely *do not reach* the PA [Public Assistance] people. . . . Only 9% of the trainees [of Manpower Development and Training programs] (28,000 people) to date have been PA recipients," and of those only some were female AFDC clients. Cohen saw these results as a failure, and he told Secretary of HEW Joseph Califano that "giving high *priority* under MDTA to PA recipients" and "going beyond the present concept of marginal training" for welfare clients was necessary if rehabilitation of welfare clients was going to succeed.[66] This never happened, and by 1967 HEW reported that only 40,000 welfare clients had found jobs as a result of the WEPs.[67]

This treatment of the WEPs within the War on Poverty caused negative outcomes for women on welfare. First, women on AFDC who wanted to train for work or to work—and many desired to, under the right conditions—were unable to get access to WEPs. Without enough federal funding of WEPs, and with a host of better-funded education, training, and employment programs for men coming out of Washington, D.C., as part of the War on Poverty, states were unlikely to use their own funds to implement or initiate new Work Experience Programs. In addition, day care funds, promised as part of the 1962 Public Welfare Amendments and Title V of the Economic Opportunity Act of

1964, were not sufficiently appropriated by Congress, creating another barrier for women on welfare who might have been able to participate in a WEP.[68]

Another negative consequence followed from this neglect. The WEPs pushed the federal commitment to encouraging women on welfare to enter the labor market the farthest it had ever gone in formal legislative language. The injunction for mothers on AFDC to work was powerfully present in the language and intent of the law, even though it was not backed by funding necessary to help welfare clients train for and find work.[69] This put women on welfare in an unfortunate position: the expectation that they should support their families financially was becoming stronger, but the opportunities and means for accomplishing this goal were becoming relatively weaker.

BY 1964 HOPES WERE dashed that liberals might approach their overlapping concerns about women and poverty similarly and produce new ways of addressing poor women. Welfare policy makers, members of the PCSW (including civil rights activists), and architects of the War on Poverty all pursued their agendas with different understandings about how gender and poverty were related and how to address that relationship. Some of their disagreements derived from their reactions to the existing program serving poor women: AFDC. It was widely recognized by policy makers and the public as unpopular and controversial. In addition, the 1962 Public Welfare Amendments and their emphasis on work for poor women struck some as ill advised and ineffective. Above all, a common framework within the Kennedy administration's emerging agendas on women and poverty—the preservation and restoration of the traditional family—reduced direct attention to both poor single women and the program that served them.

One of the most important results of the divergent approaches of liberal policy makers was that it generated a fractured policy approach to gender, race, and poverty. Policy makers divided overlapping issues and groups of people into separate categorical programs and agendas. Historians of New Deal–era social policy have long pointed to the categorization of federal income support programs by class, distinguishing between middle- and working-class people who receive social insurance and the poor who receive only means-tested public assistance.[70] More recently, feminist historians examining social programs of the Progressive Era have noted that the insurance/assistance bifurcation was also based on gender. Most women were eligible for insurance only through marriage to a working-class or middle-class man. Women who were not married were left with nothing but means-tested public assistance.[71]

In the 1960s, however, these already distinct policy categories fractured further, and new categories were created. Welfare policy makers continued on the path they took in the late 1940s, addressing the issues of women and poverty through the narrow categorical lens of the AFDC program, closely focusing on the issues of dependency and rehabilitation and on encouraging poor women to work. For their part, women's rights advocates and poverty planners ended up addressing questions of gender, race, and poverty as though they were separate categories and separate social questions rather than closely interrelated issues. The policy prescriptions of the PCSW, ostensibly directed at all women, were in fact directed mainly at *married* women who were typically white and not poor. At the same time, policy for poor people fractured, too. Poverty planners at the OEO created education, training, and empowerment programs that were consciously distinguished from, and separate from, the already existing federal welfare programs that served the poor. Even more important, poverty programs divided the target population of the poor. They avoided serving welfare clients where possible and divided the poor by gender—serving far more men than women.

In addition, because neither the PCSW nor the War on Poverty created new programs for poor single mothers, welfare policy makers remained the sole national representatives of policies for poor women, and only one rehabilitative welfare program directly served them. For their part, federal welfare administrators continued to see a rehabilitative welfare program that provided income support and a wide range of social services aimed at self-care and self-support as absolutely essential to improving the status of poor women. And they therefore still saw the goal of encouraging women on welfare to work as paramount.

Yet even rehabilitative welfare programs suffered from the divergent Kennedy-era views of poverty and women. Welfare was so overlooked by emerging policy makers that it slid to the margins of the overall liberal social agenda by 1964. Neither the PCSW nor the Consultation on the Status of Negro Women discussed welfare to any real extent, and by their silence on the subject they rendered it less visible and more vulnerable. Poverty planners actually stigmatized welfare and neglected welfare clients.

The categorization of social policy regarding gender and poverty and the marginalization of AFDC in the early 1960s was poorly timed. It occurred alongside one of the most significant demographic and economic trends of the twentieth century: the feminization of poverty. The female poor constituted the fastest growing sector of indigence in the United States in this period. In 1960 fully 70 percent of African American female-headed households were below the poverty line, as were 42 percent of white female-headed households. From 1960 to 1964 these numbers would grow while poverty rates for male heads of household of both races declined.[72] Moreover, as female-headed households were becoming more impoverished, AFDC rolls grew.[73] In the mid- to late 1960s, just when the splintering of social policy for women and the poor occurred and welfare became more isolated, the number of women on welfare rose.[74] Although more low-income women had income support than before, the numbers of women on welfare could hardly be taken as a comforting sign. The economic status of women was declining just as a new liberal social agenda was being organized so as to address their needs in a limited and piecemeal fashion.

From Rehabilitation to Responsibility

The Legacy of Postwar Welfare Reform

Walk into any supermarket, café, church, or bar in America today, and you will find that virtually everyone has an opinion about welfare. Since the 1960s, when Wilbur Cohen and his fellow reformers were frustrated in their efforts to make welfare a centerpiece in the War on Poverty, welfare has become essential to American political culture. As a matter of national policy, welfare after the 1970s became a focal point for debates about how public money is best spent to help the poor. As a matter of politics, its role was even greater. By the Reagan years, politicians regularly seized on welfare—and those who received it— as a potent tool to attack or defend government, liberalism, the poor, and one another.

Consequently, many perceive the emergence of welfare as a political and policy issue as a contemporary phenomenon. Most recent histories of welfare and poverty begin or end with the passage of the 1996 welfare reform. The Personal Responsibility and Work Opportunity Act destroyed the provision of income support to the poor by the federal government, ending the Aid to Families with Dependent Children (AFDC) program, and instituted widespread, rigorous work requirements. Recent scholarship explains the law's passage by focusing on the turbulent public debates about welfare from the late 1960s to the 1990s. Beginning with Nixon, three Republican presidencies targeted the welfare state—particularly AFDC—for demise, cutting its spending and enforcing stricter rules.[1] In the 1980s the renewed discussion about the "undeserving poor" —the so-called underclass debate—brought welfare clients to the front pages of newspapers and magazines, almost always in a negative light.[2] At the same time, the dominance of economists as poverty experts and new types of "poverty knowledge"—econometric cost-benefit analyses and studies of the individual behavior of the welfare poor—narrowed the boundaries for thinking about poverty to one question: how to force women off welfare.[3]

But this narrative tells only part of the story. The roots of the 1996 welfare reform law are older and more complicated. Recent welfare discourse is inextricably connected to the politics of welfare reform between 1945 and 1965. The sharp focus on poor women in the 1980s and 1990s, for example, was not new; the same attention was given to them by welfare professionals beginning in the 1950s. In addition, the emphasis on "personal" explanations for poverty in the recent underclass debate is arguably a direct continuation of the postwar rehabilitative conception of poverty as a matter of individual circumstance rather than a structural problem in society. Above all, the seemingly new emphasis at the federal level on mandatory work in welfare programs recalls the interest of postwar welfare professionals in rehabilitating women through work. Postwar liberal welfare reform not merely foreshadowed but created a model for a contemporary welfare policy that places the burden of escaping poverty on welfare recipients themselves.

While it is fairly easy to see that rehabilitative welfare reform in the twenty years after World War II prefigured the end of welfare as it was known in the 1990s, a reckoning of its legacy requires more extended analysis. The leaders of the liberal coalition behind postwar reform—Wilbur Cohen, Elizabeth Wickenden, Loula Dunn, and the many organizations that supported rehabilitation —did not dictate, much less advocate, the extreme transformation of welfare to mandatory workfare. To the contrary, they opposed it. The decline of their coalition in the mid-1960s, however, meant that their nuanced welfare proposals had no defenders, and the idea of rehabilitation fell prey to harsher interpretations of how welfare should evolve. Herein lies the paradox of the history of early postwar welfare. While the movement for rehabilitation ultimately contributed to today's workfare, so, too, did the diminishing power of the group of policy makers who promoted it. The members of the American Public Welfare Association (APWA), social workers, foundation leaders, and sympathetic federal administrators represented a bulwark against the transformation toward the punitive, mandatory workfare policy to which the Untied States now subscribes. When this coalition lost power, welfare policy suffered. It is an irony of postwar welfare reform that both its success and its failures fueled the distortion and destruction of AFDC.

This epilogue explores the contradictory legacy of early postwar liberal welfare reform and explains why an appreciation of that legacy is crucial to understanding recent welfare policy. The 1960s and early 1970s were a turning point in which the postwar welfare reform coalition and consensus collapsed and the contradictory effects of rehabilitative welfare reform became visible. These events occurred when new actors came to exert influence over welfare, including, most surprisingly, welfare clients themselves. Civil rights organizations and the feminists who formed the National Organization for Women also challenged welfare policy in the late 1960s and early 1970s. But, in the end, the most potent of the new actors were conservatives, who came to command enormous authority over welfare policy. As traditional welfare leaders lost power to conservatives, none of the new liberal or liberal-left groups could muster a sufficient counterweight.

When the voices in welfare reform changed, so, too, did political developments and policy proposals regarding welfare. Some innovations, such as the creation of the Medicaid program, represented victories for welfare and traditional welfare leaders. But most developments—including the attacks on the War on Poverty, the movement for a guaranteed minimum income, and the welfare reform called Work Incentive Program, or WIN—pointed in a harsh direction. The idea of rehabilitation was supplanted by the idea of responsibility —that welfare recipients must be forced to work.

Welfare Politics in the Late 1960s and 1970s

Like so many aspects of American society in the late 1960s, the world of welfare policy underwent rapid transformation. It must have disoriented the professionals who presided over welfare in the relatively quiet period that preceded it. One of the most startling changes came from an unexpected source. In 1966 the National Welfare Rights Organization (NWRO) was born. It was a historic moment. Not since the 1930s had masses of the poor banded together to demand access to government relief. The 1930s unemployed councils were not dominated by women and minorities; but of the 20,000–25,000 individuals who joined the NWRO in the late 1960s, 95 percent were women receiving AFDC, and the vast majority of them were African American.[4] The NWRO benefited from the national civil rights movement's success in the South and its subsequent turn to the northern cities for ideas and membership. In its focus on the relationship tying together economic issues, motherhood, and rights to government aid, the NWRO was, however, a distinct voice among organizations demanding democratic access in the late 1960s.[5]

The NWRO challenged the coalition of professionals, researchers, foundations, and federal administrators who had coalesced around welfare in the early post-war years. Starting in 1965, before the organization's formal establishment, welfare clients in selected cities and towns had begun meeting to protest treatment by social workers whom they deemed unfair and intrusive. After the official formation of the NWRO in 1966, the protests became organized and focused, intent on disrupting welfare provision, challenging administrative rules in the courts, and destigmatizing the receipt of relief. While the APWA, social workers, and researchers claimed expert knowledge about welfare and the poor, NWRO members countered that, in fact, they were the experts on the issues.[6]

Welfare professionals and leaders responded to the NWRO with ambivalence. They resented the organization's style and tactics, which were exhibited initially in direct confrontations at welfare offices. Many social workers and administrators were pained by, and perhaps resented, the implication of the NWRO that social workers and administrators did not understand or care about the poor. After all, they had been among the few people in the United States to pay serious attention to the poor and welfare recipients during the seemingly affluent postwar years. With regard to policy, the NWRO called into question the major liberal consensus on welfare's objective: rehabilitation. The NWRO denied that welfare clients were socially disabled individuals who needed expertise from qualified professionals. And it disputed the idea that social workers and administrators really had the best interests of clients in mind when they applied rehabilitative principles to welfare programs and imposed "services" on welfare clients.

On the other hand, many of NWRO's other criticisms were ones that welfare advocates themselves had made for decades: that welfare was stingy; that variations in states' payments were unfair; that state-level rules often crudely tried to force women off welfare; that more rather than fewer people needed access to welfare and welfare services. With these commonalities, and the power of the movement to disrupt and shame the political and welfare establishments, many in the welfare reform coalition felt compelled to support the NWRO.[7] Elizabeth Wickenden, for example, had been involved in the beginnings of welfare rights law as early as 1963 and wrote an important memorandum on welfare rights called "Poverty and the Law." She supported some of the policy positions advocated by the NWRO in the late 1960s and early 1970s.[8]

What welfare advocates thought about the NWRO was more important to them than to the NWRO itself, however. The NWRO operated without any significant alliance with the traditional postwar welfare leaders. The organization was insistent about empowering welfare clients and guarded their agenda, seeking to preserve its integrity and stem any dilution that might arise from political coalition building. Using this strategy, the NWRO unquestionably captured the attention of welfare administrators at the local, state, and federal level. In the late 1960s and early 1970s, the Department of Health, Education, and Welfare (HEW) agreed to consult with the NWRO on administrative rules and on bills before Congress. The NWRO also lobbied Congress directly, most famously in 1970 when welfare clients lambasted senators in a hearing on AFDC.[9] Yet though the organization had a powerful voice, its actions did not meet with much success. Most historians of the movement and of welfare in that period judge the policy-making power of the NWRO to have been modest, especially in light of its short life.[10] Leadership changes, funding problems, and diminishing membership caused the NWRO to decline by the early 1970s, and it closed its doors in 1975. If the policy success of the NWRO was limited, however, its political implications were great: it disrupted the status quo achieved in welfare policy making during the previous twenty years and broadened the range of actors and the terms of the debate.

The welfare policy debate gained two other parties that had a growing interest in issues related to public assistance: civil rights organizations and mainstream feminist groups. In the late 1960s and early 1970s, feminists and African American leaders were systematically addressing poverty and welfare more than they had been in the early 1960s.

In the late 1960s, the civil rights movement switched strategies, increasingly focusing on social and economic rights, which often led to a direct concern with welfare issues. As it had done in the Kennedy-Johnson era, the National Urban League (NUL) continued to attempt to influence welfare policy. But the NUL went further than before, forming ties with the NWRO, according to the historian of the NWRO, Guida West. More radical civil rights organizations, such as Congress of Racial Equality (CORE) and the Black Panthers, also had contact with the NWRO.[11] In the spring of 1968, Martin Luther King's Southern Christian Leadership Conference (SCLC) initiated the best-known economic initiative of the civil rights movement in this period, the Poor People's Campaign. SCLC organized the poor and minorities around the issue of poverty and economic rights and participated with the NWRO on the project: "NWRO launched the first demonstration—a Mother's March on May 12 (Mother's Day)—during which George [Wiley] and Coretta Scott King led some 5,000 demonstrators through the still-charred ruins of that section of Washington where rioting and burning had broken out following the assassination of Martin Luther King." In addition, for the several months that the Poor People's Campaign lasted, "NWRO coordinated many of its lobbying activities with those of SCLC."[12]

Yet relationships between the welfare rights and civil rights movements were tense. Welfare clients informed Martin Luther King just before his death in 1968 that "it was a disgrace that SCLC had ignored the welfare issue . . . for so long," and King readily admitted that he had. For SCLC and many civil rights organizations, their middle-class membership militated against a dramatic or active role in welfare policy. Even the NUL, though actively involved in welfare, differed from the NWRO and poor women in its analysis of the problem of poor women's poverty. Just as in the early 1960s, "the National Urban League's primary focus was on employment, not welfare, for blacks."[13] Gareth Davies captured the frustration of Frances Fox Piven, an NWRO activist and historian of the movement, when she tried to get the NUL to support the guaranteed minimum income movement: "We met with Whitney Young . . . and he gave us a long speech about how it was more important to get one black woman into a job as an airline stewardess than it was to get fifty poor families on to welfare."[14]

By the early 1970s, with the quieting of southern and northern African American unrest and the decline of the NWRO, it became less likely that mainstream civil rights organizations would make welfare a central component of their policy campaigns. Other civil rights goals such as antidiscrimination laws and affirmative action were seen as imperatives. New issues like drug laws and police brutality gained attention. In this context, welfare could not compete as a central issue. Civil rights groups would henceforth monitor welfare policy, but their welfare activism essentially ended.

Mainstream feminism followed a different trajectory, becoming more interested in welfare over time. Unlike the President's Commission on the Status of Women—one of the early institutions spawning second-wave feminism—the National Organization for Women (NOW), formed in 1966, made poor women a genuine focus of concern by the late 1960s. Though their original statement of purpose did not include statements on poverty or social policy per se, NOW's first conference, where it set its priorities, raised the issue of poverty. "We start with a concern for the plight of women who now live in poverty. . . . No adequate attention is being given to those women by any of the existing poverty programs."[15] NOW also paid direct attention to the issue of welfare. In 1967 it called for "revision of welfare legislation and poverty programs which deny women dignity, privacy and self-respect."[16]

NOW also began an uneasy relationship with the NWRO. Exhibiting a gap between middle-class and poor women that would persist in the feminist movement, NOW and NWRO did not agree on how to solve poor women's problems. The NWRO opposed work-based programs for women on welfare. Yet, as Martha Davis has shown, "many NOW members were ambivalent about NWRO's opposition to mandatory job-training programs and its position that women should have a right to stay home with their children." It contradicted the pivotal feminist argument that "meaningful work outside the home" was the solution to women's problems, challenged the central feminist objective of reducing sex discrimination in the labor market, and implicitly questioned the equal rights amendment. The NWRO's demand for recognition of women's right to work within the home rather than enter the labor market also seemed to legitimate traditional gender roles at a time when feminists were revealing the limitations and repression associated with them. Though this difference of opinion of poor and middle-class women emerged clearly in the early 1970s, "NOW leaders glossed over it and limited themselves to general endorsements of NWRO's positions."[17] At the same time, NOW continued, and in fact increased, its emphasis on employment as an important way to solve poor women's problems (and those of all women). The NWRO, for its part, remained wary of middle-class, white feminists.[18]

NOW retained poverty and welfare on its agenda even after the demise of the NWRO in 1975.[19] The extent and enthusiasm of their efforts to deal with welfare policy is disputed, however. In the late 1970s NOW's national leadership clearly became more attentive to questions concerning poverty as the feminization of poverty developed into a more recognized phenomenon. NOW campaigned for constructive welfare reform, job training and education, higher minimum wages, and child care for poor women.[20] Even so, welfare and poverty never became central to NOW's objectives. In the 1970s the battle for the equal rights amendment was the dominant issue for feminists. At the same time, other issues such as reproductive rights and domestic violence gained ground as major organizing and lobbying issues. These priorities reflected the direct interests of many NOW members, who never ranked poverty or welfare above other issues.[21] Additionally, as Gwendolyn Mink has argued, differences remained between poor women and feminists in their respective analyses of how to solve the problems facing poor women. The mainstream feminist agenda continued to emphasize "women's right to participate in white men's world and made work outside the home a defining element of women's full and equal citizenship." Yet, as Mink has noted, poor women were unlikely to view middle-class feminists' emphasis on work as a liberating force in their own lives: "The popular feminist claim that women earn independence, autonomy, and equality through wages long has divided feminists along class and race lines, as women of color and poor white women have not usually discovered equality in sweated labor. On the contrary: especially for women of color, wage work has been a mark of inequality: expected by the white society for whom they work; necessary because their male kin cannot find jobs or cannot earn family-supporting wages; and exploitative because their earnings keep them poor."[22]

Feminist and civil rights organizations' support for welfare and poor women in the late 1960s and 1970s had a limited effect, however, compared to the hostility voiced by conservative politicians and opinion makers. In welfare, conservatives found an issue that united antistatist, low-tax libertarians and cultural conservatives. Welfare administrators and recipients became the targets of conservative attacks. Conservative rhetoric about welfare ranged from a high-minded challenge to Great Society liberalism to a cynical code for the coarsest racial and gender demagoguery. The result was a transformation of welfare policy and the ideas that guided it.

Once Senator Barry Goldwater (R-Ariz.) made a national hero out of Joseph Mitchell, Newburgh's city manager and a self-proclaimed warrior against welfare in 1961, conservatives began to see welfare as a useful political ax to grind at the national as well as state and local levels. Starting in Louisiana and Newburgh, and accelerating in the mid- to late 1960s, conservatives made welfare the focus of numerous attacks. Some of these were congressional investigations into welfare fraud. Robert Byrd (D-W.Va.), for example, launched a much-publicized investigation into what he claimed was widespread welfare fraud in the nation's capital, Washington, D.C., in the early 1960s. During the 1964 presidential campaign, the Republican candidate, who happened to be Barry Goldwater, inveighed against welfare, telling a crowd of businessmen in Los Angeles that "workers in many other countries cannot earn as much as our welfare clients receive!"[23] Sensing the changing political mood, conservatives once willing to work with the Kennedy and Johnson administrations to expand and reform welfare and social services in the early 1960s now broke with the administration, foiling welfare bills and taking a harsher stance on AFDC.[24] Conservative publications followed the political trend (and helped create it) by increasingly publishing negative stories on welfare. "Watts: Where Welfare Bred Violence" blamed the 1965 riots in Los Angeles on welfare, and "California's Jackpot for the Jobless" suggested that welfare was causing a labor shortage by allowing the shiftless to receive welfare rather than work.[25] The vanguard publication of the postwar conservative movement, the *National Review*, also targeted welfare. Between 1965 and 1969 the magazine featured eleven major articles on welfare.[26] Conservatives felt that their attacks reflected public opinion, which was supposedly expressing a "welfare backlash" that they hoped would hurt the Democratic Party at the polls.[27]

Conservatives exploited the growing number of clients served by AFDC in order to gain political traction on the welfare issue. By all accounts, the increase was enormous. In 1960 there were approximately 3.1 million clients receiving AFDC. By 1965 there were 4.3 million, and by 1970 there were nearly 8.5 million. In 1974 almost 10.9 million clients were on AFDC. In ten years, rates had doubled; in fifteen, they had more than tripled.[28] Spending rose with growth and with the increasing federal funding of social services for welfare clients and other needy Americans. Beginning in 1962, the Public Welfare Amendments, which emphasized rehabilitation, provided federal reimbursement to states for social services to welfare clients at a rate of 75 cents on every dollar spent. As the decade progressed, changes in administrative rules authorized still further spending on social services, and in 1971 HEW approved the use of federal welfare funds to purchase a wide range of social services from state agencies or private organizations with which the department contracted, including child care, health care, job training, and other kinds of support.[29] A steep rise in social service spending followed, from $194 million in 1963 to $1.7 billion in 1972.[30] Conservatives viewed this spending with alarm and disgust.

Though criticism was nothing new for welfare advocates, the cascading attacks undermined the power of the liberal welfare establishment. As conservatives surveyed the growing welfare state, they railed against those who built it. As many had done during the welfare debacle in Newburgh, they implied that social workers and welfare administrators were hapless "do-gooders," loading the welfare rolls with undeserving clients and ignoring fraud. Of more importance was the fact that conservatives were attacking rehabilitation directly. In a 1964 campaign speech to the Economic Club of New York, Goldwater lashed out at welfare policy makers, saying that they had led the nation "to believe that relief programs can end poverty rather than only institutionalize poverty."[31] Conservatives criticized welfare administrators because rehabilitation did not move people off welfare rolls. Wilbur Mills's House Ways and Means Committee charged:

It is now 5 years since the enactment of the 1962 legislation which allowed Federal financial participation in a wide range of services to AFDC families—services which your committee was informed and believed would help reverse these trends—and your committee has had an opportunity to assess its effect on the status of the AFDC program. While the goals set for the program in 1962 were essentially sound, those amendments have not had the results which those in the administration who sponsored the amendments predicted. . . . It is . . . obvious . . . that further and more definitive action is needed if the growth of the AFDC program is to be kept under control.[32]

It was clear to critics, in other words, that welfare administrators were not following through on their own proposed reforms. If they could not make rehabilitation work, critics charged, then others—namely Congress—should intervene.

Conservative critics of welfare began to get their way, and welfare oversight was changed. In August 1967 the Johnson administration appointed a new leader for the federal welfare agency. Mary Switzer, commissioner of the Office of Vocational Rehabilitation for seventeen years, was chosen to lead the newly named and reorganized federal welfare agency called Social and Rehabilitative Services, which became the home of the AFDC program.[33] On the day after her appointment, Switzer gave an interview to the *Washington Post* in which she laid bare the diminished position of the postwar liberal welfare reform coalition. She admitted that "there has been phenomenal growth and acceptance of the principle of rehabilitation," but she insisted that she got the job implementing such ideals because she was "not a traditional welfare oriented person," not "a professional." Washington wanted a welfare outsider running welfare programs.[34] The pillars of the postwar welfare establishment had been ousted, and they rightly viewed Switzer's appointment as a defeat of their vision of welfare and as an end to their influence.[35]

Politics and Policies

Before losing direct authority over AFDC, welfare professionals did achieve a policy victory. In the spring of 1965 Wilbur Cohen was promoted from assistant secretary to undersecretary of HEW, a role in which he helped enact the Medicaid program, a medical care program for the needy poor on public assistance. At the time, it was an unheralded addition to Medicare, the larger and more publicized program that provided medical care to all elderly Americans. But Medicaid represented a victory for welfare leaders, who had long fought for it. Medical care for the needy was a central component of the defeated proposals for comprehensive social welfare in the early 1940s. Likewise, medical care for needy welfare recipients was part of the rehabilitative philosophy of the 1950s, a guarantee that health problems impairing self-sufficiency could be medically addressed to maximize independence. So its passage in 1965 buoyed Cohen and other traditional welfare leaders.[36]

Yet when Medicaid passed, Cohen and others did not get everything they wanted, and the shortcomings hampered the success of rehabilitative welfare reform. In keeping with the spirit of the broad proposals of the 1940s, welfare professionals in the 1960s wanted Medicaid to serve all needy Americans, not just those on welfare. They wanted the income level making one eligible for Medicaid to exceed the level at which one qualified for welfare. Their reasoning was simple: they wanted more poor people to have access to paid medical care. However, when passed, Medicaid was limited to those poor enough to qualify for welfare. AFDC clients under the new rehabilitative mandates of the 1962 Public Welfare Amendments were thus faced with conflicting incentives. While rehabilitative services and the Work Experience Programs encouraged them to work, earning enough to leave the AFDC program would mean a loss of medical care for themselves and their families.

Medicaid therefore represented a limited victory, but an anomalous one, as members of the postwar welfare reform coalition faced mostly defeat amid the tumult of political and policy developments in the late 1960s and early 1970s. Welfare professionals, for example, were unable to defend welfare from political attacks associated with the War on Poverty. Just as they disdained welfare, conservatives disliked the War on Poverty, viewing it as wasteful social spending. They often expressed their hostility to poverty programs by conflating them with welfare programs. Conservatives blamed the War on Poverty for directly causing the growth in welfare rolls. Favorite targets were the Community Action Programs (CAPS). The CAPS encouraged the maximum feasible participation of the poor to create their own agendas for solving poverty. Conservatives argued that they were providing funds for poor people to meet and strategize for enrolling more people on welfare. Conservatives also blamed the War on Poverty's legal services programs for enlarging AFDC because some programs advocated for welfare clients' rights to fair hearings.

In fact, such connections between poverty programs and welfare programs were spurious. Some CAPS did indeed provide the opportunity for relief recipients to organize (and the NWRO capitalized on these groups in its early years), and legal services did bring eligible people onto the welfare rolls. But the growth in welfare rolls and spending came largely from the liberalizing of eligibility rules and authorizations for further spending that welfare professionals had been advocating for years, and finally had achieved.[37]

Conservatives were nonetheless loath to let the War on Poverty off the hook. They further conflated welfare programs and poverty programs in a slightly different way, by using the rising welfare rolls to discredit the War on Poverty programs. Conservatives demanded to know why the number of poor seemed to be growing—as measured by welfare rolls—if so much was being spent on the War on Poverty. Every time the poverty programs were up for reauthorization, and every time conservatives railed against them, it seemed, they trotted out the growth in the AFDC program to "demonstrate" the failure of the War on Poverty, much to the dismay of liberal welfare and War on Poverty officials.[38]

Conservatives wrongly assumed that if welfare rolls were growing, then the War on Poverty was failing. Rising welfare rolls were a measure of the diminishment of poverty, not its deepening. By definition, those receiving welfare were less poor than they were before. More important, conservatives incorrectly associated rising welfare rolls with the War on Poverty because the War on Poverty was never aimed at individuals eligible for welfare. The Office of Economic Opportunity (OEO) had worked assiduously to distinguish between the "hand up" programs of the War on Poverty and the "handouts" identified with the AFDC program. OEO avoided serving welfare clients, neglecting them, for example, in Work Experience Programs. Poverty programs also discriminated against the population eligible for AFDC—poor women—providing only 15 percent of the War on Poverty jobs programs to women. So minimally did the War on Poverty serve poor women and welfare clients that in retrospect it is surprising that conservatives missed the opportunity to critique the War on Poverty for its most obvious failure: the failure to serve women, the fastest growing segment of the poor in the United States. Yet conservatives were not concerned about drawing distinctions between poverty and welfare programs or about enhancing women's rights. Weakening and dismantling both programs was the major goal.

During the late 1960s and early 1970s, AFDC also came under attack from the left with its proposal of a guaranteed minimum income (GMI). The GMI was a bold policy initiative compared to the modest liberal welfare politics of the 1950s and early 1960s. A GMI was an income floor, a sum to which all Americans would be entitled if they were in need and below which no one would fall. The GMI had diverse supporters. Liberal-left groups and welfare rights supporters offered the GMI as a fairer system of income support for a nation as rich as the United States. Their advocacy represented an indictment of the existing patchwork of meager programs and the administrative and legal complexities and contradictions of the contemporary welfare system. At the same time, certain conservatives, especially free-market economists, proposed the GMI in an altered form, as a negative income tax: those who earned below a certain income, they argued, were not merely excluded from paying taxes; they would receive a tax "credit" to bolster their earnings. This, economists like Milton Friedman suggested, would get income to those who needed it without burdensome red tape or government regulation.[39]

The GMI idea was hatched in the Johnson era, and discussed in liberal circles from 1966 on. But it was not until Nixon's presidency that the GMI garnered substantial support and was proposed by the administration and members of Congress. Under Nixon's unlikely leadership, the GMI concept emerged in a program proposal called the Family Assistance Plan (FAP). The FAP proposed a guaranteed minimum income for all Americans of $1,600, soon revised to $2,500, along with the abolition of existing categories of federal, state, and local public assistance. The FAP also contained other elements besides the GMI itself. It required that GMI recipients deemed "employable" either work or enroll in education or training programs.[40]

The FAP was a dramatic proposal, for it seemed to reject rehabilitation by emphasizing cash income only. But it was not a total break from the past. Like Medicaid, it echoed the early 1940s vision of "comprehensive social welfare" that the postwar welfare coalition had once supported. The Wagner-Murray-Dingell bills of 1943 and 1945 and the public welfare amendments of the late 1940s had sought to abolish the existing categorical welfare programs and re-place them with one large universal program for all the needy. They did not ar-ticulate a concept of a "guaranteed minimum income," to be sure, but they were aimed at creating a "floor" of some sort beneath which no American should fall.[41] So unsurprisingly, the National Social Welfare Assembly, the National Association of Social Workers, the APWA, and many individual welfare leaders, such as Elizabeth Wickenden, initially signed on to the FAP.

Yet their support was tentative because the FAP complicated some of the thorny issues of welfare and women's work that welfare advocates had never fully resolved: when and for whom was work an appropriate goal? On the one hand, the FAP's work recommendations were arguably consonant with rehabil-itation. Employment and job training were, after all, central elements of the re-habilitative ideal that the welfare coalition had been developing for twenty years. Although traditional welfare leaders did not support mandatory work re-quirements, they were not opposed to strongly encouraging work and training for welfare recipients, as the 1962 Public Welfare Amendments revealed. On the other hand, the work requirements of the FAP were heavy-handed and mandatory.

One of the new political forces in welfare, the NWRO, revolted when the work element of the FAP was unveiled. The NWRO viewed it as essentially co-ercive. This determination, coupled with what the NWRO deemed insufficient minimum income, prompted the organization to begin a campaign to "zap FAP."[42] When the NWRO began to attack the FAP, traditional welfare leaders equivocated. Though welfare advocates agreed that the minimum income proposed was low, many were uncomfortable with the NWRO's position that a minimum income could not be tied at all to employment or job training. Eventually, however, Wickenden and other welfare leaders followed the NWRO's lead and withdrew their support for the FAP, pointing to its insufficient income provisions and insufficient protections of the rights of welfare clients.

The debate over the FAP revealed the diminished position of welfare professionals vis-à-vis the NWRO. In the end, the ambiguous opposition of traditional welfare leaders and the staunch opposition of the NWRO were not a serious threat to the FAP and not responsible for its downfall.[43] Conservatives were the FAP's nemesis. The GMI notion, as Gareth Davies has written, struck at the heart of many Americans' opposition to welfare itself: they were suspicious of giving money to people who evidently did not deserve it. Conservatives exploited this. One of Nixon's advisers noted that "the reaction of the taxpaying public . . . would be overwhelmingly against giving money to people as a matter of right, without any questions of their ability and willingness to work." Few conservatives were convinced by free-market economists' support for the GMI, either. Conservatives saw the FAP as an unwarranted extension of the welfare state that discouraged work, despite the elements of the proposal that linked the GMI to employment. The FAP failed in Congress.[44]

The easy defeat of the GMI concept reflected the turn toward harsher, more restrictive welfare law. This was the overriding trend in welfare politics and policy in the late 1960s and early 1970s. The first step was the 1967 Work Incentive Program (WIN), quickly followed in 1971 by the Talmadge amendments to WIN, sometimes called WIN II. The 1967 welfare reform bill was a blatant attempt by Congressman Wilbur Mills (D-Ark.), the conservative chair of the Ways and Means Committee, to impose a restrictive set of rules on AFDC. The law was designed to limit perceived "welfare fraud" and reduce support for children born out of wedlock by freezing the number of additional children under age twenty-one who could receive AFDC due to the absence of the father from the home. But the hallmark of the bill was mandatory work requirements for AFDC clients. It "disqualified adults and older out of school children from AFDC payments if they refused to accept employment or participate in training programs —females and males alike, mothers as well as fathers, even in single-parent, female-headed families," though it left these determinations to the discretion of states.[45] In 1971, with WIN II, Congress removed the states' discretion, imposing mandatory registration into work programs for all except single women with children under six. And states had to place in work programs at least 15 percent of those registered for work or training or lose federal funds.[46] In the end, largely through lack of state finances, mandatory requirements did not succeed in putting women on welfare to work. No more than 10 percent of welfare clients were ever put to work through the incarnations of the WIN program. But workfare rhetoric was a powerful mandate in the minds of legislators.[47]

The shift to an aggressive work-based welfare policy in 1967 was both a continuation of and a break from the past. It was the logical result of twenty years of liberal rehabilitative welfare reform. Postwar reformers' language of independence, and the vision of welfare entitlements as essentially rehabilitative, transformed welfare debate and welfare law. By the end of 1964 liberals created a successful consensus based on the principle of rehabilitation outlined in Kennedy-era legislation. The goal of welfare was to produce independent clients. To that end, work-based goals for mothers on welfare were appropriate and useful. As we have seen, work and training programs—the Community Work and Training Programs, later called Work Experience Programs—were added to the AFDC program. Other employment-based services and incentives were also promoted. In this consensus, the "nonemployable" basis on which women historically claimed income support still existed—work was not mandatory—but it was overshadowed by the new employability goals of the AFDC program, with their rhetoric of work and independence. The rehabilitation consensus remained sharply focused on combating welfare dependency and promoting the independence of its clients.

Yet while the Kennedy-era rehabilitative welfare reform formally endorsed independence for AFDC clients for the first time in federal law, and pursued work goals for welfare mothers, it did so differently from subsequent mandatory welfare-to-work programs. Postwar welfare reform pursued rehabilitative work goals that were linked to a liberal philosophy of welfare provision rooted in the 1940s drive for "comprehensive social welfare." Liberal welfare reform of the early postwar years proposed a social service, education, and training program grafted onto expanded and equalized income support for needy women. As envisioned by liberals of the 1950s and 1960s, this program aimed to help clients achieve independence and offer them economic opportunities for self-sufficiency. Ostensibly, the means by which rehabilitation was to be accomplished reflected this philosophy: caseworkers were expected to consult with clients about pursuing education, training, and job placement, and the choice to participate was to be reserved for the client herself.

This ideal was rarely realized in practice, but before it could be more fully implemented, conservatives of the Democratic and Republican parties in the late 1960s and early 1970s set welfare along a much harsher track. Though WIN did not ultimately force most welfare clients into work, the program's rhetoric and rules nevertheless reflected the perversion of the discourse of rehabilitation and independence used by liberal welfare reform advocates for twenty years. WIN's philosophy denied the liberal intention of rehabilitation—providing opportunity on a voluntary basis—and it severed work from other rehabilitative social services not related to work (Congress cut these "soft" social services in 1967 and 1968). Above all, it was a decidedly hostile rather than a merely paternalistic assault on poor women's entitlements to government aid. With WIN, policy makers and politicians replaced the goal of rehabilitation with the goal of responsibility: welfare was not to rehabilitate welfare clients according to their needs, but to make welfare clients act "responsibly." And no responsibility was as important as the responsibility to work.

When the transformation from rehabilitation to responsibility took place in the late 1960s and early 1970s, liberals in welfare circles and their allies in foundations and interest groups objected. The APWA, the National Social Welfare Assembly, and National Association of Social Workers opposed WIN and the Talmadge amendments, regarding them with "intense dismay and anger."[48] The APWA insisted that "the participation of AFDC mothers in the work incentive program should be on a voluntary basis" only, and that "the requirement for such a provision [work incentives] . . . should be repealed."[49] Elizabeth Wickenden was "not in sympathy" with the two WIN legislative acts, predicting "tragic results from their draconian provisions."[50]

It seemed, in retrospect, that the liberal welfare reform coalition and its leaders stepped onto a slippery slope when they redefined the basic ends of welfare entitlements for low-income women. By changing the goals of welfare from supporting stay-at-home motherhood to encouraging economic independence, they opened the door to modifications to its original intent. Wickenden apparently realized this in 1968, when she repudiated the concept of rehabilitation, implying that it had been deformed by mandatory workfare: "I recognize the desirability of assisting such mothers [on AFDC] to work when this accords with their better judgment . . . but do not feel that the concepts of 'rehabilitation' are appropriate to the circumstances of responsible motherhood or that the achievement of financial independence is the primary goal of Title IV [AFDC]."[51] Only the shift toward mandatory workfare could have caused a long-time champion of rehabilitation, who only four years earlier had rejoiced in its passage, to denounce it.

By the late 1960s and early 1970s, the power of welfare advocates did not match their outrage. Their opposition to mandatory welfare-to-work programs was ineffective, and compulsory work requirements proceeded. The defeat of the postwar welfare reform coalition was critically important because no other anticonservative group was able to effectively stem the hostile tide rising against welfare. To be sure, when WIN and WIN II were passed, others also objected. The NWRO, for example, opposed it, for the WIN and WIN II programs had all of the mandatory components of workfare with none of the guaranteed income floor—however inadequate—of the FAP. But the NWRO declined in the early 1970s and was defunct by 1975. The civil rights organizations and NOW, which were more attuned than ever to welfare, also objected to mandatory work requirements for welfare clients. But in the face of growing conservative power, their concerns fell on deaf ears in Congress, too.

AS THE 1970S DREW TO a close, it seemed to welfare advocates that AFDC policy could hardly get any harsher, but the 1980s and 1990s brought still more stringent policies. Three major amendments to the law increased workfare. These were the 1981 Omnibus Budget Reconciliation Act; the 1988 Family Support Act, which created the Job Opportunities and Basic Skills program in the AFDC program; and finally the 1996 Personal Responsibility and Work Opportunity Act (PRWO).[52] After 1996 there no longer existed any guaranteed safety net for poor women and their children. Rather, federal law guaranteed that women's economic need would be met with demands for workforce participation.

At least since Democratic president Bill Clinton vowed in his 1992 election campaign to "end welfare as we know it," the march toward workfare has been trumpeted as a dramatic break from the past. Erasing decades of political and policy debate about welfare and work, late-twentieth-century welfare discourse presented workfare as a revolution in social policy. Republican New York City mayor Rudolph Giuliani, who presided over the nation's largest municipal welfare-to-work system, summed up this point of view in his endorsement of the 1996 PRWO. What made the law so novel, he declared, was that, "from 1960 to 1994, the work ethic was under attack in New York City." After 1996, however, that "perverted social philosophy" was abandoned, and New York and the nation "reawaken[ed] the respect for work."[53]

Most politicians and policy makers not only agreed with Giuliani's interpretation but also viewed workfare as an unqualified success. In the months before the reauthorization of the PRWO in the fall of 2003, welfare-to-work programs were lauded. Journalists called the PRWO "the nation's most dramatic experiment in welfare reform" and "the greatest policy achievement in recent history."[54] And from the perspective that welfare is about responsibility and not creating adequate, sustainable jobs for welfare clients, perhaps the 1996 welfare reform law was a success. Hundreds of thousands of clients were indeed forced to work as a result of the law. Republican president George W. Bush's administration believed that the PRWO could be even more effective in making clients work. In 2004 it is proposing to amend the law with even more stringent work requirements.[55]

Yet while work requirements were tightened during the past thirty years, work failed to remove poor women on welfare from poverty. As the American economy switched from a manufacturing base to a high-tech and service industries base, many of the best-paying manufacturing jobs were sent abroad.[56] Meanwhile, for twenty years after 1973, the pay rates for minimum-wage service jobs—the jobs for which most poor women now qualify—were being eroded, in real terms.[57] Basic income from sources other than wage work also declined. For example, Supplemental Security Income (1974), which provided additional federal aid to the needy, explicitly denied the benefit to women on AFDC. In-kind welfare programs—food stamps and housing supports—were cut in the 1980s, limiting further sources of support for poor women. Thus by the late 1990s the share of the poor who were women had grown. As the new millennium began, women were 40 percent more likely than men to be poor and constituted 60 percent of the "extreme poor" and "poor," as categorized by the U.S. census.[58] With the recession beginning in 2000, their economic fate worsened, as unemployment rose and poverty rates grew. Tragically, the proposals for reauthorizing the 1996 PRWO appeared to ignore these trends.

Glowing assessments of welfare reform at the turn of this century ignored the fate of the women targeted by workfare programs, and they did so in part by distorting the history of welfare and work in postwar America. They overlooked any lessons that might have been gleaned from the successes, failures, and transformation of rehabilitative welfare reform, and imagined a past in which welfare policy evolved from "handouts" to hard work. But contrary to the prevailing discourse of welfare today, those who had power over the national welfare agenda from the late 1940s onward were interested in promoting employment for welfare clients. And from 1962 onward, that interest only grew. What changed after the 1960s, however, was the nature of policy makers' interest in work, as well as the political context in which welfare and work were discussed. What began in the 1940s as an effort to encourage employment for poor women, as part of a liberal vision of an expanded, fairer, and therapeutic federal welfare system, has been transformed into a demand that poor women be required to work, as part of a conservative vision of a minimal and coercive federal welfare state.

In the last decade of her life, Elizabeth Wickenden looked back on her long career and lamented this shift toward mandatory work requirements in welfare policy in the 1970s and 1980s. Her critique captured the subtle but crucial differences between the late-twentieth-century ethos of workfare and the early postwar ethos of rehabilitation: "You have this general—almost a consensus —that the purpose of welfare is to get people off welfare," she said. "Well that may be if they're moving into a better situation[,] but if you're forcing them into a poor situation it's not the point. . . . Forcing someone to work against their will does not bring about independence."[59] This must have been a bitter and ironic conclusion after a lifetime spent fighting for what Wickenden considered a humane and reasonable social policy of aiding the nation's poorest citizens. She, Wilbur Cohen, and their allies ultimately did not realize their vision of welfare, and their unfinished work embodied the limitations of liberalism in postwar America. In particular, their experience in policy making illustrated the pitfalls of a poverty discourse narrowly focused on one welfare program and its clients. Yet their history is also a reminder that although the political debate about welfare in postwar America has never been egalitarian, it was at one time at least nuanced. Compared with today's advocates of workfare, the postwar liberal coalition of reformers was more cognizant of the difficulties facing poor women and the necessity for a robust and responsive agenda for welfare reform.

Major Federal Legislative Developments in
Aid to Dependent Children, 1935–1964

1935: Social Security Act, Title IV
   creation of public assistance fund for Aid to Dependent Children (ADC)

1939: Social Security Amendments
   revision of benefit formula for ADC, increasing federal reimbursement of states to
      half of state expenditures up to existing maximums
   creation of new social insurance program Old Age and Survivors Insurance (OASI),
      providing insurance benefits to survivors of those eligible for Old Age Insur-
      ance (Social Security), including widows and their children who had previously
      received ADC payments

1950: Social Security Amendments
   creation of caretaker provision, allowing one adult caretaker to be included as
      recipient for federal matching purposes
   requirement for a fair hearing to anyone denied ADC or faced with delay in receiv-
      ing it
   Notification of Law Enforcement Officers (NOLEO), requirement of local welfare
      offices to notify law enforcement upon granting of aid to families deserted by
      father

1952: Social Security Amendments
   increase in limit on amount of benefit to individuals to which the federal matching
      formula applies
   increase in overall federal matching funds

1956: Social Security Amendments
   new stated purpose for ADC: rather than provide income support, ADC grant is
      meant to "encourage self-care and self-support of recipient"

establishment of federal matching funds for social services to ADC clients, reimbursed at a rate of half the state cost

1961: Aid to Dependent Children–Unemployed Parent (ADC-UP)
creation of the "unemployed parent" provision allowing children of unemployed parents, usually the father, to become eligible for ADC, in addition to those children receiving funds due to the divorce, desertion, death, or incapacitation of the parent
creation of Community Work and Training Programs (CWTPS), federally funded, locally operated work and training programs designed to employ the unemployed fathers brought into the ADC program

1962: Public Welfare Amendments
requirement of minimum prescribed social services to ADC clients
revision of federal reimbursement to states for social services to ADC clients, from half of the cost to three-quarters
increased funding of CWTPS, and opening of them to adult ADC recipients who are not necessarily "unemployed parents"
incentives for demonstration projects and research on ADC through waiving federal requirements and through provision of federal funding
change in name of ADC to Aid to Families with Dependent Children (AFDC)

1964: Equal Opportunity Act of 1964, Title V
inclusion of AFDC work and training programs as part of the larger War on Poverty through the Economic Opportunity Act
change in name of CWTPS to Work Experience Programs (WEPS)

Major Federal Legislative Developments in Aid to Dependent Children Encouraging or Requiring Employment, 1956–2004

1956: Social Security Amendments
   new stated purpose for Aid to Dependent Children (ADC): rather than provide income support, ADC grant is meant to "encourage self-care and self-support of recipient"
   establishment of federal matching funds for social services to ADC clients, reimbursed at a rate of half the state cost

1961: Aid to Dependent Children–Unemployed Parent (ADC-UP)
   creation of the "unemployed parent" provision allowing children of unemployed parents, usually the father, to become eligible for ADC, in addition to those children receiving funds due to the divorce, desertion, death, or incapacitation of the parent
   creation of Community Work and Training Programs (CWTPS), federally funded, locally operated work and training programs designed to employ the unemployed fathers brought into the ADC program

1962: Public Welfare Amendments
   requirement of minimum prescribed social services to ADC clients
   revision of federal reimbursement for social services to ADC clients, from half of the cost to three-quarters
   increased funding of CWTPS, and opening of them to adult ADC recipients who are not necessarily "unemployed parents"
   incentives for demonstration projects and research on ADC through waiving federal requirements and through provision of federal funding
   change in name of ADC to Aid to Families with Dependent Children (AFDC)

1964: Equal Opportunity Act of 1964, Title V
   inclusion of AFDC work and training programs as part of the larger War on
Poverty through the Economic Opportunity Act
   change in name of CWTPS to Work Experience Programs (WEPS)

1967: Social Security Amendments
   creation of Work Incentive Program (WIN), allowing registration of AFDC clients
      for participation in work programs or working training, exempting mothers
      with children under age six

1971: Talmadge Amendments to WIN
   revision of WIN requiring that a greater number of AFDC clients register for and
      participate in work programs or work training programs, but still exempting
      mothers with children under age six

1981: Omnibus Budget Reconciliation Act
   requirement of some welfare clients to work in return for receiving welfare, effec-
      tively establishing workfare
   revision of exemptions for work participation to only mothers with toddlers and
      infants

1988: Family Support Act
   creation of federal Job Opportunities and Basic Skills Program, to require clients
      on welfare to work, train, or be educated in return for receiving welfare

1996: Personal Responsibility and Work Opportunity Act
   AFDC program replaced by Temporary Aid to Needy Families (TANF), a new tem-
      porary program providing temporary aid on a limited basis over the course of a
      lifetime to needy families who are, almost without exception, required to work

2002: Continuing Resolution extending provisions of the 1996 PRWO

2003: Continuing Resolution extending provisions of the 1996 PRWO

2004: Pending legislation to reauthorize the 1996 PRWO and expand work
   requirements

NOTES

Abbreviations in the Notes

Archives and Libraries

BL	Bentley Historical Library, University of Michigan, Ann Arbor, Mich.
CAH	Center for American History, University of Texas at Austin, Austin, Tex.
LBJL	Lyndon Baines Johnson Presidential Library, Austin, Tex.
LC	Library of Congress, Washington, D.C.
LS	Laura Schlesinger Library, Radcliffe College, Cambridge, Mass.
NA	National Archives and Records Administration, College Park, Md.
RAC	Rockefeller Archive Center, Sleepy Hollow, N.Y.
SWHA	Social Welfare History Archives, University of Minnesota, Minneapolis, Minn.
WHS	Wisconsin Historical Society, Madison, Wis.

Manuscript Collections

AFL-CIO/CSA	American Federation of Labor–Congress of Industrial Organizations Community Service Activities Collection
APWA	American Public Welfare Association Collection
AR	Abraham Ribicoff Papers
CRA	Community Research Associates Collection
CWLA	Child Welfare League of America Collection
DL/PCSW	General Records of the Department of Labor, Office of the Secretary, Secretary's Subject Correspondence, RG 174/ President's Commission on the Status of Women
EW	Elizabeth Wickenden Papers
FF	Field Foundation Collection
HEW/PCSW	General Records of the Department of Health, Education, and Welfare, Office of the Secretary, Secretary's Subject Correspondence, RG 235 / President's Commission on the Status of Women

MS   Mary Switzer Papers
NASW Supp.   National Association of Social Workers Supplement Collection
NAR   Nelson A. Rockefeller Collection
NSWA   National Social Welfare Assembly Collection
NUL   National Urban League Collection
RBF   Rockefeller Brothers Fund Collection
RF   Rockefeller Foundation Collection
UMSSW   University of Michigan School of Social Work Collection
WC   Wilbur Cohen Papers
WHCF   White House Central Files

Introduction

1. U.S. Congress, Joint Committee on the Economic Report, Subcommittee on Low-Income Families, Press Release, "Current Plans and Procedures," May 11, 1955, folder 15, box 24, APWA Collection, SWHA; U.S. Congress, Senate, Subcommittee on Low-Income Families, *Hearings on Characteristics of the Low-Income Population and Related Federal Programs*, 84th Congress, 1st session, 1955 (Washington, D.C.: U.S. Government Printing Office, 1956). James Patterson notes in his study of poverty that there was precious little in the way of quantitative studies of poverty before the 1960s. See James Patterson, *America's Struggle against Poverty, 1900–1994* (Cambridge, Mass.: Harvard University Press, 1994), 78.

2. Averell Harriman, address to New York State Legislature, January 30, 1957, folder 8, box 69, WC Papers, WHS.

3. For information on the Committee for Economic Development's poverty study, see folder 8, box 69, WC Papers, WHS. For information on the Faculty Seminar on Income Maintenance, see folder 8, box 70, WC Papers, WHS. For information on Cohen's career, an essential work is Edward Berkowitz's excellent biography, *Mr. Social Security: The Life of Wilbur J. Cohen*, (Lawrence: University Press of Kansas, 1995).

4. Although analysts measured levels of poverty differently—$2,000 annual income or less, $3,000 annual income or less—they generally agreed on some basic conclusions. The figures in the text are from James Tobin, an economist on the Council of Economic Advisers under President John F. Kennedy, quoted in Patterson, *America's Struggle against Poverty*, 79, 80.

5. Minutes of the Eleventh Meeting of the Faculty Seminar on Income Maintenance, University of Michigan, November 28, 1956, folder 8, box 70, WC Papers, WHS, 1.

6. Wilbur Cohen, "Poverty and Low Incomes in the United States," Committee for Economic Development, August 4, 1956, folder 7, box 69, WC Papers, WHS, 5.

7. No official poverty statistics exist before 1959. But extrapolating from AFDC statistics and poverty statistics from 1960, there were approximately 1.9 million mother-headed families, and they made up just over 20 percent of the nation's poor families. Michael Katz, *The Undeserving Poor: From the War on Poverty to the War on Welfare* (New York: Pantheon Books, 1989), 69.

8. Untitled draft, ca. 1957, folder 7, box 69, WC Papers, WHS, 9.

9. Two of the most influential contemporary experts on the family and psychology were Talcott Parsons and Robert Bales; see their *Family, Socialization and Interaction Process* (Glencoe, Ill.: Free Press, 1955). See also W. Allison Davis and Robert Havighurst, *Father of the Man: How Your Child Gets His Personality* (Boston: Houghton Mifflin, 1947).

10. These assessments often varied by race. Accusations of immorality drew on long-held popular notions concerning the relationship of poverty, morality, sexual behavior, and race. Conclusions about pathology drew on psychological research and studies of black family life such as E. Franklin Frazier's, which were thought to depict female-headed families as a peculiarly African American pathology. On race and single motherhood in this period, see Rickie Solinger, *Wake Up Little Susie: Race and Single Pregnancy before* Roe v. Wade (New York: Routledge, 1993). On depictions of the African American family in history, see Herbert Gutman, *The Black Family in Slavery and Freedom, 1750–1925,* (New York: Vintage, 1976); E. Franklin Frazier, *The Negro Family in Chicago* (Chicago: University of Chicago Press, 1932); and E. Franklin Frazier, *The Negro Family in the United States* (Chicago: University of Chicago Press, 1939).

11. Patterson, *America's Struggle against Poverty*, 81.

12. Nancy Cauthen and Edwin Amenta, "Not for Widows Only: Institutional Politics and the Formative Years of Aid to Dependent Children," *American Sociological Review* 61 (June 1996): 427.

13. On mothers' pensions, see Joanne Goodwin, *Gender and the Politics of Welfare Reform: Mothers' Pensions in Chicago, 1911–1929* (Chicago: University of Chicago Press, 1997); Linda Gordon, *Pitied but Not Entitled: Single Mothers and the History of Welfare* (New York: Free Press, 1994); Molly Ladd-Taylor, *Mother-Work: Women, Child Welfare, and the State, 1890–1930* (Urbana, Ill.: University of Illinois Press, 1995); and Theda Skocpol, *Protecting Soldiers and Mothers: The Political Origins of Social Policy in the United States* (Cambridge, Mass.: Belknap Press of Harvard University Press, 1992).

14. Cauthen and Amenta, "Not for Widows Only," 427–28.

15. The seminar invited researchers studying the ADC program to present their research to the group, and then the group continued to discuss the ADC program and its population. Minutes of Twelfth Meeting of the Faculty Seminar on Income Maintenance, University of Michigan, December 11, 1956, folder 8, box 70, WC Papers, WHS, 2; Minutes of Twenty-eighth Meeting of the Faculty Seminar on Income Maintenance, University of Michigan, May 9, 1957, folder 8, box 70, WC Papers, WHS. The second year of the seminar was focused much more on programs and solutions than the first. Discussions of welfare and welfare clients played a prominent role.

16. Minutes of Tenth Meeting of the Faculty Seminar on Income Maintenance, University of Michigan, November 21, 1956, folder 8, box 70, WC Papers, WHS, 2.

17. Letter to Jules Berman from Wilbur Cohen, December 30, 1957, folder 3, box 12, EW Papers, WHS, 2.

18. Ibid. Cohen's comments went on to suggest rehabilitation explicitly: "But I believe there are lots of other elements we must emphasize other than assistance, such as training, research, casework services, medical care, rehabilitation."

19. The historical literature on poverty thought and policy focuses largely on social scientists both inside and outside government. The freshest thinking on the relation-

ship between social scientists and poverty can be found in Alice O'Connor's masterful *Poverty Knowledge: Social Science, Social Policy, and the Poor in Twentieth-Century U.S. History* (Princeton, N.J.: Princeton University Press, 2001). Other treatments include Henry Aaron, *Politics and the Professors: The Great Society in Perspective* (Washington, D.C.: Brookings Institution, 1978); Gareth Davies, *From Opportunity to Entitlement: The Transformation and Decline of Great Society Liberalism* (Lawrence: University Press of Kansas, 1996), 10–53; Robert Haveman, ed., *A Decade of Federal Antipoverty Programs* (New York: Academic Press, 1977); Katz, *The Undeserving Poor*, 9–123; Sar Levitan, *The Great Society's Poor Law: A New Approach to Poverty* (Baltimore: Johns Hopkins University Press, 1969); Sar Levitan and Robert Taggart, *The Promise of Greatness* (Cambridge, Mass.: Harvard University Press, 1975); Peter Marris and Martin Rein, *Dilemmas of Social Reform: Poverty and Community Action in the United States* (London: Routledge and Kegan Paul, 1967); Daniel Patrick Moynihan, *Maximum Feasible Misunderstanding: Community Action in the War on Poverty* (New York: Free Press, 1969); Allen Matusow, *The Unraveling of America: A History of Liberalism in the 1960s* (New York: Harper Torchbooks, 1984), 97–130; Patterson, *America's Struggle against Poverty*, 99–156; Richard Pells, *The Liberal Mind in a Conservative Age: American Intellectuals in the 1940s and 1950s* (New York: Harper and Row, 1985), 117–261; James L. Sundquist, *Politics and Policy: The Eisenhower, Kennedy, and Johnson Years* (Washington, D.C.: Brookings Institution, 1968). Original writing by postwar social scientists can be found in Edward Banfield, *The Moral Basis of a Backward Society* (New York: Free Press, 1958); Herbert Gans, *The Urban Villagers* (New York: Free Press of Glencoe, 1962); Oscar Lewis, *The Children of Sanchez: Autobiography of a Mexican Family* (New York: Vintage, 1961); Richard Cloward and Lloyd Ohlin, *Delinquency and Opportunity: A Theory of Delinquent Gangs* (New York: Free Press, 1964).

20. In the standard narrative, the Progressive Era marks the birth of state-run social provision. The New Deal represents the transference of social provision to the national government and the creation of a federal system of social provision. The Great Society signifies the elaboration and extension of social provision to groups or individuals previously left out of the system. These periods were characterized by widespread reformist sentiments and powerful coalitions between grassroots support for welfare provision and elite policy leadership. On the Progressive Era, see Robert Wiebe, *The Search for Order, 1877–1920* (New York: Hill and Wang, 1967); Barbara Nelson, "Origins of the Two-Channel Welfare State: Workman's Compensation and Mothers' Aid," in *Women, the State, and Welfare*, ed. Linda Gordon (Madison, Wis.: University of Wisconsin Press, 1990), 123–51; Theda Skocpol, *Protecting Soldiers and Mothers: The Political Origins of Social Policy in the United States* (Cambridge, Mass.: Belknap Press of Harvard University Press, 1992); Linda Gordon, *Pitied but Not Entitled: Single Mothers and the History of Welfare, 1890–1935* (New York: Free Press, 1994). On the New Deal, see Steven Fraser and Gary Gerstle, *The Rise and Fall of the New Deal Order, 1930–1980* (Princeton, N.J.: Princeton University Press, 1989); Lizabeth Cohen, *Making a New Deal: Industrial Workers in Chicago, 1919–1939* (New York: Cambridge University Press, 1990). On the Great Society, see, for example, Godfrey Hodgson, *America in Our Time: From World War II to Nixon, What Happened and Why* (New York: Vintage, 1976); Allen Matusow, *The Unraveling of America: A History of Liberalism in the 1960s* (New York: Harper Torchbooks, 1984).

21. Its "Essentials of Public Welfare," first drafted in the late 1940s , became a touch-

stone of the liberal perspective on the welfare state. "Essentials of Public Welfare" was used by the APWA throughout the 1950s and, in amended form, through the 1970s. In addition, the document served as an informational and lobbying tool for other welfare organizations, such as the National Association of Social Workers (created in 1955 from a merger of two social work organizations), the National Social Welfare Assembly, the American Public Health Association, and allied interest groups like the AFL-CIO and the National Urban League. See "Essentials of Public Welfare," folder 14, box 6, APWA Collection, SWHA. The document was published as a booklet: *Essentials of Public Welfare* (Chicago: American Public Welfare Association, 1952).

22. For an account of the APWA's increased activities during the war and its aggressive campaign to become more influential at the federal level, see Elizabeth Wickenden Oral History, December 12, 1986, folder 3, box 16, EW Papers, WHS, 1–4; and Narayan Viswanathan, "The Role of the American Public Welfare Association in the Formulation and Development of Public Welfare Policies in the United States: 1930–1960" (D.S.W. thesis, Columbia University, 1961), 174–77.

23. In addition, both AFL-CIO and NUL leaders had ties to leaders of welfare organizations that reinforced their commitment to welfare policy. Katherine Ellickson and Nelson Cruikshank, respectively of the AFL and the CIO (later the AFL-CIO), had worked closely with Cohen and Wickenden on legislative proposals and lobbying during the New Deal and the early 1940s. In the late 1950s and early 1960s, Leo Perliss of the AFL-CIO's Community Service Activities became a major supporter of welfare and rehabilitation, attending APWA meetings and social work conferences and speaking on welfare at union conferences. Wickenden discusses her relationship with Cruikshank and Ellickson in her oral history. See Wickenden Oral History, 9–10. For Leo Perliss's activities, the AFL-CIO/CSA Collection at the SWHA is invaluable. The National Urban League was also involved in welfare politics by virtue of the background and relationships of its leaders. Lester Granger and Whitney Young, the two leaders of the National Urban League in the period from 1945 to 1964, had professional and personal ties to many members of the welfare–social work–philanthropy coalition behind welfare policy. The AFL-CIO supported welfare as one piece of its overall agenda —both in public policy and private contracts—to secure a "family wage" that allowed male breadwinners to support wives and children. ADC was a last-resort program to allow women without a male breadwinner to remain at home in a care-giving role. For a full statement on labor's support for welfare programs, see Resolution no. 148: Social Security: Public Assistance, adopted by the Third Constitutional Convention, AFL-CIO, San Francisco, Calif., September 17–23, 1959, folder 13, box 2, AFL-CIO/CSA Collection, SWHA, 2. In the 1950s, the National Urban League also melded welfare into its broader agenda of maximizing the benefits of the welfare state for African Americans. ADC was a program that, while hardly generous, nevertheless aided many poor African American families. For good accounts of the Urban League's interest in social programs, see Dona Hamilton and Charles Hamilton, *The Dual Agenda: Race and Social Welfare Policies of Civil Rights Organizations* (New York: Columbia University Press, 1997), 128–29; and Dennis Dickerson, *Militant Mediator: A Biography of Whitney Young, Jr.* (Lexington: University Press of Kentucky, 1998), 35–55.

24. There is no published history of the Field Foundation. But there is a wonderful,

detailed, and analytic history in the foundation's archival collection. See Charles Bourne, "History of the Field Foundation," part 1, sections 3–5, box 2F377, FF Collection, CAH.

25. Though aggressive, the Field Foundation was anomalous in the world of philanthropy. By midcentury, social welfare and, in particular, public assistance were viewed as unprofitable philanthropic ventures, palliative rather than preventative in addressing social problems like poverty. In the early twentieth century, by contrast, major national foundations such as the Russell Sage Foundation had participated in creating social welfare institutions and government programs. See Judith Sealander, *Private Wealth, Public Life: Foundation Philanthropy and the Reshaping of American Social Policy from the Progressive Era to the New Deal* (Baltimore: Johns Hopkins University Press, 1997).

26. See Julian Zelizer, *Taxing America: Wilbur D. Mills, Congress, and the State, 1945–1975* (New York: Cambridge University Press, 1998).

27. Wilbur Cohen, draft of "Social Policies and Services in an Expanding Economy," October 1957, folder 330, box 30, Rockefeller Brothers Fund Special Studies Project, series 4, subpanel IV, RBF Collection, RAC, 50–51. Such sentiments were common among welfare leaders. Charles Schottland, Social Security commissioner, testified on behalf of the rehabilitative 1956 Social Security Amendments, saying, "Today, we still have needy ... [people] ... , but our record levels of employment and our healthy economy afford much greater opportunities and rewards for intensive efforts to return them to self-support." U.S. Congress, House of Representatives, Committee on Ways and Means, *Hearings on Public Assistance Titles of the Social Security Act, 1956*, 84th Congress, 2nd session, April 12, 13, 16, 19, 20, 1956 (Washington, D.C.: U.S. Government Printing Office, 1957), 4.

28. Arthur Schlesinger, *The Vital Center* (1949; repr., Boston: Houghton Mifflin, 1962). This characterization of American liberal politics endured for many years, as historians presented a narrative of a strong, cohesive liberal coalition that dominated from the 1930s until the 1960s, after which it declined due to challenges from both the right and the left.

29. By tracing the beliefs and actions of groups or individuals who called themselves liberals, historians are plotting new maps of liberalism's progression in the twentieth century. This emerging literature takes several forms. On the general topic, see Alan Brinkley, *Liberalism and Its Discontents* (Cambridge, Mass.: Harvard University Press, 1998); Gary Gerstle, "The Protean Character of American Liberalism," *American Historical Review* 99, no. 4 (October 1994): 1043–73; and Thomas Sugrue, "Reassessing the History of Postwar America," *Prospects: An Annual of American Cultural Studies* 20 (1995): 493–509. Other literature complicates the liberal narrative, both directly and indirectly, by challenging the assumptions of liberal consensus politics in the postwar era. On disrupting racial liberalism, see, for example, Gary Gerstle, "Race and the Myth of the Liberal Consensus," *Journal of American History* 82, no. 2 (September 1995): 579–86; Thomas Sugrue, *The Origin of the Urban Crisis: Race and Inequality in Postwar Detroit* (Princeton, N.J.: Princeton University Press, 1996); Arnold Hirsch, "Massive Resistance in the Urban North: Trumbull Park, Chicago, 1953–63," *Journal of American History* 82, no. 2 (September 1995): 522–50; and Mary Dudziak, *Cold War Civil Rights: Race and the Image of American Democracy* (Princeton, N.J.: Princeton University Press, 2000). On disrupting

the consensus on gender and domesticity, and showing the overlap of gender, class, and racial politics in postwar liberal politics, see Susan Hartmann, *The Other Feminists: Activists in the Liberal Establishment* (New Haven, Conn.: Yale University Press, 1998); and Joanne Meyerowitz, ed. *Not June Cleaver: Women and Gender in Postwar America, 1945–1960* (Philadelphia: Temple University Press, 1994).

30. For information on Community Research Associates, see CRA Collection, SWHA. For information on the growth of quasi-governmental research and consulting firms and other similar "shadow government" organizations, see James Allen Smith, *The Idea Brokers: Think Tanks and the Rise of the New Policy Elite* (New York: Free Press, 1991).

31. Virtually no research on welfare was produced prior to 1945, save for a few federally funded, small-scale analyses of different aspects of the ADC program, and information produced as "an auxiliary . . . of research directed primarily to the solution of problems in the fields of health, mental health, vocational rehabilitation, education or national defense." "Social Security Research and Demonstration Program," Report of the Subcommittee on Social Research, NSWA, 4/57, folder: SIP Research, box 55, NSWA Collection, SWHA, 3. By 1961 state welfare administrator Norman Lourie could state in a research review, "The writings are so vast that any attempt to even skim or outline them here would be presumptuous." Norman Lourie, "Are We Learning How to Help Recipients Become Self-Supporting?" *Public Welfare* 20, no. 3 (July 1962): 170.

32. On the emergence of a welfare rights movement, see Frances Fox Piven and Richard Cloward, *Poor People's Movements: Why they Succeed, How they Fail* (New York: Vintage, 1977), 264–361; Guida West, *The National Welfare Rights Movement: The Social Protest of Poor Women* (New York: Praeger, 1981).

33. On the rise of postwar conservatism and the principles on which it stood, see Jerome L. Himmelstein, *To the Right: The Transformation of American Conservatism* (Berkeley: University of California Press, 1991); William B. Hixson Jr., *Search for the American Right Wing: An Analysis of the Social Science Record, 1955–1987* (Princeton, N.J.: Princeton University Press, 1992); Kari Frederickson, *The Dixiecrat Revolt and the End of the Solid South, 1932–1968* (Chapel Hill: University of North Carolina Press, 2001); Dan T. Carter, *The Politics of Rage: George Wallace, the Origins of the New Conservatism, and the Transformation of American Politics* (New York: Simon and Schuster, 1995); Lisa McGirr, *Suburban Warriors: The Origins of the New American Right* (Princeton, N.J.: Princeton University Press, 2001); Mary C. Brennan, *Turning Right in the Sixties: The Conservative Capture of the GOP* (Chapel Hill: The University of North Carolina Press, 1995); John A. Andrew III, *The Other Side of the Sixties: Young Americans for Freedom and the Rise of Conservative Politics* (New Brunswick, N.J.: Rutgers University Press, 1997); Godfrey Hodgson, *The World Turned Right Side Up: A History of the Conservative Ascendancy in America* (Boston: Houghton Mifflin, 1996); Jonathan M. Schoenwald, *A Time for Choosing: The Rise of Modern American Conservatism* (New York: Oxford University Press, 2001).

34. This also occurred after the early 1970s through the office of the assistant secretary of program evaluation (ASPE) in the Department of Health, Education, and Welfare. O'Connor, *Poverty Knowledge*, 166–95, 213–83.

35. This tension over their political authority probably also reflected a tension over their class status, which, as Daniel Walkowitz has shown, was contested terrain in twentieth-century America. Social workers struggled to define themselves as "middle class," and

the early postwar period, Walkowitz argues, was one in which "social workers reprofessionalize and reconstitute their identity as white and less equivocally middle class." Daniel Walkowitz, *Working with Class: Social Workers and the Politics of Middle-Class Identity* (Chapel Hill: University of North Carolina Press, 1999), 24.

36. Bradley Buell, "Re-tooling for Human Betterment" (draft), November 1951, folder 3, box 1, CRA Collection, SWHA, 7.

37. Ibid., 3.

38. Eisenhower quoted in U.S. Congress, House of Representatives, Committee on Ways and Means, *Hearings on Public Assistance Titles of the Social Security Act, 1957*, 84th Congress, 2nd session, April 12, 13, 16, 19, 20, 1956, 4.

39. Wilbur Cohen and Fedele Fauri, "The Social Security Amendments of 1956," *Public Welfare* 14, no. 4 (October 1956): 183–99.

40. Goodwin explains that in some periods the family-based goals have been more politically important, while in other periods work-based goals have assumed prominence. Joanne Goodwin, "'Employable Mothers' and 'Suitable Work': A Re-evaluation of Welfare and Wage-Earning for Women in the Twentieth-Century United States," *Journal of Social History* 29, no. 2 (Winter 1995): 253–74.

41. Walter Jackson, *Gunnar Myrdal and America's Conscience: Social Engineering and Racial Liberalism, 1938–1987* (Chapel Hill: University of North Carolina Press, 1990), 253–54, 279–93.

42. This was a "racialized gendered" ideology. The term is taken from Eileen Boris, "The Racialized Gendered State: Constructions of Citizenship in the United States," *Social Politics* 2, no. 2 (1994): 160–80.

Chapter 1

1. National Resources Planning Board, "Security, Work, and Relief Policies," (Washington, D.C.: U.S. Government Printing Office, 1943). It was "dubbed 'the American Beveridge Report,' after the nearly simultaneous study that led to the creation of the British welfare state." Alan Brinkley, "The New Deal and the Idea of the State," in *The Rise and Fall of the New Deal Order, 1935–1980*, ed. Steven Fraser and Gary Gerstle (Princeton, N.J.: Princeton University Press, 1989), 106.

2. The importance of the bills has been documented by historians of national politics and the welfare state. See Edwin Amenta and Theda Skocpol, "Redefining the New Deal: World War II and the Development of Social Provision in the United States," in *The Politics of Social Policy in the United States*, ed. Margaret Weir, Ann Shola Orloff, and Theda Skocpol (Princeton, N.J.: Princeton University Press, 1988), 118, 119; and Edwin Amenta, *Bold Relief: Institutional Politics and the Origins of Modern American Social Policy* (Princeton, N.J.: Princeton University Press, 1998), 191–230. Alan Brinkley called the NPRB report that inspired the Wagner-Murray-Dingell Acts "a plan that accepted, but greatly expanded upon, the outlines of the social insurance and social provision systems the New Deal had created in the 1930s. Even sixty years later, its proposals are striking for their sweep." Alan Brinkley, *The End of Reform: New Deal Liberalism in Recession and War*

(New York: Knopf, 1995), 251. See also John Jeffries, "A 'Third New Deal?' Liberal Policy and the American State, 1937–1945," *Journal of Policy History* 8, no. 4 (1996): 387–409.

3. But this consequence has been less understood by historians. Histories of ADC have either not covered this era or simply not covered the relationship of ADC to this development. See Linda Gordon, *Pitied but Not Entitled: Single Mothers and the History of Welfare, 1890–1935* (New York: Free Press, 1994); Winifred Bell, *Aid to Dependent Children* (New York: Columbia University Press, 1965); Mimi Abramowitz, *Regulating the Lives of Women: Social Welfare Policy from Colonial Times to the Present*, rev. ed. (Boston: South End Press, 1996); Joanne Goodwin, "'Employable Mothers' and 'Suitable Work': A Re-evaluation of Welfare and Wage-Earning for Women in the Twentieth-Century United States," *Journal of Social History* 29, no. 2 (Winter 1995): 258–62. Likewise, histories of the welfare state that discuss the failed efforts to expand and alter social provision during and after World War II do not deal extensively with ADC. See, for example, Amenta, *Bold Relief*. Nor do general histories of poverty and the welfare state cover the relationship between comprehensive social welfare proposals and ADC. See, for example, James Patterson, *America's Struggle against Poverty, 1900–1994* (Cambridge, Mass.: Harvard University Press, 1994); and Michael Katz, *In the Shadow of the Poorhouse: A Social History of Welfare in America* (New York: Basic Books, 1986).

4. Gordon, *Pitied but Not Entitled*, 267–68, 272. Historians of social insurance have also documented the diminished place of public assistance in the Social Security Administration. See Jerry Cates, *Insuring Inequality: Administrative Leadership in Social Security, 1934–1950* (Ann Arbor: University of Michigan Press, 1983).

5. The Social Security Board, composed of experts on social insurance, oversaw both ADC and Social Security, and its primary interest lay in promoting the new Social Security program, not welfare. Gordon, *Pitied but Not Entitled*, 4.

6. Deborah Mauldin, "Not by Bread Alone—Service Must Supplement Assistance," *Public Welfare* 5, no. 11 (November 1947): 242.

7. Good descriptions of the comprehensive nature of New Deal and Fair Deal social legislation can be found in Amenta and Skocpol, "Redefining the New Deal"; and Margaret Weir, "The Federal Government and Unemployment: The Frustration of Policy Innovation from the New Deal to the Great Society," in *The Politics of Social Policy in the United States*, ed. Margaret Weir, Ann Shola Orloff, and Theda Skocpol (Princeton, N.J.: Princeton University Press, 1988), 149–90.

8. Gordon, *Pitied but Not Entitled*, 274. In *Children's Interests/Mothers' Rights: The Shaping of America's Child Care Policy* (New Haven, Conn.: Yale University Press, 1999), Sonya Michel documents the interests of the Children's Bureau in child care policy.

9. Gordon, *Pitied but Not Entitled*, 212–13, 253–85. None of the original Progressive Era organizations played a major role in national-level welfare policy making in the 1930s or in the early postwar era. Generally speaking, private advocacy groups and social welfare groups active in the early twentieth century neither conducted research in the field of public welfare nor engaged in significant lobbying or other political action on federal welfare programs after the 1920s. They were not consulted by federal welfare officials or legislators for the major commissions on public assistance (1959, 1960,

1962), nor were they significant participants in the informal network that coalesced around national welfare policy in this period.

10. Elizabeth Wickenden Oral History, Social Security Project, interview 1, April 5, 1966, folder 5, box 16, EW Papers, WHS, 199. Both Altmeyer and Cohen were graduates of the University of Wisconsin and had mutual connections and shared ideas based on this experience. Cohen began his Washington policy career in 1934 at the Committee for Economic Security under Edwin Witte, his former professor of economics at the University of Wisconsin; Witte was a friend of Arthur Altmeyer. In 1935, when the Social Security Act was passed, Cohen went to work for Altmeyer.

11. Amenta and Skocpol, "Redefining the New Deal," 107. Berkowitz carefully charts the beginnings of Cohen's career in Social Security. Edward Berkowitz, *Mr. Social Security: The Life of Wilbur J. Cohen* (Lawrence: University Press of Kansas, 1995), 26–48.

12. Amenta and Skocpol point out that there is some dispute over who wrote the Wagner-Murray-Dingell legislation. See Amenta and Skocpol, "Redefining the New Deal," 92. Biographers of Wagner insist that he wrote it, while Martha Derthick says that Cohen wrote it. See J. Joseph Huthmacher, *Senator Robert F. Wagner and the Rise of Urban Liberalism* (New York: Atheneum, 1968), 292–93; and Martha Derthick, *Policy Making for Social Security* (Washington, D.C.: Brookings Institution, 1979), 84 n. 27. Berkowitz, Cohen's biographer, also insists that Cohen played a pivotal role in drafting the laws; Berkowitz, *Mr. Social Security*, 52, 55. Cohen's correspondence with Wagner in this period about the topic demonstrates that Cohen was drafting wording for Wagner's speeches and bills on social welfare policy. See letter to Wagner from Cohen, March 23, 1946, folder 4, box 27, WC Papers, WHS. In this letter, for example, Cohen refers to "drafting your statement" and to scheduling Wagner's testimony before congressional hearings.

13. John Jeffries's historiographical essay on the third New Deal points out the variety of motivations for and influences on the third New Deal. These ranged from liberals interested in regulatory policies, to those interested in compensatory Keynesian fiscal policy, to those interested in the welfare state. The latter two were most prominent in the NRPB's report, and were not mutually exclusive. Jeffries, "A Third New Deal?"

14. Social Security Administration, *Social Security Bulletin, Annual Statistical Supplement* (Washington, D.C.: U.S. Government Printing Office, 1973), 157. For example, ADC families increased from 162,000 in 1936 to 372,000 in 1940. Old Age Assistance recipients increased from 1,108,000 in 1936 to 2,070,000 in 1940.

15. In addition, the Wagner-Murray-Dingell Acts proposed equalizing public assistance payments among states, and increasing matching funds to states by the federal government.

16. Organizations advocating for the blind continued to be suspicious of any attempt to make a federal program noncategorical, as is evident in a letter Altmeyer wrote Cohen later in the 1940s about Altmeyer's discussions with a federal government staffer with connections to organizations for the blind: "I have been discussing our new Public Welfare Bill with Mr. Irwin. I have been trying to sell him on the idea he should support a comprehensive public welfare bill and then if he wishes to have any additional changes, like exemption of income or special provisions for the blind, to recom-

mend those special changes to the committee when hearings are held on the bill. In other words, I feel that if he would testify that he is in favor of the bill as far as it goes —rather than opposing it—we could make some progress." Memorandum to Arthur Altmeyer from Wilbur Cohen, February 17, 1947, folder 6, box 27, WC Papers, WHS.

17. From the 1940s to the 1960s, Reid of the CWLA battled, often with the support of the Children's Bureau, against proposals that combined welfare programs or functions into one program or oversight agency. Elizabeth Wickenden undertook a study called the Project on Public Services for Families and Children in 1960–61 and recommended combining welfare programs and welfare services for all people—adults and children—into one agency, for which she was excoriated publicly and privately by Reid and the CWLA and the Children's Bureau. See folder: NYSSW (Unmet Needs Project) 1960/61, box 2R382, FF Collection, CAH.

18. On organized labor, see Berkowitz, *Mr. Social Security*, 53–55; Skocpol and Amenta, "Redefining the New Deal," 115. On civil rights organizations, see Dona Hamilton and Charles Hamilton, *The Dual Agenda: Race and Social Welfare Policies of Civil Rights Organizations* (New York: Columbia University Press, 1997), 13–19.

19. Wickenden Oral History, December 12, 1986, folder 3, box 16, EW Papers, WHS, 16–18. On the founding of APWA, see Narayan Viswanathan, "The Role of the American Public Welfare Association in the Formulation and Development of Public Welfare Policies in the United States: 1930–1960" (D.S.W. thesis, Columbia University, 1961), 58–67; James Leiby, *A History of Social Welfare and Social Work in the United States, 1815–1972* (New York: Columbia University Press, 1978), 179; Blanche Coll, *Safety Net: Welfare and Social Security, 1929–1979* (New Brunswick, N.J.: Rutgers University Press, 1995), 17–18. One of the APWA's founders, Frank Bane, personally advised Harry Hopkins on FERA. Ibid., 21. Wickenden also discusses the founding of the APWA and the need for public administration. On the APWA's early activities, see Wickenden Oral History, December 12, 1986, 3.

20. Memorandum to the Commissioner of Internal Revenue, Internal Revenue Service, from American Public Welfare Association, Fred Hoehler, Director, October 6, 1941, folder 14, box 24, APWA Collection, SWHA, 2. Viswanathan, "The Role of the American Public Welfare Association," 102–18.

21. Coll, *Safety Net*, 69.

22. There are many accounts of the effects of both World War I and World War II on domestic arrangements in business, labor, education, health, and social welfare. See, for example, on World War I, David Kennedy, *Over Here: The First World War in American Society* (New York: Oxford University Press, 1980); and Allan Brandt, *No Magic Bullet: A Social History of Venereal Disease in the United States since 1880* (New York: Oxford University Press, 1985). On World War II, see Edward Berkowitz and Kim McQuaid, *Creating the Welfare State: The Political Economy of Twentieth-Century Reform* (Lawrence: University Press of Kansas, 1992), 148–51; David Brinkley, *Washington Goes to War* (New York: Knopf, 1988); Paul Koistinen, "The Hammer and the Sword: Labor, the Military and Industrial Mobilization, 1920–1945" (Ph.D. diss., University of California, Berkeley, 1965); Nelson Lichtenstein, *Labor's War at Home: The CIO in World War II* (New York: Cambridge University Press, 1983); Ruth Milkman, *Gender at Work: The Dynamics of Job Discrimination by Sex during World War II* (Urbana: University of Illinois Press, 1987).

23. Wickenden Oral History, December 12, 1986, 1–4; Viswanathan, "The Role of the American Public Welfare Association," 174–77.

24. According to Blanche Coll, "During the 1940s, the APWA greatly enlarged its interests, activities, and influence." Coll, *Safety Net*, 156.

25. Wickenden Oral History, December 12, 1986,14; Berkowitz, *Mr. Social Security*, 49, 53–55.

26. Wickenden Oral History, 9; Berkowitz, *Mr. Social Security*, 49, 53–55; Coll, *Safety Net*, 158–59, Viswanathan, "The Role of the American Public Welfare Association," 188–91.

27. The comprehensive social welfare bills were never even given hearings in Congress. Instead, when the Wagner-Murray-Dingell bill reached the floor, after being put to hearings and reported on in the Senate, it was in a different form that only emphasized medical care. See U.S. Congress, Senate, Committee on Education and Labor, *National Health Act of 1945, Report to the Committee on Education and Labor* (Washington, D.C.: U.S. Government Printing Office, 1946).

28. The growing conservativeness of the Congress in the late 1930s and 1940s is one of the most often cited explanations for the failure of the further expansion of the New Deal, and the literature referring to it is voluminous. On the specific defeat of social welfare, Jeffries provides a historiographical overview of the late New Deal and notes the role of the conservative Congress. Jeffries, "A Third New Deal?" See also Amenta and Skocpol, "Redefining the New Deal," 110, 111; A. Brinkley, *End of Reform*, 141–43.

29. On the rising power of big business during the war, see Berkowitz and McQuaid, *Creating the Welfare State*, 148. On growing power for business and the corresponding shifting goals of labor, see Nelson Lichtenstein, "The Eclipse of Social Democracy," in *The Rise and Fall of the New Deal Order*, ed. Steven Fraser and Gary Gerstle (Princeton, N.J.: Princeton University Press, 1989), 130–34, 140–45. On the privatization of the welfare state in general, see Beth Stevens, "Blurring the Boundaries: How the Federal Government Has Influenced Welfare Benefits in the Private Sector," in *The Politics of Social Policy in the United States*, ed. Margaret Weir, Ann Shola Orloff, and Theda Skocpol (Princeton, N.J.: Princeton University Press, 1988), 123–48; Jennifer Klein, *For All These Rights: Business, Labor, and the Shaping of America's Public-Private Welfare State* (Princeton, N.J.: Princeton University Press, 2003).

30. Amenta and Skocpol, "Redefining the New Deal," 111–12.

31. Winston linked her own political interests with those of the APWA and slowly and steadily directed the organization toward more active leadership and lobbying for ADC. All of her activities in the APWA in the early to mid-1950s reflected her belief that the APWA should be actively involved in promoting new ideas for legislation and supporting existing legislative proposals that met the APWA's approval. "Dr. Winston . . . emphasized the responsibility of the APWA to give leadership in meeting the needs of all the people dependent on public welfare." Minutes of the Meeting of the Committee on Welfare Policy, November 29, 1950, APWA Collection, SWHA, 2–4. Winston's stature within the APWA grew in the early 1950s as she became more active in the Welfare Policy Committee, of which she was named chair in 1953. See Marie Lane,

untitled list of members of the Committee on Welfare Policy, 1953, folder 13, box 6, APWA Collection, SWHA.

32. Dunn was aggressive in pursuing foundation grants to prop up the inefficient, ailing organization, to initiate new research, and to fund the Washington activities of Wickenden. She received substantial grants in her first few years as director from the Field Foundation. See Field Foundation, *Annual Report*, 1949 and 1951.

33. Wickenden Oral History, December 12, 1986, 5. Coll, *Safety Net*, 159.

34. Viswanathan, "The Role of the American Public Welfare Association," 213–14.

35. Wickenden Oral History, December 12, 1986, 5.

36. Ibid., 12.

37. Coll, *Safety Net*, 157; "Essentials of Public Welfare," folder 14, box 6, APWA Collection, SWHA. Regarding the APWA's "Essentials," see, above, n. 21 of the Introduction.

38. American Public Welfare Association, *Essentials of Public Welfare* (Chicago: APWA, 1952), 6.

39. Arthur Altmeyer, "Strengthening the Social Security Act," *Public Welfare* 8, nos. 8–9 (August–September 1950), 145.

40. As quoted in Coll, *Safety Net*, 159.

41. Viswanathan, "The Role of the American Public Welfare Association," 214. Viswanathan notes that "the Welfare Policy Committee's bold enunciation of the principles of public welfare contrast sharply with the evasive and sometimes clandestine approach to public welfare on the part of some individuals and groups" at the time.

42. The Cohen Papers include numerous drafts of legislation and correspondence regarding the drafts. It is clear that Cohen was one of the main authors, if not the main author, of the 1947 and 1949 bills. See folders 4 and 9, box 27, WC Papers, WHS; and HR 2892, 81st Congress, 1st session, in folder 2, box 49, WC Papers, WHS. The 1949 legislation in Cohen's papers constitutes a draft of the 1947 Forand bill, with just the date (1947) crossed out, a new definition of services written by Cohen, and a new line asking for promotion of research. For information on the 1947 proposed legislation, see HR 3636, 80th Congress, 1st session, in folder 3, box 49, WC Papers, WHS. Cohen and Wickenden communicated regularly about this legislation at formal meetings of the Welfare Policy Committee; Cohen gave the APWA the legislative proposals via the committee and told Wickenden that "before finally submitting it [the 1949 public welfare legislation draft] to Mr. Altmeyer and the Federal Security Administrator we would appreciate having any comments or suggestions from the Welfare Policy Committee of the APWA." Letter to Wickenden from Cohen, January 23, 1947, folder 6, box 48, WC Papers, WHS. But they also communicated about legislative proposals informally, outside the auspices of the Welfare Policy Committee, through informal memos and conversations. Concerning the 1947 public welfare bill alone, there are at least six memos between Cohen and Wickenden. See folder 6, box 48, WC Papers, WHS. In addition, Wickenden was often copied on Social Security Board memos and letters. See, for example, letter to Milton Patterson, Chairman, Committee on Welfare Policy, APWA, from Altemeyer, February 24, 1947, folder 6, box 27, WC Papers, WHS. Blanche Coll implies that the APWA may well have written the 1949 public welfare bill. Coll, *Safety Net*, 157.

43. Such a modest incremental approach to passing social legislation was typical of Wilbur Cohen's approach in later years, too, according to Edward Berkowitz. Berkowitz, *Mr. Social Security*, 49–93.

44. Memorandum from Cohen to Wickenden, March 12, 1948, folder 1, box 28, WC Papers, WHS, 1.

45. U.S. Congress, House of Representatives, *HR 2892*, 81st Congress, 1st session, February 21, 1949 (Washington, D.C.: U.S. Government Printing Office, 1950), 2.

46. Memorandum to APWA Welfare Policy Committee members from Wickenden, November 8, 1949, folder 3, box 49, EW Papers, WHS, 3.

47. Memorandum to Altmeyer from Goodwin, December 8, 1948, folder 2, box 49, WC Papers, WHS, 2.

48. I am grateful to Andrew Morris for sharing this quote with me. Jane Hoey, Minutes, Subcommittee on Community Organizations, 6/16/41, box 2, entry 59, RG 215, NA, copy in the possession of Andrew Morris.

49. Goodwin, for example, mentions this in her memorandum to Altmeyer, December 8, 1948, 1. Jane Hoey, director of the Bureau of Public Assistance, also made these requests in her correspondence with the Social Security commissioner and Wilbur Cohen. See memorandum to Altmeyer from Hoey, December 21, 1948, folder 2, box 49, WC Papers, WHS. In the late 1940s, the APWA repeatedly asked for greater federal monetary participation in the ADC program, the raising of ADC grants, the equalizing of grants among the states, and the inclusion of the caretaker in the ADC grant; throughout the 1950s and 1960s, the APWA continued to address these unresolved issues, both through the "Essentials of Public Welfare" statement and in the organization's legislative objectives and lobbying.

50. Titled "Future Citizens All," this was the first major national study of the ADC program. For information on the planning, execution, publication, and publicizing of the study, see folder 8, box 32, APWA Collection, SWHA.

51. Draft, Public Welfare Act of 1947: A Bill, November 27, 1946, folder 6, box 48, WC Papers, WHS, 1.

52. On casework in the early history of social work, see Clarke Chambers, *Seedtime of Reform: American Social Service and Social Action, 1918–1933* (Minneapolis: University of Minnesota Press, 1963), 87–101; Leiby, *A History of Social Welfare*, 183–86. On the Children's Bureau, see Robyn Muncy, *Creating a Female Dominion in American Reform, 1890–1935* (New York: Oxford University Press, 1991).

53. Leslie Leighninger, "Why Social Work Abandoned Public Welfare," paper presented at the *Journal of Policy History* Conference, St. Louis, Mo., May 27–30, 1999, 10. It should be noted that Hoey was not wholly antagonistic to casework; she thought it was quite useful but believed that overemphasis of social services blinded social workers to the need for income payments and structural changes in the welfare state. See Andrew Morris, "Charity, Therapy, and Poverty: Private Social Service in the Era of Public Welfare" (Ph.D. diss., University of Virginia, 2003), 201–2. For social work and public welfare in the 1930s, see Katz, *In the Shadow of the Poorhouse*, 263. Leiby discusses how social workers poured into the federal agencies in the 1930s but did not perform casework. Leiby, *A History of Social Welfare*, 243, 270–71.

54. In the 1940s, the major social work organization of the period—the American

Association of Social Workers—was not primarily concerned with public welfare, but rather with professionalization, education, and private casework. Not until the early 1960s would the renamed National Association of Social Workers play a primary role in policy making at the federal level in public welfare programs. See chap. 4.

55. Leiby, *A History of Social Welfare*, 268. On the revival of individual casework in private social work and some of its crossover into public welfare in the 1940s, see Morris, "Charity, Therapy, and Poverty," 199–218; Leiby, *A History of Social Welfare*, 272–83; Leighninger, "Why Social Work Abandoned Public Welfare." On the related trend of the growing influence of psychology during and after the war, see Nathan Hale Jr., *The Rise and Crisis of Psychoanalysis in the United States* (New York: Oxford University Press, 1995), 276–99.

56. Letter to Bane from Hoey, November 24, 1947, folder 2, box 49, WC Papers, WHS.

57. "Roundtable Conference," *Public Welfare* 12, no. 1 (January 1954), 30–31.

58. Committee on Welfare Policy, Preliminary Draft of "Statement of Welfare Principles," November 1950, folder 13, box 6, APWA Collection, SWHA, 2.

59. Wickenden Oral History, December 12, 1986, 6.

60. Memorandum to Altmeyer from Hoey, December 21, 1948.

61. Memorandum to Loula Dunn from Marie Lane, November 14, 1952, folder 13, box 6, APWA Collection, SWHA, 2. Lane refers back to the 1947 and 1949 positions of the Welfare Policy Committee in her 1952 memo.

62. Ibid.

63. Untitled memorandum, folder 6, box 48, WC Papers, WHS.

64. See U.S. Congress, House of Representatives, *HR 3636*, 80th Congress, 1st session, 1947 (Washington, D.C.: U.S. Government Printing Office, 1948).

65. The 1949 legislation in Cohen's papers is the 1947 Forand bill, with just the date (1947) crossed out, a new definition of services written by Cohen, and a new line asking for promotion of research. For information on the 1947 proposed legislation, see the bill that was to become HR 3636 of the 80th Congress, 1st session, which is marked up in Cohen's papers, folder 2, box 49, WHS. Although in 1948 a slim Democratic majority was elected in Congress, the Democrats elected were not necessarily supporters of the New Deal–Fair Deal social welfare agenda. As Skocpol and Amenta have pointed out, "If only there had been a larger urban-liberal majority in Congress," more of Truman's Fair Deal might have passed; but conservative, rural, or southern Democrats still held considerable power and voted with Republicans against welfare expansion. Amenta and Skocpol, "Redefining the New Deal," 118.

Chapter 2

1. Rudolph Danstedt, "A Possibility for Social Rehabilitation," *Public Welfare* 10, no. 2 (April 1952): 46, 48.

2. Wilbur Cohen and Fedele Fauri, "The Social Security Amendments of 1956," *Public Welfare* 14, no. 4 (October 1956): 193; U.S. Congress, House of Representatives, Committee on Ways and Means, *Hearings on Public Assistance Titles of the Social Security Act, 1956*,

84th Congress, 2nd session, April 12, 13, 16, 19, 20, 1956 (Washington, D.C.: U.S. Government Printing Office, 1957).

3. Gareth Davies, *From Opportunity to Entitlement: The Transformation and Decline of Great Society Liberalism* (Lawrence: University Press of Kansas, 1996), 10–53; Edward Berkowitz and Kim McQuaid, *Creating the Welfare State: The Political Economy of Twentieth-Century Reform* (Lawrence: University Press of Kansas, 1992), 165–92.

4. Thomas Waxter, "Aid to Dependent Children and the Public," paper presented at the APWA Annual Round Table Conference, Chicago, Ill., December 2, 1950, published in *Public Welfare* 9, no. 2 (February 1951): 44; R. Jarman, "Detroit Cracks Down on Relief Chiselers," *Saturday Evening Post*, December 10, 1949, 17–19; Hal Burton and Jacob Panker, "I Say Relief Is Ruining Families," *Saturday Evening Post*, September 30, 1950, 25, 111–15; "Why Does Relief Cost More Today Than under FDR?" (editorial), *Saturday Evening Post*, November 5, 1949, 10. Andrew Morris's research deals extensively with the local attacks in the late 1940s. He points out that in Baltimore, where Waxter was from, there was a particularly harsh backlash, and his comments at the APWA convention reflected his frustration and fear. Andrew Morris, "Charity, Therapy, and Poverty: Private Social Service in the Era of Public Welfare," (Ph.D. diss., University of Virginia, 2003), 254–76.

5. Katherine Hall Brooks, "Southeastern Regional Conference," *Public Welfare* 9, no. 10 (December 1951): 242.

6. Winifred Bell, *Aid to Dependent Children* (New York: Columbia University Press, 1965), 60.

7. Nancy Cauthen and Edwin Amenta, "Not for Widows Only: Institutional Politics and the Formative Years of Aid to Dependent Children," *American Sociological Review* 61 (June 1996): 427, 433.

8. Social Security Administration, *Social Security Bulletin, Annual Statistical Supplement* (Washington, D.C.: U.S. Government Printing Office, 1973), 157. ADC served 274,000 families in 1945 and 651,000 families in 1950.

9. Cauthen and Amenta, "Not for Widows Only," 427.

10. Morris, "Charity, Therapy, and Poverty," 254–76; Bell, *Aid to Dependent Children*, 59–61.

11. Social Security Administration, *Annual Statistical Supplement*, 157. Other welfare programs also grew: OAA grew from 2,056,000 to 2,786,000 in the same period; Aid to the Blind grew from 71,000 to 97,000; and the state programs of general assistance, not funded by the federal government, grew from 507,000 individuals per year to 866,000 recipients. None grew at the rate of ADC, however.

12. The National Association of County Officials faced the local dilemma, and its internal publications reflected this concern regarding taxes and welfare spending. See Alvin David, "New Social Security Legislation," *County Officer*, October 1950, 10–13.

13. The national Chamber of Commerce, for example, advocated ending federal grants for public assistance and forcing states and localities to bear the burden; then, public welfare rolls would be cut severely. Chamber of Commerce of the United States, Committee on Social Legislation, *Federal Grant-in-Aid Programs* (Washington, D.C.: Chamber of Commerce of the United States, 1954).

14. American Public Welfare Association, Committee on Welfare Policy, "The Cur-

rent Situation in Public Assistance," April 27, 1948, folder 14, box 6, APWA Collection, SWHA.

15. Anne Schneider and Helen Ingram, "Social Construction of Target Populations: Implications for Politics and Policy," *American Political Science Review* 87, no. 2 (June 1993): 334–47.

16. See Joanne Goodwin, *Gender and the Politics of Welfare Reform: Mothers' Pensions in Chicago, 1911–1929* (Chicago: University of Chicago Press, 1997); Linda Gordon, *Pitied but Not Entitled: Single Mothers and the History of Welfare, 1890–1935* (New York: Free Press, 1994); Molly Ladd-Taylor, *Mother-Work: Women, Child Welfare, and the State, 1890–1930* (Urbana: University of Illinois Press, 1995); and Theda Skocpol, *Protecting Soldiers and Mothers: The Political Origins of Social Policy in the United States* (Cambridge, Mass.: Belknap Press of Harvard University Press, 1992).

17. See Goodwin, *Gender and the Politics of Welfare Reform*, 73–80; Gordon, *Pitied but Not Entitled*; Gwendolyn Mink, "The Lady and the Tramp: Gender, Race, and the Origins of the American Welfare State," in *Women, the State, and Welfare*, ed. Linda Gordon (Madison: University of Wisconsin Press, 1990), 92–122.

18. Fred Steininger, "The Local Public Welfare Administrator and the Legislator," *Public Welfare* 9, no. 7 (August 1951): 165.

19. Joanne Goodwin, "'Employable Mothers' and 'Suitable Work': A Re-evaluation of Welfare and Wage-Earning for Women in the Twentieth-Century United States," *Journal of Social History* 29, no. 2 (Winter 1995): 261; James Patterson, *America's Struggle against Poverty, 1900–1994* (Cambridge, Mass.: Harvard University Press, 1994), 87–88. Welfare administrators's views regarding the negative consequences of some harsh ADC employment laws on motherhood can be found in Riley Mapes, "The Mother's Employment—Whose Decision in ADC?" *Public Welfare* 8, no. 4 (April 1950): 74.

20. Steininger, "The Local Public Welfare Administrator," 165.

21. Mary Overholt Peters, "Public Relations on a Local Level," *Public Welfare* 9, no. 3 (March 1951): 75.

22. Elroy Nelson, "A Business Man's Questions," and Herbert F. Kretchman, "How to Give the Answers," both in *Public Welfare* 13, no. 3 (July 1955): 115.

23. Fred Steininger, "Desertion and the ADC Program," *Public Welfare* 5, no. 10 (October 1947): 235. Also see, for example, Loula Dunn's editorial "What Has ADC Meant to Children?" *Public Welfare* 6, no. 4 (April 1948): 73.

24. Katherine Rickey, "Is Aid to Dependent Children Effective?" *Public Welfare* 5, no. 11 (November 1947): 249.

25. Bell, *Aid to Dependent Children*, 61.

26. Steininger, "Desertion and the ADC Program," 238. The desire of welfare professionals to bring clients further into the welfare system revealed a distinctive outcome of the revived interest in welfare dependency in the 1950s. In the late nineteenth century, poverty analysis made harsh distinctions between the worthy and unworthy, the moral and immoral poor, much as opponents of welfare did in the 1950s. However, in that earlier period, the analysis generated only a low level of social welfare provision. The more scientific interest of early social workers and reformers of the Progressive Era in dependency also focused on the problems of individuals who were poor, but generated only limited support for welfare provision, directed at individuals whose de-

pendency—primarily needy mothers—was considered acceptable. In the 1950s, by contrast, though welfare professionals focused sharply on the problems they perceived in unpopular clients, they were thoroughly committed to a large, fair, and expanding federal public welfare system. See also James Leiby, *A History of Social Welfare and Social Work in the United States, 1815–1972* (New York: Columbia University Press, 1978), 269: "The change experts had in mind was . . . toward a public welfare in which adequate and equitable assistance would combine with constructive services intended to help unfortunate people overcome the burden of deprivation and anxiety that society had hitherto misunderstood and tolerated."

27. Statement of John Tramburg, President, American Public Welfare Association, before the Senate Committee on Finance on Social Security Amendments, February 28, 1956, folder 2, box 21, APWA Collection, SWHA, 2; Leiby, *A History of Social Welfare*, 269.

28. Rickey, "Is Aid to Dependent Children Effective?" 249. As one case supervisor in Alabama, a state with very low welfare payments, noted, "The failure of our present ADC program stems not from the theory or principle on which it is based but from the inadequacy of the award." Blanche Saunders, "ADC—A Good Investment," *Public Welfare* 8, no. 5 (May 1950): 109.

29. Wilbur Cohen, "Basic Proposals and Principles of Public Assistance," paper prepared for the Central States Regional Conference of the APWA, Grand Rapids, Mich., June 16, 1954, folder 2, box 21, APWA Collection, SWHA, 9, 10.

30. Statement of John Tramburg, 9.

31. The effort to understand and reform the ADC program presented the APWA with an opportunity. Newly appointed director Loula Dunn told members in her inaugural editorial that welfare administrators had arrived at a crucial moment: "At no period during the lifetime of the APWA has its viability and clarity of purpose been more necessary or desirable." If, as Dunn hoped, the APWA took the lead in evaluating the ADC program, in investigating the changed clientele, and in gathering the expert information about the perceived trouble in the ADC program, then it would also have the advantage in interpreting and disseminating that knowledge and in making policy recommendations. See "What Has ADC Meant to Children?" 73.

32. Little has been written on Community Research Associates. James Leiby wrote briefly about the organization in 1978. See Leiby, *A History of Social Welfare*, 284. Recently, Andrew Morris has helped identify CRA as an important force in bringing private social work practices into public welfare. He emphasizes Buell's role for Community Chests in the 1930s—helping them restructure services to more efficiently handle clients—as formative for his later career in public welfare. Morris, "Charity, Therapy, and Poverty," 295–97; and Bradley Buell, "Stamford Studies Itself," *Survey Midmonthly* 53, no. 9 (September 1939): 270–73. For information on Community Research Associates, see CRA Collection, SWHA.

33. In the areas of military science and economics, RAND and the Brookings Institution are good examples. The RAND Corporation got its start after World War II in defense analysis. The Brookings Institution, although it had existed since the early twentieth century, entered a new phase of research and consulting for the federal government in the years after World War II.

34. For information on the growth of quasi-governmental research and consulting firms, and other similar "shadow government" organizations, see James Allen Smith, *The Idea Brokers: Think Tanks and the Rise of the New Policy Elite* (New York: Free Press, 1991).

35. Social welfare research consulting firms focused on public welfare policy rather than private welfare. This represented an important choice. At the time, research consulting firms probably could have made more money in private social welfare consulting. Organizations such as the Young Women's Christian Association, the Family Service Association of America, and the Child Welfare League of America, among others, were undertaking new community-based service programs in cities around the country, and often wanted help developing projects or evaluating them. Many social workers had, in fact, abandoned casework in the field of public welfare entirely, in order to take better-paying, higher-prestige jobs in private social work organizations. But the social workers of Community Research Associates and other consulting firms chose to specialize in federal public programs—focusing on how these programs were conceived and run at the federal, state, and local level. Their commitment to consulting in the field of public welfare raised the profile of welfare programs. Welfare, CRA's director Bradley Buell insisted, "is too precious a possession, too useful a community asset to take for granted." Bradley Buell, "We Know Better Than We Do," *Survey* (1951), 1 (article in the form of tear sheets in folder 3, box 1, CRA Collection, SWHA). An excellent study of this relationship between private social work and public welfare after World War II can be found in Morris, "Charity, Therapy, and Poverty," 290–333.

36. Buell, "We Know Better Than We Do," 1.

37. Ibid.

38. William T. Grant Foundation, *Modern Philanthropy and Human Welfare—A Roundtable* (New York: Grant Foundation, 1952), 5–6. Founded in 1936, the Grant Foundation engaged in a variety of activities in social welfare. The foundation funded social welfare projects ranging from health to human services, from education to recreation. In the late forties, the Grant Foundation gave a grant to CRA. The grant was for CRA's flagship study of rehabilitation in public welfare, in St. Paul, Minn. This study was the first to lay out the concepts of social disability and the first to provide the formal argument and model for the prevention of social disability and the rehabilitation of clients on welfare. After the conclusion of the St. Paul project, the Grant Foundation went on to generously fund similar CRA research projects concerning rehabilitation in welfare programs, with grants for several projects in excess of $500,000—a great deal for welfare professionals in the 1950s. It also published their findings regarding rehabilitation. See William T. Grant Foundation, *Annual Report, 1947–48* (in possession of author), 14–15. Also see folder 3, box 1, CRA Collection, SWHA.

39. Many foundations had explicitly opposed "ameliorative" or "palliative" projects that patched up existing problems in society. They preferred to undertake projects that prevented problems from occurring in the first place: public health projects, for example, that sought vaccinations or cures for worldwide diseases were model projects for many large foundations' grant making. Note that the Grant Foundation was not alone in becoming more involved in public welfare, however. Beginning in the late 1940s, the Field Foundation of Marshall Field III also became involved in welfare advocacy and

research. Its role will be discussed further in chaps. 3 and 4. In addition, the Russell Sage Foundation also funded efforts to improve public welfare in the 1940s and 1950s. In the 1950s, Russell Sage made large grants to schools of social work, such as the one at the University of Michigan, to promote the application of new social science theory and methodology to the field of public social programs. This marked a return to public welfare rather than a new entrance into the field. Russell Sage played a critical role in establishing the professional field of social work in the early twentieth century and in encouraging social work research, some of which, in turn, fostered the creation of social programs. But as federal public welfare programs were established in the 1930s, Russell Sage continued to focus more on the field of social work, social work theory, and casework rather than public welfare programs or public policy per se. On the activity of Russell Sage in the early twentieth century, see Judith Sealander, *Private Wealth and Public Life: Foundation Philanthropy and the Reshaping of American Social Policy from the Progressive Era to the New Deal* (Baltimore: Johns Hopkins University Press, 1997).

40. Grant Foundation, *Modern Philanthropy*, 5.

41. Ibid., 5–6 (emphasis added).

42. Ibid., 12 (emphasis added).

43. Bradley Buell, "Re-tooling for Human Betterment," November 1951, folder 3, box 1, CRA Collection, SWHA, 7.

44. Danstedt, "A Possibility for Social Rehabilitation," 46.

45. Stevenson quoted in Leon Lefson, "Rehabilitating Public Assistance Clients," *Public Welfare* 11, no. 2 (April 1953): 50.

46. Davies, *From Opportunity to Entitlement*, 36.

47. Interest in rehabilitation in the 1950s also recalled rehabilitation efforts in earlier eras. Quakers in the nineteenth century had hoped to change methods of criminal punishment, for example, by rehabilitating criminals to a productive life rather than simply punishing them. See David J. Rothman, "Perfecting the Prison," in *The Oxford History of the Prison: The Practice of Punishment in Western Society*, ed. Norval Morris and David J. Rothman (New York: Oxford University Press, 1995), 116–19. Edgardo Rotman has pointed out that the rehabilitative ideal, though lost in the 1930s and 1940s, was reestablished in prisons after World War II. See Edgardo Rotman, "The Failure of Reform," *The Oxford History of the Prison*, ed. Morris and Rothman, 188–89. In the late nineteenth and early twentieth centuries, the concept of rehabilitation became popular in the treatment of unwed mothers. Religiously inspired Florence Crittenden homes, for example, tried to rehabilitate "fallen women" by putting their children up for adoption and cleansing the soul of the unwed mother. See Regina Kunzel, *Fallen Women, Problem Girls: Unmarried Mothers and the Professionalization of Social Work, 1890–1945* (New Haven, Conn.: Yale University Press, 1993).

48. Berkowitz and McQuaid, *Creating the Welfare State*, 152–53. The OVR might have viewed the public welfare community's embrace of rehabilitation as a success—they had succeeded in convincing yet more people of the value of rehabilitation. But, instead, vocational rehabilitation advocates felt threatened when the public welfare community embraced rehabilitation and rehabilitative methods for their clients. Their fear of public welfare erupted in several important skirmishes over legislation and administration in the 1950s. The APWA's file on rehabilitation contains a flurry of internal

memos and letters to both state administrators and the Bureau of Public Assistance aimed at trying to determine whether state public assistance agencies can get some vocational rehabilitation (specifically, P.L. 565) funds for their rehabilitative activities. See, for example, letter to Arughru Rivers from Marie Lane, October 25, 1955; memorandum to Loula Dunn from Marie Lane, August 19, 1954; or memorandum to James Garret, Office of Vocational Rehabilitation, from Corrine Wolfe, Division of Technical Training, BPA, October 26, 1954; all in folders 18 and 19, box 25, APWA Collection, SWHA.

49. Leiby, *A History of Social Welfare*, 280.

50. Danstedt, "A Possibility for Social Rehabilitation," 48. See also Leiby, *A History of Social Welfare*, 181–84, 280–90, on the medical model of rehabilitation.

51. Frank Higgins, "Maid to Order: A Practicable Training Program to Meet a Community Need," *Public Welfare* 11, no. 3 (July 1953): 8.

52. Buell, "Re-tooling for Human Betterment," 7.

53. Deborah Mauldin, "Not By Bread Alone—Service Must Supplement Assistance," *Public Welfare* 5, no. 11 (November 1947): 242.

54. Buell, "Re-tooling for Human Betterment," 3.

55. By 1957 ADC had become the largest federal public assistance program, outstripping the Old Age Assistance program. Social Security Administration, *Annual Statistical Supplement*, 157. Moreover, as CRA noted, ADC, with its youthful clientele, offered the greatest possibilities of rehabilitating individuals to self-care and self-support.

56. Talcott Parsons and Robert Bales, *Family, Socialization and Interaction Process* (Glencoe, Ill.: Free Press, 1955); W. Allison Davis and Robert Havighurst, *Father of the Man: How Your Child Gets His Personality* (Boston: Houghton Mifflin, 1947).

57. Fears of the degeneration of youth and families flourished in the early Cold War. See James Gilbert, *A Cycle of Outrage: America's Reaction to the Juvenile Delinquent in the 1950s* (New York: Oxford University Press, 1986); William Graebner, *Coming of Age in Buffalo: Youth and Authority in the Postwar Era* (Philadelphia: Temple University Press, 1990); William Reese, "*Reefer Madness* and *A Clockwork Orange*," in *Learning from the Past: What History Teaches Us about School Reform*, ed. Maris Vinovskis and Diane Ravitch (Baltimore: Johns Hopkins University Press, 1995), 355–81; Elaine Tyler May, *Homeward Bound: American Families in the Cold War Era* (New York: Basic Books, 1988).

58. For secondary sources on the relationship between nuclear family ideology and ADC, see Bell, *Aid to Dependent Children*; Michael Katz, *The Undeserving Poor: From the War on Poverty to the War on Welfare* (New York: Pantheon Books, 1989); Kunzel, *Fallen Women*; Constance Nathanson, *Dangerous Passage: The Social Control of Sexuality in Women's Adolescence* (Philadelphia: Temple University Press, 1993); Rickie Solinger, *Wake Up Little Susie: Race and Single Pregnancy before* Roe v. Wade (New York: Routledge, 1992).

59. Kunzel, *Fallen Women*. These distinctions between social patterns and psychology were based on race. Whites were seen as having psychological problems, while African Americans were seen as playing out distinct social group patterns of sexual-familial behavior.

60. Clifford Brenner, "Illegitimacy and Aid to Dependent Children," *Public Welfare* 8, no. 10 (October 1950): 175.

61. Ibid., 174. For another example, see Mildred Stoves, "Ten Years of ADC in Tennessee," *Public Welfare* 6, no. 2 (February 1948): 33.

62. On the pathologizing of African American families, see two studies by Daryl Michael Scott: "The Politics of Pathology: The Ideological Origins of the Moynihan Controversy," *Journal of Policy History* 8, no. 1 (1996): 81–105; and *Contempt and Pity: Social Policy and the Image of the Damaged Black Psyche, 1880–1996* (Chapel Hill: University of North Carolina Press, 1997). Scott argues that the pathologizing of the African American family occurred earlier and was a product of African American as well as white researchers and commentators.

63. Brenner, "Illegitimacy and Aid to Dependent Children," 175, 176. Brenner, for example, while talking openly about race, also used these code phrases in his article.

64. Buell, "We Know Better Than We Do," 3. This fear of the connection between family degeneracy and welfare dependency must be carefully distinguished from the strain of thought that families were long-term vectors of dependency through the transmission of a "culture" of dependency, commonly referred to as the culture of poverty. Welfare professionals in this period did not use the language of culture or imply the kind of "cultural heredity" from generation to generation that is the hallmark of "culture of poverty" thinking.

65. Ibid.

66. Buell, "Re-tooling for Human Betterment," 3. Morris also discusses CRA and its Family Centered Project. See Morris, "Charity, Therapy, and Poverty," 290–333.

67. Leiby, *A History of Social Welfare*, 267.

68. Statement of John Tramburg, 11.

69. Buell, "We Know Better Than We Do," 3.

70. C. E. A. Winslow, quoted in Grant Foundation, *Modern Philanthropy*, 37.

71. U.S. Department of Health, Education, and Welfare, *Annual Report of the Department of Health, Education, and Welfare, 1955*, (Washington, D.C.: U.S. Government Printing Office, 1956), 45.

72. Bureau of Public Assistance, "Self Support and Self Care of the Needy," draft, October 11, 1955, folder 6, box 49, WC Papers, WHS, 3.

73. While many believed work was harmful for family life, they agreed that it was not as harmful for working-class and nonwhite women. These experts seemed to value white middle-class women's mothering skills more than those of working-class and nonwhite women. One of the best accounts of the debate over mothers' roles in the period can be found in Sonya Michel, *Children's Interests, Mothers' Rights: The Shaping of America's Child Care Policy* (New Haven, Conn.: Yale University Press, 1999), 150–91.

74. Miscellaneous memorandum, n.d. [ca. 1955], folder 2, box 21, APWA Collection, 2.

75. Lefson, "Rehabilitating Public Assistance Clients," 47.

76. Michel, *Children's Interests*, 187.

77. Elaine Burgess, "Some Comments on the Emphasis and Rationale of the Present Study," 1961, folder 13, box 33, APWA Collection, SWHA, 3.

78. Winifred Bell, "Casework with Chronically Dependent Families," March 1957, folder 8, box 1, EW Papers, WHS, 3. She would later become a federal policy maker and author of the first major history of the ADC program, *Aid to Dependent Children*.

79. Jo Ann Hardee, "Most ADC Families Receive Inadequate Aid, Study Finds," *Detroit News*, May 9, 1963, folder 4, box 34, APWA Collection, SWHA.

80. Danstedt, "A Possibility for Social Rehabilitation," 47.

81. Bell, "Casework with Chronically Dependent Families," 3.

82. American Public Welfare Association press release, "An American Dependency Challenge," May 9, 1963, folder 7, box 34, APWA Collection, SWHA, 3; Bell, "Casework with Chronically Dependent Families," 2.

83. Alice Mertz, "Working Mothers in the Aid to Dependent Children Program," *Public Welfare* 10, no. 3 (July 1952): 66–67.

84. Ibid. This was what some psychologists were arguing about women of the middle class who were taking up employment, too, although the argument became more common in the 1960s and 1970s.

85. Bell, "Casework with Chronically Dependent Families," 2.

86. Sydney Bernard, "Escanaba Report," speech delivered June 27, 1960, folder 3, box 73, WC Papers, WHS, 4.

87. Community Research Associates, "A New Family Rehabilitation Program," City and County of San Francisco Welfare Department, April 4, 1961, folder 10, box 17, CRA Collection, SWHA; Bell, "Casework with Chronically Dependent Families," 7.

88. Danstedt, "A Possibility for Social Rehabilitation," 48.

89. Bell, "Casework with Chronically Dependent Families," 5–6.

90. Wilbur Cohen and Sydney Bernard, "Reducing Dependency: A Report of a Demonstration and Research Project among Direct Relief Recipients in Washtenaw County, Michigan" (Ann Arbor: University of Michigan School of Social Work, 1960), chap. 8, pp. 16, 15.

91. Community Research Associates, "New Directions in ADC," Overseers of the Public Welfare, City of Boston, April 2, 1959, folder 2, box 17, CRA Collection, SWHA, 26; Community Research Associates, "A New Family Rehabilitation Program," D-13. CRA's Boston ADC study tracked caseloads each month throughout the year. Thus figures from the April 1959 report differ slightly from those of the November 1959 report in tables 1 and 2.

92. Lefson, "Rehabilitating Public Assistance Clients," 47.

93. Bernard, "Escanaba Report"; Sydney Bernard, "Presentation to Juvenile Court Advisory Council," March 14, 1960, folder 3, box 73, WC Papers, WHS; Bell, "Casework with Chronically Dependent Families," 5.

94. Welfare policy thus followed the general trend in women's labor in the 1950s. After World War II, "women were forced . . . into traditionally female occupations." Although they had experienced a temporary respite from sex-segregation during the male labor shortage during World War II, the period after the war witnessed a concerted effort to reestablish the pattern of sex-segregated occupations. Ruth Milkman, *Gender at Work: The Dynamics of Job Discrimination by Sex during World War II* (Urbana: University of Illinois Press, 1987), 1. For more on sex segregation and working women's reactions, see Dorothy Sue Cobble, "Recapturing Working-Class Feminism: Union Women in the Postwar Era," in *Not June Cleaver: Women and Gender in Postwar America, 1945–1960*, ed. Joanne Meyerowitz (Philadelphia: Temple University Press, 1994), 57–83.

95. Higgins, "Maid to Order," 88.

96. See Goodwin, *Gender and the Politics of Welfare Reform*; Gordon, *Pitied but Not Entitled*; Ladd-Taylor, *Mother-Work*; and Skocpol, *Protecting Soldiers and Mothers*.

97. Cohen and Bernard, "Reducing Dependency," 4.

98. Community Research Associates, "Family Classification Schedule," Boston ADC Project, January 1, 1959, folder 2, box 17, CRA Collection, SWHA, 12.

99. Ibid., 15.

100. Community Research Associates, "A New Family Rehabilitation Program," D-7.

101. Bernard, "Escanaba Report."

102. Case of Gerlinda Bullard, Washtenaw County Public Welfare Department Study, folder 4, box 73, WC Papers, WHS.

103. After nearly eight years of lobbying by liberals and the APWA and other welfare supporters, a federal cabinet-level department of health, education, and welfare was created in 1953. Nelson Rockefeller, undersecretary of HEW, was critical to its creation. See NAR Collection, series O—Washington, D.C., files, SCOGO, folders 421, 427, 428, box 44, and folder 386, box 45, RAC.

104. Historians have argued that the Republican Eisenhower administration supported rehabilitation in general and in welfare programs in particular, because it promised to "lower the long-range cost of assistance." See Patterson, *America's Struggle against Poverty*, 131. But the Eisenhower administration was aware that rehabilitation was, in fact, an extension of welfare provision and an expansion of federal responsibility and spending. Neither Commissioner of Social Security Charles Schottland nor Director of the Bureau of Public Assistance Jay Roney, for example, would testify before Congress that rehabilitation would reduce welfare costs. The Eisenhower administration pursued rehabilitation not so much because it promised to reduce costs, but because it promised a more effective, efficient welfare system. This was in large part due to the influence of Eisenhower's secretaries of health, education and welfare, first Oveta Culp Hobby, a wealthy publisher from Houston, Texas, and then Marion Folsom, a chief executive of the Eastman-Kodak Corporation. See U.S. Congress, House, Committee on Ways and Means, *Hearings on Public Assistance Titles*, 3–10.

105. "Further Suggestions for Additions to Mr. Cohen's Kit of Materials for Mr. Tramburg," n.d. [1953], folder 6, box 49, WC Papers, WHS.

106. Memorandum from Schottland to Roswell Perkins, September 29, 1954, folder 6, box 49, WC Papers, WHS, 1–2.

107. Bureau of Public Assistance, "Self Support and Self Care of the Needy," 1.

108. Cohen and Fauri, "The 1956 Social Security Amendments," 195.

109. On Folsom's work on unemployment and Social Security in the Eisenhower administration, see Sanford Jacoby, *Modern Manors: Welfare Capitalism since the New Deal* (Princeton, N.J.: Princeton University Press, 1997), 204, 206–7, 218–19.

110. Marion Folsom, "Stop Want at the Source," *Nation's Business*, January 1956, 44–47. He was also interviewed for a story on rehabilitation; see "Folsom's Aim: To Cut the Roots of Poverty," *Business Week*, December 24, 1955, 60–64. The articles illustrated his belief that rehabilitative welfare reform was efficient and effective; he argued that rehabilitation would "cut the roots of poverty" and "stop want at the source."

111. Cohen later commented that "the comprehensive and far-reaching character of the 1956 Amendments would not have been possible without the interest and cooperation of informed welfare personnel." See Cohen and Fauri, "The 1956 Social Security Amendments," 195, 198, 199.

112. From 1951 to 1954, when Republicans dominated Congress, Democrats had

not been able to pass any substantial welfare legislation. A series of APWA-supported bills by Aime Forand (D-R.I.) had been defeated. In 1956, however, moderate Republicans allied with the Eisenhower administration were able to work with the Democratic majority to form a bipartisan alliance on welfare. The 1950s thus marked the advent of what historian Julian Zelizer has recently demonstrated to be a "liberal alliance" founded on the basic components of state-building in the twenty-five years after World War II. Led by Representative Wilbur Mills (D-Ark.) of the House Ways and Means Committee, the bipartisan agreement on retaining the tax power of the federal government at relatively high and consistent levels allowed federal legislators to bypass antistatist state legislators who wanted to cut welfare spending. See Julian Zelizer, *Taxing America: Wilbur D. Mills, Congress, and the State, 1945–1975* (New York: Cambridge University Press, 1998), 2–3.

113. Cohen worked on the bill with the Eisenhower administration as he simultaneously consulted with his Senate contacts, thus ensuring Democratic approval. Both Cooper and Kerr had long-standing relationships with Cohen and with the American Public Welfare Association. For a good legislative history of the welfare provision of the 1956 Social Security Amendments, covering the period from 1952 to 1956, see Cohen and Fauri, "The 1956 Public Welfare Amendments," 193–98. The House passed the bill by a 372–31 vote, and the Senate passed it by a 90–0 vote. The bill that emerged from conference was also passed overwhelmingly by voice votes in both houses.

114. Ibid., 193.

115. Ibid. The law also encouraged the long-term success of rehabilitation by authorizing the training of welfare professionals and providing, "for the first time, authorization for federal money to be made available for research and demonstration projects in the field of Social Security." There were not enough professionally trained social workers to accomplish rehabilitation. See Donald Howard, "More and Better Training for Public Welfare: A Concern of Agencies and Schools" (editorial), *Public Welfare* 9, no. 7 (August 1951): 153. Almost every formal statement for rehabilitative philosophy and its application to the federal public welfare system, therefore, was accompanied by some recognition that trained social workers were required and that training needed more emphasis and funding. In addition to the call for training, rehabilitation advocates incorporated requests for federal funding of welfare research into their agenda for welfare reform. Research and demonstration projects funded by foundations had provided the means for developing the concept of rehabilitation and disseminating it. Welfare professionals were convinced that the dynamic interaction between research and demonstration and improvements in public policy must be institutionalized. See Statement of John Tramburg, 11. One last thing that the law required was that states specify what rehabilitative services they planned to use. States would have to "outline the services, if any, that they are provided under each of the four assistance programs and . . . the steps taken to assure maximum use of other agencies providing similar or related services." Cohen and Fauri, "The 1956 Public Welfare Amendments," 193.

116. Berkowitz, *Mr. Social Security*, 106, 107.

117. Letter to Elizabeth Wickenden from Wilbur Cohen, January 4, 1957, folder 3, box 12, EW Papers, WHS.

118. Letter to Jere Cooper from Wilbur Cohen, July 25, 1956, folder 2, box 60, WC Papers, WHS.

119. Loula Dunn, "1956—Year of Significance," *Public Welfare* 15, no. 2 (April 1957): 41, 42.

120. "The Work at Hand" (editorial), *Public Welfare* 15, no. 3 (July 1957): 85.

121. Ibid.

122. In 1956 the reimbursement rate of the federal government to the states for ADC payments was 14/17 of the first $17 of each individual welfare payment and one-half of the balance of payments, up to a maximum of $32, of each individual welfare payment. (Note that "individual welfare payment" refers to the amount paid to each member of a family, including the caretaker and children.) Cohen and Fauri, "The 1956 Social Security Amendments," 192.

123. Although, as the legislation acknowledged, the very idea of including social services as an important component of welfare had come from research and demonstration projects at the state or local level, states would not provide new or more services unless they received higher federal matching funds. Most states simply could not afford services on their own, and those that could subsidize some nevertheless could not afford to expand them significantly.

Chapter 3

1. These can be found in folder: Welfare Council of Metropolitan Chicago—ADC Report, 1960, box 2T6, FF Collection, CAH.

2. Race relations were then referred to as "inter-group" relations.

3. Transcript of telephone conversation between Max Hahn and Loula Dunn, April 1961, folder: APWA S.A. 1960 (ADC study) 1960–61, box 2T39, FF Collection, CAH, 2.

4. For a wonderful discussion of the use of social science techniques in not merely reflecting but also creating Americans' concepts of themselves at midcentury, see Sarah Igo, "America Surveyed: The Making of a Social Scientific Public, 1920–1960" (Ph.D. diss., Princeton University, 2001).

5. Sarah Igo, "Arguing with Gallup and Kinsey: Popular Challenges to Social Statistics, 1936–1953," paper presented at the Organization of American Historians Annual Meeting, Los Angeles, 2001.

6. Use of social science techniques to inform policy was closely related to the development of think tanks. See James Allen Smith, *The Idea Brokers: Think Tanks and the Rise of the New Policy Elite* (New York: Free Press, 1991). On social science applications to law in postwar America, particularly desegregation, see John Jackson Jr., *Social Scientists for Social Justice: Making the Case against Segregation* (New York: New York University Press, 2001); and John Jackson Jr., "Coopting the Culture Concept: Social Science in Defense of Segregation," paper presented at the Organization of American Historians Annual Meeting, Los Angeles, 2001.

7. Letter to Max Hahn from Loula Dunn, March 10, 1960, folder: APWA S.A. 1960 (ADC study), 1960–61, box 2T39, FF Collection, CAH, 1.

8. Minutes of Conference of Dr. Wilbur Cohen, Judge Justine Polier, and Maxwell Hahn, New York City, April 29, 1961, folder: Ad Hoc Committee on Public Welfare, box 4X102, FF Collection, CAH. The change of the program's name to Aid to Families with Dependent Children would officially occur on Cohen's watch as assistant sec-

retary of legislation in the Department of Health, Education, and Welfare in late 1962.

9. The APWA selected "case supervisors, program supervisors, administrators, field staff, and staff development personnel" from around the country to fan out to educate welfare departments about the new purpose of welfare. In conjunction with this, the APWA used regional and national conferences, pamphlets, bulletins, its monthly journal *Public Welfare*, and consultative services to communicate their messages to state officials. "Rockefeller Grant—Implementing 1956 Amendments," folder 12, box 27, APWA Collection, SWHA, 1. For more information on the grant and the project, see folder 623, box 93, RBF Collection, RAC. The APWA received financial help for this from the Rockefeller Brothers Fund, which provided the group with a $75,000 grant over three years, from 1957 to 1959. Traditionally, the Rockefeller Brothers Fund—unlike the Grant Foundation or the Field Foundation—was not involved in welfare reform research. The fund had, however, supported the APWA before. Moreover, the Rockefeller family had been the original sponsors of the APWA at its founding and early development through the Laura Spellman [née Rockefeller] Fund; since the Spellman grant was limited to a set term of years and expired in the early 1940s, perhaps there was a lingering sense of family obligation to help the APWA afterward.

10. "Rockefeller Grant—Implementing 1956 Amendments," folder 12, box 27, APWA Collection, SWHA, page 1.

11. Quote from Elaine Burgess, Advisory Committee Meeting of the Study of Aid to Dependent Children, APWA, Washington D.C., October 28, 1961, folder 33, box 5, APWA Collection, SWHA, 2.

12. Ibid., 2, 3, emphasis in original.

13. Institute for Research in Social Science, University of North Carolina, Chapel Hill, for American Public Welfare Association, "Study of Aid to Dependent Children Program," ca. December 1960, folder 12, box 33, APWA Collection, SWHA, 8, 10, 11.

14. Quote from Elaine Burgess, Advisory Committee Meeting of the Study of Aid to Dependent Children, 4. State public welfare directors, who wrote into the APWA regarding the focus of the study, echoed the need to answer criticisms and provide solutions. M. H. Brooks of Mississippi wrote to the APWA to point out that "we need rather urgently to have more definite information to use in program planning and evaluation, as (1) from what source and from what causes does criticism continue to come about this program; and (2) how can we in pubic welfare agencies do a better job with these families." Letter to Loula Dunn from M. H. Brooks, August 11, 1960, folder 33, box 10, APWA Collection, SWHA, 1.

15. Quote from Elaine Burgess, Advisory Committee Meeting of the Study of Aid to Dependent Children, 4–5.

16. Nora Stirling, Family Services Association of America, *The Pink Telephone*, Plays for Living (Chicago: American Public Welfare Association, n.d.), folder APWA, 1940–1962, FF Collection, CAH. Dumpson's endorsement was included in the printed edition of the play.

17. Draft statement, Foster Home Demonstration Project, Field Papers, Bound Docket, Children's Committee, January 25, 1960, FF Collection, CAH, 1.

18. Foster Home Demonstration Project, Field Papers, Bound Docket, Children's Committee, January 25, 1961, FF Collection, CAH, 4, 1.

19. Ibid., 5.

20. Draft statement, Foster Home Demonstration Project, Field Papers, Bound Docket, Children's Committee, January 25, 1960, FF Collection, CAH, 2.

21. Patricia Garland, "Public Assistance Families: A Resource for Foster Care," *Child Welfare*, September 1961, 4.

22. Ibid.

23. Ibid. Garland's six-page article in *Child Welfare*, which served as publicity for the project, includes one line on page 4 that states "the majority of these families are Negro."

24. By the 1960s, when poverty among black and white male-headed households, and among white female-headed households declined, the rate of poverty among black female-headed households rose. James Patterson, *America's Struggle against Poverty, 1900–1985* (Cambridge, Mass.: Harvard University Press, 1986), 81; National Research Council, *A Common Destiny: Blacks and American Society* (Washington, D.C.: National Academy Press, 1989), 280–81. American Public Welfare Association Board of Directors, "Public Welfare Services and Aid to Dependent Children: A Statement of Program Objectives," December 5, 1960, folder 8, box 4, APWA Collection, SWHA, 3.

25. APWA Board of Directors, "Public Welfare Services and Aid to Dependent Children," 3.

26. Wilbur Cohen, preliminary draft, "Poverty and Low Incomes in the United States," Committee for Economic Development, August 4, 1956, folder 7, box 69, WC Papers, WHS, 4; Wilbur Cohen, Agenda, Meeting of Advisory Committee on Low Income Groups, Committee for Economic Development, November 29, 1956, folder 7, box 69, WC Papers, WHS, 1.

27. Wilbur Cohen, "Low Incomes," n.d., folder 7, box 69, WC Papers, WHS, 1.

28. Marion Gross, "Preliminary Summary of Major Topics Discussed by the Faculty Seminar on Income Maintenance—1956–1957," n.d., folder 8, box 70, WC Papers, WHS, 3.

29. Advisory Council on Public Assistance, "Public Assistance," folder 9, box 38, APWA Collection, SWHA, 16. Convened by President Eisenhower, this panel was ineffective because it conducted its work just before an election year.

30. Josephine J. Williams, "Negro ADC Mothers Look for Jobs: An Attempt to Predict Employability—A Report Based on a Study of Aid to Dependent Children Cases Closed Because of the Potential Employability of the Mother, Detroit, Michigan" (Ann Arbor: University of Michigan School of Social Work, 1955), UMSSW, BL.

31. Winifred Bell, "Casework with Chronically Dependent Families," March 1957, folder 8, box 1, EW Papers, WHS, 5. On child care and racial discrimination, see Sonya Michel, *Children's Interests/Mothers' Rights: The Shaping of America's Child Care Policy* (New Haven, Conn.: Yale University Press, 1999), 170–71, 181.

32. Letter to Margaret Hickey, editor of the *Ladies Home Journal*, from Max Hahn, June 27, 1956, folder: American Public Welfare Association (ADC Study), box 2T31, FF Collection, CAH.

33. "The Negro mother has always worked in the past," a Louisiana Tax Code official proclaimed. "Now the mother has quit work. She stays at home." The official explained that in denying the African American mother welfare, "nobody wants to make the children suffer. What they want is for the mother to get out and work." Winifred

Bell, *Aid to Dependent Children* (New York: Columbia University Press, 1965), 63–64; see also Mimi Abramowitz, *Regulating the Lives of Women: Social Welfare Policy from Colonial Times to the Present*, rev. ed. (Boston: South End Press, 1996), 319–29; Joanne Goodwin, "'Employable Mothers' and 'Suitable Work': A Re-evaluation of Welfare and Wage-Earning for Women in the Twentieth-Century United States," *Journal of Social History* 29 (Winter 1995): 258–62.

34. Hahn's file in the Field Foundation Collection contains articles on ADC, letters written by ADC recipients complaining of their treatment, letters from the Cook County, Ill., director of public welfare, and letters written by Hahn trying to draw attention to the racial nature of ADC attacks. The quote from Hahn comes from letter to Hickey from Hahn, June 27, 1956.

35. Winifred Bell began her research on the suitable home provision for a Ph.D. dissertation in 1960, with funding from the Field Foundation. See folder: New York School of Social Work (Winifred Bell's dissertation) 63, and folder: NYSSW (Winifred Bell's dissertation) 61, box 2R383, FF Collection, CAH.

36. Later in the 1960s and 1970s, the Field Foundation would make civil rights within the welfare system a priority when it funded a variety of grassroots organizations, including the National Welfare Rights Organization, that were committed to this issue.

37. See folder 1, box 21, and box 20, for the yearly federal legislative objectives, APWA Collection, SWHA.

38. Welfare policy makers rarely spoke or wrote to each other openly about this ban on racial statistics. A frank exception is a discussion between Whitney Young, president of the National Urban League, and Elizabeth Wickenden in 1962. Wickenden provoked the conversation because her friend and colleague Winifred Bell was finishing up her dissertation on the suitable home provision and was having trouble finding and using racial statistics. Wickenden wrote: "She is currently doing her dissertation on suitable home requirements—in which factors of attitudes toward Negroes play a major role—and finds herself terribly handicapped by lack of studies etc. in which racial breakdown is indicated. She feels you would do well to urge HEW to get more rather than less racial identification in their studies and statistics." Letter to Whitney Young from Elizabeth Wickenden, April 16, 1962, and letter to Elizabeth Wickenden from Whitney Young, May 1, 1962, folder: NSWA, Ad Hoc Committee, 1961, box 37, series I A, part II, NUL Collection, LC.

39. The first CRA report on ADC and rehabilitation that both recorded and provided racial statistics was prepared in 1962 for the San Francisco Department of Public Welfare. See Community Research Associates, "Rehabilitation for Independence: A Report of the Family Rehabilitation Program," City and County of San Francisco Public Welfare Department, November 29, 1962, folder 10, box 17, CRA Collection, SWHA.

40. See Edwin J. Thomas and Donna McLeod, "The Effectiveness of In-Service Training and of Reduced Workloads in Aid to Dependent Children: A Report of an Experiment Conducted in Michigan" (Ann Arbor: University of Michigan School of Social Work, 1957), UMSSW Collection, BL; Donna McLeod and Lydia Hylton, "An Evaluation of a Method for Administering In-Service Training in Aid to Dependent Children: A Report of the Second of Two Experiments Conducted in Michigan" (Ann Arbor: University of Michigan School of Social Work, 1958), UMSSW Collection, BL.

On Wickenden's study, see her "Project on Public Services for Families and Children," folder 7, box 1, EW Papers, WHS. Even background materials do not mention race. On Cohen's studies, see Wilbur Cohen and Sydney Bernard, *The Prevention and Reduction of Dependency* (Ann Arbor: Washtenaw County Department of Social Welfare, 1961); and folders 3 and 5, box 73, WC Papers, WHS.

41. Letter to Young from Wickenden, April 16, 1962.

42. Letter to Max Hahn from Robert Lansdale, May 20, 1963, folder: NYSSW (Winifred Bell's dissertation) 63, box 2R383, FF Collection, CAH, 3.

43. In addition, Wilbur Mills had limited sympathy for programs like ADC whose funding came out of the general tax revenues; he preferred social programs like Social Security and unemployment insurance that were supported directly through payroll taxes. Julian Zelizer, *Taxing America: Wilbur D. Mills, Congress, and the State, 1945–1975* (New York: Cambridge University Press, 1998).

44. Wilbur Cohen Oral History, tape 6, LBJL, 17.

45. Walter Jackson, *Gunnar Myrdal and America's Conscience: Social Engineering and Racial Liberalism, 1938–1987* (Chapel Hill: University of North Carolina Press, 1990), 272; Gunnar Myrdal, *An American Dilemma: The Negro Problem and Modern Democracy* (New York: Harper and Brothers, 1944).

46. W. Jackson, *Gunnar Myrdal*, 271, 272.

47. Ibid., 271, 272; NSWA, Ad Hoc Committee, 1961, box 37, series I A, part II, NUL Collection, LC. See also Charles Bourne, "History of the Field Foundation" (unpublished manuscript), FF Collection, CAH. Bourne also describes the dilemma of Myrdalian liberalism. That liberalism was content to point out the problems of racism, believing that the mere existence of the moral contradiction would compel positive action.

48. W. Jackson, *Gunnar Myrdal*, 253.

49. Ibid., 253–54. Jackson quotes the work of Frank Tannenbaum, historian at Columbia University, and of D. W. Borgan, historian at Cambridge University, as examples of this thinking.

50. Transcript of telephone conversation between Maxwell Hahn and Joseph Reid, February 28, 1962, folder: NYSSW (Winifred Bell's dissertation), 1961, box 2R383, FF Collection, CAH, 1.

51. W. Jackson, *Gunnar Myrdal*, quotes on 286 (Williams), 288 (Adorno), with a larger discussion on 279–93. Another cogent discussion of the treatment of race by liberals appears in Frank Füredi's *The Silent War: Imperialism and the Changing Perception of Race* (New Brunswick, N.J.: Rutgers University Press, 1998).

52. Füredi, *The Silent War*, 2.

53. The study was titled "Aid to Dependent Children." Elaine Burgess, "Some Comments on the Emphasis and Rationale of the Present Study . . . ," 1961, folder 13, box 33, APWA Collection, SWHA, 4.

54. Minutes of the Advisory Committee Meeting for the Aid to Dependent Children Study, October 28, 1961, Washington, D.C., folder 5, box 33, APWA Collection, SWHA, 4.

55. Minutes of the Advisory Committee for the Aid to Dependent Children Study, June 21–22, 1962, Raleigh, N.C., folder 5, box 33, APWA Collection, SWHA, 4.

56. Such organizations as the Young Women's Christian Association, National Jewish Charities, and the Family Service Association of America were bringing in large num-

bers of social workers and developing therapeutic family services. Like the increasing interest in family rehabilitation in public welfare, private organizations' interest in family services derived from the broader cultural context of the postwar period, which emphasized the psychosocial importance of the family in American life. Unlike public welfare, however, they offered their services only to private clients; they were generally not interested in public programs. In the mid- to late 1950s, however, private social welfare organizations began to tread carefully into public welfare. This was largely due to the invention of rehabilitative discourse stressing family services in public welfare programs. What private social welfare groups, represented by the National Social Welfare Assembly (NSWA), did fell under the rubric of family services. And if the federal government was going to fund a massive effort at social services for public welfare clients, private social welfare organizations might have something to gain. For information on the growing interest of private social welfare groups in therapeutic family services, see Andrew Polsky, *The Rise of the Therapeutic State* (Princeton, N.J.: Princeton University Press, 1991), 139–87; for the way in which this interest manifested itself in an ideological and institutional relationship with public welfare in the 1950s, see Andrew Morris, "Charity, Therapy, and Poverty: Private Social Service in the Era of Public Welfare" (Ph.D. diss., University of Virginia, 2003). Elizabeth Wickenden bore some responsibility for directing private nonprofit voluntary organizations into advocacy for ADC and rehabilitation. She began working for the NSWA, the organization representing such groups, in 1955, as the head of a new Social Issues and Policies Committee. For general information on the NSWA's SIP Committee, see NSWA Collection, boxes 52 and 55, SWHA; also see folders 8 and 28, box 8, EW Papers, WHS. Although the 1956 public welfare amendments did not allow federal funding of private social welfare services for public welfare clients, it did provide for the possibility of it in the future. The Social Issues and Policies Committee created a subcommittee on research in early 1956 in anticipation of federal support for research on services in rehabilitation in welfare as a result of the 1956 Social Security Act Amendments. See Elizabeth Wickenden Oral History, February 6, 1987, folder 3, box 16, EW Papers, WHS, 7–9, and Wickenden Oral History, March 13, 1987, 4–5; see also Elizabeth Wickenden, "Evaluation of Assembly Committee on Social Issues and Policies," n.d. [ca. 1958], folder 28, box 8, EW Papers, WHS, 1.

57. The 1956 Social Security Amendments also drew on the support of the AFL-CIO. Historically, the AFL-CIO's social legislation agenda was primarily focused on social insurance, unemployment insurance, and old-age insurance. Union leaders, particularly those of the AFL, had played an important role in passing the original Social Security Act in 1935.

58. Resolution no. 148: Social Security: Public Assistance, adopted by the Third Constitutional Convention, AFL-CIO, San Francisco, Calif., September 17–23, 1959, folder 13, box 2, AFL-CIO/CSA Collection, SWHA.

59. Ibid., 2. When it came to supporting rehabilitation specifically, however, the AFL-CIO had a somewhat different take from that of public welfare advocates. The union supported the concept of rehabilitation to the extent that it promoted their larger aim of improving the independent status of male workers and their families rather than leaving them dependent and disabled. The constitutional convention of the AFL-CIO

in 1959, for example, explained this perspective on rehabilitation: "We urge that adequate funds and training be made available through federal, state, and local action so that the administration of public assistance shall respect the dignity of the individual and promote his self-reliance and his independence. Funds should be included for more effective programs of rehabilitation." See Resolution no. 148, 2. To the extent that rehabilitation encouraged mothers on welfare to become self-supporting, however, the AFL-CIO was wary of the concept. So it explicitly preferred a traditional male-bread-winner, family-based rhetoric of welfare reform. AFL-CIO Community Service Activities director Leo Perliss demanded that public assistance rehabilitative programs "train the public assistance father and assist him in getting a job" but "train the mother in proper housekeeping methods and procedures." See Leo Perliss, Keynote Address, AFL-CIO National Conference on Community Service, April 30, 1962, folder 78, box 11, AFL-CIO/CSA Collection, SWHA, 19. To the degree that rehabilitation seemed to meet these ideological criteria of the AFL-CIO, the union was willing to throw its support to ADC in congressional hearings, and speak out in favor of rehabilitation.

60. For histories of the National Urban League, see Guichard Parris and Lester Brooks, *Blacks in the City: A History of the National Urban League* (Boston: Little, Brown, 1971); Nancy J. Weiss, *Whitney Young, Jr., and the Struggle for Civil Rights* (Princeton, N.J.: Princeton University Press, 1989); Dona Hamilton and Charles Hamilton, *The Dual Agenda: Race and Social Welfare Policies of Civil Rights Organizations* (New York: Columbia University Press, 1997); Dennis Dickerson, *Militant Mediator: A Biography of Whitney Young, Jr.* (Lexington: University Press of Kentucky, 1998).

61. On the connection between emphasizing family problems and issues and expanding the welfare state, see Daryl Michael Scott, "The Politics of Pathology: The Ideological Origins of the Moynihan Controversy," *Journal of Policy History* 8, no. 1 (1996): 81–105, particularly 92–93: "Most major black leaders . . . incorporated damage imagery [of black families] in their appeals for liberal policies."

62. On the complexities and contradictions of the African American discourse of family in the 1940s, 1950s, and early 1960s, especially as it played out in the social sciences, see Scott, "The Politics of Pathology," and Daryl Michael Scott, *Contempt and Pity: Social Policy and the Image of the Damaged Black Psyche, 1880–1996* (Chapel Hill: University of North Carolina Press, 1997), 137–85.

63. Folder: Annual Conference, Program and Agenda, 1956, box 34, series IX A, part I, NUL Collection, LC.

64. Folder: Annual Conference, Program and Agenda, 1959, box 34, series IX A, Part I, NUL Collection, LC.

65. Folder: Annual Conference, Program and Agenda, 1958, box 34, series IX A, Part I, NUL collection, LC. The Urban League's files give a clear sense of their family-strengthening agenda. See Annual Reports, National Urban League, boxes 34, 35, series IX A, part I, and boxes 19, 26, 27, series VI B, part II, NUL Collection, LC. Also see Parris and Brooks, *Blacks in the City*, 379–80; Hamilton and Hamilton refer to the awareness of family-structure issues in reference to the reaction of civil rights leaders to the Moynihan report in 1965. Most civil rights leaders' first response was that there was "really nothing new or shocking in the report" from their perspective since they

had been studying and discussing these issues for years. Hamilton and Hamilton, *The Dual Agenda*, 140.

66. Scott, "The Politics of Pathology," 92–93.

67. Both leaders were themselves part of the social work profession and joined the NSWA and the APWA. In addition, Granger and particularly Young, as well as other national-level Urban League staff, were colleagues and acquaintances of key welfare reform leaders, notably Field Foundation executive director Maxwell Hahn and policy consultant Elizabeth Wickenden. Wickenden, in fact, had played a role in a 1954 internal reevaluation of the Urban League, in which she and other consultants helped the organization reorient itself as a more self-conscious social welfare and social policy institution. After that, welfare leaders regularly asked African Americans to contribute what they called the "Negro perspective" to national discussions of welfare such as the Ad Hoc Committee on Public Welfare in 1961. The NUL Collection at the Library of Congress gives a very good sense of the nature and extent of the relationship between the Urban League's civil rights agenda and its welfare agenda. Also, Elizabeth Wickenden's files on the NSWA give a sense of the relationship between the NUL's leaders and welfare interests. For information on the role of consultants, who also included Robin Williams and Eli Ginzburg, see Wickenden Oral History, February 6, 1987, 5–6, and December 12, 1986, 15–16; Parris and Brooks, *Blacks in the City*, 370–75; Hamilton and Hamilton, *The Dual Agenda*, 128, 129.

68. Parris and Brooks, *Blacks in the City*, 374, 390.

69. The Hamiltons characterize this debate as "pragmatism versus principles." They note that the NAACP debated the strategy of pursuing direct language against racial discrimination in federal legislation or pursuing less politically dangerous court rulings that circumvented the legislature and the open language in federal law. Hamilton and Hamilton, *The Dual Agenda*, 101, 107.

70. This is why, as the Hamiltons have argued, civil rights groups such as the National Urban League had historically fought for national, universal entitlements that could include African Americans, like Social Security. Hamilton and Hamilton, *The Dual Agenda*, 4–5.

71. Minutes, Evening Meeting of Race Relations Subcommittee, May 23, 1960, bound copies, board meeting docket, box 4X1, FF Collection, CAH.

72. Letter to Wickenden from Young, May 1, 1962.

73. Most historians mark the onset of the "welfare crisis" after 1964, when the size of the ADC program expanded enormously and quickly, and white people began to associate welfare with fears about black-power politics and racial violence in northern cities. See Frances Fox Piven and Richard Cloward, *Regulating the Poor: The Functions of Public Welfare* (New York: Vintage, 1971); Michael Katz, *The Undeserving Poor: From the War on Poverty to the War on Welfare* (New York: Pantheon Books, 1989); Patterson, *America's Struggle against Poverty*. Contemporary publications about welfare demonstrate clearly the rise in public interest in welfare. From 1956 to 1959 only eight articles on welfare appeared in nationally circulating periodicals; in 1960 alone, however, an equal number —eight—appeared. The next year, the number of articles on federal public welfare programs in national periodicals soared to twenty-nine, and remained high—sixty-

seven articles in national periodicals in 1969. See the index to the *Reader's Guide to Periodical Literature* for the years 1955–71. I checked on the terms "public welfare," as welfare was then referred to, and "social work," under which I picked appropriate public welfare articles (only two).

To be sure, as is described in chapter 1, hostility to welfare existed at the state level before 1960, flaring up especially during the late 1940s when welfare rolls had spiked after the war. But critiques of welfare had not achieved the intensity necessary to become a major national political issue. Conservatives in national politics never placed welfare at the top of their formal or informal political agendas. The Republican Party did not have welfare or ADC on its platform in the 1950s, and the major national conservative lobbies—the National Association of Manufacturers and the National Chamber of Commerce—did not place welfare anywhere near the top of their lobbying agendas. Publicly expressed hostility toward welfare thus continued to be a protean and largely local and regional phenomenon until 1960. In addition, Gallup polling reflects the relative lack of perceived national public interest before the 1960s. Gallup only polled on "welfare" once between 1940 and 1961, and that was in 1953 with the creation of the federal, cabinet-level Department of Health, Education, and Welfare. From 1961 to 1971 Gallup polled four times on "welfare," and also polled on poverty and the War on Poverty. See George H. Gallup, *The Gallup Poll: Public Opinion, 1935–1971*, 3 vols. (New York: Random House, 1972), index.

74. "Governor Davies Scoffs at Aid Cases," *Chicago Sun-Times*, September 23, 1960.

75. Patterson, *America's Struggle against Poverty*, 88. The Louisiana law followed a tradition of discrimination against unwed mothers in public assistance, even if previous discrimination was not as sudden or drastic. Since the time of the state-level mothers' pensions programs, local administrators had attempted to uphold white middle-class mores about the proper sexual behavior of mothers in conjunction with the distribution of public relief funds. Joanne Goodwin, *Gender and the Politics of Welfare Reform: Mothers' Pensions in Chicago, 1911–1929* (Chicago: University of Chicago Press, 1997); Linda Gordon, *Pitied but Not Entitled: Single Mothers and the History of Welfare, 1890–1935* (New York: Free Press, 1994); Gwendolyn Mink, "The Lady and the Tramp: Gender, Race, and the Origins of the American Welfare State," in *Women, the State, and Welfare*, ed. Linda Gordon (Madison: University of Wisconsin Press, 1990), 92–122; and Gwendolyn Mink, *Welfare's End* (Ithaca: Cornell University Press, 1998).

76. Mink, *Welfare's End*, 47.

77. The Child Welfare League of America argued that cutting unwed mothers off from welfare "would lead to the increased mortality, illness, shame, degradation and poverty of millions of children in an ostensible effort to coerce their parents into 'mending their ways.'" It stated further that "the aid to dependent children program can be utilized as a whip with which to beat children so that their custodians may be 'persuaded better to behave or . . . it will be used to succor needy children.'" Welfare professionals obviously preferred the latter approach, whereby families would benefit from rehabilitative services. Child Welfare League of America, Press Release, November 14, 1960, folder 4, box 71, WC Papers, WHS, 1, 3; see also folder 4, box 43, CWLA Collection, SWHA.

78. The National Urban League put the ratio at 80 percent while the commissioner

of Louisiana's State Department of Public Welfare claimed it was 95 percent. Jerome Wilson, Address at the Manhattan Central Medical Council, January 10, 1961, folder: ADC, 1960–61, container 1, series II A, part II, NUL Collection, LC; Letter to Kathryn Goodwin, Director, U.S. Bureau of Public Assistance, from Mary Evelyn Parker, Commissioner of the Department of Public Welfare, State of Louisiana, September 14, 1960, folder 4, box 71, WC Papers, WHS, 2.

79. Wilson, Address at the Manhattan Central Medical Council.

80. J. Harvey Kearns, Executive Director, Urban League of Greater New Orleans, "Report of Community Activities to Assist Children Deprived of Welfare Benefits in New Orleans . . . ," folder 4, box 71, WC Papers, WHS, 1–3.

81. Memorandum to Committee on Social Issues and Policies of the National Social Welfare Assembly, from Wickenden, October 7, 1960, folder 4, box 71, EW Papers, WHS.

82. Letter to K. Goodwin from M. E. Parker, September 14, 1960, 2.

83. Wilson, Address to the Manhattan Central Medical Council.

84. The Field Foundation also used research as a means to fight the situation in Louisiana. In the fall of 1960, the Field Foundation sponsored a research project on the situation in Louisiana to be conducted in conjunction with the Child Welfare League of America and its director Joseph Reid. The foundation gave $2,500 to a Tulane University sociologist to study the issue of illegitimacy and the ADC program in Louisiana. Reid and Hahn agreed that "we've really got to find out what's going on that's producing the increasing number of children born out of wedlock," and then they would have to explain the phenomenon and its relationship to ADC to Louisiana legislators and the federal Department of Health, Education, and Welfare. Transcript of telephone conversation between Max Hahn and Joseph Reid, October 6, 1960, folder: CWLA, ADC Louisiana Study, box 2T71, FF Collection, CAH; on the CWLA fight in Louisiana, see folder 4, box 43, CWLA Collection, SWHA.

85. Samuel Walker, *In Defense of American Liberties: A History of the ACLU* (Carbondale: Southern Illinois University Press, 1990), 313–14. William A. Donohue, *The Politics of the American Civil Liberties Union*, New Brunswick, N.J.: Transaction Press, 1985), 81–89. Much of the ACLU's work on poverty law developed around the War on Poverty and the AFDC program. The Wilcox brief was not, therefore, part of an already established ACLU tradition of poverty law and probably reflects Wilcox's own experience in the Social Security Administration and his knowledge of federal welfare administrative rules and law.

86. Elizabeth Wickenden, confidential notes on telephone conversation with Harry N. Rosenfield, Washington attorney, November 1, 1960, folder 4, box 71, WC Papers, WHS.

87. "Brief Submitted by the Child Welfare League of America, Inc., Urging that the secretary of Health, Education and Welfare find that the Louisiana plan for Aid to Dependent Children fails to comply with the provisions of Title IV of the Social Security Act," by Shad Polier, Esq., Special Counsel for the Child Welfare League of America, Inc., n.d.; and Child Welfare League of America, press release, November 14, 1960, folder 4, box 71, WC Papers, WHS.

88. Wilson, Address to the Manhattan Central Medical Council, 1; and Report of

Community Activities to Assist Children Deprived of Welfare Benefits in New Orleans Resulting from 1 of 30 Segregation Bills passed by the Louisiana State Legislature, Urban League of New Orleans, J. Harvey Kearns, Executive Director, 10/5/60, folder 4, box 71, WC Papers, WHS.

89. See arguments in memorandum from National Urban League to National Agencies, American Leaders, and Local Urban Leagues, September 19, 1960, folder: ADC, 1960–61, container 1, series II A, part II, NUL Collection, LC, which previewed the arguments of the brief.

90. A. H. Raskin, "Newburgh's Lessons for the Nation," *New York Times Magazine*, December 17, 1961, 7.

91. Raskin, "Newburgh's Lessons," 7. Joseph Ritz, *The Despised Poor: Newburgh's War on Welfare* (Boston: Beacon Press, 1966), is a good journalistic account of the attack on welfare in Newburgh.

92. See the index to the *Reader's Guide to Periodical Literature*, 1960 and 1961.

93. A wide range of articles on Newburgh can be found in the APWA Collection, folder 12, box 31, SWHA; "The Battle of Newburgh," *NBC White Paper* (New York: National Broadcasting Company, 1962).

94. Rick Perlstein, *Before the Storm: Barry Goldwater and the Unmaking of the American Consensus* (New York: Hill and Wang, 2001).

95. Quote in Raskin, "Newburgh's Lessons," 7.

96. The Gallup Poll organization conducted polling on "relief" during the Newburgh summer, asking questions about federal versus local control, work relief, and unwed mothers, issues reflecting Joseph Mitchell's thirteen-point welfare code. Gallup, *The Gallup Poll*, 3:1731–32.

97. "Who Are the People on Relief?" (editorial), *Hartford Courant*, October 1961, folder 12, box 31, APWA Collection, SWHA.

98. Quoted in Leo Perliss, "Welfare Stories—Have they Become a Scandal? or, How *Look* Cooked Up Another Newburgher," unpublished paper, December 21, 1961, folder 78, box 11, AFL-CIO/CSA Collection, SWHA. Perliss noted, perhaps rightly, that statements like this from *Look* reflected the fact that "newspapers and magazines blow up their [chiselers'] importance out of all proportion."

99. Frank Bruel, "Public Welfare: Safeguard or Free Ride?" *University of Chicago Magazine*, January 1962, 20–21.

100. Transcript of telephone conversation between Max Hahn and Raymond Houston, October 4, 1961, folder: APWA, 1942–1960, FF Collection, CAH, 1.

101. Transcript of telephone conversation between Max Hahn and Justine Polier, November 20, 1961, folder: Citizen's Committee for the Children of New York, 1961, box 2T78, FF Collection, CAH.

102. The breadth of the issues in the Newburgh incident is highlighted by Ritz in *The Despised Poor*.

103. Raskin, "Newburgh's Lessons," 7.

104. Often racial problems were portrayed as predominantly southern problems, since whites in the South maintained strict segregation laws, practiced disenfranchisement of African Americans, and reacted violently to civil rights challenges. Welfare pol-

icy makers, in keeping with this interpretation, but based as well on their own experience, also believed that racism and segregation in welfare were primarily southern problems. Southern states were generally more hostile to welfare than northern or western states, in large part because a disproportionate number of their neediest were African Americans, and southern politicians did not want to spend public funds on them. The Louisiana ADC law in 1960, as well as welfare codes in other states, seemed to underscore the racial discrimination associated with welfare in the South.

105. Joe William Trotter Jr., ed., *The Great Migration in Historical Perspective: New Dimensions of Race, Class, and Gender* (Bloomington: Indiana University Press, 1991), provides an overview of scholarship on many aspects of the great migration.

106. Raskin, "Newburgh's Lessons," 58.

107. Gareth Davies, *From Opportunity to Entitlement: The Transformation and Decline of Great Society Liberalism* (Lawrence: University Press of Kansas, 1996), 28.

108. Raskin, "Newburgh's Lessons," 58.

109. Transcript of telephone conversation between Hahn and Houston, October 4, 1961; transcript of telephone conversation between Max Hahn and Justine Polier, September 28, 1961, folder: APWA 1960 (Study of ADC), box 2T39, FF Collection, CAH, 1.

110. Leo Perliss, untitled draft of speech, December 1961, folder 78, box 11, AFL-CIO/CSA collection, SWHA. Though Perliss was an important policy ally for welfare institutions, he nevertheless took a far greater interest in the Newburgh crisis than in any welfare matters in the past.

111. See folder: NYSSW (Winifred Bell's dissertation) 63 and folder: NYSSW (Winifred Bell's dissertation) 61, box 2R383, FF Collection, CAH. When the crisis in Louisiana occurred in 1960, the Field Foundation began funding an investigation into welfare and child welfare policy by Elizabeth Wickenden through the New York School of Social Work, called the Project on Public Services for Families and Children. Through this project, the Field Foundation came to know Winifred Bell, a doctoral student at the NYSSW. Bell was Wickenden's assistant on the project. In addition to assisting Wickenden, however, Bell was beginning work on her dissertation, having chosen the suitable home provision as her topic. Since Field was already in contact with Wickenden and Bell, the foundation agreed to fund the dissertation and its conversion into a publishable manuscript, giving the New York School of Social Work $9,250 to subsidize Bell in September 1961. The Field officials hoped that the study would educate policy makers and the public about the proper and improper uses of the suitable home provision by the states over the years.

112. Transcript of telephone conversation between Max Hahn and Justine Polier, July 29, 1963, folder: NYSSW (Winifred Bell's dissertation) 63, box 2R383, FF Collection, CAH.

113. Memorandum to Whitney Young from Elizabeth Wickenden, April 16, 1962, folder: NSWA, 1062, box 37, series I A, part II, NUL Collection, LC.

114. Elizabeth Wickenden, "The Recurrent Crises of Public Welfare—Asset or Handicap?" *Public Welfare* 21, no. 4 (October 1963): 174.

115. See, for example, New York State Board of Social Welfare, untitled press statement, July 18, 1961, folder 10, box 31, APWA Collection, SWHA, 1.

116. The quote is from AFL-CIO representative Leo Perliss, who derided the euphemistic terms because they covered up the ugly reality of blatant racial discrimination. See Perliss, untitled draft of speech, December 1961.

117. Letter to Hahn from Lansdale, May 20, 1963, 3.

118. Transcript of telephone conversation between Max Hahn and Joseph Reid, June 11, 1963, folder: NYSSW (Winifred Bell's dissertation) 63, box 2R383, FF Collection, CAH. Reid elaborated on this theme in a follow-up letter to Hahn: "The study is marred in my opinion by a kind of historical intolerance. . . . Although she clearly documents that practically all social welfare leaders favored the suitable home concept, there is somewhat of an air of regarding them as fools rather than trying to understand the limitations of their views at that point in history." Letter to Hahn from Reid, June 12, 1963, folder: NYSSW (Winifred Bell's dissertation) 63, box 2R383, FF Collection, CAH. Bell was clearly hitting a sore point, perhaps even guilt, when she wondered why federal policy makers had failed to speak explicitly about racial discrimination.

119. Apparently convinced by Reid, Hahn recommended to the Field board that the foundation not fund the publication of Bell's dissertation. Except for Justine Polier, they agreed. Whether or not Bell's open treatment of the issue of race discouraged Hahn from wanting to sponsor the dissertation's publication is not openly addressed in the foundation's records. Historically, the foundation was an unequaled supporter of civil rights issues, funding the most controversial grass roots organizations in the South, including the Highlander Folk School, from the 1940s onward. The foundation officials and Hahn were also closely associated with many civil rights leaders in the South, scholars such as Robin M. Williams and Gordon Allport, and national figures in the civil rights movement such as Martin Luther King Jr. and Whitney Young. So it seems unlikely that Hahn was put off simply by Bell's discussion of racial rights.

120. Memorandum to Executive Secretaries, Local Affiliates, National Urban League, from Lester Granger, July 25, 1961, folder: Public Welfare Situation . . . 1962, box 47, series I A, Part II, NUL Collection, LC.

121. See index and ADC files, NUL Collection, LC. Edith Evans Asbury, "Newburgh Chided by Urban League," *New York Times*, September 6, 1961, 20.

122. U.S. Department of Health, Education, and Welfare, Transcript of Proceedings of the Conference with the National Urban League, Washington D.C., May 17, 1962, folder: U.S. Dept of HEW Conference with NUL, 1962, box 26, series V A, part II, NUL Collection, LC, 171.

123. Ibid., 171, 173, 174.

124. Ibid., 174. Others in the coalition of welfare advocates apparently sensed that the NUL was still sensitive about the race-welfare connection. When Joseph Reid of the Child Welfare League of America disparaged Winifred Bell's suitable home provision study to the Field Foundation, he argued to Max Hahn that "the Urban League would take quite a bit of exception to the fact that she talks about the convergence of family patterns [with ADC] . . . (and what she means by family patterns is the very, very high illegitimacy among Negroes)." Transcript of telephone conversation between Hahn and Reid, June 11, 1963.

125. Ritz, *The Despised Poor*, 50–52.

126. Bruel, "Public Welfare," 21.

127. Jonathan Spivak, "Ribicoff's Strategy: He Tries to Restore Relief Critics' Faith by Tying Economy Hope to More Charity," *Wall Street Journal*, November 21, 1961: "Critics contend the program encourages unwed mothers to bear illegitimate children."

128. Quoted in Bruel, "Public Welfare," 21.

129. On the one hand, federal law seemed to make it clear that work relief—a policy whereby needy people worked on locally created work projects in return for a welfare check or a low wage—could not be implemented in conjunction with the federally funded categorical assistance programs—Old Age Assistance, Aid to the Blind, Aid to the Totally and Permanently Disabled, and Aid to Dependent Children. The state-level general assistance programs with which work relief projects were solely associated were noncategorical programs aimed primarily at single and married men who did not qualify for federal categorical public assistance programs. On the other hand, rehabilitation implied that self-support through employment was a legitimate goal of the ADC program.

130. The APWA sent out its own defense of welfare to reporters in the form of a policy statement. Dunn told Hahn, "We have had very heavy demand for the policy statement we developed . . .: could we reprint your policy statement on Newburgh?" Transcript of telephone conversation between Max Hahn and Loula Dunn, October 4, 1961, folder: APWA 1960 (Study of ADC), box 2T39, FF Collection, CAH, 1.

131. Spivak, "Ribicoff's Strategy."

132. "To Help Them Help Themselves" (editorial), *Chicago Sun-Times*, May 12, 1962; Ruth Dunbar, "Relief Recipients Take to Schooling Program," *Chicago Sun-Times*, May 13, 1962.

133. M. W. Newman, "How ADC Families Get Back on Feet," *Chicago Daily News*, September 5, 1962.

134. *Philadelphia Enquirer*, September 14, 1961, folder 11, box 31, APWA Collection, SWHA.

135. Letter to Reverend Joseph Becker from Elizabeth Wickenden, March 8, 1962, folder 7, box 12, EW Papers, WHS, 1; see Wickenden's letters to Winifred Bell when Bell took over the Social Security research projects office at HEW, folder 17, box 1, EW Papers, WHS.

136. Folder: NSWA, Ad Hoc Committee, 1961, box 37, series I A, part II, NUL Collection, LC. Wickenden sent the plan to Whitney Young, of the National Urban League, and to other social welfare leaders. Young was skeptical about Hilliard's proposed project, particularly the "compulsory nature of it." See letter to Wickenden from Young, May 1, 1962, same folder.

137. Letter to Maxwell Hahn from Wilbur Cohen, October 16, 1962, folder 1, box 133, WC Papers, WHS. The Field Foundation provided the government with $200,000 in seed money to begin ADC research before Congress appropriated funds.

138. Pete Ivy, "Welfare Study," *Chapel Hill Weekly*, May 8, 1963, 2.

139. Jim Whitfield, "Child Welfare Aide Solutions Posed—Education and Training," *Christian Science Monitor*, May 10, 1963.

140. See n. 95 above.

141. This bias was recognized at the time. See "Newburgh TV Show Stirs Controversy," *New York Times*, February 1, 1962, 41.

Chapter 4

1. Wilbur Cohen Oral History, May 10, 1969, LBJL, 5, 38–39.

2. The Kennedy presidency represented what political scientists call a "policy window" in welfare—a period when several factors expediting policy reform coincide and produce legislative change. As defined by John Kingdon, what opens a policy window includes the following factors: that perceived and real social problems achieve political notice; that well-thought-out policy agendas exist; and that policy makers actively assess policy alternatives and formulate new legislation. John Kingdon, *Agendas, Alternatives, and Public Policies*, 2nd ed. (Boston: Little, Brown, 1995). With these conditions present in the early 1960s, changes in welfare law could be made.

3. Letter to Wilbur Cohen from Julius Edlestein, Oct. 4, 1960, folder 4, box, 70, WC Papers, WHS. Kennedy's administration was shaped by this early recession and its attendant problems. He planned to use both economic policy to create jobs for the unemployed and social programs to ameliorate the circumstances of the unemployed and poor, and to train or retrain them for new jobs. Allen Matusow, *The Unraveling of America: A History of Liberalism in the 1960s* (New York: Harper Torchbooks, 1984), 18–19.

4. See Cohen's papers from the period at the University of Michigan, boxes 59–73, WC Papers, WHS.

5. "Health and Social Security for the American People: A Report to President-Elect John F. Kennedy by the Task Force on Health and Social Security," January 10, 1961, folder 7, box 1, EW Papers, WHS.

6. In the two months during which it operated, the task force formulated nine recommendations on health and social security legislation. Three of them dealt solely with federal public assistance programs. The relatively large emphasis on assistance policy came from Cohen and his expert on assistance for the task force, Elizabeth Wickenden.

7. "Health and Social Security for the American People," 10.

8. See U.S. Congress, House of Representatives, *Aid to Dependent Children of Unemployed Parents*, 87th Congress, 1st session, 1961, H. Rep. 28 (Washington, D.C.: U.S. Government Printing Office, 1962).

9. "Health and Social Security for the American People," 10; also see James Patterson, *America's Struggle against Poverty, 1900–1994* (Cambridge, Mass.: Harvard University Press, 1994), 130.

10. Kennedy cited in U.S. Congress, House, *Aid to Dependent Children of Unemployed Parents*, 2.

11. *Congressional Quarterly Almanac*, 87th Congress, 1st session, 17:282. In the hearings on the ADC-UP program, Secretary Ribicoff, John Tramburg, president of the American Public Welfare Association, and Nelson Cruikshank of the AFL-CIO testified similarly. This was a widely advocated justification for ADC-UP.

12. Draft of letter written by Wilbur Cohen for President Kennedy to Governor Hughes of New Jersey, June 14, 1963, folder 3, box 131, WC Papers, WHS, 1–2. HEW wanted to encourage more states to adopt the ADC-UP program. See also U.S. Congress, Senate, *ADC Benefits to Children of Unemployed Parents*, 87th Congress, 1st Session, 1961, S. Rep. (Washington, D.C.: U.S. Government Printing Office, 1962), 165. Also see Patterson, *America's Struggle against Poverty*, 130.

13. U.S. Congress, House of Representatives, *Public Welfare Amendments of 1962*, 87th Congress, 2nd session, 1962, H. Rep. 1414 (Washington, D.C.: U.S. Government Printing Office, 1963), 15. Federal public assistance was still, in 1961, officially a collection of government programs for people designated as nonemployable—that is, the elderly, the totally and permanently disabled, the blind, and mothers with dependent children. There was no language in the federal ADC program that required employment rehabilitation services.

14. See memorandum to William Mitchell, Commissioner of Social Security, from Andrew Trueleson, Acting Director of the Bureau of Public Assistance, May 19, 1961, folder 6, box 135, WC Papers, 1 and attachment. General relief programs, also identified as general assistance programs, the nonfederal, state and locally funded public assistance programs, could not serve as adequate substitutes for the robust, relatively high-paying New Deal work relief programs. Although government spending on general assistance began to grow in the 1940s and continued to do so thereafter, the disbursements were lower than those of the federal categorical assistance programs, and the criteria for eligibility were stricter. See Patterson, *America's Struggle against Poverty*, 200.

15. U.S. Congress, House, *Public Welfare Amendments of 1962*, H. Rep. 1414, 15.

16. U.S. Congress, House, *Aid to Dependent Children of Unemployed Parents*, 3–4.

17. Federal law authorized states to force fathers to participate in work relief or work training programs. But it did not authorize federal funds for those programs. Since the New Deal, the federal government had refused to establish federally funded work relief programs. Thus, as they had in the past, states would have to subsidize work relief for the new unemployed men on the ADC program with their own funds.

18. Memorandum to Mitchell from Trueleson, 1 and attachment; "Statement by Secretary Ribicoff on the Relationship between State Work Relief Programs and the Public Assistance Provisions of Federal Law," folder: Secretary's Statement—Work Relief Programs and Public Assistance, July 1961, box 21, AR Papers, LC.

19. These comments came from the Ad Hoc Committee on Public Welfare, a federal advisory committee to be discussed later in the chapter. Minutes of Meeting, August 1, 1961, folder: Ad Hoc Committee on Public Welfare, box 11, NASW Supp. Collection, SHWA, 2, 9.

20. Quoted in Patterson, *America's Struggle against Poverty*, 132. Unlike many welfare administrators and social workers, Cohen was an experienced political operative. Throughout his life, Cohen was an open Democratic Party supporter and campaigner, and in the late 1950s, while at the University of Michigan, he was particularly active in national campaigns. He advised presidential and senatorial campaigns on social policy, including Adlai Stevenson's presidential campaign, Hubert Humphrey's senatorial campaign, John Kennedy's senatorial campaign, and, of course, Kennedy's presidential campaign. Edward Berkowitz, *Mr. Social Security: The Life of Wilbur J. Cohen* (Lawrence: University Press of Kansas, 1995), 94–113.

21. Memo to Wilbur Cohen from Bess Furman Armstrong, September 27, 1961, Report on the Meeting of the Ad Hoc Committee with Secretary Ribicoff . . . , folder 2, box 144, WC Papers, WHS, 2.

22. Ribicoff quoted in Minutes of Meeting of the Ad Hoc Committee on Public

Welfare, June 30–July 1, 1961, dated July 12, 1961, folder: Ad Hoc Committee on Public Welfare, box 11 NASW, Supp. Collection, WHS, 3.

23. Ibid.

24. Wayne Vasey, the secretary of the Ad Hoc Committee on Public Welfare, told the meeting that Cohen and Ribicoff were in the position of having to make clear statements about work relief because of Newburgh. Minutes of Meeting, June 30–July 1, 1961, dated July 12, 1961, Ad Hoc Committee on Public Welfare, 7; and Draft of Minutes, Ad Hoc Committee Meeting, Tuesday, August 1, 2; both documents in folder: Ad Hoc Committee on Public Welfare, box 11, NASW Supp. Collection, SWHA. "The secretary emphasized that he would particularly appreciate guidance in dealing with ... the policies governing work relief programs for able-bodied unemployed assistance recipients." Memorandum to NASW Board of Directors from Joseph Anderson, August 18, 1961, folder: Ad Hoc Committee on Public Welfare, box 11, NASW Supp. Collection, SWHA, 2.

25. See Minutes of Meeting, June 30–July 1, 1961, Ad Hoc Committee on Public Welfare, July 12, 1961, 3. In an attempt to clarify these questions, committee consultant Wayne Vasey on several occasions laid out the options for the federal government and for the kinds of work-welfare programs that might exist. In terms of payments, the federal government could either leave things the way they were, with no federal participation in work relief payments or programs; allow federal funds to be used in projects created at the local level; or provide federal funds for federally controlled and monitored public work projects. In terms of types of work-welfare programs that might exist, there were work-out-relief programs in which recipients "worked out" their relief payments. A step up were work-relief programs of the type similar to the New Deal–era Works Progress Administration in which unemployed or dependent individuals were paid minimum wages on locally administered and monitored projects. And, finally, there were large-scale federal public works projects like those of the New Deal–era Public Works Administration, which created the Hoover Dam and which paid prevailing rather than minimum wages. Consultant Vasey asked the committee to consider whether and how the federal government and the ADC program should be drawn into one or more of these payments and activities. See Preliminary Agenda for Meeting, Ad Hoc Committee on Public Welfare, August 1–2, 1961; and Minutes of Meeting, August 1–2, 1961, Ad Hoc Committee on Public Welfare, 5–6 in particular; both in folder: Ad Hoc Committee on Public Welfare, box 11, NASW Supp. Collection, SWHA. "A Report of the Conference with HEW Secretary Ribicoff, Friday, September 8, 1961," September 11, 1961, folder: Ad Hoc Committee on Public Welfare, box 11, NASW Supp. Collection, SWHA, 3–4.

26. Good accounts of the genesis of the Ad Hoc Committee on Public Welfare can be found in the Field Foundation Collection. See folder: Memorandum for Conference of Children's Committee ... April 4, 1961 ..., box 4X101, and folder: Ad Hoc Committee ... 1961, box 4X102, FF Collection, CAH. Although the Ad Hoc Committee operated under governmental auspices, it was in fact underwritten by the Field Foundation. When welfare advocate Wilbur Cohen was named assistant secretary for legislation of Kennedy's Department of Health, Education, and Welfare in early 1961, Cohen and the Field Foundation together used the opportunity to convince the secretary to under-

take a large-scale professional and expert review of the ADC program. The Field Foundation clearly saw the Kennedy administration as having the potential to accomplish the kinds of reforms that the foundation and its welfare advocate allies had been promoting throughout the 1950s. The Ad Hoc Committee would be the vehicle by which new reforms would be created and worked into legislation.

All of the important groups and individuals active in welfare policy for the previous ten to fifteen years—and especially those active in opposing the draconian Louisiana welfare law of 1960—were asked to join: the American Public Welfare Association and its leader, Loula Dunn; the National Social Welfare Assembly and its leader, Robert Bondy; the Child Welfare League of America and its leader, Joseph Reid; the AFL-CIO and its representatives, Nelson Cruikshank and Katherine Ellickson; and the National Urban League and its director, Whitney Young. Other members included deans of schools of social work, and social work and social science researchers such as Fedele Fauri, Herman Somers, and Eveline Burns. The Field Foundation provided the funding to undertake the Ad Hoc Committee's studies, hire staff people, and pay for committee members' travel. Soon after the committee was formed, a second venue for review was also created. There was some question as to whether one committee should be responsible for all of the legislative and administrative aspects of a full-scale welfare evaluation and recommendation. The Field Foundation agreed, therefore, to fund a second report. Whereas the Ad Hoc Committee would focus on legislation, a study performed by one individual, George Wyman, would address solely the administration of welfare and how it could be changed and improved.

27. Leslie Leighninger points out how surprised and happy the NASW was to be tapped for the position and welcomed directly into HEW. See Leslie Leighninger, "Why Social Work Abandoned Public Welfare," paper presented at the *Journal of Policy History* Conference, St. Louis, Mo., May 27–30, 1999. Information on the NASW and its limited involvement in welfare policy making in this period can be found in the NASW Supplement Collection, which specifically concerns the Washington, D.C., office created to act on legislative issues. The NASW's Social Action Workshop was a brainchild of the Washington office, an attempt to interest the general NASW membership in the legislative process and create lobbying priorities. See folder: Social Action Workshop, 1957–1963, box 2, NASW Supp. Collection, SWHA. Certain key leaders of the Washington office were in favor of rehabilitation, such as Rudolph Danstedt, who wrote often about rehabilitation for the APWA's journal, *Public Welfare*.

28. Minutes of Meeting, August 1, 1961, Ad Hoc Committee on Public Welfare, 8.

29. Ad Hoc Committee on Public Welfare, "A Report of the Conference with HEW Secretary Ribicoff, Friday, September 8, 1961," 3.

30. Ibid.

31. Ibid., 3–4.

32. Ribicoff quoted in Vasey, Draft of Ad Hoc Committee Report, n.d. [ca. mid-July 1961], folder: Ad Hoc Committee on Public Welfare, box 11, NASW Supp. Collection, SWHA, 3.

33. Young and his most vocal allies—Ernest Witte of Rutgers University, Trude Lash of the Citizens Committee of the Children of New York, and James Dumpson, commissioner of New York City's Department of Public Welfare—refused to yield to

the secretary and filed official objections on this issue alongside the Ad Hoc Committee report. They made no difference, however. The discomfort of other members who did agree to the work relief provision was still evident, however. They begged committee secretary Wayne Vasey to make their endorsement palatable: "Try to come up with a new way of phrasing it," they asked, "so that the words might be fresh and have better possibilities for understanding." See Minutes of Meeting, June 30–July 1, 1961, dated July 12, 1961, Ad Hoc Committee on Public Welfare, 7.

34. Both the APWA and the NASW quoted in a review of work relief positions among welfare groups in "Proposed NASW Federal Legislative Objectives for 1962," folder: Legislative Objectives 1962–63, box 5, NASW Supp., SWHA, 3–4.

35. Although the discussion of work and welfare had provoked dissension in the Ad Hoc Committee's discussion, it did not in the congressional hearings or reports of the pending 1962 public welfare amendments. Even though the APWA, the NASW, and other groups advocating for welfare, such as the National Urban League, remained privately unenthusiastic about work relief programs in the ADC program, and even though these organizations formally stated objections to other aspects of the proposed legislation, such as residence requirements and the use of vouchers rather than cash payments, none of them challenged the Community Work and Training Programs in their testimony. The APWA, the NASW, the Child Welfare League of American, and even the NUL, whose president Whitney Young had so eloquently attacked federal work relief in the Ad Hoc Committee, gave their tacit approval to the Community Work and Training Programs as the necessary sacrifice for allowing "employable" unemployed men to be eligible for ADC under the Unemployed Parent provision.

36. U.S. Congress, House, *Public Welfare Amendments of 1962*, H. Rep. 1414, 15.

37. National Association of Social Workers, "Recommendations for Public Welfare Reorganization," based on Ad Hoc Committee on Public Welfare Report, November 30, 1961, folder: Ad Hoc Committee on Public Welfare, box 11, NASW Supp. Collection, SWHA, 2.

38. Ibid.

39. Ibid.; and Vasey, Draft of Ad Hoc Committee Report, n.d. [ca. mid-July 1961], folder: Ad Hoc Committee on Public Welfare, box 11, NASW Supp. Collection, SWHA, 2, 5.

40. Wilbur Cohen and Robert Ball, "The Public Welfare Amendments of 1962," *Public Welfare* 20, no. 4 (October 1962): 191.

41. Not only did the law state that rehabilitative services were the central component of welfare—even more important than cash payments—but it also funded those services at a 50 percent higher rate than services had ever been funded in the past. For any rehabilitative service offered to a welfare client, the federal government agreed to pay 75 cents of each dollar the service cost. The law also required a minimum level of service provision in each state and opened those services for the first time to people likely to become welfare clients, not just people already on welfare. The services were created primarily for the ADC program, but there was also a large expansion of child welfare services such as protective services and day care in the bill. The amendments required, in addition, that each state establish a minimum level of services provision for welfare clients. The law even authorized welfare departments to contract with other state agen-

cies, such as vocational education, in order to purchase rehabilitative services for clients.

42. "Resolution of the National Urban League re: 1962 Public Welfare Amendments Bill, May 24, 1962," folder: 1962—NUL Resolutions re: welfare and medicine, box 5, series IV A, part II, NUL Collection, LC. Wilbur Cohen and Robert Ball referred to the 1962 legislation, after its passage, in nearly the same terms, as "the most comprehensive revision of federal provision for public welfare since the Social Security Act became law in 1935." See Cohen and Ball, "The Public Welfare Amendments of 1962," 191.

43. "Statement of Wayne Vasey for the National Association of Social Workers to the Committee on Finance of the United States Senate on H.R. 10606—The Public Welfare Amendments of 1962, May 15, 1962," folder: Public Welfare Proposals 1962, box 11, NASW Supp. Collection, SWHA, 2.

44. Memorandum to William Mitchell from Abraham Ribicoff, December 6, 1961, folder 2, box 136, WC Papers, WHS, 2.

45. U.S. Congress, House, *Public Welfare Amendments of 1962*, H. Rep. 1414, 23; and U.S. Congress, Senate, *Public Welfare Amendments of 1962*, 87th Congress, 2nd session, 1962, S. Rep. 1589 (Washington, D.C.: U.S. Government Printing Office, 1962), 20. Ribicoff's promises apparently did not satisfy Robert Byrd, and he established a congressional committee to investigate welfare abuses in Washington, D.C.

46. The interrelationship between Cohen's views on welfare, work, and women, and the political climate in Washington, D.C., were captured in a 1964 memo Cohen wrote to Washington's welfare commissioner. "Nearly ever day when I complete my legislative work 'on the hill' with members of Congress, I walk back the few blocks to my office to clear my mind. As I walk along I have noticed two things: the absence of 1, any benches to sit down and rest, and 2, wastebaskets. . . . Why doesn't the District accept the . . . community work and training programs and put some employable adult persons on aid to dependent children to work making such benches and wastebaskets. . . . Washington would be a more beautiful city." See letter to Walter Tobriner from Cohen, June 9, 1964, folder 9, box 132, WC Papers, WHS. One can imagine as well how much political mileage Cohen would have gotten from pointing out the welfare mothers' work to legislators on Capitol Hill.

47. N.A. [no author], untitled draft of potential questions for the secretary of health, education, and welfare in the House Ways and Means Committee hearings on HR 10032, February 6, 1962, folder 10, box 135, WC Papers, WHS, 1, section B.

48. Ibid., 3, section B; 2, section A.

49. U.S. Congress, House, *Public Welfare Amendments of 1962*, H. Rep. 1414, 16.

50. U.S. Congress, Senate, *Public Welfare Amendments of 1962*, S. Rep. 1589, 18.

51. It is also worth noting that women on ADC gained little in the redefinition of their official employable status in the ADC program. Though designated as "employable," they were not officially "unemployed," a status that would have recognized their lifetime status as workers (as most ADC mothers were) and made them eligible for unemployment insurance.

52. Elizabeth Wickenden quoted in U.S. Department of Health, Education, and Welfare, Work Group on Exemption of Earned Income, "Recommendations Referred to This Group for Consideration," September 12, 1961, folder 2, box 144, WC Papers, WHS.

53. U.S. Congress, Senate, *Public Welfare Amendments of 1962*, S. Rep. 1589, 18.

54. U.S. Congress, House, *Public Welfare Amendments of 1962*, H. Rep. 1414, 5.

55. Sonya Michel, *Children's Interests, Mothers' Rights: The Shaping of America's Child Care Policy* (New Haven: Yale University Press, 1999), 118–280.

56. U.S. Congress, House, *Public Welfare Amendments of 1962*, H. Rep. 1414, 21, 20.

57. *Congressional Quarterly Almanac*, 87th Congress, 2nd session, 1962, 884.

58. Testimony of Ellen Winston, American Public Welfare Association, before the House Committee on Ways and Means on "The Public Welfare Amendments of 1962," February 13, 1962, folder 5, box 144, WC Papers, WHS, 9.

59. Although Congress had authorized federal funding before, it had never appropriated funding.

60. Wilbur Cohen, "Welfare—A Challenge and a Responsibility," paper delivered at the opening session of the 1961 American Public Welfare Association Northeast Regional Conference, Boston, Mass., September 13, 1961, folder 3, box 130, WC Papers, WHS, 9.

61. Cohen contacted, for example, colleagues at the APWA, NASW, the New York School of Social Work, the University of Michigan, and the Field Foundation to encourage applications for federal funding of research on welfare.

62. Winston had overseen two major national studies of ADC by the APWA and had great faith in the possibilities of federal funding.

63. Letter to Max Hahn from Wilbur Cohen, October 16, 1962, folder 1, box 133, WC Papers, WHS. Hahn was the executive director of the Field Foundation, which provided the government with $200,000 in seed money to begin ADC research before Congress appropriated funds.

64. Ellen Winston, untitled proposal, ca. October 1961, folder 17, box 1, EW Papers, WHS, 1.

65. Wickenden originally passed on information about the Georgia project in 1962 and followed up in a letter to Bell in 1963. Letter to Winifred Bell from Elizabeth Wickenden, May 7, 1963, folder 17, box 1, EW Papers, WHS.

66. Winifred Bell, "Casework with Chronically Dependent Families," March 1957, folder 8, box 1, EW Papers, WHS.

67. Winifred Bell, "Demonstration, Research and Related Project Reports Received, December 1–December 30, 1962," folder 17, box 1, EW Papers, WHS.

68. Winifred Bell, "Activities in Public Welfare: Digest of Recent Press Reports, Bureau of Family Services," February 1963, folder 17, box 1, EW Papers, WHS, 3, 5.

69. Letter to Elizabeth Wickenden from Winifred Bell, January 17, 1963, folder 17, box 1, EW Papers, WHS, 3. As Bell's comments suggested, there remained among these women a commitment to multiple goals in welfare research. Their increasing preoccupation with research projects in which rehabilitation represented education and job training, or job placement and job support programs, did not spell a total abandonment of their goals for strengthening family life. For example, the 1962 Public Welfare Amendments, in their official rehabilitative language, reflected the priorities that liberal welfare advocates' desired—both strengthening family life and encouraging independence. Moreover, while Cohen, Wickenden, and Winston became increasingly preoccupied with employment services for ADC mothers, the major welfare organizations such as

the APWA and the NASW continued to be firmly committed to legislative priorities that mixed strengthening family life with encouraging independence and remained cautious about aggressive approaches to employment in ADC, such as the work-relief-type Community Work and Training Programs. The legislative priorities for both the APWA and the NASW from 1961 through 1964 reflect a strong commitment to a well-rounded view of rehabilitation and a continuing commitment to other facets of improving ADC, such as those they had always fought for: higher payments, no residence requirements, and money payments only. See American Public Welfare Association, "Federal Legislative Objectives," folder 1, box 21, APWA Collection, SWHA. Also see National Association of Social Workers, folder: "Legislative Objectives, 1962–63," box 5, NASW Supp. Collection, SWHA. National voluntary organizations—members of the National Social Welfare Assembly such as the Child Welfare League of America and the National Urban League—were also firmly committed to the more comprehensive view of rehabilitation and hesitant about language that appeared to prioritize work over family in the rehabilitation of welfare clients. Joseph Reid, for example, contacted Wilbur Cohen when he detected in the testimony of the National Conference of Catholic Charities the idea that welfare mothers be expected to work. See letter to Rt. Reverend Monseigneur Joseph Springbob, Director, Catholic Social Welfare Bureau, from Joseph Reid, February 21, 1962, folder 16, box 143, WC Papers, WHS, 2. Former Social Security commissioner Arthur Altmeyer, a close friend and confidante of Wilbur Cohen and Elizabeth Wickenden, and himself a member of the APWA, confided to Wickenden that he was worried about "taking away from a mother the right to determine whether or not it is in the best interests of her children for her to work outside the home," which he saw as coming out of a "general growth in coercion and control of public assistance clients" in the 1962 Public Welfare Amendments. See letter to Elizabeth Wickenden from Arthur Altmeyer, September 10, 1962, folder 21, box 1, EW Papers, WHS.

70. Interview of Secretary Abraham Ribicoff by Edwin Newman, *Today* (NBC-TV), December 13, 1961, folder: Secretary's Interview, NBC, Today Program, box 21, AR Papers, LC.

71. *Congressional Quarterly Almanac*, 87th Congress, 2nd session, 1962, 18:218, 212.

72. Ibid., 217.

73. A. H. Raskin, "Newburgh's Lessons for the Nation," *New York Times Magazine*, December 17, 1961, 58. The quote is from an article on Newburgh's city manager Joseph Mitchell, who became a conservative Republican star when he launched his crusade against welfare in late 1961.

74. *Congressional Quarterly Almanac*, 87th Congress, 2nd session, 1962, 18:216.

75. Ibid., 217, 212.

76. U.S. Congress, House, *Public Welfare Amendments of 1962*, H. Rep. 1414; U.S. Congress, Senate, *Public Welfare Amendments of 1962*, S. Rep. 1589; and U.S. Congress, House, *Public Welfare Amendments of 1962*, 87th Congress, 2nd session, 1962, Conference Rep. 2006 (Washington, D.C.: U.S. Government Printing Office, 1963). Keeping costs down and maintaining state discretion were, in fact, conservative selling points for the social service provisions, stated openly in the House and Senate reports. Note that conservatives' efforts to keep down costs even at the outset of the legislation calls into question again the assertion by some historians that conservatives supported rehabilitation

as a cost-cutting, long-term venture. The evidence remains that conservatives supported it, quite rationally, for its language and message regarding independence and work.

77. Ribicoff's December 1 speech to the APWA was copied in HEW's *Regional and Field Letter*, no. 453, December 11, 1961, folder 2, box 136, WC Papers, WHS.

78. Joel Handler and Ellen Hollingsworth quoted in Patterson, *America's Struggle against Poverty*, 133. Some historians have posited that this was in part because the Bureau of Family Assistance "had no end of trouble trying to define 'services.'" But the cost component and the reluctance of states to spend on ADC were probably more important. Martha Derthick's work on social service spending shows that rather than impede the growth of social services, the lack of definition caused a flowering of social service spending. Notably, however, the spending, though it was supposed to be for welfare services, was spent on all kinds of other social services not directly associated with welfare. It was, therefore, clearly, *welfare* spending that states did not want to undertake. See Martha Derthick, *Uncontrollable Spending for Social Service Grants* (Washington, D.C.: Brookings Institution, 1975).

Chapter 5

1. John Kenneth Galbraith, *The Affluent Society* (Boston: Houghton Mifflin, 1958).

2. Case study of Gerlinda Bullard, Washtenaw County Public Welfare Study, 1959–1962, folder 4, box 73, WC Papers, WHS, 1–5.

3. Case study of Gerlinda Bullard, 5.

4. Senator Robert Byrd (D-W.Va.) led an investigation into welfare fraud in Washington, D.C. In addition, the 1962 Public Welfare Amendments authorized a congressional inquiry into the entire federal welfare program one year after the passage of the amendments.

5. On the women's rights agenda from the mid-1940s onward, see Cynthia Harrison, *On Account of Sex: The Politics of Women's Issues, 1945–1968* (Berkeley: University of California Press, 1988); Leila Rupp and Verta Taylor, *Survival in the Doldrums: The American Women's Rights Movement, 1945 to the 1960s* (New York: Oxford University Press, 1987); Dorothy Sue Cobble, "Recapturing Working-Class Feminism: Union Women in the Postwar Era," in *Not June Cleaver: Women and Gender in Postwar America, 1945–1960*, ed. Joanne Meyerowitz (Philadelphia: Temple University Press, 1994), 57–83; Susan Hartmann, "Women's Employment and the Domestic Ideal in the Early Postwar Years," in *Not June Cleaver: Women and Gender in Postwar America, 1945–1960*, ed. Joanne Meyerowitz (Philadelphia: Temple University Press, 1994), 88–90; Susan Hartmann, *The Other Feminists: Activists in the Liberal Establishment* (New Haven: Yale University Press, 1998); Dennis Deslippe, *Rights, Not Roses: Unions and the Rise of Working-Class Feminism, 1945–80* (Urbana: University of Illinois Press, 2000). One exception to this was temporary support for the equal rights amendment by key Republicans in Congress during debates over the federal income tax codes during World War II. See Alice Kessler-Harris, *In Pursuit of Equity: Women, Men, and the Quest for Economic Citizenship in Twentieth-Century America* (New York: Oxford University Press, 2001), 190.

6. After the passage of the Nineteenth Amendment giving women the right to vote, some feminists turned their attention to passing an equal rights amendment to the

Constitution. Most feminists opposed the equal rights agenda on the basis that it would repeal special protections won for women in areas like labor legislation.

7. Harrison, *On Account of Sex*, 109–13.

8. Ibid., xii, 138, 109–68; Kessler-Harris, *In Pursuit of Equity*, 213–34.

9. Hartmann, "Women's Employment," 86.

10. Harrison, *On Account of Sex*, 138–68.

11. Elizabeth Wickenden, for example, laughed at the notion that she was qualified to speak on women's issues. In this respect, women in the world of welfare like Wickenden and APWA leaders Loula Dunn and Ellen Winston typified the nonfeminist stance of women in politics of the 1950s.

12. "Members of the President's Commission on the Status of Women," n.d., folder 8, box 194, WC Papers, WHS. Eleanor Roosevelt was chosen as formal head of the commission, but she died before the commission completed its work.

13. Harrison, *On Account of Sex*, section 3, has a good account of the political setting that produced the PCSW and an analysis of its political outcomes. Harrison does not focus on the contributions of and the contention between welfare advocates and Department of Labor staff and PCSW members. Her work emphasizes the thorny issue of the definition of women's rights and the controversy over the equal rights amendment among women's advocates.

14. *American Women: A Report of the President's Commission on the Status of Women and Other Publications of the Commission* (New York: Charles Scribner and Sons, 1965), 254–58; Harrison, *On Account of Sex*, 138 (see 109–68 for a full discussion of all of the committees mentioned in the text).

15. Minutes of Fifth Meeting—February 11–12, 1963, President's Commission on the Status of Women, box 145, RG 235, HEW/PCSW Records, NA.

16. Ibid., 11.

17. *American Women*, 113, 116, 111–17.

18. Memorandum to Wilbur Cohen from Grace Hewell, June 4, 1963, folder 1, box 195, WC Papers, WHS.

19. Memorandum to Wilbur Cohen from Grace Hewell, May 14, 1963, folder 8, box 194, WC Papers, WHS, 2–3.

20. Letter to Esther Peterson from Philip Des Marais, Deputy Assistant Secretary, HEW, April 22, 1963, folder: Status of Women, April–June 1963, box 144, RG 235, HEW/PCSW Records, NA.

21. Memorandum to Ivan Nestigen from Grace Hewell, through Assistant Secretary Cohen, June 4, 1963, folder: Status of Women, April–June 1963, box 144, RG 235, HEW/PCSW Records, NA, 1.

22. *American Women*, 17, 21, 38, 39, 40. Reference to these same issues can be found in the archival sources, too. See "American Women," the final report of the President's Commission on the Status of Women, October 11, 1963, folder: 1963 Commission—President's Commission on the Status of Women (May–October), box 52, RG 174, DL/PCSW Records, NA, 19–23.

23. Harrison, *On Account of Sex*, 109–37.

24. I am grateful to Cynthia Harrison for alerting me to this document and discussing it with me. Letter to David Ball from Arthur Goldberg, January 24, 1962, in

possession of Cynthia Harrison, 2, 3. Interestingly, Peterson was correct to worry about the effect of ADC-UP on ADC and encouraging women to work, as chapter 4 of this book demonstrates.

25. Peterson might still have discussed poor women and AFDC even if she opposed the 1962 Public Welfare Amendments. If Peterson subscribed to the view of AFDC as primarily a family program that was supposed to help poor mothers in their stay-at-home mothering duties, there were still services that it offered that she could support. Although the 1962 Public Welfare Amendments encouraged women more strongly than ever before to work outside the home, AFDC continued to support in rhetoric and in practice "improving family life." Furthermore, the Community Work and Training Programs were not mandatory. And mothering was still compelling to many in HEW. Grace Hewell and other HEW staff pressing Peterson to include welfare in the PCSW report were asking her to make reference to the family services part of the 1962 Public Welfare Amendments, not the employment services. Peterson might have seen an opportunity to reinforce her opinion of the 1962 Public Welfare Amendments by taking the opposite tack, discussing what an important and necessary program AFDC was in terms of helping low-income women raise families. She might have demanded that it be enlarged and strengthened. This strategy would have remained consonant with her beliefs without undermining the administration. *American Women*, 36.

26. Harrison, *On Account of Sex*, 138. For more on the effects of this assumption, see ibid., 138–68.

27. *American Women*, 35, 32.

28. Ibid., 111 (emphasis added). A footnote linked to the word "others" in the quote says, "The Committee included in this description women who are heads of families or in low-income groups."

29. Memorandum to Wilbur Cohen from Irvin Walker, May 3, 1963, folder: Status of Women, April–June, 1963, box 144, RG 235, HEW/PCSW Records, NA, 1.

30. Memorandum to Cohen from Hewell, May 14, 1963, 4. Though Grace Hewell may have been genuinely interested in ensuring a fair hearing for African American women, it was likely that her concern—and that of her boss, Wilbur Cohen—was strategic: they hoped that by discussing African American women they could force welfare onto the commission agenda. At the time, national welfare leadership both within HEW and in organizations like the APWA and the NSWA were addressing racial issues minimally at best. Only recently, when lobbying for the 1962 Public Welfare Amendments, Cohen and other leaders of welfare organizations had remained silent on how the program affected growing numbers of African Americans and how the racially motivated attacks on AFDC like the ones in Louisiana in 1960 and in Newburgh, New York, in 1961 affected the future of AFDC.

31. Memorandum to Grace Hewell from Lisle Carter, May 17, 1963, folder 1, box 195, WC Papers, WHS.

32. See arguments in memorandum from National Urban League to National Agencies, American Leaders, and Local Urban Leagues, September 19, 1960, folder: ADC, 1960–61, container 1, series II A, part II, NUL Collection, LC, which previewed those of the brief.

33. Allen Matusow, *The Unraveling of America: A History of Liberalism in the 1960s* (New York: Harper Torchbooks, 1984), 85–96.

34. The first quotation comes from Wilbur Cohen's handwritten notes on the meeting, June 1, 1963, folder 9, box 114, WC Papers, WHS, 3. The second quotation comes from a memorandum by Anthony Celebrezze, secretary of HEW, to John Kennedy, June 10, 1963, folder 9, box 114, WC Papers, WHS, 1.

35. Draft memorandum by Cohen, June 3, 1963, folder 9, box 114, WC Papers, WHS, 1.

36. Memorandum to Cohen from Hewell, June 4, 1963.

37. Harrison, *On Account of Sex*, 161–62; "Problems of Negro Women," Press Release: "News of the PCSW," May 10, 1963, folder: 1963 Commission—President's Commission on the Status of Women (May–October), box 52, RG 174, DL/PCSW Records, NA. Department of Labor staffer Daniel Patrick Moynihan, who would write the infamous "Moynihan Report," was on the consultation committee.

38. "Problems of Negro Women," 1, 3–4. See also Tracey Fitzgerald, *The National Council of Negro Women and the Feminist Movement, 1935–1975* (Washington, D.C.: Georgetown University Press, 1985). Fitzgerald explains the nuances of the National Council on Negro Women's position on gender, racism, and social policy. Although the NCNW was unusual among African American women's organizations for taking a gender and race perspective on its mission, historically, the NCNW negotiated the swirling eddies of sexism and racism cautiously, especially in the late 1950s, 1960s, and 1970s, when these issues became part of national politics. "The loyalties of black women," Fitzgerald says, "remained with their men" (41). She also explains that this ideological perspective manifested itself in political agendas, such that the NCNW and many individual African American women were willing to support the male-biased, male-dominated mainstream civil rights agenda and organizations for quite some time before objecting to sexism (35–41).

39. See Jacqueline Jones, *Labor of Love, Labor of Sorrow* (New York: Vintage, 1985). The NUL had been concerned about the relationship between family structure and poverty for a couple of decades. Its annual reports feature projects and symposiums on this issue for most of the 1950s and early 1960s. See, Annual Reports, National Urban League, boxes 34, 35, series IX A, part I, and boxes 19, 26, 27, series VI B, part II, NUL Collection, LC.

40. On the ways in which African American leaders and organizations viewed the African American family, see Daryl Michael Scott, "The Politics of Pathology: The Ideological Origins of the Moynihan Controversy," *Journal of Policy History* 8, no. 1 (1996): 81–105.

41. U.S. Department of Health, Education, and Welfare, Transcript of Proceedings, Conference with the National Urban League, May 17, 1962, Washington, D.C. (Washington, D.C.: Federal Reporting Company, 1962), folder: US Dept. of HEW Conference with NUL 1962 (transcript), box 26, series V A, part II, NUL Collection, LC. For more on the Domestic Marshall Plan and the agenda of the NUL, see Hamilton and Hamilton, *The Dual Agenda*, 128–29; and Dickerson, *Militant Mediator*, 255.

42. There are many works addressing the history of the War on Poverty. See Alice O'Connor, *Poverty Knowledge: Social Science, Social Policy, and the Poor in Twentieth-Century U.S.*

History (Princeton, N.J.: Princeton University Press, 2001), 139–95; Henry Aaron, *Politics and the Professors: The Great Society in Perspective* (Washington, D.C.: Brookings Institution, 1978); Gareth Davies, *From Opportunity to Entitlement: The Transformation and Decline of Great Society Liberalism* (Lawrence: University Press of Kansas, 1996), 10–53; Robert Haveman, ed., *A Decade of Federal Antipoverty Programs* (New York: Academic Press, 1977); Michael Katz, *The Undeserving Poor: From the War on Poverty to the War on Welfare* (New York: Pantheon Books, 1989), 9–123; Sar Levitan, *The Great Society's Poor Law: A New Approach to Poverty* (Baltimore: Johns Hopkins University Press, 1969); Sar Levitan and Robert Taggart, *The Promise of Greatness* (Cambridge, Mass.: Harvard University Press, 1975); Peter Marris and Martin Rein, *Dilemmas of Social Reform: Poverty and Community Action in the United States* (London: Routledge and Kegan Paul, 1967); Daniel Patrick Moynihan, *Maximum Feasible Misunderstanding: Community Action in the War on Poverty* (New York: Free Press, 1969); Matusow, *The Unraveling of America*, 97–130; James Patterson, *America's Struggle against Poverty, 1900–1994* (Cambridge, Mass.: Harvard University Press, 1994), 99–156; Richard Pells, *The Liberal Mind in a Conservative Age: American Intellectuals in the 1940s and 1950s* (New York: Harper and Row, 1985), 117–61; James L. Sundquist, *Politics and Policy: The Eisenhower, Kennedy, and Johnson Years* (Washington, D.C.: Brookings Institution, 1968), 57–154.

43. Elizabeth Wickenden Oral History, February 27, 1987, folder 3, box 16, EW Papers, WHS, 23. The Economic Opportunity Act, as the poverty legislation came to be called, "distribute[d] funds to existing agencies to operate a variety of programs authorized under the [Economic Opportunity Act of 1964]." See U.S. Congress, Senate, *Economic Opportunity Act of 1964*, 88th Congress, 2nd session, 1964, S. Rep. 1218 (Washington, D.C.: U.S. Government Printing Office, 1965). The programs were incorporated into the Economic Opportunity Act and the OEO but were administered by existing departments included manpower training and development programs in the Department of Labor; small business loans for poor communities in the Small Business Administration; adult basic education and work study programs through the Department of Health, Education, and Welfare; and rural antipoverty programs though the Department of Agriculture. See Aaron, *Politics and the Professors*, chap. 2. Wilbur Cohen's biographer also presents an informative account of the collection of programs that came to be the War on Poverty; see Edward Berkowitz, *Mr. Social Security: The Life of Wilbur J. Cohen* (Lawrence: University of Press of Kansas, 1995), 188–211.

44. The Community Action Programs (CAPs) were formed on the model of community empowerment developed by Lloyd Ohlin and Richard Cloward on the Lower East Side of New York City. The CAPs theorized that what the poor needed was the ability to form their own representative organizations and take a place at the decision-making table in cities and counties across America. Because the CAPs ended up either challenging existing power structures in cities or being co-opted by powerful city governments, their legacy has been controversial. But many other newly created programs were just as important, financially and otherwise, to the War on Poverty. The Job Corps, employment programs, and education grants offered education and job training for low-income youth. Volunteers in Service to America (VISTA) brought volunteers into low-income communities. There were programs to combat poverty among migrant agricultural laborers. All of these programs were brought together under the author-

ity of the newly created Office of Economic Opportunity (OEO), an executive office of the president (as opposed to a new cabinet department).

45. On the efforts of Wilbur Cohen and Elizabeth Wickenden to influence the federal war on poverty, see Wickenden Oral History, February 27, 1987, 23; and O'Connor, *Poverty Knowledge*, 155–56. Wickenden was developing her own ideas about the relationship of welfare to poverty at this time. But she was moving out of lobbying for legislation and into the realm of litigation, working to develop the new legal field of welfare or poverty law. Her memorandum "Poverty and the Law" was an influential text describing the civil rights discrimination suffered by welfare clients and the poor in general within the AFDC program and other government programs. See folder 7, box 2, EW Papers, WHS.

46. Wilbur Cohen, "Poverty and Low Incomes in the United States," Committee for Economic Development, August 4, 1956, folder 7, box 69, WC Papers, WHS, 5.

47. Patterson, *America's Struggle against Poverty*, 81.

48. Wilbur Cohen and Sydney Bernard, "Reducing Dependency: A Report of a Demonstration and Research Project among Direct Relief Recipients in Washtenaw County, Michigan," (Ann Arbor: University of Michigan School of Social Work, 1960), chap. 8, p. 5.

49. Berkowitz, *Mr. Social Security*, 194.

50. Davies called poverty programs "little more than an extension and repackaging of a concern that was by now a decade old," a concern with "rehabilitating the dependent poor." Davies, *From Opportunity to Entitlement*, 31.

51. While the Council on Economic Advisers argued that poverty in America was in large part the result of structural problems in the macroeconomy—unemployment due to shifts in economic sectors, changes in technology, and uneven regional economic development—it also agreed with many other influential Kennedy's appointees in the Department of Labor and the Department of Health, Education, and Welfare that poverty was also often the result of social factors, so-called social disabilities. These included problems of a more personal, community, or cultural nature such as lack of education or job skills, family disorganization, racial discrimination, and physical or mental illness. In action, the War on Poverty programs spoke to the social disabilities analysis of poverty rather than to the macroeconomic approach. Solving structural problems in the economy would have required drastic and far-reaching solutions, such as a redistribution of wealth or a full-employment policy. But solving "social" problems related to poverty was more suited to smaller programs, less spending, and less politically controversial approaches—approaches such as rehabilitation in welfare (for example, the 1962 Public Welfare Amendments, which passed so easily) and those of the later War on Poverty. The fact that the War on Poverty took the rehabilitative approach to the dependent poor calls into question stories that focus on the its origins in Mobilization for Youth, the community youth program modeled on the work of Lloyd Ohlin and Richard Cloward that eventually spawned the Community Action Programs. Since CAPs were but one part of the War on Poverty—albeit the one with the highest profile—it is important to note that the remainder of the programs were largely the result of the faith that national welfare leaders and other liberals had developed in rehabilitating the dependent poor on welfare.

52. Patterson, *America's Struggle against Poverty*, 136–37.

53. Berkowitz, *Mr. Social Security*, 196.

54. Patterson, *America's Struggle against Poverty*, 144. This strategy of degrading welfare in order to curry political favor for a new program reprised the old efforts of Social Security advocates to gain support for insurance at the expense of public assistance. See Jerry Cates, *Insuring Inequality: Administrative Leadership in Social Security, 1934–1950* (Ann Arbor: University of Michigan Press, 1983), 104–35.

55. Patterson, *America's Struggle against Poverty*, 144.

56. Agency was pitted against agency as a result of the OEO's disdain for existing agencies. The OEO and other departments often fought over control of government programs. Wilbur Cohen's oral history reveals the extreme tensions generated by the OEO's takeover of existing programs in the Department of Health, Education, and Welfare and the Department of Labor. Cohen himself commented that he approved of having an executive office like OEO exist, but he felt that it should exist solely to generate new programs. After the new programs were created, however, he thought they should be transferred back to old-line agencies. Cohen said, "I favor, when OEO programs are . . . determined and something has been worked out, transfer[ring] them to the old-line agency and keep[ing] OEO as a creative innovative type agency." See Wilbur Cohen Oral History, tape 5, May 10, 1969, LBJL, 7. Cohen also commented on the hostility the OEO caused between its leaders and Secretary of Labor Willard Wirtz. Wirtz eventually came to think that Cohen, too, was against him. According to Cohen, Wirtz was "extremely possessive and bureaucratic about his role in these areas. . . . During this period of time, Secretary Wirtz's and my personal relationship deteriorated very badly because he felt that I was the one who was not concurring in his views and making it difficult for him to get his views both in Congress and at the White House." See Ibid., 18.

57. Eileen Boris, "Contested Rights: How the Great Society Crossed the Boundaries between Home and Work," in *The Great Society and the Rights Revolution*, ed. Sidney Milkis and Jerome Mileur (Amherst: University of Massachusetts Press, forthcoming [2005]); manuscript in possession of author.

58. Boris, "Contested Rights"; Jill Quadagno and Catherine Fobes, "The Welfare State and the Cultural Reproduction of Gender: Making Good Girls and Boys in the Job Corps," *Social Problems* 42, no. 2 (May 1995): 171–90.

59. For the Moynihan report, written by Daniel Patrick Moynihan in his role as a staffer in the Department of Labor, see U.S. Department of Labor, Office of Policy Planning and Research, *The Negro Family: The Case for National Action* (Washington, D.C.: U.S. Government Printing Office, 1965). There has been no comprehensive scholarly inquiry into the gendered basis of the War on Poverty. But its male bias has been explored by Gwendolyn Mink, *Welfare's End* (Ithaca, N.Y.: Cornell University Press, 1998), 24, 25; Joanne Goodwin, "'Employable Mothers' and 'Suitable Work': A Re-evaluation of Welfare and Wage-Earning for Women in the Twentieth-Century United States," *Journal of Social History* 29, no. 2 (Winter 1995): 265; Nancy Naples, *Grassroots Warriors: Activist Mothering, Community Work, and the War on Poverty* (New York: Routledge, 1998); Quadagno and Fobes, "The Welfare State"; and Boris, "Contested Rights."

60. Memorandum to Joseph Califano from Wilbur Cohen, December 14, 1965, folder: November 22, 1965–August 31, 1967, box 164, WE 6, WHCF, LBJL, 7.

61. Liberals in Congress, such as Senator Abraham Ribicoff (D-Conn.), the former HEW secretary, had tried to expand the Community Work and Training Programs throughout 1963 but got nowhere. According to Elizabeth Wickenden's legislative updates, for example, Ribicoff proposed "Work and Training for Public Assistance Recipients, . . . S 1803 (HR 7262) to authorize an additional $50,000,000 to help in meeting extra costs involved in developing work and training projects for public assistance recipients under the demonstration authority of the 1962 Public Welfare Amendments." Actual appropriations never came near this amount. See memorandum to Committee on Social Issues and Policies, Participating Councils and Others Concerned with Public Welfare, from Wickenden, July 1, 1963, folder 7, box 2, EW Papers, WHS, 1.

62. U.S. Congress, House of Representatives, *Economic Opportunity Act of 1964*, 88th Congress, 2nd session, 1964, H. Rep. 1458 (Washington, D.C.: U.S. Government Printing Office, 1965), 1–2.

63. The WEPs were never administrated in a stable fashion. Initially, in 1964–65, the OEO administered the program, taking charge of legislative matters. In 1965, as part of the amendments to the poverty programs, administration of the WEPs was transferred to HEW. But in 1966 control was again shifted, so that it was now shared between the Department of Labor and HEW. The OEO retained responsibility for bringing the EOA amendments before Congress, however, and so regardless of which agency held day-to-day administrative control, the legislative agenda for the WEPs was largely determined by the OEO's priorities. *Congressional Quarterly Almanac*, 89th Congress, 1st session, 1965, 21:416; *Congressional Quarterly Almanac*, 89th Congress, 2nd session, 1966, 22:252.

64. U.S. Congress, House, *Economic Opportunity Act of 1964*, 32.

65. There was a difference between authorization and appropriations. Though funding authorizations for other OEO programs were raised to the amount requested, appropriations, as is often the case, were lower. *Congressional Quarterly Almanac*, 21:406–20; U.S. Department of Health, Education, and Welfare, Welfare Administration, "Fact Sheet on Work Experience and Training Programs," ca. 1967, folder: June 15–July 12, 1967, box 29, WE 9, WHCF, LBJL, 2.

66. Memorandum to Califano from Cohen, December 14, 1965, 7, 8.

67. U.S. Department of Health, Education, and Welfare, Welfare Administration, "Fact Sheet on Work Experience and Training Programs," 1.

68. Day-care funding was a crucial component of the 1962 Public Welfare Amendments, meant to assist women on welfare who wanted to work or take training. Although funding for day care in 1963 was supposed to be $10 million, it was reduced to $8 million. Then, for 1964, when the amount was supposed to have increased from $10 million (on its way to $30 million in 1969 through yearly increments), it was decreased from $8 million to $4 million. *Congressional Quarterly Almanac*, 88th Congress, 1st session, 1963, 19:157.

69. The Work Experience Programs of the Economic Opportunity Act focused sharply on women on welfare, encouraging them to gain work experience and become independent of welfare. The Senate report on the EOA of 1964, for example, justified

the Title V WEPs exclusively in terms of their service for single mothers on welfare: "Of the over 700,000 women heading families receiving AFDC, about 14 percent are now employed and another 13 percent, or approximately 100,000, could work if employment were available. Many more would seek employment if adequate day-care facilities were available." U.S. Congress, Senate, *Economic Opportunity Act of 1964*, 32.

70. The first major historical treatment of Social Security to address this issue was Edwin Witte, *The Development of the Social Security Act* (Madison: University of Wisconsin Press, 1963). Cates's *Insuring Inequality* directly addresses this issue.

71. The seminal text on this topic is Barbara Nelson's "Origins of the Two-Channel Welfare State: Workman's Compensation and Mother's Aid," in *Women, the State, and Welfare* ed. Linda Gordon (Madison: University of Wisconsin Press, 1990), 123–51.

72. By the 1960s, when poverty among black and white male-headed households and among white female-headed households declined, the rate of poverty among black female-headed households rose. Patterson, *America's Struggle against Poverty*, 81; National Research Council, *A Common Destiny: Blacks and American Society* (Washington, D.C.: National Academy Press, 1989), 280–81.

73. ADC overtook Old Age Assistance (OAA) as the largest federal public assistance program as early as 1957.

74. In 1960 there were 3.05 million people receiving AFDC; in 1965 there were 4.3 million; and by 1970 there were 8.46 million. In 1974 10.86 million clients received AFDC. In ten years, rates had doubled; in fifteen, they had more than tripled. Social Security Administration, *Social Security Bulletin, Annual Statistical Supplement, 1977–1979* (Washington, D.C.: U.S. Government Printing Office, 1979), 248.

Epilogue

1. James Patterson, *America's Struggle against Poverty, 1900–1994* (Cambridge, Mass.: Harvard University Press, 1994), 210–41; Patterson focuses on Reagan and George H. W. Bush, and the conservative Congress from 1994 to 1996. See also Michael Katz, *In the Shadow of the Poorhouse: A Social History of Welfare in America*, rev. ed. (New York: Basic Books, 1996), 283–334; and Walter Trattner, *From Poor Law to Welfare State: A History of Social Welfare in America*, 5th ed. (New York: Free Press, 1994), 338–85. All emphasize the importance of conservative politics and the initiatives of Republican presidencies in explaining harsher welfare policies.

2. The vast literature on the underclass is mainly written from a sociological or economics perspective. The most thorough recent history addressing the rise of the concept of the underclass is Alice O'Connor, *Poverty Knowledge: Social Science, Social Policy, and the Poor in Twentieth-Century U.S. History* (Princeton, N.J.: Princeton University Press, 2001), 242–83. See also Michael Katz, *The Undeserving Poor: From the War on Poverty to the War on Welfare* (New York: Pantheon Books, 1989). For original work on this subject, see Ken Auletta, *The Underclass* (New York: Random House, 1982); and Nicholas Lemann, "Origins of the Underclass," *Atlantic Monthly*, June 1986, 31–61, and July 1986, 54–68. Lemann continued his work on the underclass in *The Promised Land: The Great*

Black Migration and How it Changed America (New York: Knopf, 1991). Here he argued that origins of underclass behaviors could be traced to the agricultural South.

3. O'Connor, *Poverty Knowledge*, 213–96.

4. Different historians give different numbers, but all are between 20,000 and 25,000.

5. The classic accounts of the NWRO are Frances Fox Piven and Richard Cloward, *Poor People's Movements: Why They Succeed, How They Fail* (New York: Vintage, 1977), 290–98; and Guida West, *The National Welfare Rights Movement: The Social Protest of Poor Women* (New York: Praeger, 1981).

6. Piven and Cloward, *Poor People's Movements*, 290–98.

7. Most did so cautiously and with reservations, however. Some younger social workers from the New Left and African American social workers signed on enthusiastically.

8. On Wickenden and welfare rights, see Elizabeth Wickenden Oral History, February 27, 1987, folder 3, box 16, EW Papers, WHS, 25–28; and Index to Field Foundation Collection, FF Collection, CAH. On qualified support for NWRO positions, see American Public Welfare Association, "Federal Legislative Objectives, 1968," folder 1, box 21, APWA Collection, SWHA; Gareth Davies, *From Opportunity to Entitlement: The Transformation and Decline of Great Society Liberalism* (Lawrence: University Press of Kansas, 1996), 121–23.

9. West, *National Welfare Rights Movement*, 366–68. Local welfare offices built cooperative relationships with the NWRO regarding treatment of clients and policy. Officials of the NWRO attended state-level welfare administration and social work conferences. The NWRO consulted at the federal level in such venues as the White House Conference on Hunger and Malnutrition; it also received a grant for monitoring welfare-work programs from the Department of Labor. See Piven and Cloward, *Poor People's Movements*, 322, 325, 326, 328. On the congressional hearing in 1970, see Patterson, *America's Struggle against Poverty*, 195.

10. Piven and Cloward, *Poor People's Movements*, 343–49.

11. West, *National Welfare Rights Movement*, 217–23. The black power movement that began at that time also dealt with the issue of poverty, but it was undermined in many of its attempts to effectively advocate for antipoverty programs or perform community service by government infiltration and attack.

12. Piven and Cloward, *Poor People's Movements*, 325.

13. Johnnie Tilmon quoted in West, *National Welfare Rights Movement*, 215; ibid., 227–28, 223.

14. Davies, *From Opportunity to Entitlement*, 118; West, *National Welfare Rights Movement*, 245.

15. National Organization for Women, "NOW Statement of Purpose, 1966," in *Major Problems in American Women's History: Documents and Essays*, ed. Mary Beth Norton and Ruth Alexander (Boston: Houghton Mifflin, 2003), 432; Martha Davis, "Welfare Rights and Women's Rights in the 1960s," *Journal of Policy History* 8, no. 1 (1996): 150.

16. M. Davis, "Welfare Rights and Women's Rights," 151.

17. Ibid., 151–52.

18. West, *National Welfare Rights Movement*, 234–60; M. Davis, "Welfare Rights and Women's Rights," 152, 155–57, 160–62. For a look at the feminist politics of African

American NWRO members and their contribution to second-wave feminism, see Premilla Nadasen, "Expanding the Boundaries of the Women's Movement: Black Feminism and the Struggle for Welfare Rights," *Feminist Studies* 28, no. 2 (2002): 271–301.

19. See Marisa Chappell, "Rethinking Women's Politics in the 1970s: The League of Women Voters and the National Organization for Women Confront Poverty," *Journal of Women's History* 13, no. 4 (Winter 2002): 155–79.

20. West, *National Welfare Rights Movement*, 234, 235, 246, 258, 259, 260.

21. Ibid., 245–46, 259, 260; M. Davis, "Welfare Rights and Women's Rights," 151, 156–57.

22. Gwendolyn Mink, *Welfare's End* (Ithaca, N.Y.: Cornell University Press, 1998), 24, 25. See also West, *National Welfare Rights Movement*, 245. Moreover, in emphasizing the importance of wage earning, feminists have not equally emphasized the importance of the choice to stay at home and care for families. While mainstream feminists do not dispute the legitimacy of that choice, they have not perhaps supported it as much as wage earning. In this way, the desire of women on welfare to care for their families at home receives somewhat less philosophical or political support from mainstream feminists than it might. In her analysis of the role of feminists in the 1996 welfare reform, Gwendolyn Mink takes a strong stance on this issue, arguing that "if racism has permitted policymakers to negate poor single mothers as citizens and mothers, white middle-class feminism has provided those policymakers with an excuse. White middle-class feminists' emphasis on women's right to work outside the home—accompanied by women's increased presence in the labor force—gave cover to conservatives eager to require wage work of single mothers even as they championed the traditional family." Mink, *Welfare's End*, 23–24. Mink also notes the small scale of mainstream feminist lobbying on the issue of welfare versus that of domestic violence or reproductive rights (25). Moreover, Mink points out that the support of feminist members of Congress—including two co-chairs of the Congressional Women's Caucus—for the 1996 Personal Responsibility and Work Opportunity Act abolishing AFDC and creating mandatory work requirements for women on welfare substantially undermined feminist claims to support poor women and welfare. "One hundred fifty-nine House Democrats voted for this baleful assault on the rights of poor mothers, including co-chair of the Congressional Women's Caucus (Nita Lowey, D-New York), the former Democratic co-chair of the Caucus (Patricia Schroeder, D-Colorado), the only woman in the Democratic leadership (Barbara Kennelly, D-Connecticut), twenty-three of twenty-eight other Democratic women. . . . As one congressional feminist admitted of her colleagues, when it comes to welfare 'nobody cares about women'" (3).

23. Barry Goldwater, speech to American Petroleum Institute in Los Angeles, April 29, 1964, courtesy of Rick Perlstein.

24. This is what Wilbur Mills (D-Ark.) and Russell Long (D-La.) did in 1967 when they suddenly replaced a rehabilitative social services bill proposed by the administration with the harsher workfare WIN program. See discussion in text below.

25. E. Selby and A. Selby, "Watts: Where Welfare Bred Violence," *Reader's Digest*, May 1966, 67–71; and E. Selby and A. Selby, "California's Jackpot for the Jobless," *Reader's Digest*, June 1965, 67–70.

26. Index to *Reader's Guide to Periodical Literature*, 1955–71. Note that this count does

not include articles on poverty in general or the War on Poverty, or single-parent house-holds, or any other topic that might be related to welfare. The articles were on AFDC alone.

27. Davies cites the *Wall Street Journal* as saying "that irritation about supposed welfare chiseling by Negroes was hurting Democrats even more than the backlash against integrated housing." Davies, *From Opportunity to Entitlement*, 159. Also see Patterson, *America's Struggle against Poverty*, 109, 172–73.

28. Social Security Administration, *Social Security Bulletin, Annual Statistical Supplement, 1977–1979* (Washington, D.C.: U.S. Government Printing Office, 1979), 248.

29. Patterson, *America's Struggle against Poverty*, 182; James Leiby, *A History of Social Welfare and Social Work in the United States* (New York: Columbia University Press, 1978), 325, 326, 328; Martha Derthick, *Uncontrollable Spending for Social Service Grants* (Washington, D.C.: Brookings Institution, 1975).

30. Katz, *In the Shadow of the Poorhouse*, 261. Katz notes that though social services spending to alleviate poverty rose, with the transference of government funds to private agencies that provided social services, a lower share of government funds allocated actually made its way to needy people (262).

31. Barry Goldwater, speech to Economic Club of New York, January 16, 1964, courtesy of Rick Perlstein.

32. U.S. Congress, House of Representatives, Committee on Ways and Means, *House Report on the Social Security Amendments of 1967, August 7, 1967*, 90th Congress, 1st session (Washington, D.C.: U.S. Government Printing Office, 1967), 96.

33. The change represented the culmination of a simmering bureaucratic turf war between welfare advocates in public assistance and civil servants in the field of vocational education. Since 1954, the American Public Welfare Association had been intermittently sparring with Switzer and the National Rehabilitation Association, who wanted to obtain some or all of the federal funds for rehabilitative services in public welfare programs, and to administer those programs. Vocational rehabilitation advocates believed that the Office of Vocational Rehabilitation was the only agency truly qualified to provide vocational rehabilitation to welfare clients. Welfare professionals had successfully argued that their concept of rehabilitation was far broader than Vocational Rehabilitation's programs were capable of handling: OVR handled the ill and physically handicapped while welfare clients were, in addition to being physically disabled, more often "socially disabled" in the minds of welfare administrators. Different and more appropriate social work and social service expertise, therefore, were required. Though welfare officials had won the disputes handily in the previous decades, they lost in 1967. For Mary Switzer's ascension to the leadership of the federal welfare agency, see folders 51 and 53, box 5, MS Papers, LS.

34. Elizabeth Shelton, "'Old Bureaucrat' for New," *Washington Post*, August 16, 1967, folder: Press clippings, MS Papers, LS. James Leiby has also written about the significance of Switzer's appointment in ushering in a more hard-nosed, cost-conscious approach to welfare and services than in the previous twenty years. Leiby, *A History of Social Welfare*, 330.

35. Elizabeth Wickenden reported that when welfare was "brought under [the control] of Vocational Rehabilitation . . . I had some real doubts about that. . . . My crite-

rion for what belonged in the Welfare Administration were any functions in which the profession of Social Work was central." Coming from a vocational rehabilitation background, Mary Switzer clearly did not meet that criterion. Wickenden Oral History, March 6, 1987, 17. In 1962 Secretary of HEW Abraham Ribicoff asked Assistant Secretary Wilbur Cohen to consider Mary Switzer for the position of head of the new Welfare Administration; even at that time, Cohen opposed Switzer's appointment to run welfare programs. Memorandum to Ribicoff from Cohen, November 20, 1962, folder 2, box 137, WC Papers, WHS, 2.

36. Edward Berkowitz, *Mr. Social Security: The Life of Wilbur J. Cohen* (Lawrence: University Press of Kansas, 1995), 212–38. Berkowitz details the passage of Medicare and Medicaid and Cohen's pivotal role in lobbying for both. The history of Medicaid is also covered in Edward Berkowitz, *America's Welfare State: From Roosevelt to Reagan* (Baltimore: Johns Hopkins University Press, 1991); and Sheri I. David, *With Dignity: The Search for Medicare and Medicaid* (Westport, Conn.: Greenwood Press, 1985).

37. Patterson, *America's Struggle against Poverty*, 180–82.

38. Trattner, *From Poor Law to Welfare State*, 329. As an example of the dismay this caused, an exchange between the heads of HEW and the OEO is instructive. In 1967 Secretary of HEW Joseph Califano made a statement regarding the numbers of clients on AFDC and how the War on Poverty was not targeting them. Sargent Shriver, director of the OEO, wrote him back, begging him to correct the statement. "Forgive my temerity in writing you," he scrawled on the bottom of the letter in his own handwriting, "but I hope you'll understand I don't want anyone to have ammunition against OEO!" Letter to Joseph Califano from Sargent Shriver, April 25, 1967, folder: 1966–1967, box 98, WE 9, WHCF, LBJL.

39. Milton Friedman, "The Case for the Negative Income Tax," *National Review*, March 7, 1967, 239–40. Gareth Davies has a detailed account of the political origins and legislative history of the GMI. Davies, *From Opportunity to Entitlement*, 211–32.

40. Davies, *From Opportunity to Entitlement*, 213–14; Patterson, *America's Struggle against Poverty*, 192–98; Katz, *In the Shadow of the Poorhouse*, 269; Piven and Cloward, *Poor People's Movements*, 335–43.

41. The spirit of the original Wagner-Murray-Dingell Acts was in the air among social workers and welfare leaders even before the FAP. In 1966 the Advisory Council on Public Welfare, in which Elizabeth Wickenden participated, recommended something quite similar to the 1940s proposals: "to improve the existing system by a federal minimum in all states or perhaps outright federalization." Leiby, *A History of Social Welfare*, 326.

42. Davies, *From Opportunity to Entitlement*, 212, 213–14, 221–22; Patterson, *America's Struggle against Poverty*, 195; Piven and Cloward, *Poor People's Movements*, 343–49.

43. Piven and Cloward, *Poor People's Movements*, 343–49; Patterson, *America's Struggle against Poverty*, 196.

44. Davies, *From Opportunity to Entitlement*, 220–21; Patterson, *America's Struggle against Poverty*, 196.

45. Trattner, *From Poor Law to Welfare State*, 331. U.S. Congress, *Conference Report on the Social Security Amendments of 1967, December 11, 1967*, 90th Congress, 1st session (Washington, D.C.: U.S. Government Printing Office, 1968), 58.

46. Trattner, *From Poor Law to Welfare State*, 347.

47. Patterson, *America's Struggle against Poverty*, 201.

48. Davies, *From Opportunity to Entitlement*, 198. Adding to this dismay was the fact that the original WIN bill proposed by the administration was not advocating mandatory work. Instead, the House Ways and Means Committee suddenly replaced the administration bill, HR 5710, with HR 12080, a much harsher one. See folder 4: Legislative, HR 12080, 1967, box 42, CWLA Collection, SWHA.

49. American Public Welfare Association, "Federal Legislative Objectives, 1968," folder 1, box 21, APWA Collection, SWHA, 3.

50. Memorandum to Chester Jones from Elizabeth Wickenden, May 13, 1968, folder: Social Issues/Politics, correspondence and memos, January–June 1968, box 53, NSWA Collection, SWHA; Wickenden quoted in Davies, *From Opportunity to Entitlement*, 198.

51. Memorandum to Jones from Wickenden, May 13, 1968.

52. In 1996 the entire AFDC program was abolished and replaced with a new program that provided aid on a time-limited basis to needy families who were, in turn, required to work, almost without exception. It is called Temporary Aid to Needy Families (TANF).

53. The first two quotations are from Giuliani, quoted in Jason DeParle, "What Welfare-to-Work Really Means," *New York Times Magazine*, December 20, 1998, 53. The third quotation is a paraphrase of Giuliani from DeParle (53).

54. Crocker Stephenson, "Hardest Cases Define Welfare's Next Challenge," *Milwaukee Journal Sentinel Online*, December 12, 1999, ‹http://www.jsonline.com/news/state/dec99/welfare12121199a.asp›. Wisconsin's welfare-to-work program was among the most researched and lauded in the nation. Katherine Boo, "The Black Gender Gap," *Atlantic Monthly Online*, January/February 2003, 1, ‹http://www.theatlantic.com/issues/2003/01/boo.htm›.

55. The reauthorization of the 1996 PRWO Act was postponed through two continuing resolutions by Congress, one in the fall of 2002 and another in the fall of 2003. The reauthorization was thus pushed to 2004. The Bush administration's proposals have been on the table since 2002. It proposed to increase the work-participation requirement of recipients of TANF to 70 percent. The administration is supported in its view by conservative think tanks such as the Heritage Foundation. See Brian Riedel and Robert Rector, "Work: The Key to Welfare," *Washington Post*, August 5, 2003. The administration also advocated providing $300 million for encouraging marriage among the poor, a proposal aimed not so much at encouraging work or reducing poverty as furthering a conservative Republican pro-family agenda, according to the Republican House majority whip Tom DeLay of Texas. For an excellent article on the proposal to fund marriage classes, and its political supporters, see Chisun Lee, "Unholy Matrimony: Politics and the President's Marriage Proposal," *Village Voice*, May 1–7, 2002. While many commentators over the years have implied that marriage may help reduce poverty, it is an arguable contention.

56. William Julius Wilson has written about the connection between jobs and poverty, but his work focuses disproportionately on the effects of job loss on men, rather than women. See William Julius Wilson, *When Work Disappears: The World of the New Urban Poor* (New York: Vintage, 1996).

57. For an analysis that links female poverty to the decline in real wages, see Gary L. Bowen, Laura M. Desimone, and Jennifer K. McKay, *Poverty and the Single-Mother Family: A Macroeconomic Perspective* (Binghamton, N.Y.: Haworth Press, 1995), 116–42. Compounding the decline in real wages has been the growing gap between the rich and the poor during the last decade. Mark Elliot, Mae Watson Grote, and Oren M. Levin-Waldman, "Deepening Disparity: Income Inequality in New York City," a report published by Public/Private Ventures (New York, September 2001), 1, ⟨http://www.ppv.org/ppv/publications/assets/90_publication.pdf⟩.

58. U.S. Census Bureau, *Poverty in the United States, 2001*, Current Population Reports, P60–219 (Washington, D.C.: U.S. Government Printing Office, 2002), ⟨http://www.census.gov/prod/2002pubs/p.60–219.pdf⟩.

59. Wickenden Oral History, March 6, 1987, 34.

SELECTED BIBLIOGRAPHY

Primary Sources

Manuscript Collections

Ann Arbor, Mich.
    Bentley Historical Library, University of Michigan
        University of Michigan School of Social Work Collection
Austin, Tex.
    Center for American History, University of Texas at Austin
        Field Foundation Collection
    Lyndon Baines Johnson Presidential Library
        White House Central Files, War on Poverty Papers, part I, WE 9, WE 6,
            Congressional Documents
        Wilbur Cohen Oral History
        Elizabeth Wickenden Oral History
Cambridge, Mass.
    Laura Schlesinger Library, Radcliffe College
        Mary Switzer Papers
College Park, Md.
    National Archives and Records Administration
        General Records of the Department of Health, Education, and Welfare, Office
            of the Secretary, RG 235
        General Records of the Department of Labor, Office of the Secretary, RG 174
Madison, Wis.
    Wisconsin Historical Society
        Arthur Altmeyer Papers
        Wilbur J. Cohen Papers
        Elizabeth Wickenden Papers
Minneapolis, Minn.
    Social Welfare History Archives, University of Minnesota

American Federation of Labor–Congress of Industrial Organizations
(AFL-CIO) Community Service Activities Collection
American Public Welfare Association Collection
Child Welfare League of America Collection
Community Research Associates Collection
National Association of Social Workers Collection
National Social Welfare Assembly Collection
Sleepy Hollow, N.Y.
Rockefeller Archive Center
Nelson Rockefeller Papers
Rockefeller Brothers Fund Collection
Rockefeller Foundation Collection
Russell Sage Foundation Collection
Washington, D.C.
Library of Congress
National Urban League Collection
Abraham Ribicoff Papers

Periodicals

Congressional Quarterly Almanac, 1945–65.
The County Officer, 1950–62.
Field Foundation, *Annual Report*, 1947–64.
Public Welfare, 1945–65.
Reader's Guide to Periodical Literature, 1955–71.
Social Security Bulletin, 1938–79.
Survey Midmonthly and *Survey*, various years.
William T. Grant Foundation, *Annual Report*, 1947–64.

Government Documents

U.S. Census Bureau. *Poverty in the United States, 2001.* Current Population Reports,
P60–219. Washington, D.C.: U.S. Government Printing Office, 2002. ⟨http://www.
census.gov/prod/2002pubs/p60-219.pdf⟩.
U.S. Congress. House of Representatives. *Aid to Dependent Children of Unemployed Parents.* 87th Congress, 1st session, 1961. H. Rep. 28. Washington, D.C.: U.S. Government Printing Office, 1962.
———. *Economic Opportunity Act of 1964.* 88th Congress, 2nd session, 1964. H. Rep.
1458. Washington, D.C.: U.S. Government Printing Office, 1965.
———. *HR 2892.* 81st Congress, 1st session, February 21, 1949. Washington, D.C.:
U.S. Government Printing Office, 1950.
———. *HR 3636.* 80th Congress, 1st session, May 27, 1947. Washington, D.C.: U.S.
Government Printing Office, 1948.
———. *Public Welfare Amendments of 1962.* 87th Congress, 2nd session, 1962. H. Rep.
1414. Washington, D.C.: U.S. Government Printing Office, 1963.

———. *Public Welfare Amendments of 1962.* 87th Congress, 2nd session, 1962. Conference Rep. 2006. Washington, D.C.: U.S. Government Printing Office, 1963.

———. Committee on Ways and Means. *Hearings on Public Assistance Titles of the Social Security Act, 1956.* 84th Congress, 2nd session, April 12, 13, 16, 19, 20, 1956. Washington, D.C.: U.S. Government Printing Office, 1957.

U.S. Congress. Senate. *ADC Benefits to Children of Unemployed Parents.* 87th Congress, 1st session, 1961. S. Rept. 165. Washington, D.C.: U.S. Government Printing Office, 1962.

———. *Economic Opportunity Act of 1964.* 88th Congress, 2nd session, 1964. S. Rept. 1218. Washington, D.C.: U.S. Government Printing Office, 1965.

———. *Public Welfare Amendments of 1962.* 87th Congress, 2nd session, 1962. S. Rept. 1589. Washington, D.C.: U.S. Government Printing Office, 1963.

———. Joint Committee on the Economic Report. *Hearings before the Subcommittee on Low-Income Families.* 81st Congress, 1st session, December 12–17, 19–22, 1949. Washington, D.C.: U.S. Government Printing Office, 1950.

———. Subcommittee on Low-Income Families. *Hearings on Characteristics of the Low-Income Population and Related Federal Programs.* 84th Congress, 1st session, November 18, 19, 21–23, 1955. Washington, D.C.: U.S. Government Printing Office, 1956.

U.S. Department of Labor. Office of Policy Planning and Research. *The Negro Family: The Case for National Action.* Washington, D.C.: U.S. Government Printing Office, 1965.

U.S. Federal Security Agency/U.S. Department of Health, Education, and Welfare. *Annual Report.* Washington D.C.: U.S. Government Printing Office, 1945–1960.

Articles, Books, Reports, and Miscellaneous Items

American Public Welfare Association. *Essentials of Public Welfare.* Chicago: American Public Welfare Association, 1952.

———. *Future Citizens All.* Chicago: American Public Welfare Association and the Field Foundation, 1952.

American Women: A Report of the President's Commission on the Status of Women and Other Publications of the Commission. New York: Charles Scribner and Sons, 1965.

Banfield, Edward. *The Moral Basis of a Backward Society.* New York: Free Press, 1958.

"Battle of Newburgh." Television documentary shown on the *NBC White Paper* series. 16mm film. New York: National Broadcasting Company, 1962.

Bruel, Frank. "Public Welfare: Safeguard or Free Ride?" *University of Chicago Magazine,* January 1962, 19–23.

Burgess, M. Elaine, and Daniel O. Price. *An American Dependency Challenge.* Chicago: American Public Welfare Association, 1963.

Burton, Hal, and Jacob Panker. "I Say Relief Is Ruining Families." *Saturday Evening Post,* September 30, 1950, 25, 111–15.

Chamber of Commerce of the United States. Committee on Social Legislation. *Federal Grant-in-Aid Programs.* Washington, D.C.: Chamber of Commerce of the United States, 1954.

Cloward, Richard, and Lloyd Ohlin. *Delinquency and Opportunity: A Theory of Delinquent Gangs.* New York: Free Press, 1964.

Cohen, Wilbur, and Sydney Bernard. *The Prevention and Reduction of Dependency*. Ann Arbor, Mich.: Washtenaw County Department of Social Welfare, 1961.

Cohen, Wilbur, and Sydney Bernard. "Reducing Dependency: A Report of a Demonstration and Research Project among Direct Relief Recipients in Washtenaw County, Michigan." Ann Arbor: University of Michigan School of Social Work, 1960.

Cohen, Wilbur, and Fedele Fauri. "The Social Security Amendments of 1956." *Public Welfare* 14, no. 4 (October 1956): 183–99.

Community Research Associates. *Current Social Research*. New York: Community Research Associates, 1957.

David, Alvin. "New Social Security Legislation." *County Officer*, October 1950, 10–13.

Davis, W. Allison, and Robert Havighurst. *Father of the Man: How Your Child Gets His Personality*. Boston: Houghton Mifflin, 1947.

Dunbar, Ruth. "Relief Recipients Take to Schooling Program." *Chicago Sun Times*, May 13, 1962.

Folsom, Marion. "Stop Want at the Source." *Nation's Business*, January 1956, 44–47.

"Folsom's Aim: To Cut the Roots of Poverty." *Business Week*, December 24, 1955, 60–64.

Galbraith, John Kenneth. *The Affluent Society*. Boston: Houghton Mifflin, 1958.

Gallup, George H. *The Gallup Poll: Public Opinion, 1935–1971*. 3 vols. New York: Random House, 1972.

Gans, Herbert. *Urban Villagers: Group and Class in the Life of Italian Americans*. New York: Free Press of Glencoe, 1962.

Garland, Patricia. "Public Assistance Families: A Resource for Foster Care." *Child Welfare*, September 1961, 1–6.

Goodwin, Kathryn, et al. *ADC: Problem and Promise*. Chicago: American Public Welfare Association, 1959.

Greenleigh Associates. *ADC: Facts, Fallacies, and Future*. Chicago: Field Foundation, 1960.

Harrington, Michael. *The Other America: Poverty in the United States*. New York: Penguin Books, 1963.

Jarman, R. "Detroit Cracks Down on Relief Chiselers." *Saturday Evening Post*, December 1949, 17–19.

Lewis, Oscar. *Children of Sanchez: Autobiography of a Mexican Family*. New York: Vintage, 1961.

Lundberg, Ferdinand, and Marynia Farnham. *Modern Woman: The Lost Sex*. New York: Harper and Brothers, 1947.

McLeod, Donna, and Lydia Hylton. "An Evaluation of a Method for Administering In-Service Training in Aid to Dependent Children: A Report of the Second of Two Experiments Conducted in Michigan." Ann Arbor: University of Michigan School of Social Work, 1958.

Myrdal, Gunnar. *An American Dilemma: The Negro Problem and Modern Democracy*. New York: Harper and Brothers, 1944.

National Organization for Women. "NOW Statement of Purpose, 1966." In *Major*

Problems in American Women's History: Documents and Essays, edited by Mary Beth Norton and Ruth Alexander, 432. Boston: Houghton Mifflin, 2003.

Newman, M. W. "How ADC Families Get Back on Feet." *Chicago Daily News*, September 5, 1962.

Parsons, Talcott and Robert Bales. *Family, Socialization and Interaction Process.* Glencoe, Ill.: Free Press, 1955.

Project on Public Services for Families and Children. "Public Welfare: Time for a Change; report by Elizabeth Wickenden and Winifred Bell [of the project]." New York, 1961.

Raskin, A. H. "Newburgh's Lessons for the Nation." *New York Times Magazine*, December 17, 1961, 7–8, 57–60.

Rockefeller Brothers Fund. *Prospect for America: The Rockefeller Panel Reports.* New York: Doubleday, 1961.

Schlesinger, Arthur. *The Vital Center: The Politics of Freedom.* Boston: Houghton Mifflin, 1949.

Selby, E., and A. Selby. "California's Jackpot for the Jobless." *Reader's Digest*, June 1965, 67–70.

———. "Watts: Where Welfare Bred Violence." *Reader's Digest*, May 1966, 67–71.

Spivak, Jonathan. "Ribicoff's Strategy: He Tries to Restore Relief Critics' Faith by Tying Economy Hope to More Charity." *Wall Street Journal*, November 21, 1961.

Stirling, Nora. Family Services Association of America. *The Pink Telephone.* Plays for Living (series). Chicago: American Public Welfare Association, n.d.

Task Force on Health and Social Security. "Health and Social Security for the American People: A Report to President-Elect John F. Kennedy." January 10, 1961.

Thomas, Edwin, and Donna McLeod. "The Effectiveness of In-Service Training and of Reduced Workloads in Aid to Dependent Children: A Report of an Experiment Conducted in Michigan." Ann Arbor: University of Michigan School of Social Work, 1957.

"Why Does Relief Cost More Today Than under FDR?" editorial. *Saturday Evening Post*, November 5, 1949, 11.

Williams, Josephine J. "Negro ADC Mothers Look for Jobs: An Attempt to Predict Employability—A Report Based on a Study of Aid to Dependent Children Cases Closed Because of the Potential Employability of the Mother, Detroit, Michigan." Ann Arbor: University of Michigan School of Social Work, 1955.

William T. Grant Foundation. *Modern Philanthropy and Human Welfare: A Roundtable.* New York: Grant Foundation, 1952.

Winston, Ellen. "Values of the Aid to Dependent Children Program." *Social Forces* 28, no. 1 (October 1949), 50–53.

Secondary Sources

Aaron, Henry. *Politics and the Professors: The Great Society in Perspective.* Washington, D.C.: Brookings Institution, 1978.

Abramowitz, Mimi. *Regulating the Lives of Women: Social Welfare Policy from Colonial Times to the Present*. Rev. ed. Boston: South End Press, 1996.

Amenta, Edwin. *Bold Relief: Institutional Politics and the Origins of Modern American Social Policy*. Princeton, N.J.: Princeton University Press, 1998.

Amenta, Edwin, and Theda Skocpol. "Redefining the New Deal: World War II and the Development of Social Provision in the United States." In *The Politics of Social Policy in the United States*, edited by Margaret Weir, Ann Shola Orloff, and Theda Skocpol, 81–122. Princeton, N.J.: Princeton University Press, 1988.

Amott, Teresa. "Black Women and AFDC: Making Entitlement Out of Necessity." In *Women, the State, and Welfare*, edited by Linda Gordon, 280–98. Madison: University of Wisconsin Press, 1990.

Anderson, Karen. *Wartime Women: Sex Roles, Family Relations, and the Status of Women during World War II*. Westport, Conn.: Greenwood Press, 1981.

Andrew, John A., III. *The Other Side of the Sixties: Young Americans for Freedom and the Rise of Conservative Politics*. New Brunswick, N.J.: Rutgers University Press, 1997.

Auletta, Ken. *The Underclass*. New York: Random House, 1982.

Bell, Winifred. *Aid to Dependent Children*. New York: Columbia University Press, 1965.

Berkowitz, Edward. *America's Welfare State: From Roosevelt to Reagan*. Baltimore: Johns Hopkins University Press, 1991.

——. *Mr. Social Security: The Life of Wilbur J. Cohen*. Lawrence: University Press of Kansas, 1995.

Berkowitz, Edward, and Kim McQuaid. *Creating the Welfare State: The Political Economy of Twentieth-Century Reform*. Lawrence: University Press of Kansas, 1992.

Boo, Katherine. "The Black Gender Gap." *Atlantic Monthly Online*, January/February 2003. ⟨http://www.theatlantic.com/issues/2003/01/boo.htm⟩.

Boris, Eileen. "Contested Rights: How the Great Society Crossed the Boundaries between Home and Work." In *The Great Society and the Rights Revolution*, edited by Sidney Milkis and Jerome Mileur. Amherst: University of Massachusetts Press, forthcoming [2005].

——. "The Racialized Gendered State: Constructions of Citizenship in the United States." *Social Politics* 2, no. 2 (1994): 160–80.

Bowen, Gary L., Laura M. Desimone, and Jennifer K. McKay. *Poverty and the Single-Mother Family: A Macroeconomic Perspective*. Binghamton, N.Y.: Haworth Press, 1995.

Brandt, Allan. *No Magic Bullet: A Social History of Venereal Disease in the United States since 1880*. New York: Oxford University Press, 1985.

Brennan, Mary C. *Turning Right in the Sixties: The Conservative Capture of the GOP*. Chapel Hill: University of North Carolina Press, 1995.

Brinkley, Alan. *The End of Reform: New Deal Liberalism in Recession and War*. New York: Knopf, 1995.

——. *Liberalism and Its Discontents*. Cambridge, Mass.: Harvard University Press, 1998.

——. "The New Deal and the Idea of the State." In *The Rise and Fall of the New Deal Order, 1930–1980*, edited by Steven Fraser and Gary Gerstle, 85–121. Princeton, N.J.: Princeton University Press, 1989.

Brinkley, David. *Washington Goes to War*. New York: Knopf, 1988.

Brownmiller, Susan. *In Our Time: Memoir of a Revolution*. New York: Dial Press, 1999.

Burns, Nancy. "Locating Gender in the Paths to Politics." May 1997. Unpublished paper in possession of the author.

Carter, Dan T. *The Politics of Rage: George Wallace, the Origins of the New Conservatism, and the Transformation of American Politics*. New York: Simon and Schuster, 1995.

Cates, Jerry. *Insuring Inequality: Administrative Leadership in Social Security: 1934–1950*. Ann Arbor: University of Michigan Press, 1983.

Cauthen, Nancy, and Edwin Amenta. "Not for Widows Only: Institutional Politics and the Formative Years of Aid to Dependent Children." *American Sociological Review* 61 (June 1996): 427–48.

Chafe, William H., ed. *The Achievement of American Liberalism: The New Deal and Its Legacies*. New York: Columbia University Press, 2003.

Chambers, Clarke. *Seedtime of Reform: American Social Service and Social Action, 1918–1933*. Minneapolis: University of Minnesota Press, 1963.

Chappell, Marisa. "The Radical Potential of Conservative Family Values: The Guaranteed Income Campaign, 1964–72." Paper presented at the Social Science History Association Annual Conference, November 15, 2003, Baltimore, Md.

———. "Rethinking Women's Politics in the 1970s: The League of Women Voters and the National Organization for Women Confront Poverty." *Journal of Women's History* 13, no. 4 (Winter 2002): 155–79.

Cmiel, Kenneth. "On Cynicism, Evil, and the Discovery of Communication in the 1940s." *Journal of Communication* 46, no. 3 (1996): 88–107.

Cobble, Dorothy Sue. "Recapturing Working-Class Feminism: Union Women in the Postwar Era." In *Not June Cleaver: Women and Gender in Postwar America, 1945–1960*, edited by Joanne Meyerowitz, 57–83. Philadelphia: Temple University Press, 1994.

Cochran, David Carroll. *The Color of Freedom: Race and Contemporary American Liberalism*. Albany: State University of New York Press, 1999.

Cohen, Lizabeth. *Making a New Deal: Industrial Workers in Chicago, 1919–1939*. New York: Cambridge University Press, 1990.

Coll, Blanche. *Safety Net: Welfare and Social Security, 1929–1979*. New Brunswick, N.J.: Rutgers University Press, 1995.

Collins, Robert M. *More: The Politics of Economic Growth in Postwar America*. New York: Oxford University Press, 2002.

Coontz, Stephanie. *The Way We Never Were: American Families and the Nostalgia Trap*. New York: Basic Books, 1992.

Critchlow, Donald. *The Brookings Institution, 1916–1952: Expertise and the Public Interest in a Democratic Society*. DeKalb: Northern Illinois University Press, 1985.

Critchlow, Donald, and Ellis Hawley, eds. *Federal Social Policy: The Historical Dimension*. University Park: Pennsylvania State University Press, 1988.

David, Sheri I. *With Dignity: The Search for Medicare and Medicaid*. Westport, Conn.: Greenwood Press, 1985.

Davies, Gareth. *From Opportunity to Entitlement: The Transformation and Decline of Great Society Liberalism*. Lawrence: University Press of Kansas, 1996.

Davis, Flora. *Moving the Mountain: The Women's Movement since 1960*. New York: Simon and Schuster, 1991.

Davis, Martha. "Welfare Rights and Women's Rights in the 1960s." *Journal of Policy History* 8, no. 1 (1996): 144–65.

DeParle, Jason. "What Welfare-to-Work Really Means." *New York Times Magazine*, December 20, 1998, 50–59, 70–74, 88–89.

Derthick, Martha. *The Influence of Federal Grants: Public Assistance in Massachusetts*. Cambridge, Mass.: Harvard University Press, 1970.

———. *Policy Making for Social Security*. Washington, D.C.: Brookings Institution, 1979.

———. *Uncontrollable Spending for Social Service Grants*. Washington, D.C.: Brookings Institution, 1975.

De Hart, Jane. "Gender on the Right: Meanings beyond the Existential Scream." *Gender and History* 3, no. 3 (1991): 246–67.

Dickerson, Dennis. *Militant Mediator: A Biography of Whitney Young, Jr.* Lexington: University Press of Kentucky, 1998.

Donohue, William A. *The Politics of the American Civil Liberties Union*. New Brunswick, N.J.: Transaction Press, 1985.

Dudziak, Mary L. *Cold War Civil Rights: Race and the Image of American Democracy*. Princeton, N.J.: Princeton University Press, 2000.

DuPlessis, Rachel Blau, and Ann Snitow, eds. *The Feminist Memoir Project: Voices from Women's Liberation*. New York: Three Rivers Press, 1998.

Echols, Alice. *Daring to Be Bad: Radical Feminism in America, 1967–1975*. Minneapolis: University of Minnesota Press, 1989.

Edsall, Thomas Byrne, and Mary Edsall. *Chain Reaction: The Impact of Race, Rights, and Taxes on American Politics*. New York: W. W. Norton, 1991.

Elliot, Mark, Mae Watson Grote, and Oren M. Levin-Waldman. "Deepening Disparity: Income Inequality in New York City." A report issued by Public/Private Ventures. New York, September 2001. ⟨http://www.ppv.org/ppv/publications/assets/90_publication.pdf⟩

Esping-Anderson, Gøsta. *The Three Worlds of Welfare Capitalism*. Princeton, N.J.: Princeton University Press, 1990.

Evans, Sara. *Personal Politics: The Roots of Women's Liberation in the Civil Rights Movement and the New Left*. New York: Vintage, 1979.

Feldstein, Ruth. *Motherhood in Black and White: Race and Sex in American Liberalism, 1930–1965*. Ithaca, N.Y.: Cornell University Press, 2000.

Fitzgerald, Tracey. *The National Council of Negro Women and the Feminist Movement, 1935–1975*. Washington, D.C.: Georgetown University Press, 1985.

Folbre, Nancy. *The Invisible Heart: Economics and Family Values*. New York: New Press, 2001.

Fraser, Nancy. "Struggle over Needs: Outline of a Socialist-Feminist Critical Theory of Late-Capitalist Political Culture." In *Women, the State, and Welfare*, edited by Linda Gordon, 199–225. Madison: University of Wisconsin Press. 1990.

Fraser, Nancy, and Linda Gordon. "A Genealogy of Dependency." *Signs* 19, no. 2 (1994): 309–36.

Fraser, Steven, and Gary Gerstle. *The Rise and Fall of the New Deal Order, 1930–1980*. Princeton, N.J.: Princeton University Press, 1989.

Frazier, E. Franklin. *The Negro Family in Chicago*. Chicago: University of Chicago Press, 1932.

———. *The Negro Family in The United States*. Chicago: University of Chicago Press, 1939.

Frederickson, Kari. *The Dixiecrat Revolt and the End of the Solid South, 1932–1968*. Chapel Hill: University of North Carolina Press, 2001.

Freeman, Jo. *The Politics of Women's Liberation: A Case Study of an Emerging Social Movement and its Relation to the Policy Process*. New York: David McKay, 1975.

Füredi, Frank. *The Silent War: Imperialism and the Changing Perception of Race*. New Brunswick, N.J.: Rutgers University Press, 1998.

Gerstle, Gary. "The Protean Character of American Liberalism." *American Historical Review* 99, no. 4 (October 1994): 1043–73.

———. "Race and the Myth of the Liberal Consensus." *Journal of American History* 82, no. 2 (September 1995): 579–86.

Gilbert, James. *A Cycle of Outrage: America's Reaction to the Juvenile Delinquent in the 1950s*. New York: Oxford University Press, 1986.

Goodwin, Joanne. "'Employable Mothers' and "Suitable Work': A Re-evaluation of Welfare and Wage-Earning for Women in the Twentieth-Century United States." *Journal of Social History* 29, no. 2 (Winter 1995): 253–74.

———. *Gender and the Politics of Welfare Reform: Mothers' Pensions in Chicago, 1911–1929*. Chicago: University of Chicago Press, 1997.

Gordon, Linda. *Pitied but Not Entitled: Single Mothers and the History of Welfare*. New York: Free Press, 1994.

———, ed. *Women, the State, and Welfare*. Madison: University of Wisconsin Press, 1990.

Graebner, William. *Coming of Age in Buffalo: Youth and Authority in the Postwar Era*. Philadelphia: Temple University Press, 1990.

Greenstein, Fred I. *The Hidden-Hand Presidency: Eisenhower as Leader*. New York: Basic Books, 1982.

Gutman, Herbert. *The Black Family in Slavery and Freedom, 1750–1925*. New York: Vintage, 1976.

Hale, Nathan, Jr. *The Rise and Crisis of Psychoanalysis in the United States*. New York: Oxford University Press, 1995.

Hamilton, Dona Cooper, and Charles V. Hamilton. *The Dual Agenda: Race and Social Welfare Policies of Civil Rights Organizations*. New York: Columbia University Press, 1997.

Handler, Joel, and Yesheskel Hasenfeld. *The Moral Construction of Poverty: Welfare Reform in America*. Newbury Park, Calif.: Sage Publications, 1991.

Harrison, Cynthia. *On Account of Sex: The Politics of Women's Issues, 1945–1968*. Berkeley: University of California Press, 1988.

Hartmann, Susan. *The Home Front and Beyond: American Women in the 1940s*. Boston: Twayne, 1982.

———. *The Other Feminists: Activists in the Liberal Establishment*. New Haven, Conn.: Yale University Press, 1998.

————. "Women's Employment and the Domestic Ideal in the Early Postwar Years." In *Not June Cleaver: Women and Gender in Postwar America, 1945–1960*, edited by Joanne Meyerowitz, 84–127. Philadelphia: Temple University Press, 1994.

Haveman, Robert, ed., *A Decade of Federal Antipoverty Programs: Achievements, Failures, and Lessons.* New York: Academic Press, 1977.

Heclo, Hugh. "Poverty Politics." In *Confronting Poverty: Prescriptions for Change*, edited by Sheldon Danziger, 396–437. Cambridge, Mass.: Harvard University Press and Russell Sage Foundation, 1994.

Himmelstein, Jerome L. *To the Right: The Transformation of American Conservatism.* Berkeley: University of California Press, 1991.

Hirsch, Arnold. "Massive Resistance in the Urban North: Trumbull Park, Chicago, 1953–63." *Journal of American History* 82, no. 2 (September 1995): 522–50.

Hixson, William B., Jr. *Search for the American Right Wing: An Analysis of the Social Science Record, 1955–1987.* Princeton, N.J.: Princeton University Press, 1992.

Hodgson, Godfrey. *America in Our Time: From World War II to Nixon, What Happened and Why.* New York: Vintage, 1976.

————. *The World Turned Right Side Up: A History of the Conservative Ascendancy in America.* Boston: Houghton Mifflin, 1996.

Huthmacher, J. Joseph. *Senator Robert F. Wagner and the Rise of Urban Liberalism.* New York: Atheneum, 1968.

Igo, Sarah E. "America Surveyed: The Making of a Social Scientific Public, 1920–1960." Ph.D. diss., Princeton University, 2001.

Igo, Sarah. "Arguing with Gallup and Kinsey: Popular Challenges to Social Statistics, 1936–1953." Paper presented at the Organization of American Historians Annual Meeting, Los Angeles, 2001.

Jackson, John, Jr. "Coopting the Culture Concept: Social Science in Defense of Segregation." Paper presented at the Organization of American Historians Annual Meeting, Los Angeles, 2001.

————. *Social Scientists for Social Justice: Making the Case against Segregation.* New York: New York University Press, 2001.

Jackson, Walter. *Gunnar Myrdal and America's Conscience: Social Engineering and Racial Liberalism, 1938–1987.* Chapel Hill: University of North Carolina Press, 1990.

Jacoby, Sanford. *Modern Manors: Welfare Capitalism since the New Deal.* Princeton, N.J.: Princeton University Press, 1997.

Jeffries, John. "A 'Third New Deal?' Liberal Policy and the American State, 1937–1945." *Journal of Policy History* 8, no. 4 (1996): 387–409.

Jones, Jacqueline. *Labor of Love, Labor of Sorrow: Black Women, Work, and the Family from Slavery to the Present.* New York: Vintage, 1985.

Kaledin, Eugenia. *Mothers and More: American Women in the 1950s.* Boston: Twayne, 1984.

Katz, Michael. *In the Shadow of the Poorhouse: A Social History of Welfare in America.* Rev. ed. New York: Basic Books, 1996.

————. *The Undeserving Poor: From the War on Poverty to the War on Welfare.* New York: Pantheon Books, 1989.

Kennedy, David. *Over Here: The First World War in American Society.* New York: Oxford University Press, 1980.

Kessler-Harris, Alice. *In Pursuit of Equity: Women, Men, and the Quest for Economic Citizenship in Twentieth-Century America*. New York: Oxford University Press, 2001.

Kingdon, John. *Agendas, Alternatives, and Public Policies*. 2nd ed. Boston: Little, Brown, 1995.

Klatch, Rebecca. *Women of the New Right*. Philadelphia: Temple University Press, 1987.

Klein, Jennifer. *For All These Rights: Business, Labor, and the Shaping of America's Public-Private Welfare State*. Princeton, N.J.: Princeton University Press, 2003.

Koven, Seth, and Sonya Michel. *Mothers of a New World: Maternalist Politics and the Origins of the Welfare State*. New York: Routledge, 1993.

Krieg, Joann P., ed. *Dwight D. Eisenhower: Soldier, President, Statesman*. New York: Greenwood Press, 1987.

Kunzel, Regina. *Fallen Women, Problem Girls: Unmarried Mothers and the Professionalization of Social Work, 1890–1945*. New Haven, Conn.: Yale University Press, 1993.

Ladd-Taylor, Molly. *Mother-Work: Women, Child Welfare, and the State, 1890–1930*. Urbana: University of Illinois Press, 1995.

Leiby, James. *A History of Social Welfare and Social Work in the United States*. New York: Columbia University Press, 1978.

Leighninger, Leslie. "Why Social Work Abandoned Public Welfare." Paper presented at the *Journal of Policy History* Conference, St. Louis, Mo., May 27–30, 1999.

Lemann, Nicholas. "Origins of the Underclass." *Atlantic Monthly*, June 1986, 31–61, and July 1986, 54–68.

———. *The Promised Land: The Great Black Migration and How It Changed America*. New York: Knopf, 1991.

Levitan, Sar. *The Great Society's Poor Law: A New Approach to Poverty*. Baltimore: Johns Hopkins University Press, 1969.

Levitan, Sar, and Robert Taggart. *The Promise of Greatness*. Cambridge, Mass.: Harvard University Press, 1975.

Lichtenstein, Nelson. *Labor's War at Home: The CIO in World War II*. New York: Cambridge University Press, 1983.

Lindenmeyer, Kriste. *"A Right to Childhood": The U.S. Children's Bureau and Child Welfare, 1912–46*. Urbana: University of Illinois Press, 1997.

Marris, Peter, and Martin Rein. *Dilemmas of Social Reform: Poverty and Community Action in the United States*. London: Routledge and Kegan Paul, 1967.

Marshall, Thomas H. *Citizenship and Social Class, and Other Essays*. Cambridge: Cambridge University Press, 1950.

Matusow, Allen. *The Unraveling of America: A History of Liberalism in the 1960s*. New York: Harper and Row, 1984.

May, Elaine Tyler. *Homeward Bound: American Families in the Cold War Era*. New York: Basic Books, 1988.

McDonald, Terrence J. "The Burdens of Urban History: The Theory of the State in Recent American Social History." *Studies in American Political Development* 3 (Spring 1989): 3–55.

McGirr, Lisa. *Suburban Warriors: The Origins of the New American Right*. Princeton, N.J.: Princeton University Press, 2001.

McKeown, Elizabeth. "Claiming the Poor." In *With Us Always: A History of Private*

Charity and Public Welfare, edited by Donald Critchlow and Charles N. Parker, 145–60. Lanham, Md.: Rowman and Littlefield, 1998.

Mead, Lawrence. *Beyond Entitlement: The Social Obligations of Citizenship*. New York: Free Press, 1986.

Meyerowitz, Joanne, ed. *Not June Cleaver: Women and Gender in Postwar America, 1945–1960*. Philadelphia: Temple University Press, 1994.

Michel, Sonya. *Children's Interests/Mother's Rights: The Shaping of America's Child Care Policy*. New Haven, Conn.: Yale University Press. 1999.

Milkman, Ruth. *Gender at Work: The Dynamics of Job Discrimination by Sex during World War II*. Urbana: University of Illinois Press, 1987.

Mink, Gwendolyn. "The Lady and the Tramp: Gender, Race, and the Origins of the American Welfare State." In *Women, the State, and Welfare*, edited by Linda Gordon, 92–122. Madison: University of Wisconsin Press, 1990.

———. *Welfare's End*. Ithaca, N.Y.: Cornell University Press, 1998.

Misra, Joya, Stephanie Moller, and Chris Lenzo. "Race, Class, and Gender and the U.S. Welfare State: Explaining State-Level Variations in Welfare Comprehensiveness." Paper presented at the Social Science History Association Annual Meeting, Chicago, Ill., November 1998.

Mittelstadt, Jennifer. "Educating Our Girls and Welfare Mothers: Discussions of Education Policy for Pregnant Teenagers in Congressional Hearings, 1975–1995." *Journal of Family History* 22, no. 3 (Summer 1997): 326–53.

Morris, Andrew. "Charity, Therapy, and Poverty: Private Social Service in the Era of Public Welfare," Ph.D. diss., University of Virginia, 2003.

Morris, Norval, and David J. Rothman, eds. *The Oxford History of the Prison: The Practice of Punishment in Western Society*. New York: Oxford University Press, 1995.

Moya, Sara. "Growth Management in Maricopa County, 1988–1992: An Application of Kingdon's Agenda-Setting Model." *Social Science Journal* 35, no. 4 (1998): 525–42.

Moynihan, Daniel Patrick. *Maximum Feasible Misunderstanding: Community Action in the War on Poverty*. New York: Free Press, 1969.

Muncy, Robyn. *Creating a Female Dominion in American Reform, 1890–1935*. New York: Oxford University Press, 1991.

Murray, Charles. *Losing Ground: American Social Policy, 1950–1980*. New York: Basic Books, 1984.

Nadasen, Premilla. "Expanding the Boundaries of the Women's Movement: Black Feminism and the Struggle for Welfare Rights." *Feminist Studies* 28, no. 2 (2002): 271–301.

Naples, Nancy. *Grassroots Warriors: Activist Mothering, Community Work, and the War on Poverty*. New York: Routledge, 1998.

Nash, George. *The Conservative Intellectual Movement in America, since 1945*. New York: Basic Books, 1976.

Nathanson, Constance. *Dangerous Passage: The Social Control of Sexuality in Women's Adolescence*. Philadelphia: Temple University Press, 1993.

National Research Council. *A Common Destiny: Blacks and American Society*. Washington, D.C.: National Academy Press, 1989.

Nelson, Barbara. "The Origins of the Two-Channel Welfare State: Workmen's Compensation and Mothers' Aid." In *Women, the State, and Welfare*, edited by Linda Gordon, 123–51. Madison: University of Wisconsin, 1990.

Newman, Louise Michele. *White Women's Rights: The Racial Origins of Feminism in the United States*. New York: Oxford University Press, 1999.

Nordquist, Joan, comp. *The Feminization of Poverty: Contemporary Social Issues: A Bibliographic Series*. Santa Cruz, Calif.: Reference and Research Services, 1987.

O'Connor, Alice. "Neither Charity nor Relief: The War on Poverty and the Effort to Redefine the Basis of Social Provision." In *With Us Always: A History of Private Charity and Public Welfare*, edited by Donald Critchlow and Charles N. Parker, 191–210. Lanham, Md.: Rowman and Littlefield, 1998.

———. *Poverty Knowledge: Social Science, Social Policy, and the Poor in Twentieth-Century U.S. History*. Princeton, N.J.: Princeton University Press, 2001.

O'Connor, Julia, Ann Shola Orloff, and Sheila Shaver. *States, Markets, Families: Gender, Liberalism and Social Policy in Australia, Canada, Great Britain and the United States*. New York: Cambridge University Press, 1999.

Parris, Guichard, and Lester Brooks. *Blacks in the City: A History of the National Urban League*. Boston: Little, Brown, 1971.

Patterson, James. *America's Struggle against Poverty, 1900–1994*. Cambridge, Mass.: Harvard University Press, 1994.

Pearce, Diana. "Welfare Is Not *for* Women: Why the War on Poverty Cannot Conquer the Feminization of Poverty." In *Women, the State, and Welfare*, edited by Linda Gordon, 265–79. Madison: University of Wisconsin Press, 1990.

Pells, Richard. *The Liberal Mind in a Conservative Age: American Intellectuals in the 1940s and 1950s*. New York: Harper and Row, 1985.

Perlstein, Rick. *Before the Storm: Barry Goldwater and the Unmaking of the American Consensus*. New York: Hill and Wang, 2001.

Piven, Frances Fox, and Richard Cloward. *Poor People's Movements: Why They Succeed, How They Fail*. New York: Vintage, 1977.

———. *Regulating the Poor: The Functions of Public Welfare*. New York: Vintage, 1971.

Polsky, Andrew. *The Rise of the Therapeutic State*. Princeton, N.J.: Princeton University Press, 1991.

Quadagno, Jill. *The Color of Welfare: How Racism Undermined the War on Poverty*. New York: Oxford University Press, 1994.

———. "From Old Age Assistance to Supplemental Security Income: The Political Economy of Relief in the South, 1935–1972." In *The Politics of Social Policy in the United States*, edited by Margaret Weir, Ann Orloff, and Theda Skocpol, 235–63. Princeton, N.J.: Princeton University Press, 1988.

Quadagno, Jill, and Catherine Fobes. "The Welfare State and the Cultural Reproduction of Gender: Making Good Girls and Boys in the Job Corps." *Social Problems* 42, no. 2 (May 1995): 181–96.

Rabinowitz, Alan. *Social Change Philanthropy in America*. New York: Quorum Books, 1990.

Reese, William. "*Reefer Madness* and *A Clockwork Orange*." In *Learning from the Past: What History Teaches Us about School Reform*, edited by Maris Vinovskis and Diane Ravitch, 355–81. Baltimore: Johns Hopkins University Press, 1995.

Reichard, Gary W. *Politics as Usual: The Age of Truman and Eisenhower.* Arlington Heights, Ill.: Harlan Davidson, 1988.

Ricci, David. *The Transformation of American Politics: The New Washington and the Rise of Think Tanks.* New Haven, Conn.: Yale University Press, 1993.

Riedel, Brian, and Robert Rector. "Work: The Key to Welfare." *Washington Post,* August 5, 2003.

Ritz, Joseph. *The Despised Poor: Newburgh's War on Welfare.* Boston: Beacon Press, 1966.

Rose, Sonya, and Jane Lewis. "Let England Blush: Protective Labor Legislation, 1820–1914." In *Protecting Women: Labor Legislation in Europe, the United States, and Australia, 1880–1920,* edited by Ulla Wikander, Alice Kessler-Harris, and Jane Lewis, 91–124. Urbana: University of Illinois Press, 1995.

Rupp, Leila, and Verta Taylor. *Survival in the Doldrums: The American Women's Rights Movement, 1945 to the 1960s.* New York: Oxford University Press, 1987.

Rymph, Catherine. "Neither Neutral nor Neutralized: Phyllis Schlafly's Battle against Sexism." In *Women's America: Refocusing the Past,* edited by Jane Sherron De Hart and Linda Kerber, 501–7. New York: Oxford University Press, 2000.

Sapiro, Virginia. "The Gender Basis of American Social Policy." In *Women, the State, and Welfare,* edited by Linda Gordon, 36–54. Madison: University of Wisconsin Press, 1990.

Schneider, Anne, and Helen Ingram. "Social Construction of Target Populations: Implications for Politics and Policy." *American Political Science Review* 87, no. 2 (June 1993): 334–47.

Schoenwald, Jonathan M. *A Time for Choosing: The Rise of Modern American Conservatism.* New York: Oxford University Press, 2001.

Schor, Juliet. *The Overworked American: The Unexpected Decline of Leisure.* New York: Basic Books, 1991.

Schriftgiesser, Karl. *Business and Public Policy: The Role of the Committee for Economic Development, 1942–1967.* Englewood Cliffs, N.J.: Prentice-Hall, 1967.

Scott, Daryl Michael. *Contempt and Pity: Social Policy and the Image of the Damaged Black Psyche, 1880–1996.* Chapel Hill: University of North Carolina Press, 1997.

———. "The Politics of Pathology: The Ideological Origins of the Moynihan Controversy." *Journal of Policy History* 8, no. 1 (1996): 81–105.

Sealander, Judith. *Private Wealth and Public Life: Foundation Philanthropy and the Reshaping of American Social Policy from the Progressive Era to the New Deal.* Baltimore: Johns Hopkins University Press, 1997.

Skocpol, Theda. *Protecting Soldiers and Mothers: The Political Origins of Social Policy in the United States.* Cambridge, Mass.: Belknap Press of Harvard University Press, 1992.

Smith, James Allen. *The Idea Brokers: Think Tanks and the Rise of the New Policy Elite.* New York: Free Press, 1991.

Solinger, Rickie. *Wake Up Little Susie: Race and Single Pregnancy before Roe v. Wade.* New York: Routledge, 1993.

Soule, Sarah, and Yvonne Zylan. "Runaway Train? The Diffusion of State-Level Reform in ADC/AFDC Eligibility Requirements, 1950–1967." *American Journal of Sociology* 103, no. 3 (1997): 733–62.

Stefanic, Jean, and Richard Delgado. *No Mercy: How Conservative Think Tanks and Foundations Changed America's Social Agenda*. Philadelphia: Temple University Press, 1996.

Steinmetz, George. *Regulating the Social: The Welfare State and Local Politics in Imperial Germany*. Princeton, N.J.: Princeton University Press, 1993.

Stephenson, Crocker. "Hardest Cases Define Welfare's Next Challenge." *Milwaukee Journal Sentinel Online*, December 12, 1999, ‹http://www.jsonline.com/news/state/dec99/welfare12121199a.asp›.

Sugrue, Thomas. *The Origin of the Urban Crisis: Race and Inequality in Postwar Detroit*. Princeton, N.J.: Princeton University Press, 1996.

————. "Reassessing the History of Postwar America." *Prospects: An Annual of American Cultural Studies* 20 (1995): 493–509.

Sundquist, James L. *Politics and Policy: The Eisenhower, Kennedy, and Johnson Years*. Washington, D.C.: Brookings Institution, 1968.

Titmuss, Richard. *Essays on the Welfare State*. London: Allen and Unwin, 1963.

Trattner, Walter I., ed. *Biographical Dictionary of Social Welfare in America*. Westport, Conn.: Greenwood Press, 1986.

————. *From Poor Law to Welfare State: A History of Social Welfare in America*. 5th ed. New York: Free Press, 1994.

Trotter, Joe William, Jr., ed. *The Great Migration in Historical Perspective: New Dimensions of Race, Class, and Gender*. Bloomington: Indiana University Press, 1991.

Vinovskis, Maris. *An "Epidemic" of Adolescent Pregnancy? Some Historical and Policy Considerations*. New York: Oxford University Press, 1988.

Viswanathan, Narayan. "The Role of the American Public Welfare Association in the Formulation and Development of Public Welfare Policies in the United States: 1930–1960." D.S.W. thesis, Columbia University, 1961.

Wagner, Steven. "Eisenhower's Pursuit of the Middle Way." Paper presented at the *Journal of Policy History* Conference, St. Louis, Mo., May 27–30, 1999.

Walker, Samuel. *In Defense of American Liberties: A History of the ACLU*. Carbondale: Southern Illinois University Press, 1990.

Walkowitz, Daniel. *Working with Class: Social Workers and the Politics of Middle-Class Identity*. Chapel Hill: University of North Carolina Press, 1999.

Weir, Margaret, Ann Shola Orloff, and Theda Skocpol, eds. *The Politics of Social Policy in the United States*. Princeton, N.J.: Princeton University Press, 1988.

Weisbrot, Robert. *Freedom Bound: A History of America's Civil Rights Movement*. New York: Norton, 1990.

Weiss, Nancy J. *Whitney Young, Jr., and the Struggle for Civil Rights*. Princeton, N.J.: Princeton University Press, 1989.

West, Guida. *The National Welfare Rights Movement: The Social Protest of Poor Women*. New York: Praeger, 1981.

Wiebe, Robert. *The Search for Order: 1877–1920*. New York: Hill and Wang, 1967.

Wikander, Ulla, Alice Kessler-Harris, and Jane Lewis, eds. *Protecting Women: Labor Legislation in Europe, the United States, and Australia, 1880–1920*. Urbana: University of Illinois Press, 1995.

Wilson, Greg. S. "The Area Redevelopment Act and Postwar Social Policy in the

United States, 1940–1956." Paper presented at the *Journal of Policy History* Conference, St. Louis, Mo., May 27–30, 1999.

Wilson, William Julius. *The Truly Disadvantaged: The Inner City, the Underclass, and Public Policy.* Chicago: University of Chicago Press, 1986.

———. *When Work Disappears: The World of the New Urban Poor.* New York: Knopf, 1996.

Witte, Edwin. *The Development of the Social Security Act.* Madison: University of Wisconsin Press, 1963.

Zelizer, Julian. *Taxing America: Wilbur C. Mills, Congress, and the State, 1945–1975.* New York: Cambridge University Press, 1998.

INDEX

ADC. *See* Aid to Dependent Children

Addams, Jane, 35

Ad Hoc Committee on Public Welfare: origins of, 220–21 (n. 26); and Public Welfare Amendments of 1962, 118, 119, 120; and racial discrimination, 120; and work relief, 116–17

Adorno, Theodor, 81

AFDC. *See* Aid to Families with Dependent Children

Affluent society, 131

AFL. *See* American Federation of Labor; American Federation of Labor–Congress of Industrial Organizations

AFL-CIO. *See* American Federation of Labor–Congress of Industrial Organizations

African Americans, 69; and Aid to Dependent Children, 95, 141–42; and discrimination, 77, 78, 80; and employment, 77, 78, 143–44; and families, 83; and Louisiana welfare crisis, 88–90; and migration to North, 94; and Newburgh, N.Y., 105; and poverty, 76, 83, 145; and President's Commission on the Status of Women, 141–42; and single motherhood, 143–44; and unwed motherhood, 54–55

Aid to Dependent Children (ADC): attacks on, 43, 45, 61, 70, 71, 86, 87,

155; and change of name, 13, 18, 73, 108; during 1940s, 21, 34, 43, 93; and employment, 13, 16, 46, 57, 58, 63, 71, 101, 103, 104, 108, 109, 116, 118–19, 128, 140, 223 (nn. 46, 51), 225–25 (n. 69); and family life, 13, 53, 63, 72, 73, 75, 76, 87, 101, 110, 111; and federal-state relationship, 97–98; and foster care, 75, 76; and income incentives, 122–23; isolation of, 19, 153; legislative changes in, 4, 42, 108; and men, 113; and noncategorical public assistance, 110; origins of, 3, 22, 24; and payments, 58; perceived abuses in, 14; and President's Commission on the Status of Women, 18, 136; promotion of, 13, 14, 16, 68, 70, 71, 72, 75, 83, 87, 99, 101, 110; publicity regarding, 69, 70, 86, 211–12 (n. 73); purpose of, 42, 45, 62, 63; and racial discrimination, 13, 77, 78, 79, 88, 97–98, 120; research on, 71, 72, 74, 124–25, restrictions of, 46, 86; size of, 3, 43, 73, 146, 153; stigmatization of, 13, 84, 99; treatment of issue of race in, 14, 16, 27, 71, 76, 79, 82, 90, 96, 105, 207 (nn. 38, 39); and War on Poverty, 18. *See also* Aid to Dependent Children–Unemployed Parent provision; Aid to Families with Dependent Children; Family Support

habilitation, 77; and research on Aid to Dependent Children/Aid to Families with Dependent Children, 97–98, 125, 215 (n. 111), 216 (nn. 118, 119)

Berkowitz, Edward, 25

Bernard, Sydney, 59, 63

Birmingham, Ala., 142

Black Panthers, 159

Boris, Eileen, 148

Brown v. Board of Education, 15, 72, 81

Buell, Bradley, 9, 48, 56

Bureau of Family Services, 99, 124, 138. *See also* Bureau of Public Assistance

Bureau of Public Assistance, 99, 24; change in name of, 73, 138; and comprehensive social welfare, 25; and noncategorical public assistance, 33, 34; and services in Aid to Dependent Children, 56, 57, 64; and Wagner-Murray-Dingell bills, 29; and welfare legislation in 1940s, 37, 38. *See also* Bureau of Family Services

Burgess, Elaine, 57, 73–74, 82

Bush, George W., 172

Byrd, Robert (D-W.Va.), 79, 121, 162

Califano, Joseph, 150

California: and Aid to Dependent Children, 61–62

Capron, William, 147

Carter, Lisle, 90, 142

Casework, 35, 36. *See also* Rehabilitation; Social services; Social work

Cauthen, Nancy, 44

Celebrezze, Anthony, 137

Chapel Hill Weekly, 103

Chicago Daily News, 102

Chicago Sun-Times, 69, 91, 102

Chicago Tribune, 69

Children's Bureau, 3, 22, 24, 27, 35, 56, 124

Children's Committee of the City of New York, 117

Child Welfare League of America (CWLA), 26; and Louisiana welfare

crisis, 88–89, 212 (n. 77); attitude toward racial discrimination, 81, 97; and support for Aid to Dependent Children, 9

Christian Science Monitor, 104

CIO. *See* American Federation of Labor–Congress of Industrial Organizations (AFL-CIO); Congress of Industrial Organizations (CIO)

Civil rights movement, 80; agenda in early 1960s, 142; attitude toward single mothers, 143–45; attitude toward welfare, 84–85, 141–45; opposition to workfare, 157

Clinton, Bill, 171

Cloward, Richard, 145

Cohen, Wilbur, 8, 9, 12, 15, 33, 37, 38, 39, 64, 66, 134, 155, 173; and Ad Hoc Committee on Public Welfare, 120; and Aid to Dependent Children–Unemployed Parent provision (ADC-UP), 110, 111, 113, 114, 115, 116; and Congress, 80; connections with American Public Welfare Association, 28, 31, 191 (n. 42); and Department of Health, Education, and Welfare, 94, 107, 108; during 1940s, 25, 34, 35; early career of, 5; encouraging employment of Aid to Dependent Children clients, 19, 29, 103, 119, 121, 122, 125–26, 128, 129, 223 (n. 46); and Medicaid, 164; and Newburgh, N.Y., welfare crisis, 94; and opposition to workfare, 156; and President's Commission on the Status of Women, 137, 138, 139, 141; and promotion of rehabilitation, 71, 73, 120, 181 (n. 18); and Public Welfare Amendments of 1962, 119, 121, 122, 124, 125–26; and Rockefeller Brothers Fund Special Studies Project, 7; and Social Security Administration, 6; studies of poverty, 1, 2, 146; studies of rehabilitation, 59, 60, 62, 63, 71, 124, 125–26; understanding of racial discrimination, 77,

79, 96–97, 100; and War on Poverty, 145, 146, 149; and welfare reform, 4, 17; and work relief, 117, 118

Committee for Economic Development, 1, 2, 77, 146

Committee on Economic Security, 24

Community Action Program, 145, 165

Community Chests and Councils of America, 48

Community Research Associates (CRA), 11, 70; origins of, 9, 48; advocacy of rehabilitation, 51, 56; research on Aid to Dependent Children, 9, 61, 62, 71; and use of racial statistics, 79, 207 (n. 39)

Community Work and Training Programs, 118, 119, 169; opening to women, 121, 122; opposition to, 139–140; and War on Poverty, 149

Comprehensive social welfare, 15–16, 21, 23, 25, 28, 167, 169. See also Wagner-Murray-Dingell bills

Congress of Racial Equality (CORE), 159

Congress, 67, 85; and Aid to Dependent Children, 111, 113; and Aid to Families with Dependent Children, 170; during 1950s, 67; during 1940s, 22, 23, 29, 34; encouraging Aid to Dependent Children clients to work, 108, 122, 168; and National Welfare Rights Organization, 159, and Public Welfare Amendments of 1962, 121, 122, 126, 128; southerners in, 80; and War on Poverty, 150

Congress of Industrial Organizations (CIO), 27, 29. See also American Federation of Labor–Congress of Industrial Organizations

Conservatives, 29, 37, 44, 61, 105; opposition to welfare, 9–10, 162, 163; and Public Welfare Amendments of 1962, 126, 127; and support for workfare, 157, 168, 169–70; and War on Poverty, 165

Consultation on the Status of Negro Women (of President's Commission on the Status of Women), 143–45

Cook County Department of Public Aid, 102–3

CORE. See Congress of Racial Equality

Council of Economic Advisers, 10, 146, 147

Council of State Governments, 36

Danstedt, Rudolph, 41, 42, 147

Davies, Gareth, 147, 160, 168

Davis, Jimmie, 85, 86

Davis, Martha, 161

Day care, 78, 123–24, 150, 233 (n. 68)

Democratic Party, 31, 105, 108, 126, 135. See also Democrats

Democrats, 29, 79, 80, 108, 127, 128. See also Democratic Party

Department of Health, Education, and Welfare, 43, 64, 99, 107, 111, 114, 129, 134–35; and Aid to Dependent Children–Unemployed Parent provision, 118; and Louisiana welfare crisis, 89; and National Welfare Rights Organization, 159; and President's Commission on the Status of Women, 136, 137, 139, 141; and spending, 163; use of racial statistics, 79; and War on Poverty, 145, 146, 150

Department of Labor, 27, 135, 136, 145

Dependency, 56

Des Marais, Philip, 138, 139

Detroit, Mich., 60, 77, 125

Dingell, John (D-Mich.), 24

Du Bois, W. E. B., 83

Dumpson, James, 75, 94, 117

Dunn, Loula, 5, 31, 39, 67, 72, 73, 88, 94, 102, 156

East St. Louis, Ill., 62

Economic Opportunity Act of 1964, 147, 149, 150, 151

Economists, 156. See also Social scientists

Eisenhower, Dwight, 10, 11, 64, 109, 132

Employment: of women, 57, 58, 59, 200 (n. 73). *See also* Aid to Dependent Children: and employment; Aid to Families with Dependent Children: and employment; Community Work and Training Programs; Mothers: and employment; Work Experience Programs; Workfare

"Essentials of Public Welfare" (APWA), 32, 33, 34, 38, 182–83 (n. 21)

Evers, Medgar, 142

Fair Deal, 37

Family Assistance Plan, 167–68

Family Service Association of America, 9, 83

Family Services, 56. *See also* Rehabilitation: and family life; Social services; Welfare services

Family Service Society, 89

Family structure, 53, 134, 151–52. *See also* Single mothers; Unwed mothers

Family Support Act of 1988, 171

Farm Security Agency, 6

Federal Emergency Relief Administration, 5, 27

Federal Security Agency, 27

Feminism, 135–36, 160, 161, 236 (n. 22)

Feminization of poverty, 152–53, 172.

Field, Marshall III, 6

Field Foundation, 43; attitude toward racial discrimination, 81, 84, 96, 97; and Louisiana welfare crisis, 88–89, 102, 213 (n. 84); and Newburgh, N.Y., welfare crisis, 94; origins and mission of, 6–7, 69; and promotion of Aid to Dependent Children, 75, 76, 220–21 (n. 26); and research on Aid to Dependent Children, 72, 74, 75, 76; and Winifred Bell, 96, 215 (n. 111), 216 (nn. 118, 119)

Flemming, Arthur, 89, 90, 142

Foster care, 75–76

Foundations, 4, 156, 184 (n. 25), 197–98 (n. 39). *See also* Field Foundation;

Laura Spellman Fund; Rockefeller Brothers Fund; Russell Sage Foundation; William T. Grant Foundation

Frazier, E. Franklin, 55, 83

Friedman, Milton, 166–67

Full Employment Act of 1946, 29

Fulton County, Ga., 125

"Future Citizens All" (APWA), 72

Galbraith, John Kenneth, 131

Gallup Poll, 16, 72, 92, 212 (n. 73)

General assistance, 26, 34, 114, 194 (n. 11), 217 (n. 129)

General Federation of Women's Clubs, 24

General relief. *See* General assistance

Giuliani, Rudolph, 171

Goldwater, Barry (R-Ariz.), 85, 92, 162, 163

Goodwin, Joanne, 13, 45

Goodwin, Kathryn, 33, 34

Gordon, Linda, 22, 34

Granger, Lester, 8, 84, 98, 211 (n. 67)

Grant Foundation. See William T. Grant Foundation

Great Britain, 89

Great Depression, 29, 113

Great Society, 5, 15, 19, 162

Greene, Edith (D-Ore.), 148

Greenleigh Associates, 48

Guaranteed minimum income (GMI), 166–67. *See also* Family Assistance Plan

Hackett, David, 145

Hahn, Maxwell, 69; and attitude toward employment of Aid to Dependent Children clients, 103; and attitude toward racial discrimination, 78, 81, 84, 95, 96; and Louisiana welfare crisis, 88; and Newburgh, N.Y., welfare crisis, 94, 102; and promoting Aid to Dependent Children, 69–71; and reform of Aid to Dependent Children, 72–73; and Winifred Bell, 96

Ohlin, Lloyd, 145
Old Age Assistance (OAA), 3, 26, 73, 110
Omnibus Budget Reconciliation Act of 1981, 171

Page, Harry O., 9, 48, 51
Parsons, Talcott, 81
Perliss, Leo, 94, 96
Personal Responsibility and Work Opportunity Act of 1996 (PRWO), 155, 156, 171, 172, 239 (nn. 52, 55)
Peterson, Esther, 135, 139–40, 142, 143
Philadelphia Inquirer, 102
Pink Telephone, The, 74–75
Piven, Frances Fox, 160
"Platform for Public Welfare" (APWA), 32, 33, 38
Polier, Justine, 89, 94, 96
Polier, Shad, 89–90
Poor People's Campaign, 159, 160
Poverty: explanations for, 2, 4, 42, 156; measures of, 2, 172; and single mothers, 146, 152–53; and African Americans, 152–53; relationship to rehabilitation, 133; social scientists and, 4; studies of, 1–3. *See also* Feminization of poverty
President's Commission on the Status of Women (PCSW), 8, 18, 132, 160; administration and scope of, 136, 137; and African Americans, 142–43; and Aid to Dependent Children, 133, 137, 138, 145, 152; gender ideology of, 140–41, 144–45, 151; and poor, single mothers, 137, 152; specialized committees of, 137
Progressive Era, 5, 35, 135, 151
"Prospect for America," 7. *See also* Rockefeller Brothers Fund
Public assistance, 25; attacks on, 91, 92; clientele of, 22, 26, 39; during 1940s, 6, 33, 34, 35, 38, 39, 44; extension of, 65, 67, 110; federal payments for, 65, 67; gender differentials in, 113; public-

ity about, 91, 102; racial discrimination in, 94, 95; size of, 22, 33, 44. *See also* Aid to Dependent Children; Aid to Dependent Children–Unemployed Parent provision; Aid to Families with Dependent Children; General assistance; Noncategorical public assistance
Public welfare. *See* Aid to Dependent Children; Aid to Dependent Children–Unemployed Parent provision; Aid to Families with Dependent Children; General assistance; Noncategorical public assistance; Public assistance
Public Welfare, 36, 41, 46, 47, 54, 55, 58, 62, 67, 96
Public Welfare Amendments of 1962, 108, 115, 119, 121, 132, 133, 134, 144, 151, 163; and day care, 123–24, 151; and employment of Aid to Families with Dependent Children clients, 109, 122, 149, 165, 167; federal funding of, 124, 125, 126–27; opposition to, 127, 134; outcomes of, 129; passage of, 126; and President's Commission on the Status of Women, 137, 138, 139; and rehabilitation, 128; and War on Poverty, 147
Puerto Ricans, 77, 95, 96

Reagan, Ronald, 155
Recessions, 19, 110, 112
Rehabilitation, 116, 124, 132; challenges to, 88, 91, 105, 108, 158; costs of, 202 (n. 104), 222–23 (n. 41), 225–26 (n. 76); and employment, 12, 13, 57, 59, 60, 61, 62, 63, 67, 116, 117–18, 121, 156, 157, 170; and family life, 53, 55, 56, 67, 70, 72, 87, 108, 224–25 (n. 69); ideology of, 11, 12, 13, 63, 146–47, 169–70; in legislation, 12, 16, 42, 65, 67, 116, 117–18, 119, 222–23 (n. 41); legacy of, 128–29, 156, 164; origins of, 11, 52, 198 (n. 47), 217 (n. 129), 224–25 (n. 69); and Presi-

nizations; Congress of Industrial
Organizations
U.S. Chamber of Congress, 126, 194
(n. 13), 212 (n. 73)
U.S. Committee for the Care of Euro-
pean Children, 28
U.S. House of Representatives, 11, 123,
127
U.S. House of Representatives, Commit-
tee on Ways and Means, 79, 121, 122,
163–64, 168–69
U.S. News and World Report, 115
U.S. Senate, 127
U.S. Senate, Committee on Finance, 79–
80, 121, 122
U.S. War Department, 27
University of Alabama, 142
University of Chicago Magazine, 92
University of Michigan, 1–2, 9, 59, 71,
77, 79, 103, 146
University of North Carolina at Chapel
Hill, 72, 103
University of Wisconsin, 5
Unwed mothers, 46, 54, 87, 133. *See also*
Aid to Dependent Children; Aid to
Families with Dependent Children;
Single mothers; Welfare clients

Vasey, Wayne, 120, 220 (n. 25)
Vital Center, The (Schlesinger), 7, 184
(n. 28)

Wagner, Robert (D-N.Y.), 24
Wagner-Murray-Dingell bills, 24, 25,
27, 28, 29, 30, 34, 38, 110, 167, 190
(n. 27)
Walker, Irvin, 141
Wall Street Journal, 91, 102
Ware, Caroline, 137
War on Poverty, 4, 18, 132–33, 155, 157,
165; administration of, 230 (n. 43),
232 (n. 56); and Aid to Families with
Dependent Children, 133, 134, 147,
150, 152; gender ideology of, 148, 151,
152, 166; in New York, 1; origins of,

145, 146; and rehabilitation, 147, 231
(n. 51)
Washington, D.C., 162
Washington Post, 164
Washtenaw County, Mich., 60
Welfare Administration, 6, 31, 138
Welfare administrators. *See* American
Public Welfare Association
Welfare clients, 9, 13–14, 75–76, 77, 91,
100–101, 149–50, 158; employment
of, 60, 108, 122, 129, 157; single moth-
ers as, 133; studies of, 11, 74. *See also*
Aid to Dependent Children; Public
assistance: clientele of
Welfare reform. *See* Aid to Dependent
Children: legislative changes in; Fam-
ily Support Act of 1988; Omnibus
Budget Reconciliation Act of 1981;
Personal Responsibility and Work Op-
portunity Act of 1996; Public Welfare
Amendments of 1962; Rehabilitation;
Social Security Amendments of 1956;
Work Incentives Program
Welfare reform coalition, 4–6, 18–19,
156–57, 164, 170–71
Welfare rights, 9. *See* National Welfare
Rights Organization
Welfare services, 36, 37, 39, 120, 127,
163. *See also* Public Welfare Amend-
ments of 1962; Rehabilitation; Social
Security Amendments of 1956; Social
services
Welfare state, 5, 8, 38, 182 (n. 20)
West, Guida, 159
Wickenden, Elizabeth, 15, 18, 29, 31, 33,
38, 39, 43, 66, 125, 158; attitude toward racial discrimination, 77, 79, 96–
97, 100; defense of Aid to Dependent
Children, 70, 88, 94, 156, 167, 170,
173; early career of, 6; employment
with American Public Welfare Association, 28, 32; encouraging employment of Aid to Dependent Children
clients, 102, 122; and guaranteed minimum income, 167, 168; lobbying in

GENDER AND AMERICAN CULTURE

Imagining Medea: Rhodessa Jones and Theater for Incarcerated Women, by Rena Fraden (2001).

Painting Professionals: Women Artists and the Development of Modern American Art, 1870–1920, by Kirsten Swinth (2001).

Remaking Respectability: African American Women in Interwar Detroit, by Victoria W. Wolcott (2001).

Ida B. Wells-Barnett and American Reform, 1880–1930, by Patricia A. Schechter (2001).

Taking Haiti: Military Occupation and the Culture of U.S. Imperialism, 1915–1940, by Mary A. Renda (2001).

Before Jim Crow: The Politics of Race in Postemancipation Virginia, by Jane Dailey (2000).

Captain Ahab Had a Wife: New England Women and the Whalefishery, 1720–1870, by Lisa Norling (2000).

Civilizing Capitalism: The National Consumers' League, Women's Activism, and Labor Standards in the New Deal Era, by Landon R. Y. Storrs (2000).

Rank Ladies: Gender and Cultural Hierarchy in American Vaudeville, by M. Alison Kibler (1999).

Strangers and Pilgrims: Female Preaching in America, 1740–1845, by Catherine A. Brekus (1998).

Sex and Citizenship in Antebellum America, by Nancy Isenberg (1998).

Yours in Sisterhood: Ms. Magazine and the Promise of Popular Feminism, by Amy Erdman Farrell (1998).

We Mean to Be Counted: White Women and Politics in Antebellum Virginia, by Elizabeth R. Varon (1998).

Women Against the Good War: Conscientious Objection and Gender on the American Home Front, 1941–1947, by Rachel Waltner Goossen (1997).

Toward an Intellectual History of Women: Essays by Linda K. Kerber (1997).

Gender and Jim Crow: Women and the Politics of White Supremacy in North Carolina, 1896–1920, by Glenda Elizabeth Gilmore (1996).

Delinquent Daughters: Protecting and Policing Adolescent Female Sexuality in the United States, 1885–1920, by Mary E. Odem (1995).

U.S. History as Women's History: New Feminist Essays, edited by Linda K. Kerber, Alice Kessler-Harris, and Kathryn Kish Sklar (1995).

Common Sense and a Little Fire: Women and Working-Class Politics in the United States, 1900–1965, by Annelise Orleck (1995).

How Am I to Be Heard?: Letters of Lillian Smith, edited by Margaret Rose Gladney (1993).

Entitled to Power: Farm Women and Technology, 1913–1963, by Katherine Jellison (1993).

Revising Life: Sylvia Plath's Ariel Poems, by Susan R. Van Dyne (1993).

Made From This Earth: American Women and Nature, by Vera Norwood (1993).

Unruly Women: The Politics of Social and Sexual Control in the Old South, by Victoria E. Bynum (1992).

The Work of Self-Representation: Lyric Poetry in Colonial New England, by Ivy Schweitzer (1991).

Labor and Desire: Women's Revolutionary Fiction in Depression America, by Paula Rabinowitz (1991).

Community of Suffering and Struggle: Women, Men, and the Labor Movement in Minneapolis, 1915–1945, by Elizabeth Faue (1991).

All That Hollywood Allows: Re-reading Gender in 1950s Melodrama, by Jackie Byars (1991).

Doing Literary Business: American Women Writers in the Nineteenth Century, by Susan Coultrap-McQuin (1990).

Ladies, Women, and Wenches: Choice and Constraint in Antebellum Charleston and Boston, by Jane H. Pease and William H. Pease (1990).

The Secret Eye: The Journal of Ella Gertrude Clanton Thomas, 1848–1889, edited by Virginia Ingraham Burr, with an introduction by Nell Irvin Painter (1990).

Second Stories: The Politics of Language, Form, and Gender in Early American Fictions, by Cynthia S. Jordan (1989).

Within the Plantation Household: Black and White Women of the Old South, by Elizabeth Fox-Genovese (1988).

The Limits of Sisterhood: The Beecher Sisters on Women's Rights and Woman's Sphere, by Jeanne Boydston, Mary Kelley, and Anne Margolis (1988).